Theory of Value, Prices and Accumulation

A mathematical integration of Marx, von Neumann and Sraffa

Theory of Value, Prices and Accumulation

A mathematical integration of Marx, von Neumann and Sraffa

GILBERT ABRAHAM-FROIS
PROFESSEUR D'ÉCONOMIE POLITIQUE
UNIVERSITÉ DE PARIS X, NANTERRE

EDMOND BERREBI
PROFESSEUR
UNIVERSITÉ DE PARIS X, NANTERRE

Translated by M. P. Kregel-Javaux

CAMBRIDGE UNIVERSITY PRESS
CAMBRIDGE
LONDON · NEW YORK · MELBOURNE

Published by the Syndics of the Cambridge University Press
The Pitt Building, Trumpington Street, Cambridge CB2 1RP
Bentley House, 200 Euston Road, London NW1 2DB
32 East 57th Street, New York, NY 10022, USA
296 Beaconsfield Parade, Middle Park, Melbourne 3206, Australia

First published 1979

Printed in Great Britain at the University Press, Cambridge

This book was originally published in French in 1976
by Ed. Economica under the title *Théorie de la valeur, des prix et de l' accumulation.*

Library of Congress Cataloguing in Publication Data

Abraham-Frois, Gilbert.

Theory of value, prices, and accumulation.

Translation of Théorie de la valeur, des prix et de
l'accumulation.

Bibliography: p.

Includes index.

1. Value. 2. Prices. 3. Saving and investment.
4. Marxian economics. I. Berrebi, Edmond, joint author.
II. Title.
HB97.5.A2713 335.4'12 78-16277
ISBN 0 521 22385 7 hard covers
ISBN 0 521 29467 3 paperback

Contents

Preface to the English edition ix
Introduction xi
Symbols xv

1 From the theory of value to the explanation of profit **1**
1.1 The theory of value 1
1.1.1 Use-value and exchange-value 1
1.1.2 The measure of value 3
1.1.3 From exchange-value to surplus-value and the theory of exploitation 10
1.2 The problems of the 'transformation' of surplus-value into profit and of values into prices of production 17
1.2.1 Karl Marx's solution 20
1.2.2 Marx's error 22
1.2.3 The fundamental Marxian theorem 29

2 Prices of production: single-product industries and circulating capital **32**
2.1 Production for subsistence 32
2.2 Production with a surplus 35
2.2.1 Prices and distribution 35
2.2.2 Basic and non-basic products 39
2.3 Effects of changes in wages on the rate of profit and on prices 44
2.4 The standard commodity 47
2.4.1 Why a particular standard commodity? 47
2.4.2 The construction of the standard commodity 48
2.4.3 Properties of the standard commodity and the wage–profit relation 51
2.4.4 The existence and uniqueness of the standard system 53
2.5 Conditions for the existence, uniqueness, and positiveness of the prices of production . . . 54
2.5.1 . . . of basic commodities 54
2.5.2 . . . of non-basic commodities 55

3 General analysis of prices: joint production, fixed capital, land and natural resources **59**
3.1 Equilibrium prices and the rate of profit in a von Neumann model 59
3.1.1 Description of the model 59

3.1.2 Economic expansion of the system 61
3.1.3 The system of equilibrium prices 62
3.1.4 Economic goods and free goods 63
3.1.5 The introduction of labour in von Neumann's model 64
3.2 A system with circulating capital and joint production: Sraffa's analysis 65
3.2.1 Basic and non-basic commodities 66
3.2.2 The standard commodity 76
3.2.3 Prices and the standard ratio in joint production 80
3.3 Fixed capital 82
3.3.1 Fixed capital as a special case of joint production 82
3.3.2 Value of machines with constant efficiency in time 82
3.3.3 The notion of an integrated sector 86
3.3.4 Efficiency and obsolescence 87
3.3.5 Construction of the standard commodity 90
3.3.6 Special cases: everlasting machines 92
3.4 Land and natural resources 93
3.4.1 Various types of rents 95
3.4.2 Specialisation of land 98
3.4.3 'Land' and the standard system 99
3.4.4 Some particular cases 101
3.5 Determination of prices and values: a summing-up 102
3.5.1 Price determination 102
3.5.2 Determination of values in Marx's sense 105

4 Proportional growth—duality **112**
4.1 Technological expansion of the system 112
4.2 Decomposable and indecomposable models 118
4.2.1 Technological decomposability 118
4.2.2 Economic decomposability 120
4.3 Comparison of the rate of growth G and the rate of profit R 123
4.4 Determination of R, $\mathbf{p}(r)$, G and $\mathbf{y}(G)$ when $m = n$ 124
4.4.1 Matrix **B** is diagonal and has an inverse 125
4.4.2 Matrix **B** has an inverse and $\mathbf{B}^{-1}\mathbf{A} \geq \mathbf{0}$ 128
4.4.3 Matrix **A** is diagonal and has an inverse 129
4.4.4 Matrix **A** has an inverse and $\mathbf{A}^{-1}\mathbf{B} \geq \mathbf{0}$ 132
4.5 Exclusion relations 135

5 Accumulation, conflicts and quasi-duality **137**
5.1 Social conflicts and the 'trade-off' between the distributive variables 137
5.1.1 The relation between the rate of profit and the wage 137
5.1.2 The relation between the rate of profit, wages and rent 143
5.2 Conflicts between accumulation and consumption and quasi-duality 149
5.2.1 The 'trade-off' between the rate of growth and the level of consumption 149
5.2.2 Effects of changes in the level of consumption on the rate of growth and the activity levels 150

5.2.3 Construction of the standard commodity for activity levels 155
5.2.4 Antibasic and non-antibasic processes 160
5.3 Commodity prices and activity levels—dual norms 164
5.3.1 Price equations and rate-of-profit–wage curves 167
5.3.2 Equations of activity levels and accumulation–consumption curves 169
5.3.3 Equivalence of the rate-of-profit–wage curve and the accumulation–consumption curves 172
5.4 Interdependence of the 'trade offs' 173
5.4.1 First case: workers consume the whole of their wages 174
5.4.2 Second case: workers save part of their wages 177
5.4.3 The influence of the behaviour of the owners of natural resources 179
5.5 Changes of technique and conflicts of objectives 181
5.5.1 The choice of the technique of production 181
5.5.2 Conflicts of objectives and the wage–consumption relation 189

6 Value: duality and 'transformation' **195**
6.1 Accumulation in the capitalist production system 197
6.2 Duality: the second fundamental Marxian theorem 203
6.3 The standard commodity and 'transformation' 206
6.3.1 The transformation of values into prices of production in a Marx–von Neumann system 206
6.3.2 The relation between the rate of profit and the rate of exploitation 210
6.4 'Transformation' and the proportion of labour to means of production 218
6.5 Conclusion 227

Mathematical appendix **230**

Notes 244

Bibliography 257

Preface to the English edition

This English edition of our *Théorie de la valeur, des prix et de l'accumulation* is not a simple translation of the original French edition published in 1976. The entire text has been revised, and the last two chapters have been altered substantially.

These alterations relate, first, to the analysis of the existence of 'differential quasi-rents' when a particular commodity may be produced by several processes (in a simple production system). The revised formulation allows a more lucid exposition of Marx's analysis of 'extra' surplus-value and super profit as well as of the relations between prices of production and market prices.

Secondly, we have given additional emphasis to the importance of the choice of the normalisation vectors for prices *and* activity levels. The result is the formulation of special normalisation conditions which assure the coincidence of the wage–profit and the consumption–accumulation curves.

Finally, we have identified all those special cases in which 'transformation' is possible. These cases are intimately related to the existence of a standard commodity for prices constructed under the assumption of wages being paid in advance. It would thus appear that the old 'transformation' problem might now be left behind.

These are the essential differences between the French and the English versions. Of course, this edition would not have been possible without the contribution of M. P. Kregel-Javaux, who carried out the translation with remarkable accuracy and clarity. We would like to take this opportunity to express our gratitude to her. The content of this edition has also greatly benefited from comments by L. L. Pasinetti and the anonymous referees of the Cambridge University Press, to whom we also wish to express our gratitude. Finally, we are particularly indebted to Dr Colin Day, editor for the Press, for his valuable suggestions.

January 1978

Introduction

Although the capital theory debates have popularised the work of P. Sraffa they have done so in a way that has tended to diminish Sraffa's contribution to economic theory to a mere critique of neo-classical theory, overlooking the more essential aspects such as the formulation of the theory of the prices of production and the construction of the standard commodity whose 'particular proportions ... may give transparency to a system and render visible what was hidden' (P. S., §31, p. 23).[1] *Production of Commodities by Means of Commodities* presents a point of departure for a reconsideration of Classical Economics. This has been confirmed in recent years by the publication of diverse contributions to Marxian analysis, in particular those of A. Brody[2] and M. Morishima.[3]

It is tempting to try to build on the previous analyses in order to provide a more profound analysis of the problems of distribution, the formation of prices, and accumulation in the capitalist mode of production. Such an integration requires great care for it should not involve analysing Marx in Sraffian terms,[4] or reformulating his theory in terms of general equilibrium.[5] On the other hand, to simply point out the similarities between the recent formalisations of Marx and Sraffa's approach would be of little interest. Rather the problem should be approached by determining more exactly the points at which there is difference or even opposition in order to construct a more general system which integrates both positions.

This attempt at integration can also be justified by the fact that Frobenius' theorem[6] can be applied to both Marx's and Sraffa's analysis. From this point of view Marx's prices of production appear, *in a sense*, as a particular case of Sraffa's prices of production, but only in the mathematical sense, for there is a basic difference concerning the treatment of wages. The assumptions on this matter adopted by Marx and Sraffa are mutually exclusive and, at the same time, extreme, for in Marx's analysis the wage is *completely* advanced, while for Sraffa it is paid from the produced surplus. It seems possible, however,[7] to consider a system in which wages are composed of two parts, one 'advanced', the other paid from the surplus; such a system, which Sraffa, in fact, suggested (*op. cit.* p. 10), contains the two extreme assumptions as special cases. It seems to us that such an approach bears closer investigation and we shall make frequent use of it in what follows.

Both the first and the last chapter of this book are devoted to Marx's analysis, primarily that of *Capital* because it seemed to us that a certain number of problems posed by Marx could not be correctly resolved except with reference to concepts developed by Sraffa. The first chapter simply summarises the recent reformulation (in terms of linear algebra) of the theory of labour value and the problems raised by the 'transformation' of surplus-value into profit and values into prices. These problems are re-examined in Chapter 6 where it is shown that 'transformation' takes place under the hypothesis concerning the technology (identical organic composition of capital in all sectors), the savings behaviour of capitalists (accumulation of all the surplus-value), or in other special cases which will be defined in the last section of that chapter.

In the most general case 'transformation' cannot be proven. This demonstrates the interest and the necessity of reference to a 'standard commodity' based on an 'advanced' wage. The rate of profit of the actual system is determined by the conditions of production in the reconstructed standard system and not, as Marx supposed, on the basis of the 'average' conditions of production.

Since the wage is totally advanced it is therefore the 'standard ratio' of this system which determines the rate of profit of the actual system.

These examples should be enough to explain why a simple repetition of Sraffa's analysis would not have been sufficient; it seemed to us essential to spell out the full mathematical structure of *Production of Commodities by Means of Commodities*. This task was greatly simplified by the very remarkable work of B. Schefold[8] and we would like to record our particular admiration of his analysis.

The determination of prices and of the endogenous distributive variable, the specification of basic goods, and the construction of the standard system are carried out in two stages. Chapter 2 studies the simple case of single-product industries and circulating capital where the Frobenius theorem allows a clear and simple exposition. The more complex problems of joint-production, fixed capital and land are dealt with in Chapter 3. It is here that use of a mathematical formulation is of great relevance for it allows a precise judgement of the implications of these problems for Sraffa's analysis. We know that in joint-production systems the existence of the standard system and the standard commodity is no longer guaranteed,[9] these 'anomalies' cannot appear in single-product industries using fixed capital and we have shown in a simple case that the standard ratio exists.

The construction of the standard system leads us to the analysis of von Neumann's[10] dynamic model which has the same mathematical structure as the auxiliary structure created by Sraffa to resolve the problem posed by Ricardo. Von Neumann's model will thus appear at the centre of our study, even more so because Sraffa's treatment of fixed capital is the same as that used by von Neumann, so that there would seem to be only advantages in treating fixed capital within Marx's analysis in the same way. The developments of Chapter 4, which deals with proportional growth and duality, also demonstrate the importance, for von Neumann's analysis, of the assumptions of technological and economic indecomposability, as well as the concept of duality: between goods and activities, prices and levels of activity, each activity being characterised by its level of utilisation just as each good (or commodity) is characterised by its price (of production).

In fact, duality is only completely ensured by assuming both the economic and technological indecomposability of the system *and* the reinvestment of the entire produced surplus. Von Neumann's analysis ignores all conflict for, on the one hand, the capitalists claim the entire surplus, and, on the other, they completely reinvest the surplus. There is neither capitalist consumption (which would reduce accumulation), nor wage paid out of the surplus (which would reduce profits). Relaxing these assumptions brings out the problem of 'conflicts' treated in Chapter 5.

It is in this respect that we note the special role played by certain activities which we call 'anti-basic'. It is already known that when the wage is fixed exogenously the rate of profit and the prices of basic goods are determined simultaneously; the prices of non-basics can be deduced from the basic goods' prices. It can be shown, in the same way, that for an exogenously given level of consumption the rate of growth of means of production and the levels of 'anti-basic' activities are simultaneously determined; the activity levels of the other activities can be deduced from the levels of activity of anti-basics. When the system is not basic a basic and anti-basic sector can be identified; the first to determine prices, the second the levels of activity. This leads to the notion of a 'quasi-duality' between prices of production and levels of activity.

Sraffa's composite commodity cannot be used directly for the analysis of distribution in an economic system where, as Marx supposed, the wage is 'advanced'. A reformulation of Sraffa's concept is necessary. The same will obviously be true for the 'virtual' commodity that we propose to use as the standard of levels of activity. It is remarkable, in this respect, that the assumption of a totally advanced wage leads to an identification of prices of production and the structure of the 'virtual' commodity.

Part of the problems dealt with here have already been discussed in the lectures that we have given at the University of Paris X, Nanterre. We would like to express sincere thanks to the students and colleagues who took an active part in these discussions, especially G. Ballot, Ph. de Lavergne, O. Favereau, our assistants. We would also like to acknowledge the benefit of the recent works of G. Dumesnil, G. Faccarello, R. Ferreira dos Santos, D. Lacaze, P. Maurisson, F. Meunier and B. Rosier (see Bibliography).

To help the reader through the maze of mathematical equations required for the discussion in the pages that follow, a list of symbols is appended to this introduction. Matrices and vectors are distinguished from scalars by heavy type.

Obviously, we alone are responsible for any errors, omissions, or imprecisions which might remain. We offer thanks in advance for any criticism or suggestion from our readers.

There is only one remaining point of clarification. The reader interested in the respective responsibility of each of the authors will be disappointed, for this book is the result of an intellectual collaboration which could be explained in the same way as the analysis of joint production. It remains to be seen whether or not it is a 'basic good'.

Symbols

A vector with a subscript (e.g. $\mathbf{a}_i$) denotes a row vector, a vector with a superscript (e.g. $\mathbf{a}^i$) a column vector

$\mathbf{A}$	input matrix
$\mathbf{A}^* = \mathbf{A} + \mathbf{Ld}$	socio-technological matrix
$\mathbf{B}$	output matrix
c	constant capital
$\mathbf{D}$	real-wage vector
$\mathbf{d}$	vector of real wages per hour
e	rate of exploitation
$\mathbf{E}$	capital gains
F_h	total charge of a machine at period h
G	maximum rate of growth
g	uniform rate of growth of means of production
g'	rate of growth (in value)
i	ratio of new share issues to investment expenditures
$\mathbf{I}$	identity matrix
k	organic composition of capital
k_q	organic composition of the standard commodity
$\mathbf{L}$	vector of direct labour
$\mathbf{M}$	Manara matrix
m	surplus-value
N	number of shares
$\mathbf{p}$	price vector
$\hat{\mathbf{p}} = \mathbf{p}/w$	wage prices
$\mathbf{p}_s$	prices expressed in Sraffa's standard
$p_{m,0}$	price of a new machine
$p_{m,h}$	price of a machine of age h
p_T	price of land
$\bar{\mathbf{p}}$	virtual commodity standard of the activity levels
$\mathbf{q}$	composite commodity standard of prices (Sraffa)
R	maximum rate of profit
r	uniform rate of profit
s_c	propensity to save of the capitalists
s_p	propensity to save of the owners of natural resources
s_w	propensity to save of wage-earners

supp($\mathbf{y}$)	support of the vector $\mathbf{y}$
$\mathbf{T}$	quantity vector of land
T	working life of a machine
$\mathbf{u}$	$=[1, 1, \ldots, 1]$
v	variable capital
V	valuation ratio
w	wage
w_o	'advanced' wage
w'	wage paid from the surplus
w_s	wage expressed in Sraffa's standard
$\mathbf{x}$	input vector
$\mathbf{X}$	output vector
$\mathbf{y}$	vector of activity levels or technique of production
$\hat{\mathbf{y}} = \mathbf{y}/\xi$	vector of activity levels expressed in 'consumption'
$\mathbf{y}_s$	vector of activity levels expressed in the standard
α^*	dominant eigenvalue of a square matrix
γ	propensity of the capitalists to save surplus-value
$\boldsymbol{\delta}$	structure of consumption
ξ	level of consumption
ξ_s	level of consumption expressed in the standard
ξ_0	'advanced' consumption
ξ'	consumption out of surplus
$\boldsymbol{\Lambda}$	value vector
$\lambda_{m,0}$	value of a new machine
$\lambda_{m,h}$	value of a machine of age h
Π	total profit
ρ	rent
ρ_s	rent expressed in Sraffa's standard
σ	vector of net product
$\boldsymbol{\Omega}$	'height' vector
ω	prices of securities
$\mathbf{A} \geqq \mathbf{0}$	$\mathbf{A}$ is nonnegative
$\mathbf{A} \geq \mathbf{0}$	$\mathbf{A}$ is semi-positive
$\mathbf{A} > \mathbf{0}$	$\mathbf{A}$ is positive

NOTES ON SOURCES AND ABBREVIATIONS

(a) References to Karl Marx's *Capital* are given by volume number and page only and to *A Contribution to the Critique of Political Economy* by C and page number of the Lawrence & Wishart editions, London.

(b) References to P. Sraffa's *Production of Commodities by Means of Commodities* are given by the initials P. S. followed by the number of the relevant page, section or chapter.

1

From the theory of value to the explanation of profit

1.1 The theory of value

1.1.1 Use-value and exchange-value

The fact that Marx adopted the classical economists' distinction between use-value and exchange-value suggests that the concept of 'utility' was not foreign to Marx's own analysis.[1]

For Marx, an object would not be manufactured unless it was likely to be *useful*, that is, unless it could satisfy a particular need, which is precisely what gives it a 'use-value': 'The utility of a thing makes it a use-value' (I, p. 36). Marx viewed use-value as an 'intrinsic virtue' of objects, as a material quality; while from the neo-classical viewpoint 'use-value' became a relation of subject to object, a judgement passed on the object by the subject. In a certain sense use-value is in itself objective from the Marxian perspective: 'this utility is not a thing of air. Being limited by the physical properties of the commodity, it has no existence apart from that commodity' (I, p. 36).

Use-value therefore rests on the intrinsic characteristics of the commodity, on its own qualities: 'As use-values, commodities are, above all, of different qualities, but as exchange-values they are merely different quantities' (I, pp. 37–8).

According to Marx, since use-values are qualities each is different from the other, therefore they cannot be compared. Use-values cannot then exchange for use-values because exchange implicitly means comparison and thus the possibility of finding an equivalence between quantities. This explains the definition of exchange-value which 'at first sight, presents itself as a quantitative relation, as the proportion in which values in use of one sort are exchanged for those of another sort' (I, p. 36). It is also evident that only a commodity with use-value can have exchange-value since only commodities that have utility will be exchanged.

How then can the various commodities be measured? We must keep in mind that, for Marx, the measure of value exists before exchange: 'It becomes plain, that it is not the exchange of commodities which regulates the magnitude of their value; but, on the contrary, that it is the magnitude of their value which controls their exchange proportions' (I, p. 63).

We therefore have to find a way of comparing various commodities with different use-values: 'the exchange-values of commodities must be capable of being expressed in terms of something common to them all' (I, p. 37). 'If then we leave out of consideration the use-value of commodities, they have only one common property left, that of being products of labour' (I, p. 38).

Labour is therefore the only source of value or, to be more exact, the substance of value. Before going on to demonstrate how value is to be measured we must first exactly define those categories to which the theory of labour-values applies. Only goods regularly produced to be sold on a market, i.e. commodities in the strict sense, and goods produced and reproducible by labour have an exchange-value. On this point Marx follows strictly Ricardo's analysis. Neither works of art nor land have exchange-value. Let us consider these two categories separately.

Marx's position concerning works of art is the same as Ricardo's. Marx refers to Ricardo approvingly on numerous occasions in *The Poverty of Philosophy.* The following quotations are explicit and require no further comment:

> Utility then is not the measure of exchangeable value, although it is absolutely essential to it.
>
> Possessing utility, commodities derive their exchangeable value from two sources: from their scarcity, and from the quantity of labour required to obtain them.
>
> There are some commodities, the value of which is determined by their scarcity alone. No labour can increase the quantity of such goods, and therefore their value cannot be lowered by an increased supply. Some rare statues and pictures, scarce books and coins, wines of a peculiar quality, which can be made only from grapes grown on a particular soil, of which there is a very limited quantity, are all of this description. Their value is wholly independent of the quantity of labour originally necessary to produce them, and varies with the varying wealth and inclinations of those who are desirous to possess them.
>
> These commodities, however, form a very small part of the mass of commodities daily exchanged in the market. By far the greatest part of those goods which are the objects of desire, are procured by labour; and they may be multiplied, not in one country alone, but in many, almost without any assignable limit, if we are disposed to bestow the labour necessary to obtain them.

> In speaking then of commodities, of their exchangeable value, and of the laws which regulate their relative prices, we mean always such commodities only as can be increased in quantity by the exertion of human industry, and on the production of which competition operates without restraint [pp. 11 and 12].*

For Ricardo, as for Marx, a work of art has no real exchange-value as previously defined. Of course, it will have a price but this price comes from the market, from the relation of exchange, while the exchange-value of a commodity exists prior to its exchange in the market. The factors that explain the formation of such prices are totally different from those that determine the value of commodities in the strict sense.

Land, similarly, has no exchange-value, yet it also can be exchanged, bought or sold. But its price is only the income it brings, the rent its landlord receives, capitalised at the current rate of interest: 'For instance, if the average rate of interest is 5%, then an annual ground-rent of 200 may be regarded as interest on a capital of 4,000. Ground-rent so capitalised constitutes the purchase price or value of the land, a category which like the price of labour is *prima facie* irrational, since the earth is not the product of labour and therefore has no value' (III, p. 608).

Having clarified the position of these two categories, the class of goods that is the object of the analysis is clearly specified and we can proceed to show how their value is to be measured.

1.1.2 The measure of value

'How, then, is the magnitude of this value to be measured? Plainly, by the quantity of the value-creating substance, the labour, contained in the article' (I, p. 38).

But this passage from labour to value cannot be made directly, for two quite different reasons. The first involves a *process of abstraction*, the second, a *process of socialisation*. Again, quoting Marx: 'Regarded as exchange-values all commodities are merely definite quantities of congealed *labour-time*' (C, p. 30); or: 'As objectification of social labour, all commodities are crystallisations of the same substance' (C, p. 29).

The first form of labour, which is essentially concerned with making an object useful, i.e. capable of satisfying human needs, Marx calls 'useful

* (The quotations are taken from Vol. I of the Sraffa edition of Ricardo. The quotes that appear on p. 49 of Marx's *The Poverty of Philosophy* (Chicago: Kerr & Co) which is the English translation of the reference cited by the authors, appear to be re-translations into English of an unknown translation of Ricardo used by Marx and thus do not correspond to their original source.)

labour' (C, p. 43) or 'concrete labour'. It is the labour which gives exchange-value to an object by modifying it in some particular way. This type of labour can be identified with the particular labour of specific workers: 'Different use-values are, moreover, products of the activity of different individuals and therefore the result of individually different kinds of labour. But as exchange-values they represent the same homogeneous labour, i.e., labour in which the individual characteristics of the workers are obliterated. Labour which creates exchange-value is thus *abstract general* labour' (C, p. 29).

There is then a state of the world typified by concrete labour and use-value, where concrete labour provides use-values. This state of the world may have existed in past history (the problem of the actual existence of historical antecedents is not, however, pertinent to our argument). Nonetheless, the requirements of exchange and private ownership of the means of production have profoundly modified the concrete conditions of labour which is replaced, as Marx shows, by its 'abstract' social form. Just as production is no longer production of use-value but production of exchange-value, the product of labour becomes a commodity, and concrete labour is transformed into abstract labour. We then have, in the beginning, so to speak, concrete labour of every possible variety and skill level. The commodity economy succeeds in masking these qualitative differences of labour, or, more exactly in transforming the products of labour into 'the same unsubstantial reality... a mere congelation of homogeneous human labour' (I, p. 38). This process is described by Marx several lines earlier: 'Along with the useful qualities of the products themselves, we put out of sight both the useful character of the various kinds of labour embodied in them, and the concrete forms of that labour; all are reduced to one and the same sort of labour, human labour in the abstract' (I, p. 38).

The differences in the quality of labour are also translated into differences in quantity. Marx distinguishes simple labour from skilled labour, defining the latter as 'labour-power whose production has cost more time and labour, and which therefore has a higher value' (I, p. 197). 'Skilled labour counts only as simple labour intensified, or rather, as multiplied simple labour, a given quantity of skilled being considered equal to a greater quantity of simple labour' (I, p. 44).

Labour called 'skilled' is therefore reduced to simple labour equivalents through a social process which is invisible to the producers.[2] Notice, however, as Marx emphasises, that this reduction does not in any way involve 'the wages or value that the labourer gets for a given labour-time, but...the value of the commodity in which that labour-time is materialised' (I, p. 44 n. 2).

Thus since skilled labour is just a multiple of simple labour, the exchange-value created by a skilled labourer can be expressed as being *x* times that created during the same time by a non-skilled labourer. All that is left is to identify the base of such a calculation. But on this point Marx is far from clear. It is possible to explain the equivalence on the basis of the cost of training in terms of labour-time. This view is supported by the following passage: 'All labour of a higher or more complicated character than average labour is expenditure of labour-power of a more costly kind, labour-power whose production has cost more time and labour' (I, p. 197). This is, in fact, nothing more than an indication. Marx does not define clearly the process that should be used to reduce skilled to simple labour. In what follows we shall suppose that this problem has been resolved and thus always reason in terms of simple labour equivalents. In this way the problem can be temporarily avoided; it nonetheless awaits a final resolution.[3]

There is thus a process which transforms concrete labour into abstract labour, i.e. different qualities of labour into multiples of a single quantity of a sort of numeraire: labour-time. This process of 'abstraction' is a social phenomenon that takes place in society, but is invisible to producers.

There is also an associated process, which we have assumed to be known, by which skilled labour is reduced to simple labour equivalents.

This phenomenon of socialisation also exists in another, analytically distinct, problem. The exchange-value of a commodity is not in fact determined by the conditions of production of each individual producer. If this were the case, 'Some people might think that if the value of a commodity is determined by the quantity of labour spent on it, the more idle and unskilful the labourer, the more valuable would his commodity be, because more time would be required in its production' (I, p. 39). In fact, 'no more time than is needed on an average, no more than is socially necessary' (I, p. 39) for a commodity's production should be considered, not the actual amount of time expended in production.

But just exactly how is this 'socially necessary' labour-time to be defined? The general idea seems clear enough, yet difficulties arise in its precise definition. In this respect consider the passage from *Capital* which follows that given above:

> The labour-time socially necessary is that required to produce an article under the normal conditions of production, and with the average degree of skill and intensity prevalent at the time. The introduction of power-looms

into England probably reduced by one-half the labour required to weave a given quantity of yarn into cloth. The hand-loom weavers, as a matter of fact, continued to require the same time as before; but for all that, the product of one hour of their labour represented after the change only half an hour's social labour, and consequently fell to one-half its former value [I, p. 39].

This passage should be considered with care. First, it makes the obvious point that value and wealth should not be confused. The fact that the quantity of cloth produced by one hour of unskilled labour stays constant does not prevent the value that is created during the same amount of time from being diminished as a result of the modifications in the conditions of production, i.e. of technical progress. It then stresses the important point that the value of a given quantity of a commodity diminishes with technical progress and innovation. But difficulties appear when the consequences of innovation (in this case the introduction of power-looms) on value are analysed more closely. If production with the new technique requires half the time previously necessary to turn a given amount of thread into cloth, is the value created by a traditional weaver simply one-half of what it was before the appearance of the new technology? This seems to be the implication of the final part of the passage. Yet, the first sentence of the passage seems to imply that the value should be an average of the new and the old technologies. But then, how is the average to be calculated?

Having recognised this difficulty (which will be dealt with in Chapter 3) we shall simply note how it underlines the extent to which the existence of exchange-value appears as a social phenomenon. What Marx calls the 'law of value' constitutes the fundamental law of exchange in commodity production. In the (imaginary ?) case of 'simple commodity production' (composed of individuals who exchange their products among themselves and who own their own means of production) the law of value is the law that directly determines prices. In such a society there are no capitalists and therefore there is no exploitation of labour. The prices or the ratios of exchange between commodities should be equal to the ratios of their values. In this case then the law of value implies the determination of prices. But it is more than this. A system of prices is, in fact, a system of exchange ratios, a relative system; while Marx's theory of value defines, given the problem already cited, an absolute measure, an absolute value for each product.

If the law of value, then, is also the law that directly determines price (while being more than this) in the case of simple commodity production, it can be seen that it only serves this function indirectly in the case of capitalist commodity production.[4]

Further, it should be noted that it would be an error to attribute:

> to Marx the idea that commodities *ought to* exchange according to the amounts of labour embodied in them. That is, this state of affairs will be eventually reached in a future, collectivist, society, when exploitation and profits have been eliminated and all the social product accrues to labourers... Now, this view simply rules out the contrast between Marx and the Utopian scholars. Marx makes it clear that his theory of value—and indeed his theory *tout court*—should not be interpreted as a *moral claim* or a normative proposition referring to the new post-capitalist society, but he emphasized that it was intended to be a tool of analysis of the *present* society.[5]

Having reviewed the significance of the law of value in Marx's theory it is now necessary to proceed to a precise demonstration of the measurement of the value of any commodity in terms of labour-time. We will assume in the argument that follows that the several problems cited above have been resolved, i.e. that all skilled labour has been converted into simple labour equivalents, and that the argument is formulated in terms of socially necessary labour.

It is also necessary to point out that we must take into account indirect labour as well as direct labour, i.e. the value incorporated in the means of production employed during the productive process. Marx is repeatedly perfectly explicit on this point: 'The labour required for the production of the cotton, the raw material of the yarn, is part of the labour necessary to produce the yarn, and is therefore contained in the yarn. The same applies to the labour embodied in the spindle, without whose wear and tear the cotton could not be spun' (I, p. 187). And further on, 'the quantity of labour expended in the production of the consumed article, forms a portion of the quantity of labour necessary to produce the new use-value; this portion is therefore *labour transferred from the means of production to the new product*' (I, p. 200).

The problem can be more easily understood with reference to Morishima's very simplified example.[6] Suppose that the society produces only two commodities, wheat (commodity 1) and fertiliser (commodity 2). The production of a unit of wheat (a bushel for example, or a ton, the actual unit is unimportant) requires a_{11} units of wheat, a_{12} units of fertiliser and l_1 units of direct labour (recall that skilled labour has already been reduced to simple labour equivalents).

Let λ_1 be the exchange-value of a unit of wheat, λ_2 the exchange-value of a unit of fertiliser. Since the a_{11} units of wheat and the a_{12} units of fertiliser consumed in the production of a unit of wheat represent $a_{11}\lambda_1$ and $a_{12}\lambda_2$ hours of labour, and l_1 additional hours of labour are required directly for the production of a unit of wheat, the total quantity of labour incorporated in a unit of wheat can be represented by λ_1, which is defined as the value of a unit of wheat

$$\lambda_1 = a_{11}\lambda_1 + a_{12}\lambda_2 + l_1 \tag{1}$$

In this example we have only wheat and fertiliser. Marx takes an example in which there are three commodities (yarn, cotton, spindles), but the same idea, expressed differently, can be seen in both.

> The labourer adds fresh value to the subject of his labour by expending upon it a given amount of additional labour, no matter what the specific character and utility of that labour may be. On the other hand, the values of the means of production used up in the process are preserved, and present themselves afresh as constituent parts of the value of the product; the values of the cotton and the spindle, for instance, re-appear again in the value of the yarn. The value of the means of production is therefore preserved, by being transferred to the product [I, p. 199].

Obviously, the value of wheat cannot be determined from the single equation (1) above, for there are two unknowns (the values of wheat and fertiliser) and only one equation (note that a_{11}, a_{12}, l_1 are supposed to be known parameters which express the social conditions of production for a given period in history). But we can also establish an equation for the definition of the value of a unit of fertiliser (a kilogram or a sack).

Let : a_{21} be the quantity of wheat (commodity 1) necessary to produce one unit of fertiliser (commodity 2);

a_{22} be the quantity of fertiliser necessary to produce one unit of fertiliser, and

l_2 the number of hours of direct labour required for the production of one unit of fertiliser.

Thus $\lambda_2 = a_{21}\lambda_1 + a_{22}\lambda_2 + l_2$. (2)

The values of wheat (λ_1) and fertiliser (λ_2) can now be determined from equations (1) and (2). It thus appears that no one commodity's value can be determined independently of the values of the other commodities (except for the case, of little economic interest, where the system is completely decomposable into independent sectors, i.e. where $a_{ij} = 0$ for all i, such that $i \neq j$).

The fact that value is a social phenomenon can now be presented in a different way. Value is determined in a given historical epoch by the conditions of production, the structure of technology (represented here by the values of a_{ij} and l_i), independent of any other factors.

More generally, for an economy of n sectors, if we call a_{ij} the quantity of good j used to produce a unit of good i and l_i the quantity of direct labour necessary to produce a unit of good i (in simple-labour equivalents) the technological structure of the economy could be presented as follows:

$$\begin{bmatrix} a_{11} & a_{12} & a_{1j} & a_{1n} \\ \cdots & \cdots & \cdots & \cdots \\ a_{i1} & a_{i2} & a_{ij} & a_{in} \\ \cdots & \cdots & \cdots & \cdots \\ a_{n1} & a_{n2} & a_{nj} & a_{nn} \end{bmatrix}, \quad \begin{bmatrix} l_1 \\ \cdots \\ l_i \\ \cdots \\ l_n \end{bmatrix}$$

The unit values of the different commodities can then be expressed as the consumption of indirect labour and necessary direct labour (socially necessary, of course) using the technological structure described above:

$$\begin{cases} \lambda_1 = a_{11}\lambda_1 + a_{12}\lambda_2 + \ldots + a_{1i}\lambda_i + \ldots + a_{1n}\lambda_n + l_1 \\ \lambda_2 = a_{21}\lambda_1 + a_{22}\lambda_2 + \ldots + a_{2i}\lambda_i + \ldots + a_{2n}\lambda_n + l_2 \\ \cdots\cdots\cdots\cdots\cdots\cdots\cdots\cdots\cdots\cdots\cdots\cdots \\ \lambda_j = a_{j1}\lambda_1 + a_{j2}\lambda_2 + \ldots + a_{ji}\lambda_i + \ldots + a_{jn}\lambda_n + l_j \\ \cdots\cdots\cdots\cdots\cdots\cdots\cdots\cdots\cdots\cdots\cdots\cdots \\ \lambda_n = a_{n1}\lambda_1 + a_{n2}\lambda_2 + \ldots + a_{ni}\lambda_i + \ldots + a_{nn}\lambda_n + l_n \end{cases}$$

or $\mathbf{\Lambda} = \mathbf{A\Lambda} + \mathbf{L}$ with $\mathbf{\Lambda} = \begin{bmatrix} \lambda_1 \\ \vdots \\ \lambda_i \\ \vdots \\ \lambda_n \end{bmatrix}$ and $\mathbf{L} = \begin{bmatrix} l_1 \\ \vdots \\ l_i \\ \vdots \\ l_n \end{bmatrix}$

Therefore $\mathbf{\Lambda} = [\mathbf{I} - \mathbf{A}]^{-1}\mathbf{L}$

if $\mathbf{I} - \mathbf{A}$ is nonsingular i.e. det $[\mathbf{I} - \mathbf{A}] \neq 0$. We assume that the system is productive (see below).

Several important points concerning value which Marx notes in the very first pages of Volume I of *Capital* (I, pp. 40–1) allow a more precise definition of the meaning of this approach. First, 'A thing can be a use-value, without having value. This is the case whenever its utility to man is not due to labour. Such are air, virgin soil, natural meadows, etc.' On the other hand:

> A thing can be useful and the product of human labour, without being a commodity. Whoever directly satisfies his wants with the produce of his own labour, creates, indeed, use-values, but not commodities. In order to produce the latter, he must not only produce use-values, but use-values for

> others, social use-values.[7] Lastly, nothing can have value, without being an object of utility. If the thing is useless, so is the labour contained in it; the labour does not count as labour, and therefore creates no value.

The readers' attention is drawn, in particular, to these latter points.

Thus the system $\mathbf{\Lambda} = \mathbf{A\Lambda} + \mathbf{L}$ does not apply to all 'things', to paraphrase Marx. First, because all 'things' which are not the product of human labour do not have value, thus they cannot have value by themselves. Further, because, even if human labour is involved, social use-values are not necessarily produced. Finally, because 'nothing can have value, without being an object of utility'. But, if something is (a) the product of human labour, (b) capable of satisfying a social need, and (c) useful, then its value will be determined by the matrix system

$$\mathbf{\Lambda} = \mathbf{A\Lambda} + \mathbf{L}$$

or $$\mathbf{\Lambda} = [\mathbf{I} - \mathbf{A}]^{-1}\mathbf{L} \qquad \text{if } \det[\mathbf{I} - \mathbf{A}] \neq 0$$

The assumptions that we have made in deriving this formulation may be stated more precisely as follows:[8]

(a) in each industry there is only one available method of production, such that there is no problem of the 'choice of techniques'. Furthermore, each technique exhibits constant returns to scale.[9]
(b) each industry produces only one type of good, i.e. an assumption of simple production or absence of joint-production.
(c) labour is the only primary productive factor (it is labour-power that is reproduced).
(d) there are no durable capital goods that exist for more than one period, i.e. there is only circulating capital.
(e) all goods have the same unit-period of production.
(f) each method of production is such that by starting with inputs at the beginning of the period, output is obtained at the end of the period, in such a way that labour is applied only once during the period.

We will see below how each of these assumptions may be relaxed.

1.1.3 From exchange-value to surplus-value and the theory of exploitation

Abstract labour is at one and the same time the substance and the measure of value. But how can surplus-value, 'the conversion of money into capital' (I, p. 161), be explained? The change in value expressed by M–C–M′ cannot be explained, according to Marx, either by the exchange M–C (purchase of a commodity with money) or by the exchange C–M′ (sale of a commodity for money) since all exchange must be exchange of equals.

> We are, therefore, forced to the conclusion that the change originates in the use-value, as such, of the commodity, i.e., in its consumption [I, p. 167].
>
> In order to be able to extract value from the consumption of a commodity, our friend, Moneybags, must be so lucky as to find, within the sphere of circulation, in the market, a commodity, whose use-value possesses the peculiar property of being a source of value ... [ibid.]
>
> The possessor of money does find on the market such a special commodity in capacity for labour or labour-power [ibid.].

The distinction that Marx draws between abstract labour and labour-power is evidently fundamental. Under capitalist production there is private ownership of the means of production, that is, the capitalist puts abstract labour to work and is the owner of the product produced by such labour. But the capitalist does not buy the abstract labour that is performed from the worker, but rather his, 'capacity for labour or labour-power'. 'By labour-power or capacity for labour is to be understood the aggregate of those mental and physical capabilities existing in a human being, which he exercises whenever he produces a use-value of any description' (ibid.).

This labour-power is a commodity. Certainly it possesses a particular characteristic, that has already been pointed out, of being the source of exchange-value. But, it is a commodity and, 'Like all others it has a value. How is that value determined? The value of labour-power is determined, as in the case of every other commodity, by the labour-time necessary for the production, and consequently also the reproduction, of this special article' (I, pp. 170–1).

This conception is more specifically defined in the following passages: 'the labour-time requisite for the production of labour-power reduces itself to that necessary for the production of those means of subsistence; in other words, the value of labour-power is the value of the means of subsistence necessary for the maintenance of the labourer' (I, p. 171). Marx adds:

> His natural wants, such as food, clothing, fuel, and housing, vary according to the climatic and other physical conditions of his country. On the other hand, the number and extent of his so-called necessary wants, as also the modes of satisfying them, are themselves the product of historical development, and depend therefore to a great extent on the degree of civilisation of a country ... In contradistinction therefore to the case of other commodities, there enters into the determination of the value of labour-power a historical and moral element. Nevertheless, in a given country, at a given period, the average

> quantity of the means of subsistence necessary for the labourer is practically known [I, p. 171].

This last point is important and will form an integral part of the argument that follows.

Also known for any period are, 'the sum of the means of subsistence necessary for the production of labour-power must include the means necessary for the labourer's substitutes, i.e., his children' (I, p. 172); and 'The expenses of his education (excessively small in the case of ordinary labour-power), enter *pro tanto* into the total value spent in its production' (ibid.). Obviously, then, 'The value of labour-power resolves itself into the value of a definite quantity of the means of subsistence. It therefore varies with the value of these means or with the quantity of labour requisite for their production' (I, p. 172).

With the value of labour-power determined in this way, surplus-value will appear as a difference or a gap between the value of labour-power and the value produced by that labour-power. If six hours' work a day suffice to produce the goods necessary to support a worker's family, the wage will be the equivalent of six hours' work. But the head of the family will work twelve hours under the regime of capitalist production. The capitalist appropriates the difference which is the surplus-value.

Surplus-value represents a deduction from the production of labour which constitutes what Marx calls the exploitation of labour-power by capital and which is a necessary consequence of the private ownership of the means of production and the transformation of labour-power into a commodity. Exploitation characterises the relations that emerge in production and separate men into two classes, those who own the means of production and those who own nothing but their own labour-power. The interests of the two groups are thus fundamentally antagonistic. For Marx the 'capitalist mode of production' is characterised by specific relations of production[10] in an economic system which is historically specific: 'Production of surplus-value is the absolute law of this mode of production' (I, p. 618).

At the aggregate level surplus-value is shared out among the capitalists under different forms (profits, rents, interest): '*Rent, Interest, and Industrial Profit* are only *different names* for *different parts* of the *surplus-value* of the commodity, or the *unpaid labour enclosed in it*, and they are *equally derived from this source, and from this source alone*' (Marx, *Wages, Price and Profit*, p. 39).

But, further precision is required for a complete analysis, for example, how is this surplus-value 'produced'? How can the capitalist increase surplus-value? What are the factors that explain changes in surplus-value?

First, it should be noticed that Marx does not employ Ricardo's distinction between *fixed* and *circulating capital* in his analysis of the process of production: 'According as capital is rapidly perishable, and requires to be frequently reproduced, or is of slow consumption, it is classed under the heads of circulating, or of fixed capital' (Sraffa edn, p. 31). Although Marx does not really reject this framework of analysis which he adopts later (Volume II) in his analysis of the turnover of capital, he does not think the distinction pertinent to the explanation of surplus-value. To treat the same phenomenon Marx instead defines *constant* and *variable* capital.

Constant capital is made up of the aggregate means of production that the capitalist buys or puts to work in each production process. This includes not only those goods considered by the classical economists as fixed capital but also the physical part of circulating capital (raw materials, energy...). It is simply 'dead labour' previously accumulated (during previous cycles of production) as constant capital: 'Therefore the means of production can never add more value to the product than they themselves possess' (I, p. 205). This type of capital can then only transfer value already created in a previous period to goods currently being produced, which is why it is identified as 'constant'.

Variable capital, on the contrary, is 'living labour' at work in the current cycle of production, it is the only capital that is productive in the literal sense, and it alone is the creator of value, and therefore surplus-value.

On this point Marx is perfectly explicit:

> That part of capital then, which is represented by the means of production, by the raw material, auxiliary material and the instruments of labour, does not, in the process of production, undergo any quantitative alteration of value. I therefore call it the constant part of capital, or, more shortly, *constant capital*.
>
> On the other hand, that part of capital, represented by labour-power, does, in the process of production, undergo an alteration of value. It both reproduces the equivalent of its own value, and also produces an excess, a surplus-value, which may itself vary, may be more or less according to circumstances. This part of capital is continually being transformed from a constant into a variable magnitude. I therefore call it the variable part of capital, or shortly, *variable capital* [I, p. 209].

We can now understand the importance that Marx attaches to the definition of the rate of surplus-value as 'an exact expression for the degree of exploitation of labour-power by capital, or of the labourer by the capitalist' (I, p. 218), that is, as a causal relation which shows the amount of surplus-value produced by a given variable capital. Surplus-value is related to variable capital as surplus labour is to necessary labour. Thus the rate of exploitation (surplus-value) can be expressed as

$$e = \frac{m}{v} = \frac{\text{surplus labour}}{\text{necessary labour}}$$

We can now proceed to a definition of those factors which determine the rate of surplus-value or the rate of exploitation, using a slightly different notation. (It is still supposed that the analysis is carried out in terms of socially necessary labour reduced to simple labour equivalents.) Assume that

– the average labourer has a working-day of T hours. The working-day is a function of historical conditions and social factors which vary over long periods of time. But, at any given instant T may be considered as given. The additional value created during the working-day is equal, by definition, to T.

– the worker receives daily, for his own maintenance and that of his family, means of subsistence made up of given quantities of particular goods, i.e. a basket of goods

$$\mathbf{D} = (D_1, D_2, D_3, \ldots, D_n)$$

representing a given physical quantity of good i (e.g. so many loaves of bread, or yards of cloth). The analysis could (but need not) be simplified by supposing that the worker only consumes one type of good, for example, bread, which he receives each day in a given amount (e.g., D_3).

– each of these goods has a value $(\lambda_1, \lambda_2, \lambda_3, \ldots, \lambda_n)$ which can be determined in the manner shown above, given the social conditions of production.

– the amount of labour necessary for the reproduction of labour-power is, then, in the general case $\sum_{i=1}^{i=n} D_i\lambda_i = \mathbf{D\Lambda}$ and in the simplified case where there is only one good in the consumption basket, $D_3\lambda_3$. This expression then represents the *value of daily labour-power* or the *necessary labour* required for daily maintenance and reproduction of labour-power, or the value of variable capital (for a working-day).

– *surplus-value* or *surplus labour* is then simply the difference between the actual labour performed, the value created (i.e. the length of the working-day, T), and the value of labour-power, the value (expressed in labour) of the workers' consumption ($\mathbf{D\Lambda}$ or $D_3\lambda_3$ in the simplified case).

This can be written as $m = T - \mathbf{D\Lambda}$ (or $m = T - D_3\lambda_3$ for the simplified case). From this the expression for the *rate of surplus-value* can be rewritten as

$$e = \frac{(T - \mathbf{D\Lambda})}{\mathbf{D\Lambda}} \quad \text{or} \quad e = \frac{(T - \Sigma D_i\lambda_i)}{\Sigma D_i\lambda_i}$$

and $e = \dfrac{(T - D_3\lambda_3)}{D_3\lambda_3}$ for the simplified case of the one-good consumption basket.

It is thus clear that the rate of surplus-value is a function of three distinct elements:

(a) the *quantitative importance of the various goods in the consumption basket* $(D_1, \ldots, D_n)$ (or D_3) that the worker receives. This basket is fixed for any given historical epoch but it can vary over the long period. This is the 'historical and moral element' incorporated in labour-power that Marx mentions. It is thus evident that, other things being equal, the rate of exploitation will be reduced if the basket of consumption goods expands.

(b) *the length of the working-day*, T. For $T' > T$, given $\mathbf{\Lambda}$ and $\mathbf{D}$ $e' = (T' - \mathbf{D\Lambda})/\mathbf{D\Lambda} > e = (T - \mathbf{D\Lambda})/\mathbf{D\Lambda}$. Therefore, any lengthening of the working-day implies, *ceteris paribus* (i.e. given $\mathbf{D}$ and $\mathbf{\Lambda}$), an increase in the rate of exploitation.

(c) *the value of wage goods* (i.e. the λ_i) or the social productivity of labour, keeping in mind that 'The value of commodities is in inverse ratio to the productiveness of labour' (I, p. 319).

This formulation allows us to specify more precisely the distinction between the production of absolute surplus-value (b) and the production of relative surplus-value (c). Here again it is necessary to cite Marx to show how the preceding analysis simply formalises (and possibly clarifies) his analysis:

> The prolongation of the working-day beyond the point at which the labourer would have produced just an equivalent for the value of his labour-power, and the appropriation of that surplus-labour by capital, this is production of absolute surplus-value. It forms the general groundwork of the capitalist system, and the starting-point for the production of relative surplus-value. The latter presupposes that the working-day is already divided into two parts, necessary labour, and surplus-labour. In order to prolong the surplus-labour, the necessary labour is shortened by methods whereby the equivalent for wages is produced in less time. The production of absolute surplus-value turns exclusively upon the length of the working-day; the production of relative surplus-value, revolutionises out and out the technical processes of labour, and the composition of society. It therefore pre-supposes a specific mode, the capitalist mode of production [I, pp. 509–10].

We can now see that the expression given above for the rate of exploitation can be reformulated even more simply. Up to this point we have assumed that the worker received a basket of consumption goods $(D_1, \ldots, D_n)$ (or D_3 in the simplified example with only one good in the consumption basket) for T hours of daily work. If we now write **d** for the goods that the worker receives for each hour of work (or d_3 for the simplified case) with **d** defined as $d_i = D_i/T$, the expression for the rate of exploitation becomes $e = (1 - \mathbf{d\Lambda})/\mathbf{d\Lambda}\,[= (1 - d_3\lambda_3)/d_3\lambda_3$ for the simplified case]. As long as $T - \mathbf{D\Lambda} > 0$ or $1 - \mathbf{d\Lambda} > 0$ (the two expressions are strictly equivalent) it is evident that there is exploitation.

The importance of a clear analysis of the factors determining the rate of surplus-value can now be recognised. To the extent that only variable capital is 'productive' in the sense of creating value, we know that another element is fundamentally important to Marx's analysis. This element is the *composition of capital,* the ratio of constant to variable capital, c/v.

A certain number of difficulties are encountered in rigorous presentation of Marx's analysis. A rather long passage is necessary to start with.

> The composition of capital is to be understood in a two-fold sense. On the side of value, it is determined by the proportion in which it is divided into constant capital or value of the means of production, and variable capital or value of labour-power, the sum of total wages. On the side of material, as it functions in the process of production, all capital is divided into means of production and living labour-power. This latter composition is determined by the relation between the mass of the means of production employed, on the one hand, and the mass of labour necessary for their employment on the other. I call the former the *value-composition,* the latter the *technical-composition* of capital. Between the two there is a strict correlation. To express this, I call the value-composition of capital, in so far as it is determined by its technical composition and mirrors the change of the latter, the *organic composition* of capital. Wherever I refer to the composition of capital, without further qualification, its organic composition is always understood [I, p. 612].

The formal schema set out above allows us to exactly determine the meaning of this passage and to identify the distinction Marx makes between the technical composition and the value composition of capital. From the value equations set out above, the organic composition of capital, k_i, for the ith branch or sector of production, can be written generally as:

$$k_i = \frac{\sum_{j=1}^{n} a_{ij}\lambda_j}{\left(\sum_{j=1}^{n} d_j\lambda_j\right) l_i} = \frac{\mathbf{a}_i\mathbf{\Lambda}}{l_i\mathbf{d\Lambda}}$$

where $\mathbf{a}_i = (a_{i1}, \ldots, a_{in})$ represents the quantity vector of goods necessary to produce a unit of good i, and l_i (a scalar) the quantity of direct labour required per unit.

The numerator of this expression simply represents the values of the different sorts of constant capital used in the production process. While this formulation is perfectly general it is probable that a certain number of the a_{ij} coefficients will be zero (e.g. consumption goods are not normally used as instruments of production, and, in addition, there is no necessity for all raw materials or production goods to be used in each branch of production considered).

The denominator represents variable capital, expressed in values, used in the ith sector. In this sector each of the l_i units of simple labour used receives a basket of consumption goods $(d_1, \ldots, d_j, \ldots, d_n)$ with values, respectively, of $(\lambda_1, \ldots, \lambda_j, \ldots, \lambda_n)$. Again, it is likely that a number of the ds will be zero for workers consume neither production goods nor luxury goods.

Taking a simple example of an economy with just four sectors producing, respectively, means of production, raw materials, wage goods and luxury goods consumed only by capitalists, the organic composition of capital in the second sector, k_2, defined as the ratio of the value of the means of production and the constant capital used up in that sector $(\mathbf{a}_2\mathbf{\Lambda})$ to the value of the variable capital $(l_2\mathbf{d}\mathbf{\Lambda})$ would be given by the following expression since $\mathbf{a}_2 = (a_{21}, a_{22}, 0, 0)$:

$$k_2 = \frac{a_{21}\lambda_1 + a_{22}\lambda_2}{l_2 d_3 \lambda_3} \left(= \frac{\mathbf{a}_2\mathbf{\Lambda}}{l_2\mathbf{d}\mathbf{\Lambda}} \right)$$

Now let us return to the difference between technical composition and value composition. The preceding analysis has dealt only with value composition. The technical composition of industry i represents the relation between the total means of production employed $(a_{i1}, a_{ii}, \ldots, a_{in})$ and the total labour employed in the same industry; any change in the technical coefficients of type a_{ij}, or in the coefficient of labour utilisation l_i due to a technical innovation would produce a change in the technical composition of capital. But such a change would also affect the values of commodities $(\lambda_1, \lambda_2, \ldots, \lambda_n)$ in such a way that the value composition of capital reflects not only changes in the technical composition, but also induced changes in the value system.

1.2 The problems of the 'transformation' of surplus-value into profit and of values into prices of production

Under conditions of simple commodity production, defined by the absence of capitalists (and thus absence of exploitation) and workers' ownership of their own means of production, the law of value directly explains the price system:

> it is quite appropriate to regard the values of commodities as not only theoretically but also historically *prius* to the prices of production.[11] This applies to conditions in which the labourer owns his means of production, and this is the condition of the landowning farmer living off his own labour and the craftsman, in the ancient as well as in the modern world... It holds not only for this primitive condition, but also for subsequent conditions, based on slavery and serfdom, and for the guild organization of handicrafts, so long as the means of production involved in each branch of production can be transferred from one sphere to another only with difficulty [III, p. 174].

But things will be rather different under the capitalist mode of production. The fundamental characteristic of this system is the transformation of the instruments of work into capital that is separate from the workers operating them. This is the result of the private ownership of the means of production and the exclusive emphasis of the system on the production of exchange-values.

In a letter to Engels, Marx writes: 'What competition between the various masses of capital—differently composed and invested in different spheres of production—is striving to produce is *capitalist communism,* namely that the *mass of capital belonging to each sphere of production* should snatch an aliquot part of the total surplus value proportionate to the part of the total social capital which it forms' (Marx and Engels, *Selected Correspondence*, Letter no. 101, 30 April 1868, p. 206).

It is from this last requirement that profit appears as a 'converted form of surplus-value' (III, p. 47) and the rate of profit differs from the rate of surplus-value. Again, in Marx's words:

> The rate of surplus-value measured against the variable capital is called rate of surplus-value. The rate of surplus-value measured against the total capital is called rate of profit. These are two different measurements of the same entity, and owing to the difference of the two standards of measurement they express different proportions or relations of this entity.
>
> The transformation of surplus-value into profit must be deduced from the transformation of the rate of surplus-value into the rate of profit, not vice versa. And in fact it was rate of profit which was the historical point of departure. Surplus-value and rate of surplus-value are, relatively, the invisible and unknown essence that wants investigating, while rate of profit and therefore the appearance of surplus-value in the form of profit are revealed on the surface of the phenomenon [III, pp. 42–43].

Obviously, surplus-value is created solely on the social level by living labour. This fact is embodied in the rate of surplus-value or the rate of exploitation (e) which represents the causal relation between the mass of surplus-value created and the amount of variable capital ($e = m/v$). But,

> So far as the individual capitalist is concerned, it is evident that he is only interested in the relation of the surplus-value, or the excess value at which he sells his commodities, to the total capital advanced for the production of the commodities, while the specific relationship and inner connection of this surplus with the various components of capital fail to interest him, and it is, moreover, rather in his interests to draw the veil over this specific relationship and this intrinsic connection [III, p. 43].

The rate of profit on the social level will thus be given by the ratio of total surplus-value to the total capital advanced. The capitalist makes no distinction between constant or variable capital for the particular nature of the total capital advanced is of no interest to him. It is here that we find the justification of what is commonly considered as the 'Marxian' assumption that the 'wage is advanced' by the capitalist while it is generally considered as being paid 'post-factum' in other theoretical approaches and in actual practice. Here again the discussion may be clarified by reference to a passage in Volume III of *Capital*:

> The capitalist does not care whether it is considered that he advances constant capital to make a profit out of his variable capital, or that he advances variable capital to enhance the value of the constant capital; that he invests money in wages to raise the value of his machinery and raw materials, or that he invests money in machinery and raw materials to be able to exploit labour. Although it is only the variable portion of capital which creates surplus-value, it does so only if the other portions, the conditions of production, are likewise advanced. Seeing that the capitalist can exploit labour only by advancing constant capital and that he can turn his constant capital to good account only by advancing variable capital, he lumps them all together in his imagination, and much more so since the actual rate of his gain is not determined by its proportion to the variable, but to the total capital, not by the rate of surplus-value, but by the rate of profit [III, pp. 41–2].

The rate of profit $r = m/(c + v)$ is thus seen to be distinct from the rate of exploitation $e = m/v$. Their relationship is shown by: $r = m/(c + v) = ev/(c + v) = e/(k + 1)$ where k, as previously defined, is the organic composition of capital c/v.

The rate of profit so defined ensures that the redistribution of the total surplus-value is in proportion to the total mass of capital. But this requirement of the capitalist mode of production at the same time implies that the operation of the law of value can only be identified indirectly through the intermediary of *prices of production*, which are defined by Marx in the following passage: 'The price thus equalised, which divides up the social surplus value equally among the individual capitals in proportion to their sizes, is the *price of production* of commodities, the centre around which the oscillation of the market prices move' (Marx and Engels, *ibid.*).

And in the second section of Volume III, 'the tendency necessarily prevails to make the prices of production merely converted forms of value, or to turn profits into mere portions of surplus-value. However, these are not distributed in proportion to the surplus-value produced in each special sphere of production, but rather in proportion to the mass of capital employed in each sphere' (III, pp. 170–1).

The disposal of commodities at their value would not ensure to each capitalist the average profit, 'the profit accruing...to any capital of a given magnitude, whatever its organic composition' (III, p. 156). 'It is *prima facie* two entirely different matters whether commodities are sold at their values (i.e., exchanged in proportion to the value contained in them at prices corresponding to their value), or whether they are sold at such prices that their sale yields equal profits for equal masses of the capitals advanced for their respective production' (III, p. 172).

Obviously, it is assumed that the rate of exploitation is the same in each sector of the economy: 'Such a general rate of surplus-value—viewed as a tendency, like all other economic laws—has been assumed by us for the sake of theoretical simplification.... In reality there exists only approximation' (III, p. 172).

In such conditions if all commodities sold at their values there would be a different rate of profit in each different sphere of production unless the organic composition of capital were the same in each (which is equivalent to assuming that there is only one sphere of production and one produced commodity...). Now, 'The whole difficulty arises from the fact that commodities are not exchanged simply as *commodities*, but as *products of capitals*, which claim participation in the total amount of surplus-value, proportional to their magnitude. And this claim is to be satisfied by the total price for commodities produced by a given capital in a certain space of time' (III, p. 172).

The problem to be resolved is clearly stated in this last quotation. What solution does Marx propose for it?

1.2.1 Karl Marx's solution

In Volume III Marx gives a number of arithmetical examples[12] to illustrate his analysis. They can be presented more generally as follows:

Write the value system as $\mathbf{\Lambda} = \mathbf{A\Lambda} + \mathbf{L}$ and define the rate of exploitation as $e = \frac{1 - \mathbf{d\Lambda}}{\mathbf{d\Lambda}}$ which when written as

$$(1 + e)\,\mathbf{d\Lambda} = 1 \text{ yields}^{13}$$

$$\mathbf{\Lambda} = \mathbf{A\Lambda} + \mathbf{L}(1 + e)\,\mathbf{d\Lambda} = \mathbf{A\Lambda} + \mathbf{Ld\Lambda} + e\mathbf{Ld\Lambda}$$

Let $\mathbf{y} = [y_1, y_2, \dots, y_n]$ be the vector of the quantities produced of each good.

Then we have:

$$\mathbf{y\Lambda} = \mathbf{yA\Lambda} + \mathbf{yLd\Lambda} + e\mathbf{yLd\Lambda}$$

with $\mathbf{y\Lambda}$ = the aggregate value of all produced commodities
$\mathbf{yA\Lambda}$ = the value of the total means of production employed, i.e. the total constant capital[14] expressed in values,
$\mathbf{yLd\Lambda}$ = the total of variable capital in values,
$e\mathbf{yLd\Lambda}$ = the total surplus-value.

Thus the rate of profit, r, defined by Marx as the ratio of the total surplus-value to the total capital advanced by the capitalists can be written as

$$r = \frac{e\mathbf{yLd\Lambda}}{\mathbf{yLd\Lambda} + \mathbf{yA\Lambda}} = \frac{e}{1 + k}$$

where $k = \mathbf{yA\Lambda}/\mathbf{yLd\Lambda}$ is the organic composition of capital.

The prices of production, $\mathbf{p}$, can be determined by applying this average rate of profit to the total capital advanced in each branch of production.

$$\mathbf{p} = (1 + r)(\mathbf{A\Lambda} + \mathbf{Ld\Lambda})$$

It can easily be seen that the determination of the prices of production requires previous knowledge of the values that appear in the expression for the rate of profit. It is also obvious that the rate of profit has been defined as a ratio of quantities measured in value terms.

Finally, it is easy to verify the two classic relations of Marxian analysis:
(a) *the sum of profits is of necessity equal to the total surplus-value.*

Total profit $\Pi = r(\mathbf{yLd\Lambda} + \mathbf{yA\Lambda})$ can in fact be written by using the definition of the rate of profit as

$$\Pi = \frac{e\mathbf{yLd\Lambda}}{\mathbf{yLd\Lambda} + \mathbf{yA\Lambda}}(\mathbf{yLd\Lambda} + \mathbf{yA\Lambda}) = e\mathbf{yLd\Lambda} = m$$

Of course, there will be a difference between the surplus-value created in each sector and the total profit of each sector since the norm for the distribution of surplus-value (i.e. total capital) is different from the norm for the creation of surplus-value (variable capital multiplied by the rate of exploitation). More precisely profit will be greater than surplus-value in those sectors where the organic composition of capital is greater than the average,[15] and less than surplus-value in those sectors where the organic composition is less than the average. Obviously, the two will be equal where the organic composition is equal to the average. The surplus-value created in each process of production (by variable capital alone) is thus redistributed in order to ensure the formation of a general rate of profit which rules in the long term as an average rate. By the same process the values of commodities are converted into prices of production so that the redistribution of the total surplus-value could be envisaged as taking place to the detriment of those branches with a relatively low organic composition of capital and to the benefit of those branches with a relatively high organic composition of capital.

(b) '*the sum of the prices of production of all commodities produced in society* [the totality of all branches of production] *is equal to the sum of their values*' (III, p. 157)

Thus:

$$\mathbf{yp} = (1 + r)\mathbf{y}(\mathbf{A\Lambda} + \mathbf{Ld\Lambda}) = \mathbf{y}(\mathbf{A\Lambda} + \mathbf{Ld\Lambda}) + r(\mathbf{yA\Lambda} + \mathbf{yLd\Lambda})$$

By taking (a) into account this can be written:

$$\mathbf{yp} = \mathbf{y}(\mathbf{A\Lambda} + \mathbf{Ld\Lambda}) + e\mathbf{yLd\Lambda} = \mathbf{y}(\mathbf{A\Lambda} + \mathbf{Ld\Lambda} + e\mathbf{Ld\Lambda}) = \mathbf{y\Lambda}$$

and

$$\mathbf{yp} = \mathbf{y\Lambda}$$

1.2.2 Marx's error

Marx was himself aware of the 'approximate' character of his solution: 'We had originally assumed that the cost-price of a commodity equalled the *value* of the commodities consumed in its production. But for the buyer the price of production of a specific commodity is its cost-price, and may thus pass as cost-price into the prices of other commodities' (III, p. 162).

The equations for the prices of production that Marx's analysis implies are not therefore correct because they are of the form

$$\mathbf{p} = (1 + r)(\mathbf{A\Lambda} + \mathbf{Ld\Lambda}) \text{ i.e. } p_i = (1 + r)(\mathbf{a}_i\mathbf{\Lambda} + l_i\mathbf{d\Lambda})$$

A few lines after the passage given above Marx himself notes that the approach followed in this equation is logically faulty: 'It is necessary to remember this modified significance of the cost-price, and to bear in mind that there is always the possibility of an error if the cost-price of a commodity in any particular sphere is identified with the value of the means of production consumed by it'. But having pointed out this possibility of error Marx immediately adds: 'Our present analysis does not necessitate a closer examination of this point' (III, p. 162).

It is precisely on this particular point that the controversy on the transformation of values into prices of production has developed. Von Bortkiewicz,[16] a German economist writing at the beginning of this century, was the first to emphasise the importance of the problem. The general idea is very simple. The equations that determine prices on the basis of values are, as Marx noted, logically inconsistent. The cost of production which enters the price of production of a commodity should itself be calculated in terms of its price of production. Thus the 'inputs' of these costs should also be measured in prices of production and not in values.

In the solution that Marx proposes the same commodity is considered in two different ways. As an 'input', an element in the process of production, it is measured in value. As an 'output', the result of the production process, in terms of prices of production. Let us make the assumption that there is no net accumulation, that the system is self-replacing (this assumption does not affect the generality of the analysis). If the *i*th commodity is neither a capitalist luxury good nor a workers' subsistence good then a quantity $\mathbf{y}\mathbf{a}^i$ of this commodity will be used, with

$$\mathbf{a}^i = \begin{bmatrix} a_{1i} \\ a_{2i} \\ \vdots \\ a_{ni} \end{bmatrix}$$

to produce quantity, y_i. The equilibrium conditions in terms of physical quantities can then be written $y_i = \mathbf{y}\mathbf{a}^i$ which becomes, in Marx's proposed solution, $y_i p_i = \mathbf{y}\mathbf{a}^i \lambda_i$.

The inconsistency of the system can easily be seen from the fact that this equilibrium condition now expresses a relation between quantities measured in terms of prices on one side, and of values on the other.

In fact, the values and the prices of production appear in two 'valuation spaces', the labour-value space (where the rate of exploitation appears) and the price of production space (where the rate of profit appears). In matrix notation the value system is written $\mathbf{\Lambda} = \mathbf{A}\mathbf{\Lambda} + \mathbf{L}$

while the price system is written

$$\mathbf{p} = (1 + R)[\mathbf{Ap} + \mathbf{L}w]$$

where $\mathbf{p}$ = the vector of prices of production
$\mathbf{A}$ = the technology matrix (as previously defined)
$\mathbf{L}$ = the vector of labour coefficients (as previously defined)
w = the wage rate defined as the money sum which allows the worker to buy consumption goods and must obviously be measured in prices of production $w = \mathbf{dp}(= \Sigma d_i p_i)$
R = the rate of profit, assumed to be uniform

The system of prices of production set out here is simply a representation in modern language of the principal result of von Bortkiewicz's study of the problem. There are no particular difficulties involved in its solution. If there are n goods we have a classic system of equations where:

(i) there are n independent equations (one for each good)
(ii) there are n unknowns, composed of $(n - 1)$ prices; since only relative prices have to be determined, one of the goods (any one) may serve as numeraire leaving $(n - 1)$ prices to be determined; and
(iii) 1 distributive variable, the rate of profit (since w is already given by $w = \mathbf{dp}$).

There are then n equations to determine the $(n - 1) + 1 = n$ unknowns.

While the mathematical solution of the problem presents no difficulties, the economic interpretation of the 'correction' of the transformation problem proposed by von Bortkiewicz does have three particularly important consequences.

1*st consequence*: contrary to Marx's thesis, not all branches of production participate in the *determination of the general rate of profit*, which is determined exclusively by the conditions of production in the sectors producing production goods on one hand, and wage goods on the other. The general rate of profit is exclusively determined by the direct and indirect production of the commodities of these two sectors while *the conditions of production of luxury goods have no influence whatsoever on the determination of the general rate of profit.*

This can be shown simply in an economy with only three sectors, the first producing instruments of production, the second, wage goods and the third, luxury goods (the generalisation to n sectors can be easily made).

Let

$$\mathbf{p} = \begin{bmatrix} p_1 \\ p_2 \\ p_3 \end{bmatrix}, \mathbf{A} = \begin{bmatrix} a_{11} & 0 & 0 \\ a_{21} & 0 & 0 \\ a_{31} & 0 & 0 \end{bmatrix} \text{ and } \mathbf{L} = \begin{bmatrix} l_1 \\ l_2 \\ l_3 \end{bmatrix}$$

with $w = d_2 p_2$ (the workers only consume wage goods produced by the second sector); d_2 is given for the period under consideration. The system of prices of production can then be written, taking account of the definition of w, as

$$p_1 = (a_{11}p_1 + l_1 d_2 p_2)(1 + R) \qquad \text{(a)}$$

$$p_2 = (a_{21}p_1 + l_2 d_2 p_2)(1 + R) \qquad \text{(b)}$$

$$p_3 = (a_{31}p_1 + l_3 d_2 p_2)(1 + R) \qquad \text{(c)}$$

$$\Leftrightarrow \mathbf{p} = (1 + R)[\mathbf{Ap} + \mathbf{L}w]$$

In the following table the endogenous variables used in each of the equations are identified:

Table 1

Equations	Endogenous variables			
	p_1	p_2	p_3	R
(a)	x	x		x
(b)	x	x		x
(c)	x	x	x	x

It is clear that one of the endogenous variables, p_3, the price of production of luxury goods, only appears in equation (c), while the other three endogenous variables appear in all the equations. Further, the two equation system composed of (a) and (b) is an independent system in two unknowns since any good can be taken as numeraire (e.g. wage goods). This leaves the price of production of means of production (constant capital) and the rate of profit as the two unknowns which can be determined by the sub-system of production (a) and (b) independently of (c).

The price of production of luxury goods is thus determined by the prices of production of (1) and (2) and the rate of profit but does not enter into their determination or have any kind of influence on them. There is thus a unique causal relation that runs from the variables determined by sub-system [(a), (b)] to those determined in the rest of the system.[17]

Commodities of type (3), the luxury goods, are neither used as means of production nor as means of subsistence for the production of other goods. Since these goods do not enter the determination of the system and are completely passive they can be classed as 'non-basics'. In other words, the price of a 'non-basic' product depends on the prices of its means of production (in the general sense, that is, taking into account the price of the basket of goods necessary for the reproduction of the labour power used in the production process) and is completely determined by them, but has no role in determining them. For a 'basic' good, on the contrary, the price of its means of production depends on its own price just as its price depends on the prices of its means of production. *The rate of profit and the prices of basic goods and only basic goods are determined simultaneously*, while the prices of non-basic goods are determined by them, as previously explained.

An exact formulation of the prices of production thus permits precision of the manner in which the rate of profit is determined. It does not produce any fundamental criticism of Marxian theory.

2nd consequence: we have already seen that the scheme of 'transformation' of values into prices of production set out by Marx emphasises on the one hand *the equality between the sum of profits and the sum of surplus-value and the equality between the sum of prices and the sum of values* on the other. Once the system of prices of production is written in a logically consistent manner and not in the approximate way that Marx suggested (although with caveats as noted above) *there is no longer any logical reason why these equalities should be true in general.*

Let us return to the notation used above. The value equations can be written, in matrix notation, as:

$$\mathbf{\Lambda} = \mathbf{A}\mathbf{\Lambda} + \mathbf{L}$$

The price equations are written in matrix notation as:

$$\mathbf{p} = (1 + R)(\mathbf{A}\mathbf{p} + \mathbf{L}w) \qquad \text{with } w = \mathbf{d}\mathbf{p}$$

It is in the price system that the rate of profit is defined.

We thus have two distinct systems of valuation, two disjoint 'spaces': the system of values (or the 'value space') where the rate of exploitation is defined, and the system of prices of production (or the 'price space') where the rate of profit is determined. As a result, aggregate profits and the mass of surplus-value on one hand and the sum of prices and the sum of values on the other are, in the strict sense, both *non commensurable* pairs. This does not mean that the equalities are not true. Rather it means, as a logical consequence of the construction of the price system and the value system, that no comparison is possible, the equality cannot be verified. It is essential to note that the 'value system' represents 'labour contents', i.e. absolute values, while the price system determines relative prices (defined up to the multiplication by scalars). (Relative) prices and (absolute) values are incommensurable *a priori.*

However, it is possible to make them commensurable by normalising the price system. We can, for example, set $p_i = \lambda_i$, i.e. normalise the price system in such a way that the price of a certain quantity of a commodity (3 ounces of gold, for example, or 4 kilos of wheat) is set equal to its value. This normalisation condition is always possible and does not require any other assumption. But we can also set $\mathbf{yp} = \mathbf{y\Lambda}$ as a normalisation condition. This means that the value in terms of prices of production of the aggregate output is, by assumption, equal to its labour-value or in other words, that 'the sum of prices equals the sum of values'. But we cannot in general affirm that the sum of profits is equal to the sum of surplus-value.

Let the value system be

$$\mathbf{\Lambda} = \mathbf{A\Lambda} + \mathbf{L} = \mathbf{A\Lambda} + (1 + e)\mathbf{Ld\Lambda}$$

The total surplus-value is written as:

$$e\mathbf{yLd\Lambda} = \mathbf{y\Lambda} - \mathbf{yA\Lambda} - \mathbf{yLd\Lambda} = \mathbf{y\Lambda} - \mathbf{y}(\mathbf{A} + \mathbf{Ld})\mathbf{\Lambda}$$

$$e\mathbf{yLd\Lambda} = \mathbf{y\Lambda} - \mathbf{yA}^*\mathbf{\Lambda}, \qquad \text{with } \mathbf{A}^* = \mathbf{A} + \mathbf{Ld}.$$

The price system is written

$$\mathbf{p} = (1 + R)(\mathbf{Ap} + \mathbf{Ldp}) = (1 + R)(\mathbf{A} + \mathbf{Ld})\mathbf{p} = (1 + R)\mathbf{A}^*\mathbf{p}$$

Thus the aggregate profit is

$$R\mathbf{y}(\mathbf{A} + \mathbf{Ld})\mathbf{p} = \mathbf{yp} - \mathbf{y}(\mathbf{A} + \mathbf{Ld})\mathbf{p} = \mathbf{yp} - \mathbf{yA}^*\mathbf{p}.$$

Using the normalisation condition $\mathbf{yp} = \mathbf{y\Lambda}$, it is obvious that the aggregate profit cannot be equal to the mass of surplus-value since (at least generally) $\mathbf{yA}^*\mathbf{\Lambda} \neq \mathbf{yA}^*\mathbf{p}$.

We could, however, use another normalisation condition for prices such as, for example, $\mathbf{y}(\mathbf{I} - \mathbf{A}^*)\mathbf{p} = \mathbf{y}(\mathbf{I} - \mathbf{A}^*)\mathbf{\Lambda}$; this means that aggregate profit is set equal to surplus-value. In this case, we can show without difficulty that, generally, the equality between 'the sum of prices and the sum of values' does not hold:

$$\mathbf{y}(\mathbf{I} - \mathbf{A}^*)\mathbf{\Lambda} = \mathbf{y\Lambda} - \mathbf{yA}^*\mathbf{\Lambda} = e\mathbf{yLd\Lambda}$$

$$\mathbf{y}(\mathbf{I} - \mathbf{A}^*)\mathbf{p} = \mathbf{yp} - \mathbf{yA}^*\mathbf{p} = R\mathbf{yA}^*\mathbf{p}$$

It is obvious that the normalisation condition 'aggregate profits equal the mass of surplus-value' only implies $\mathbf{yp} = \mathbf{y\Lambda}$ if $\mathbf{yA}^*\mathbf{p} = \mathbf{yA}^*\mathbf{\Lambda}$ and there is no reason for this latter equality to be satisfied.

It is therefore always possible to obtain *either* the equality between the sum of profits and the mass of surplus-value *or* the equality between the sum of prices and the sum of values, depending on the choice of the normalisation condition. But it is impossible for the two equalities (associated with different normalisation conditions for the prices of production) to be simultaneously satisfied. We shall show, however, that in a certain number of particular cases (see Chapter 6) both equalities can hold simultaneously. But this is not the problem; the simultaneous realisation of these two equalities is *in general* impossible.

3rd consequence: the modern presentation of the system of prices of production shows clearly the problem that emerged after von Bortkiewicz pointed out Marx's logical error.

Since the system of prices is written

$$\mathbf{p} = (1 + R)(\mathbf{Ap} + \mathbf{Ldp}) = (1 + R)\mathbf{A}^*\mathbf{p}$$

it is obvious that the value equations are not in any way needed to write the system. The system of prices (of production) is thus independent of the value system; this poses a fundamental challenge to Marxian theory since for Marx the 'transformation' problem gave at the same time an explanation and a causal relation of the following type:

$$\text{value} \longrightarrow \text{rate of profit} \longrightarrow \text{prices of production}$$

But we have already shown that prices of production and the rate of profit are simultaneously determined, thus the rate of profit cannot be considered as essential to the determination of the prices of production.

The consequences of this were seen immediately by neoclassical writers. At the end of the last century Böhm-Bawerk concluded that Marx's theory of value was useless and inconsistent since prices of production could be determined without reference to the law of value, and that Volume III of *Capital*, where the theory of prices of production is spelled out, is in direct contradiction with (or at best, has no relation to) Volume I where the theory of labour-value is presented, this latter being without interest.

More recently a similar position has been taken by Paul Samuelson[18]:

> I should perhaps explain in the beginning why the words 'so-called transformation problem' appear in the title. As the present survey shows, better descriptive words than 'the transformation problem' would be provided by the 'problem of comparing and contrasting the mutually-exclusive alternatives of "values" and "prices".' For when you cut through the maze of algebra and come to understand what is going on, you discover that the 'transformation algorithm' is precisely of the following form: 'Contemplate two alternative and discordant systems. Write down one. Now transform by taking an eraser

and rubbing it out. Then fill in the other one. Voilà! You have completed your transformation algorithm.'

It is true that the 'transformation' such as it was envisaged by Marx is logically impossible, that there is no algorithm that permits the move from value-space to price-space, the 'transformation' of values into prices. But this does not signify that the theory of value is without importance or useless. In fact, a 'bridge', a 'passage' between the Marxist theory of prices of production and the Marxist theory of value exists. This bridge exists in what has now commonly come to be called the Okishio–Morishima 'Fundamental Marxian Theorem'.

1.2.3 The 'Fundamental Marxian Theorem'[19]

This 'theorem' is both very simple and very important. Its application is seemingly limited since it only allows the demonstration that *positive profits will exist in all sectors of production only if there is exploitation of labour*. This proposition that *the exploitation of labour by capitalists is a necessary condition for the existence of positive profits* may seem tautologous if one refers to Marx's definition of the rate of profit:

$$r = \frac{m}{c+v} = e\frac{v}{c+v}$$

where it is clear that r is positive only if e, the rate of exploitation, is positive.

But we have already seen that this expression does not determine the rate of profit R. The rate of profit is in fact defined in price 'space' and the rate of exploitation in value 'space' and it seems impossible to find a way from one to the other. Further, even if we argue in prices of production normalised by the condition 'the sum of prices equals the sum of values'. the mass of surplus-value ($m = ev$) will not in general be equal to the aggregate profit.

The link between the rate of exploitation and the rate of profit thus cannot possibly be tautologous. It involves a demonstration of the conditions for the existence of a positive profit in all sectors (prices of production also being positive) which allows a link to be established between the theory of distribution, the existence of a positive profit in the price system and the theory of labour-values or, more precisely, with the theory of exploitation.

Demonstration

Recall that the system of values can be written as

$$\mathbf{\Lambda} = \mathbf{A\Lambda} + (1+e)\mathbf{Ld\Lambda} = \mathbf{A\Lambda} + \mathbf{Ld\Lambda} + e\mathbf{Ld\Lambda}$$

given the definition of the rate of exploitation.

Define $\mathbf{A}^*$ as the 'socio-technological' matrix obtained from the technology matrix $\mathbf{A}$ and the vectors $\mathbf{d}$ and $\mathbf{L}$ representing respectively the means of subsistence 'advanced' to the labourers and the socially necessary direct labour required per unit of output such that

$$\mathbf{A}^* = \mathbf{A} + \mathbf{Ld} \qquad \text{or } a_{ij}^* = a_{ij} + l_i d_j$$

Then

$$\mathbf{\Lambda} = \mathbf{A}^*\mathbf{\Lambda} + e\mathbf{Ld\Lambda}$$

The system of prices of production can then be written in the same notation as:

$$\mathbf{p} = (1+R)(\mathbf{Ap} + \mathbf{Ldp}) = (1+R)(\mathbf{A} + \mathbf{Ld})\mathbf{p} = (1+R)\mathbf{A}^*\mathbf{p}$$

$\mathbf{p}$ is therefore the eigenvector corresponding to the dominant eigenvalue $\alpha^* = 1/(1+R)$ of the $\mathbf{A}^*$ matrix (see mathematical appendix). We also know that $\mathbf{p}$ will be strictly positive if $\mathbf{A}^*$ is indecomposable and semi-positive if $\mathbf{A}^*$ is decomposable.

With the rate of profit R determined simultaneously with the prices of basic products[20] we can, for simplicity, distinguish two cases:

(a) all goods are basic (no luxuries) which means that the $\mathbf{A}^*$ matrix is indecomposable and that $\mathbf{p}$ is strictly positive (see mathematical appendix).

Thus

$$R > 0 \Leftrightarrow \alpha^*(\mathbf{A}^*) = \frac{1}{1+R} < 1$$

$$\alpha^*(\mathbf{A}^*) < 1 \Leftrightarrow e > 0$$

since we have

$$\mathbf{\Lambda} = (\mathbf{A}^* + e\mathbf{Ld})\mathbf{\Lambda} \qquad \text{or } \alpha^*(\mathbf{A}^* + e\mathbf{Ld}) = 1$$

and therefore $\alpha^*(\mathbf{A}^*) < 1$ is equivalent to $\mathbf{A}^* \leq \mathbf{A}^* + e\mathbf{Ld}$ where $\mathbf{Ld} \geq 0$ (see mathematical appendix, Section 5 theorem 2)

Thus R is positive if, and only if, e is positive (the fact that e is positive if R is positive is mathematically true but without any interest in this case). We can therefore conclude that in a productive system without joint production[21] the necessary and sufficient condition to have a uniform positive rate of profit in every sector producing 'basic' goods is the exploitation of labour.

(b) Not all goods are basic (luxuries consumed only by capitalists exist) which means that $\mathbf{A}^*$ is decomposable (see Chapters 2 and 3). Let $\bar{\mathbf{A}}^*$ be the (indecomposable) matrix of only basic goods which is the same as the preceding case.

It may be observed in passing that this necessity of distinguishing basic from non-basic products[22] is linked to the very definition of a commodity given by Marx in the opening lines of *Capital*: 'A commodity is, in the first place, an object outside us, a thing that by its properties satisfies human wants of some sort or another... whether directly as means of subsistence, or indirectly as means of production' (I, p. 35). Commodities in this sense are a sub-set of the set of produced goods. This sub-set is represented by the basic sector $\bar{\mathbf{A}}^*$ of the $\mathbf{A}^*$ matrix.

Obviously, in order for profit to actually arrive in the capitalists' hands the products must first be sold. If not, the labourer is indeed exploited in the sense that the working-day is longer than the time he need work to produce his own subsistence, but surplus-value is not realised for the capitalist fails to convert commodities produced into money capital.

For realisation to take place and the profit to arrive in the hands of the capitalists certain supplementary conditions must be satisfied; there must be a sufficient demand for the surplus products which constitute the surplus to be sold. We shall return to the conditions required for realisation of surplus-value in Chapters 5 and 6. Obviously, the object of the fundamental Marxian theorem is not the problem of the realisation of surplus-value. Furthermore, the theorem does not assure the transformation of values into prices of production and of surplus-value into profit.

We have already seen that in Marx's analysis a relation between the rate of exploitation and the rate of profit is established by means of the concept of the average or social organic composition of capital. No similar relation is proposed here. The 'fundamental Marxian theorem' does not establish a relation between the rate of profit and the rate of exploitation, it only shows that for the rate of profit to be positive it is necessary (and sufficient) that the rate of exploitation be positive. We shall examine below (Chapter 6) what kind of functional relation can be derived between the rate of profit (R) and the rate of exploitation (e) and we shall identify those special cases in which Marx's analysis is valid.

The study of the prices of production is the object of the two following chapters.

2

Prices of production: single-product industries and circulating capital

This chapter will examine the problem of the determination of prices of production taking the analysis presented by P. Sraffa in his *Production of Commodities by Means of Commodities*[1] as a starting point.

The examination is limited to the study of systems with single-product industries and circulating capital. Each industry, process or activity (the three classifications are considered as equivalent) is assumed to produce one single commodity by means of circulating capital and labour. We are therefore able to use the main points of the analysis of Part I of Sraffa's book.[2] By amplifying the mathematical formulation of Sraffa's approach it can be compared and analysed by reference to certain properties of decomposable or indecomposable matrices and to the Perron–Frobenius theorem.[3]

It should be pointed out immediately that the presentation of Sraffa's theory which will be given here is not completely 'faithful'. In the preface to his book Sraffa stresses that 'no question arises as to the variation or constancy of returns',[4] yet we shall explicitly assume that constant returns prevail in every industry. This 'unfaithfulness', which was anticipated and partially accepted by the author,[5] is first of all mathematically convenient and, further, it has no important consequences in the present context since we do not propose any additional contribution to the critique of the neoclassical theory of capital that has already been developed.[6] Finally, it is necessary for the analysis of the activity levels of the system which will be considered below. The assumption of constant returns will therefore be used in our examination of the principal topics developed by Sraffa in relation to single-product industries and circulating capital. The more complex problems of joint production, fixed capital and land will be investigated more thoroughly in Chapter 3.

2.1 Production for subsistence

Consider a society which produces just enough to maintain itself; every commodity produced is entirely consumed either as a means of production or as a subsistence good. Such a system which just replaces those commodities that have been used up in the process of production is said to be 'self-replacing'.

More generally, let us suppose that there are k commodities each of which is produced by a different industry. Calling a_{ij} the quantity of j necessary to produce a unit of i, the vector of inputs necessary to produce a unit of i is $(a_{i1}, a_{i2}, \ldots, a_{ij}, \ldots, a_{ik})$. We do not have to suppose that every commodity enters directly in the production of every other, so some of the a_{ij} may be zero.

The quantity produced of each commodity can be used as the unit of output, without making the analysis any less general. Thus, if the three industries of the economy produce respectively 450 quarters of wheat, 21 tons of iron, and 60 pigs, this assumption means that the unit of output produced by the first industry is made up of 450 quarters of wheat, by the second, of 21 tons of iron...etc. The a_{ij} are accordingly identified: the vector of inputs necessary to produce a unit of wheat is the vector of inputs necessary to produce 450 quarters of wheat. We note that for all commodities, $\sum_{i=1}^{k} a_{ij} = 1$ since, by assumption, in a self-replacing system the consumed quantity of j, $\sum_{i=1}^{k} a_{ij}$, equals the produced quantity of j (which equals 1 as seen above).

Every quantity produced and consumed is known, by assumption. The unknowns to be determined are $p_1, p_2, \ldots, p_k$, the values of the units of output of the k commodities which, if adopted, restore the 'original distribution of the products and make it possible for the process to be repeated; such values spring directly from the methods of production' (P. S. §1, p. 3).

The k prices are the solution of the following system:

$$\begin{cases} a_{11}p_1 + \ldots + a_{1j}p_j + \ldots + a_{1k}p_k = p_1 \\ \cdots\cdots\cdots\cdots\cdots\cdots\cdots\cdots\cdots\cdots\cdots\cdots \\ a_{i1}p_1 + \ldots + a_{ij}p_j + \ldots + a_{ik}p_k = p_i \\ \cdots\cdots\cdots\cdots\cdots\cdots\cdots\cdots\cdots\cdots\cdots\cdots \\ a_{k1}p_1 + \ldots + a_{kj}p_j + \ldots + a_{kk}p_k = p_k \end{cases}$$

or

$$\mathbf{Ap} = \mathbf{p} \qquad \text{where} \quad \underset{(k \times k)}{\mathbf{A}} = [a_{ij}] \quad \text{and} \quad \underset{(k \times 1)}{\mathbf{p}} = [p_i]$$

The price vector **p** appears as the eigenvector of matrix **A**[7] corresponding to the dominant eigenvalue 1 of **A**. The vector **p** is defined up to the multiplication by scalars since one can choose the value of any commodity (or any combination of commodities) as the standard of value. Therefore there are only $k-1$ unknowns.[8]

On the other hand, there are k equations but only $(k-1)$ are independent. Since we have supposed that the system replaces what has been consumed in production, the sum of each column equals 1. If we sum the equations, the same quantities will appear on both sides, therefore any one of these equations can be inferred from the sum of the $(k-1)$ other equations. This leaves only '$k-1$ independent linear equations which uniquely determine the $k-1$ prices' (P. S. §3, p. 5). Thus the system of k equations has rank $(k-1)$.

The fact that the number of equations is equal to the number of unknowns is not sufficient to ensure that every price is strictly positive. But it is implicitly assumed here that matrix **A** is indecomposable. (We will return to this important point below.) Given this assumption the eigenvector corresponding to the dominant eigenvalue of an indecomposable matrix is strictly positive. Every price is then strictly positive and defined uniquely, up to the multiplication by scalars.

Sraffa gives two examples to illustrate 'an extremely simple society which produces just enough to maintain itself. Commodities are produced by separate industries and are exchanged for one another at a market held after the harvest' (P. S. §1, p. 3). For a system producing three commodities:

$$\begin{aligned} 240 \text{ qr wheat} + 12 \text{ t iron} + 18 \text{ pigs} &\rightarrow 450 \text{ qr wheat} \\ 90 \text{ qr wheat} + 6 \text{ t iron} + 12 \text{ pigs} &\rightarrow 21 \text{ t iron} \\ 120 \text{ qr wheat} + 3 \text{ t iron} + 30 \text{ pigs} &\rightarrow 60 \text{ pigs} \end{aligned}$$

'The exchange-values which ensure replacement all round are 10 quarters of wheat = 1 ton iron = 2 pigs' (P.S. §1, p. 4). Using the notation previously defined we have:

$$\mathbf{A} = \begin{bmatrix} \frac{8}{15} & \frac{4}{7} & \frac{3}{10} \\ \frac{3}{15} & \frac{2}{7} & \frac{1}{5} \\ \frac{4}{15} & \frac{1}{7} & \frac{1}{2} \end{bmatrix}$$

The dominant eigenvalue of **A** is 1 because the sum of the elements in each column is equal to 1 and the corresponding eigenvector up to the multiplication by scalars is $\mathbf{p} = \begin{bmatrix} 15 \\ 7 \\ 10 \end{bmatrix}$. This means that if 15 is the 'cost' of 450 quarters of wheat, 7 the 'cost' of 21 tons of iron and 10 the 'cost' of 60 pigs, then 1 is at the same time the 'cost' of 30 quarters of wheat (450/15), of 3 tons of iron (21/7), and of 6 pigs (60/10).

30 quarters of wheat are then being exchanged for three tons of iron or six pigs. The exchange-values are therefore those indicated above: 10 quarters of wheat = 1 ton of iron = 2 pigs.

In production for replacement, 'there is a unique set of exchange-values which if adopted by the market restores the original distribution of the products and makes it possible for the process to be repeated; such values spring directly from the methods of production' (P.S. §1, p. 3).

The problem is more difficult when there is a surplus.

2.2 Production with a surplus

If the economy produces more than the minimum necessary for replacement of what has been used up in production and if there is a surplus to be distributed (i.e. $\sum_{i=1}^{k} a_{ij} \leq 1$ for all j, with a strict inequality for at least one j), then exchange-values cannot be determined as in the case of production for subsistence. We now have a system of equations of rank k to determine $k - 1$ prices. The k equations are independent, that is, none of them can be inferred from the rest of the system and we only have $k - 1$ prices as unknowns.

2.2.1 Prices and distribution

The problem of the distribution of surplus demonstrates the interaction between prices and the distributive variables. Sraffa assumes that 'the surplus (or profit) must be distributed in proportion to the means of production (or capital) advanced in each industry' and he shows that 'the distribution of the surplus must be determined through the same mechanism and at the same time as are the prices of commodities' (P.S. §4, p. 6).

When we introduce the rate of profit r (assumed to be uniform for all industries) as an additional unknown, the system becomes:

$$\begin{cases} (a_{11}p_1 + \dots + a_{1j}p_j + \dots + a_{1k}p_k)(1+r) = p_1 \\ \dots\dots\dots\dots\dots\dots\dots\dots\dots\dots\dots\dots \\ (a_{i1}p_1 + \dots + a_{ij}p_j + \dots + a_{ik}p_k)(1+r) = p_i \\ \dots\dots\dots\dots\dots\dots\dots\dots\dots\dots\dots\dots \\ (a_{k1}p_1 + \dots + a_{kj}p_j + \dots + a_{kk}p_k)(1+r) = p_k \end{cases}$$

Or, in matrix notation:

$$\mathbf{Ap}(1+r) = \mathbf{p} \Leftrightarrow \mathbf{Ap} = \frac{1}{1+r}\mathbf{p}$$

which means that **p** is the eigenvector corresponding to the dominant eigenvalue $1/(1+r)$.[9] In this way we determine simultaneously the dominant eigenvalue of **A**, $1/(1+r)$, i.e. the rate of profit r and the corresponding eigenvector **p**, i.e. the $(k-1)$ relative prices.[10]

To show this, let us use the example given by Sraffa of a two-commodity system, wheat and iron, where there is a surplus of 175 quarters of wheat and no surplus of iron. By assumption, we have the following production equations:

$$\begin{cases} 280 \text{ quarters wheat} + 12 \text{ tons iron} \rightarrow 575 \text{ qr wheat} \\ 120 \text{ quarters wheat} + 8 \text{ tons iron} \rightarrow 20 \text{ t iron} \end{cases}$$

The simultaneous determination of prices and rate of profit does not present any difficulty once we have written the system as $\mathbf{Ap} = 1/(1+r)\mathbf{p}$ or

$$\begin{bmatrix} \frac{56}{115} & 0.6 \\ \frac{24}{115} & 0.4 \end{bmatrix} \begin{bmatrix} p_1 \\ p_2 \end{bmatrix} = \frac{1}{1+r} \begin{bmatrix} p_1 \\ p_2 \end{bmatrix}$$

Let us call $\alpha^* = 1/(1+r)$ the dominant eigenvalue of matrix **A**. Using the characteristic equation $|\mathbf{A} - \alpha\mathbf{I}| = 0$ we get $\alpha^* = (92/115)$ and therefore $r = 25\%$.[11]

The eigenvector $\begin{bmatrix} p_1 \\ p_2 \end{bmatrix}$ corresponding to $1/(1+r) = 92/115$ is such that $(56/115)p_1 + 0.6p_2 = (92/115)p_1$ or $0.6p_2 = (36/115)p_1$. Therefore $p_2 = (60/115)p_1 = (12/23)p_1$ or $\begin{bmatrix} p_1 \\ p_2 \end{bmatrix} = \begin{bmatrix} 23 \\ 12 \end{bmatrix}$. These results mean that 575 quarters of wheat are exchanged for 20 tons of iron with a relative price ratio for these two quantities as shown in the equation above. In other words, the value of 20 tons of iron is equivalent to the value of 12/23 of 575 quarters of wheat or a ton of iron is exchanged for 20 times less wheat: $[(12/23) \times 575](1/20) = 15$ qr.[12] 'The exchange-ratio which enables the advances to be replaced and the profits to be distributed to both industries in proportion to their advances is 15 quarters of wheat for 1 ton of iron; and the corresponding rate of profits in each industry is 25%' (P.S. §5, p. 7).

How can workers' wages be taken into account? 'We have up to this point regarded wages as consisting of the necessary subsistence of the workers and thus entering the system on the same footing as the fuel for the engines or the feed for the cattle'[13] (P.S. §8, p. 9). We can also assume that wages include a share of the surplus. Sraffa continues: 'In view of this double character of the wages it would be appropriate ... to separate the two component parts of the wage and regard only the "surplus" part as variable' (P.S. §8, p. 9). However, Sraffa abandons this assumption as soon as it is suggested[14] and goes on to consider the whole of the wage as variable, with three immediate consequences:

(a) the necessaries of consumption are relegated 'to the limbo of non-basic products[15] ... so that an improvement in the methods of production of necessaries of life will no longer directly affect the rate of profits and the prices of other products' (P.S. §8, p. 10). Sraffa points out that 'necessaries however are essentially basic and if they are prevented from exerting their influence on prices and profits under that label, they must do so in devious ways (e.g., by setting a limit below which the wage cannot fall ...)' (P.S. §8, p. 10). We will subsequently suggest a more general treatment which avoids the contradiction that Sraffa refers to in the preceding quotation.

(b) Sraffa assumes that wages are paid *post factum* as a share of the annual product whereas the classics assumed wages to be 'advanced' by the capitalist.[16]

(c) quantities of commodities necessary for workers' subsistence no longer appear in the technology matrix. The quantity of labour employed in each industry (with labour of uniform quality) must now enter explicitly. Sraffa assumes that 'any differences in quality have been previously reduced to equivalent differences in quantity so that each unit of labour receives the same wage' (P.S. §8, p. 10).

Let $l_1, l_2, \ldots, l_k$ be the annual quantities of labour respectively employed in the industries 1, 2, ..., k and assume $l_1 + l_2 + \ldots l_k = 1$, i.e. define the l_js as fractions of the total annual labour of society which is equal to unity.

Let w be the wage per unit of labour which, just as for prices, will be expressed in terms of the chosen standard. On this basis the production equations will take the form:

$$\begin{cases} (a_{11}p_1 + \ldots + a_{1j}p_j + \ldots + a_{1k}p_k)(1+r) + wl_1 = p_1 \\ \ldots\ldots\ldots\ldots\ldots\ldots\ldots\ldots\ldots\ldots\ldots\ldots \\ (a_{i1}p_1 + \ldots + a_{ij}p_j + \ldots + a_{ik}p_k)(1+r) + wl_i = p_i \\ \ldots\ldots\ldots\ldots\ldots\ldots\ldots\ldots\ldots\ldots\ldots\ldots \\ (a_{k1}p_1 + \ldots + a_{kj}p_j + \ldots + a_{kk}p_k)(1+r) + wl_k = p_k \end{cases}$$

which can be written as $(1+r)\mathbf{Ap} + w\mathbf{L} = \mathbf{p}$

with

$$\mathbf{p} = \begin{bmatrix} p_1 \\ \vdots \\ p_i \\ \vdots \\ p_k \end{bmatrix} \qquad \mathbf{L} = \begin{bmatrix} l_1 \\ \vdots \\ l_i \\ \vdots \\ l_k \end{bmatrix}$$

and $\sum_{i=1}^{k} a_{ij} \leq 1, j = 1, 2, \ldots k$ with $\sum_{i=1}^{k} a_{ij} < 1$ for at least one j.

Sraffa calls the 'national income of a system in a self-replacing state… the set of commodities which are left over when from the gross national product we have removed item by item the articles which go to replace the means of production used up in all the industries' (P.S. §12, p. 11).

Thus $\left(1 - \sum_i a_{i1}, \ldots, 1 - \sum_i a_{ij}, \ldots, 1 - \sum_i a_{ik}\right) \geq 0$

By assumption the value of this set of commodities which forms the national income is set equal to 1 and it is called the 'composite commodity'. It thus becomes the standard in terms of which the wage and the prices are expressed. We therefore have the additional equation:

$$\left[1 - \sum_i a_{i1}\right]p_1 + \left[1 - \sum_i a_{i2}\right]p_2 + \ldots + \left[1 - \sum_i a_{ij}\right]p_j + \ldots$$
$$+ \left[1 - \sum_i a_{ik}\right]p_k = 1$$

We thus have a system of $(k+1)$ equations (k price equations and the equation given above) and $(k+2)$ unknowns: the wage, w, the rate of profit, r, and the k prices, p_i. Since the wage is considered exogenous, the number of unknowns exceeds the number of equations by one, so the system has one degree of freedom. We only have to fix one of the $k+2$ unknowns to determine the $k+1$ others.

2.2.2 Basic and non-basic products

The existence of surplus production introduces the notion of '"luxury" products which are not used, whether as instruments of production or as articles of subsistence, in the production of others' (P.S. §6, p. 7). This category of products could not exist in simple reproduction where, the surplus being zero by assumption, each commodity 'had to be' at the same time product and instrument of production.

Now not all products have necessarily to be on the same level. Luxury products have a purely passive role. They have no part in the determination of the system. If an invention allows a reduction in the quantity of the means of production necessary to produce a unit of a luxury commodity, the price of this commodity will decrease but there will not be any other consequences in the system as a whole. The price relations of the other products and the distributive variables will not be affected as they would have been had an invention improved the methods of production of these other products.

The distinction between basic and non-basic products now clearly appears as very important. The term non-basic is more appropriate than 'luxury' good because their passive role can be extended to such luxuries generally used for their own production, directly or indirectly, or for the production of other luxuries. 'The criterion is whether a commodity enters (no matter whether directly or indirectly) into the production of *all commodities*. Those that do we shall call *basic*, and those that do not, *non-basic* products' (P.S. §6, p. 8).

The utilisation of this definition can be related, as will be seen, to the concept of a decomposable matrix. We must identify and classify commodities in the two distinct sectors of basic products on the one hand, and non-basic on the other. Once we have thus identified commodities we can rearrange the technology matrix by simultaneous permutations of rows and columns.

When there are non-basic products it is possible to obtain the following configuration (such matrices are called quasi-triangular):[17]

$$\mathbf{A} = \begin{array}{|c|c|l}\hline \mathbf{A}_1^1 & 0 & (k-m) \\ \hline \mathbf{A}_2^1 & \mathbf{A}_2^2 & (m) \\ \hline \multicolumn{1}{c}{(k-m)} & \multicolumn{1}{c}{(m)} & \end{array} \qquad \text{for example} \qquad \begin{array}{r|ccc|cc|} \cline{2-6} (5-2) & 0.3 & 0.1 & 0.4 & 0 & 0 \\ & 0.2 & 0 & 0.1 & 0 & 0 \\ & 0.1 & 0.2 & 0.1 & 0 & 0 \\ \cline{2-6} (2) & 0.2 & 0.4 & 0 & 0.3 & 0 \\ & 0.1 & 0.1 & 0.2 & 0.5 & 0.1 \\ \cline{2-6} \multicolumn{1}{c}{} & \multicolumn{3}{c}{(5-2)} & \multicolumn{2}{c}{(2)} \end{array}$$

If m is the maximum number of columns for which block $\mathbf{A}_1^2$ contains only zeros,[18] then there exist m non-basic products and $(k-m)$ basic products (entering directly or indirectly in the production of the other commodities). If $m = 0$ it is impossible to obtain such a configuration by permuting simultaneously rows and columns. The system is indecomposable, the economy only contains basic products.

If $m > 0$ block $\mathbf{A}_1^1$ represents an indecomposable system made up of all the basic products. The higher the value of m (with $m \leq k$), the higher is the number of non-basic products and thus the smaller the number of basics.

If $m = k - 1$ then there are $(k-1)$ non-basic products and one basic; $\mathbf{A}_1^2$ which generally has $(k-m)$ rows and m columns becomes a row-vector $(k - m = k - (k-1) = 1)$ with $m = k - 1$ components, all of them zero.

If matrix $\mathbf{A}$ is completely decomposable, then there are only non-basic products; therefore no product is basic. In this case the production system could be decomposed into several sub-sets, without any technical inter-relations, which represent as many independent 'sub-economies' as there are sub-sets, each with at least one specific basic product. The configuration of the technology matrix would then be the following:

$$\begin{array}{|c|c|c|c|}\hline \mathbf{A}_1^1 & & & \\ \hline & \mathbf{A}_2^2 & & \\ \hline & & \mathbf{A}_3^3 & \\ \hline & & & \mathbf{A}_4^4 \\ \hline \end{array}$$

There would thus be several elementary economies separately defined by their basic products, represented above by sub-matrices of the type $\mathbf{A}_1^1$, $\mathbf{A}_2^2$, $\mathbf{A}_3^3$, $\mathbf{A}_4^4$. We can now understand Sraffa's assumption that: 'We shall assume throughout that any system contains at least one basic product' (P.S. §6, p. 8).

We can now decompose the system of price equations $(1 + r)\mathbf{Ap} + w\mathbf{L} = \mathbf{p}$. Recall the new configuration of the technology matrix

$$\mathbf{A} = \begin{bmatrix} \mathbf{A}_1^1 & \mathbf{0} \\ \mathbf{A}_2^1 & \mathbf{A}_2^2 \end{bmatrix}$$

Let us now distinguish between $\mathbf{L}_1$ and $\mathbf{L}_2$, vectors of the quantities of direct labour used respectively in the basic and non-basic sectors. Thus $\mathbf{L} = \begin{bmatrix} \mathbf{L}_1 \\ \mathbf{L}_2 \end{bmatrix}$. Similarly, we have $\mathbf{p} = \begin{bmatrix} \mathbf{p}_1 \\ \mathbf{p}_2 \end{bmatrix}$ with $\mathbf{p}_1$ and $\mathbf{p}_2$ price vectors respectively in the basic and non-basic sectors.

$$(1 + r)\begin{bmatrix} \mathbf{A}_1^1 & \mathbf{0} \\ \mathbf{A}_2^1 & \mathbf{A}_2^2 \end{bmatrix}\begin{bmatrix} \mathbf{p}_1 \\ \mathbf{p}_2 \end{bmatrix} + w\begin{bmatrix} \mathbf{L}_1 \\ \mathbf{L}_2 \end{bmatrix} = \begin{bmatrix} \mathbf{p}_1 \\ \mathbf{p}_2 \end{bmatrix}$$

We get two vector systems

$$(1 + r)\ \mathbf{A}_1^1\mathbf{p}_1 + w\mathbf{L}_1 = \mathbf{p}_1$$

$$(1 + r)(\mathbf{A}_2^1\mathbf{p}_1 + \mathbf{A}_2^2\mathbf{p}_2) + w\mathbf{L}_2 = \mathbf{p}_2$$

The first system of $(k - m)$ equations simultaneously determines the $(k - m - 1)$ relative prices of the basic products and the two distributive variables. Given an adequate standard (this problem will be taken up below), there are $(k - m)$ equations for $(k - m - 1 + 2) = (k - m + 1)$ unknowns. Therefore, the system has one degree of freedom and we only have to fix one of the $(k - m + 1)$ unknowns to determine the $(k - m)$ others.

The second system of m equations determines the m prices of the non-basic products as functions of the prices of the basic products and the distributive variables already derived from the first system.

It is now easy to understand, in relation to Sraffa's text,

> why the ratios which satisfy the conditions of production have been called 'values' or 'prices' rather than, as might be thought more appropriate, 'costs of production'.
>
> The latter description would be adequate so far as *non*-basic products were concerned, since ... their exchange ratio is merely a reflection of what must be paid for means of production, labour and profits in order to produce them—there is no mutual dependence ...

> In other words, the price of a non-basic product depends on the prices of its means of production, but these do not depend on it. Whereas in the case of a basic product the prices of its means of production depend on its own price no less than the latter depends on them [P. S. §7, pp. 8–9].

The prices of the non-basic products are determined by the conditions of their production whereas, with a known and unaltered technology matrix, the prices of the basic products determine the distributive variables as much as they are determined by them.

A further characteristic of the technological configuration which will be useful in the case of joint production can now be demonstrated. Up to this point we have put the emphasis on the input matrix and have neglected the presentation of the output matrix. This is easily justified since, by assuming simple production, the output matrix **B** is the diagonal identity matrix.

$$\mathbf{B} = \mathbf{I} = \begin{bmatrix} 1 & & & & 0 \\ & \ddots & & & \\ & & 1 & & \\ & & & \ddots & \\ 0 & & & & 1 \end{bmatrix}$$

and the general system of equations is similarly

$$(1 + r)\mathbf{Ap} + w\mathbf{L} = \mathbf{Bp} = \mathbf{Ip} = \mathbf{p}$$

However (and in a purely formal way for the present), we can simultaneously permute rows and columns of matrix **B** and obtain the same grouping by blocks:

$k - m$ industries	$\mathbf{A}^1_1$	$\mathbf{0}$		$\mathbf{B}^1_1$	$\mathbf{B}^2_1$
m industries	$\mathbf{A}^1_2$	$\mathbf{A}^2_2$		$\mathbf{B}^1_2$	$\mathbf{B}^2_2$

By taking into account the assumption of simple production we have:

$$\mathbf{B}^1_1 = \begin{bmatrix} 1 & & & & 0 \\ & \ddots & & & \\ & & 1 & & \\ & & & \ddots & \\ 0 & & & & 1 \end{bmatrix} \quad \mathbf{B}^2_1 = [\mathbf{0}] \quad \mathbf{B}^1_2 = [\mathbf{0}] \quad \mathbf{B}^2_2 = \begin{bmatrix} 1 & & & & 0 \\ & \ddots & & & \\ & & 1 & & \\ & & & \ddots & \\ 0 & & & & 1 \end{bmatrix}$$

$$\text{or } \mathbf{B} = \begin{array}{|ccc|ccc|l} \hline 1 & & 0 & & & & \\ & \ddots & & & & & \\ & 1 & & & \mathbf{0} & & (k-m) \\ & & \ddots & & & & \\ 0 & & 1 & & & & \\ \hline & & & 1 & & 0 & \\ & & & & \ddots & & \\ & \mathbf{0} & & & 1 & & (m) \\ & & & & & \ddots & \\ & & & 0 & & 1 & \\ \hline \multicolumn{3}{c}{(k-m)} & \multicolumn{3}{c}{(m)} & \end{array}$$

We can form the $k \times 2m$ $[\mathbf{A}^2, \mathbf{B}^2]$ matrix by putting together the m last columns of $\mathbf{A}$ and $\mathbf{B}$.

$$[\mathbf{A}^2, \mathbf{B}^2] = \left[\begin{array}{c|ccc} \mathbf{0} & & \mathbf{0} & \\ \hline & 1 & & 0 \\ & & \ddots & \\ \mathbf{A}_2^2 & & 1 & \\ & & & \ddots \\ & 0 & & 1 \end{array}\right] \begin{array}{l} (k-m) \\ \\ \\ (m) \\ \\ \\ \end{array}$$

$$\qquad\qquad (m) \qquad\qquad\qquad (m)$$

The rank of $[\mathbf{A}^2, \mathbf{B}^2]$ is obviously inferior or equal to m (there are a maximum of m independent vectors since $k-m$ vectors are already zero). In the case of joint production (i.e. when $\mathbf{B}$ is different from the diagonal matrix) we shall define a system $[\mathbf{A}, \mathbf{B}]$ as non-basic if there exists a permutation of the columns and a number m such that the matrix $[\mathbf{A}^2, \mathbf{B}^2]$ composed of the m last columns $(1 \leq m \leq k-1)$ of $\mathbf{A}$ and $\mathbf{B}$ is at most of rank m (see Section 3.2).

This general definition can of course be applied to the particular case of 'simple' production: the system $[\mathbf{A}, \mathbf{I}]$ is non-basic since there exists a permutation of columns and a number m such that matrix $[\mathbf{A}^2, \mathbf{I}^2]$ composed of the last m columns $(1 \leq m \leq k-1)$ of $\mathbf{A}$, and $\mathbf{I}$ is at most of rank m.

We note again that the assumption that there is at least one basic good in the system eliminates the cases where matrix $\mathbf{A}$ is completely decomposable.

2.3 Effects of changes in wages on the rate of profit and on prices

This problem, fundamental in Sraffa's analysis, can be considered by supposing the wage, w, to take on successive values ranging from 1 to 0. We have already mentioned that the variables (the wage and the k prices) have been expressed in terms of a standard composed of the national income. The successive values given to w therefore represent fractions of the national income.

– If we assume that $w = 1$, the whole national income goes to wages $(r = 0)$. We thus revert, in effect, to the system of linear equations from which we started (of the type $\mathbf{Ap} = \mathbf{p}$ used in simple reproduction) with the difference that the quantities of labour are explicitly introduced instead of being represented by the quantities of goods necessary for subsistence (cf. the $\mathbf{A}^*$ matrix used in the analysis of labour values in Chapter 1). At this level of wages ($w = 1$, $r = 0$) the relative values of commodities are proportional to their labour cost, i.e. to the quantity of direct or indirect labour used in their production. The determination of labour values is then a particular case of the determination of prices.

From $w = 1, r = 0, \mathbf{Ap}(1 + r) + \mathbf{L}w = \mathbf{p}$, we have

$$\mathbf{Ap}(1 + 0) + \mathbf{L}.1 = \mathbf{p} \qquad \text{or} \qquad [\mathbf{I} - \mathbf{A}]\mathbf{p} = \mathbf{L}$$

and if $\det[\mathbf{I} - \mathbf{A}] \neq 0$

$$\mathbf{p} = [\mathbf{I} - \mathbf{A}]^{-1}\mathbf{L}$$

– If we assume $w = 0$, the whole national income is paid as profit ($r = R =$ maximum rate of profit). The price system becomes

$$\mathbf{Ap}(1 + R) = \mathbf{p} \Leftrightarrow \mathbf{Ap} = \frac{1}{1 + R}\mathbf{p}$$

$\mathbf{p}$, the eigenvector corresponding to the dominant eigenvalue $\alpha^* = 1/(1 + R)$ of matrix $\mathbf{A}$, is strictly positive (every price is positive) when there are only basic products (matrix $\mathbf{A}$ is indecomposable). When matrix $\mathbf{A}$ is decomposable (i.e. there are at the same time basic and non-basic products) the vector $\mathbf{p}$ is semi-positive; some prices can be zero. (Note that $\alpha^* = 1/(1 + R) < 1 \Rightarrow R > 0$.)

Now that these two extreme cases have been examined the question is to determine how a change in wages w (i.e. a change in the share of wages in national income) affects prices. Starting from the situation where the whole of the national income goes to labour ($w = 1$) we assume a reduction of the wage ($w < 1$), which implies that a rate of profit will thereby arise ($r > 0$).

Under what conditions will the prices in the system remain unchanged? The proportion in which labour and means of production are employed in the various industries of the system would have to be the same in all industries. In this case equal reductions of the wages of all industries will bring equivalent increases of the net product which can be paid as profits on the means of production. In this way 'in each industry an equal deduction from the wage would yield just as much as was required for paying the profits on its means of production at a uniform rate without need to disturb the existing prices' (P.S. §15, p. 13).

However, there is no reason for the proportion of labour to means of production to be the same in all industries. As a consequence, in order for the rate of profit to be uniform in the system, it is impossible for prices to remain unchanged when the wage varies. Variations in prices must therefore occur. There will be a decrease in the prices of the commodities produced by processes, or industries, with a relatively high proportion of labour to means of production when the wage falls. On the contrary, prices in industries with a relatively low proportion of labour to means of production will increase. And finally, prices of 'average' commodities characterised by a 'critical proportion' of labour to means of production will remain constant whatever the level of the wage and the rate of profit.

Let us take as an example the case of an industry using more labour than the 'critical proportion'. A wage reduction would leave a net product larger than that necessary (at the new uniform rate of profit) to remunerate the means of production (which by assumption enter in the process in a smaller proportion than the 'critical proportion'). Therefore, the price of the commodity produced in this industry will have to fall in order to decrease the value of the surplus of the industry so as to conform to the unique rate of profit for the system.

This conclusion would be challenged if the processes that produce the means of production necessary for production in the industry considered were to use labour in a smaller proportion than the critical proportion. This would lead to an increase in the price of the commodity. Such a fall would compensate the rise in value of the means of production necessary to get the final product. It is therefore impossible to reach a general conclusion on the reaction of prices to changes in wages when industries have proportions of labour to means of production superior or inferior to the 'critical proportion'. When wages fall the price of a 'high proportion' industry ('surplus' industry in Sraffa's terminology) can fall or rise. It can even rise and fall alternately. Similarly, the price of a 'low-proportion' product (or 'deficit') can rise or fall or alternate in its variations: 'what neither of such products can do... is to remain stable in price relative to its means of production throughout any range, whether long or short, of the wage-variation' (P.S. §19, p. 15).

It must be pointed out that for an industry to be characterised by the 'critical proportion' it is necessary that the same proportion be respected in the whole series of industries producing the necessary means of production (condition of 'recurrence' in Sraffa's terminology). A commodity produced in these conditions shows all the properties required of a unique standard of value since its price is necessarily invariant to changes in the wage or the rate of profit. This commodity could then be used as a standard, for example, to compare the variations in prices of the other commodities of the system. Since it is unlikely that such a commodity exists, Sraffa proceeds to construct a 'composite commodity' possessing all the desired properties. This composite he calls the 'standard commodity'.

Before examining this problem, let us revert to the definition of the 'critical proportion' or 'equilibrium proportion'. Up to now the 'proportion' between the quantity of labour and the value of the means of production was of a hybrid nature. Sraffa proposes its replacement by a 'pure' ratio between homogeneous quantities, more precisely by the value-ratio of net product to means of production. Let us quote Sraffa's proposition (P.S. §22, p. 17): 'While the rate of profits is uniform in all industries, and depends only on the wage, the value-ratio of the net product to the means of production is in general different for each industry and mainly depends on its particular circumstances of production.' The price equation for the ith commodity is the following:

$$\mathbf{a}_i\mathbf{p}(1+r) + l_i w = p_i$$

with $\mathbf{a}_i$ the row vector of intermediate consumptions

$$\mathbf{a}_i = (a_{i1}, a_{i2}, \dots, a_{ij}, \dots, a_{ik}).$$

Hence the expression of the ratio of net product $(p_i - \mathbf{a}_i\mathbf{p})$ to the means of production $(\mathbf{a}_i\mathbf{p})$:

$$\left[\frac{p_i - \mathbf{a}_i\mathbf{p}}{\mathbf{a}_i\mathbf{p}}\right] = r + \frac{l_i w}{\mathbf{a}_i\mathbf{p}}$$

is different according to the industry considered and depends on the particular circumstances of production.

Let us quote Sraffa again:

> There is however an exception to this. When we make the wage equal to zero and the whole of the net product goes to profit, in each industry the value-ratio of net product to means of production necessarily comes to coincide with the general rate of profits. However different from one another they may have been at other wage levels, at this level the 'value-ratios' of all industries are equal [P. S. §21, p. 17].

Thus for $w = 0$ we have $r = R$, the maximum rate of profits with

$$\mathbf{Ap}(1+R) = \mathbf{p} \text{ or } \mathbf{a}_i\mathbf{p}(1+R) = p_i \qquad \text{or } \frac{p_i - \mathbf{a}_i\mathbf{p}}{\mathbf{a}_i\mathbf{p}} = R = \text{constant.}$$

Sraffa concludes: 'it follows that the only "value-ratio" which can be invariant to changes in the wage... is the one that is equal to the rate of profits which corresponds to zero wage. And *that* is the "balancing ratio' (P.S. §21, p. 17).

2.4 The standard commodity

2.4.1 Why a particular standard commodity?

The reason for this is very clearly exposed by Sraffa at the beginning of Chapter 5.

> The necessity of having to express the price of one commodity in terms of another which is arbitrarily chosen as standard, complicates the study of the price-movements which accompany a change in distribution. It is impossible to tell of any particular price-fluctuation whether it arises from the peculiarities of the commodity which is being measured or from those of the measuring standard. The relevant peculiarities as we have just seen, can only consist in the inequality of the proportions of labour to means of production in the successive 'layers' into which a commodity and the aggregate of its means of production can be analysed; for it is such an inequality that makes it necessary for the commodity to change in value relative to its means of production as the wage changes.
>
> The 'balanced' commodity which we have just considered would present no peculiarities of this type, since the same proportion would be found in all its 'layers'. It is true that, as wages fall, such a commodity would be no less susceptible than any other to rise or fall in price relative to other individual commodities; but we should know for certain that any such fluctuation would originate exclusively in the peculiarities of production of the commodity which was being compared with it, and not in its own. If we could discover such a commodity we should therefore be in possession of a standard capable of isolating the price-movements of any other product so that they could be observed as in a vacuum [P.S. §23, p. 18].

2.4.2 The construction of the standard commodity

It is unlikely that we can find an *individual* commodity fulfilling even approximately the requisite conditions. But a mixture of commodities, a 'composite commodity' would do equally well. Can we construct such a commodity?

Any standard commodity must respect the critical proportion of net product to means of production. This critical proportion $\alpha^* = 1/(1+R)$ has been previously defined as the dominant eigenvalue of the technology matrix **A**. The quantities which respect the critical proportion still have to be determined, that is, a vector $\mathbf{q} = (q_1, \ldots, q_i, \ldots, q_k)$ must be defined such that

$$\mathbf{qA} = \alpha^*\mathbf{q} = \frac{1}{1+R}\mathbf{q}$$

q appears as the eigenvector (on the left) corresponding to the dominant eigenvalue of matrix **A**. Such a system will contain, by construction, the critical proportion of net product to means of production, since we have $(\mathbf{q} - \mathbf{qA})/\mathbf{qA} = (1 - \alpha^*)/\alpha^* = R$. The various commodities will be represented among the aggregate means of production in the same proportions as they are produced as products.

Let us use the example given by Sraffa (P.S. §25–26, pp. 19–20): the actual system from which we start includes only basic industries producing respectively iron, coal and wheat in the following way:

$$90 \text{ t iron} + 120 \text{ t coal} + 60 \text{ qr wheat} + \frac{3}{16} \text{ labour} \rightarrow 180 \text{ t iron}$$

$$50 \text{ t iron} + 125 \text{ t coal} + 150 \text{ qr wheat} + \frac{5}{16} \text{ labour} \rightarrow 450 \text{ t coal}$$

$$40 \text{ t iron} + 40 \text{ t coal} + 200 \text{ qr wheat} + \frac{8}{16} \text{ labour} \rightarrow 480 \text{ qr wheat}$$

Totals: 180 285 410 1

In such a system the price equations are of the form:

$$\mathbf{Ap}(1+r) + \mathbf{L}w = \mathbf{p}$$

Thus we have:

$$\begin{bmatrix} \frac{1}{2} & \frac{12}{45} & \frac{1}{8} \\ \frac{5}{18} & \frac{5}{18} & \frac{5}{16} \\ \frac{2}{9} & \frac{4}{45} & \frac{5}{12} \end{bmatrix} \begin{bmatrix} p_1 \\ p_2 \\ p_3 \end{bmatrix} (1+r) + \begin{bmatrix} \frac{3}{16} \\ \frac{5}{16} \\ \frac{8}{16} \end{bmatrix} w = \begin{bmatrix} p_1 \\ p_2 \\ p_3 \end{bmatrix}$$

The dominant eigenvalue $\alpha^* = 1/(1+R)$ of matrix $\mathbf{A}$ is 5/6 which corresponds to a maximum rate of profits or surplus rate of $R = 20\%$.[19] The eigenvector corresponding to the dominant eigenvalue is such that we have:

$$\mathbf{qA} = \frac{1}{1+R}\mathbf{q} \quad \text{where } \frac{1}{1+R} = \frac{5}{6}, \quad \text{and } \mathbf{q} = \left(1, \frac{3}{5}, \frac{3}{4}\right).$$

Thus, the 'constructed system' consists of the whole of the iron industry ($q_1 = 1$), $\frac{3}{5}$ of the coal industry and $\frac{3}{4}$ of the wheat industry. The resulting system is:

$$\begin{cases} 90\text{ t iron} + 120\text{ t coal} + 60\text{ qr wheat} + \frac{3}{16}\text{ labour} \rightarrow 180\text{ t iron} \\ 30\text{ t iron} + 75\text{ t coal} + 90\text{ qr wheat} + \frac{3}{16}\text{ labour} \rightarrow 270\text{ t coal} \\ 30\text{ t iron} + 30\text{ t coal} + 150\text{ qr wheat} + \frac{6}{16}\text{ labour} \rightarrow 360\text{ qr wheat} \end{cases}$$

$$\text{Totals} = 150 \qquad 225 \qquad 300 \qquad \frac{12}{16}$$

'The proportions in which the three commodities are produced in the new system (180/270/360) are equal to those in which they enter its aggregate means of production (150/225/300). The composite commodity sought for is accordingly made up in the proportions 1 ton iron: $1\frac{1}{2}$ tons coal: 2 quarters wheat' (P.S. §26, p. 20).

Sraffa calls 'a mixture of this type the *Standard composite commodity*, or, for short, the *Standard commodity*; and the set of equations (or of industries), taken in the proportion that produce the Standard commodity, the Standard system'[20] (P.S. §26, p. 20).

Of course, the standard system has been constructed in such a way that the various commodities are produced in the same proportions as they enter the aggregate means of production; again by construction the percentage of the excess quantity produced over the quantity used up in production is the same for every commodity. In the preceding example the rate for every commodity is 20%.

$$\left.\begin{cases} 180\text{ t iron} = (1+0.2)\,150\text{ t iron} \\ 270\text{ t coal} = (1+0.2)\,225\text{ t coal} \\ 360\text{ qr wheat} = (1+0.2)\,300\text{ qr wheat} \end{cases}\right\} \Leftrightarrow \mathbf{q} = (1+R)\mathbf{q}A \text{ with } R = 20\%$$

To sum up, the problem of constructing the standard commodity consists in finding the eigenvector on the left corresponding to the dominant eigenvalue of matrix **A**, $\mathbf{qA} = 1/(1+R)\mathbf{q}$. The ratio R, the maximum rate of profits of the system, is called the standard ratio. Since we want the quantity of labour employed in the standard system to be the same as in the actual system, we must add an equation taking this condition into account: $\mathbf{qL} = q_1 l_1 + q_2 l_2 + \ldots + q_k l_k = 1$ with $\mathbf{q}$ defined up to the multiplication by scalars. We have therefore $k+1$ equations determining the k multipliers and R.[21]

The application of the k multipliers to the equations of the actual system transforms it into the standard system as follows:

$$\begin{cases} q_1[(a_{11}p_1 + a_{12}p_2 + \ldots + a_{1k}p_k)(1+r) + l_1 w] = q_1 p_1 \\ q_2[(a_{21}p_1 + a_{22}p_2 + \ldots + a_{2k}p_k)(1+r) + l_2 w] = q_2 p_2 \\ \cdots\cdots\cdots\cdots\cdots\cdots\cdots\cdots\cdots\cdots \\ q_k[(a_{k1}p_1 + a_{k2}p_2 + \ldots + a_{kk}p_k)(1+r) + l_k w] = q_k p_k \end{cases}$$

which can be written in a more compact equivalent form:

$$\mathring{\mathbf{q}}[\mathbf{Ap}(1+r) + \mathbf{L}w] = \mathring{\mathbf{q}}\mathbf{p} \quad \text{where } \mathring{\mathbf{q}} = \begin{bmatrix} q_1 & 0 & 0 & \ldots & 0 \\ 0 & q_2 & 0 & \ldots & 0 \\ 0 & 0 & q_3 & \ldots & 0 \\ \cdots & \cdots & \cdots & \cdots & \cdots \\ 0 & 0 & 0 & \ldots & q_k \end{bmatrix}$$

From this we derive the standard national income which Sraffa adopts as the unit of wages and prices in the original system of production. Thus we normalise the system by putting

$$\left[q_1 - \sum_{j=1}^{k} q_j a_{j1}\right]p_1 + \left[q_2 - \sum_{j=1}^{k} q_j a_{j2}\right]p_2 + \ldots + \left[q_k - \sum_{j=1}^{k} q_j a_{jk}\right]p_k = 1$$

or $[\mathbf{q} - \mathbf{qA}]\mathbf{p} = 1 \Leftrightarrow \mathbf{q}[\mathbf{I} - \mathbf{A}]\mathbf{p} = 1$ which is strictly equivalent. This composite commodity is the standard of wages and prices that we have been seeking.

With the introduction of this normalisation condition into the system we have $(k+1)$ equations (k price equations and 1 normalisation equation) and $k+2$ unknowns (k prices and 2 distributive variables). Thus there is no difficulty in solving the system for the rate of profits and the k prices, given w. The k prices and the wage are, of course, expressed in terms of the standard net product. To avoid any ambiguity we shall call them hereafter p_s and w_s.

With this notation we have:

$$\mathring{\mathbf{q}}[\mathbf{A}\mathbf{p}_s(1+r)+\mathbf{L}w_s]=\mathring{\mathbf{q}}\mathbf{p}_s$$

The normalisation condition can be written as either

$$\mathbf{q}(\mathbf{I}-\mathbf{A})\mathbf{p}_s=\mathbf{q}(\mathbf{I}-\mathbf{A})\frac{\mathbf{p}}{\mathbf{q}(\mathbf{I}-\mathbf{A})\mathbf{p}}=1 \quad \text{or} \quad \mathbf{p}_s=\frac{\mathbf{p}}{\mathbf{q}(\mathbf{I}-\mathbf{A})\mathbf{p}}$$

2.4.3 Properties of the standard commodity and the wage–profit relation

We called the *standard ratio* the ratio of net product to means of production.

But

> The possibility of speaking of a ratio between two collections of miscellaneous commodities without need of reducing them to the common measure of price arises of course from the circumstances that both collections are made up in the same proportions—from their being in fact quantities of the same composite commodity.
>
> The result would therefore not be affected by multiplying the individual component commodities by their prices. The ratio of the values of the two aggregates would inevitably be always equal to the ratio of the quantities of their several components. Nor, once the commodities had been multiplied by their prices, would the ratio be disturbed if those individual prices were to vary in all sorts of divergent ways.
>
> Thus in the Standard system the ratio of the net product to the means of production would remain the same whatever variations occurred in the division of the net product between wages and profits and whatever the consequent price changes [P.S. §28, p. 21].

Now suppose the standard net product to be divided between wages and profits keeping in mind that wages w_s are expressed in terms of standard net product and represent at the same time wages and the share of wages in the standard net product. In the example given previously where the standard ratio was 20%, if $\frac{3}{4}$ of the standard national income goes to wages and $\frac{1}{4}$ to profits, then the rate of profits will be 5% ($\frac{1}{4}\times 20\%$); if half goes to each, it will be 10%. It will reach the maximum level of 20% coinciding with the standard ratio when $w_s=0$.

We have reached a double conclusion. On one hand, the rate of profits in the standard system appears as a pure number, as a ratio between quantities of commodities irrespective of their prices. On the other hand, we have seen that we obtain a very simple linear relation between r and $w_s: r=R(1-w_s)$

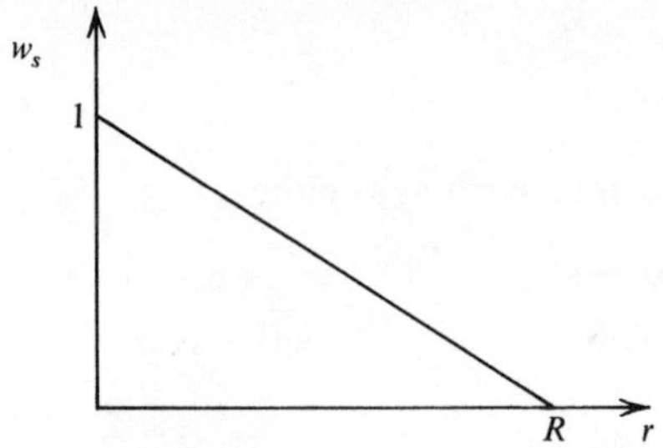

Fig. 2.1

This very famous relation can be shown directly by starting from the definition of prices and wages in terms of the standard net product. Thus

$$\mathbf{A}\mathbf{p}_s(1+r)+\mathbf{L}w_s=\mathbf{p}_s$$

Hence

$$r\mathbf{A}\mathbf{p}_s+\mathbf{L}w_s=\mathbf{p}_s-\mathbf{A}\mathbf{p}_s=[\mathbf{I}-\mathbf{A}]\mathbf{p}_s$$

Since we have the normalisation condition as

$$\mathbf{q}(\mathbf{I}-\mathbf{A})\mathbf{p}_s=1$$

we have

$$1=r\mathbf{q}\mathbf{A}\mathbf{p}_s+\mathbf{q}\mathbf{L}w_s=\frac{r}{R}\mathbf{q}R\mathbf{A}\mathbf{p}_s+(\mathbf{q}\mathbf{L})w_s$$

but $\mathbf{q}[\mathbf{I}-\mathbf{A}]=\mathbf{q}R\mathbf{A}$ (since by construction $\mathbf{q}\mathbf{A}(1+R)=\mathbf{q}$) and $(\mathbf{q}\mathbf{L})=1$ (the quantity of labour employed in the standard system is the same as in the actual system). By substitution, we have

$$1=\frac{r}{R}\mathbf{q}[\mathbf{I}-\mathbf{A}]\mathbf{p}_s+w_s=\frac{r}{R}+w_s$$

$$1=\frac{r}{R}+w_s \qquad \text{or} \qquad r=R(1-w_s)$$

Such a relation is more interesting than it may look at first sight because its validity, far from being limited to the imaginary standard system, can be extended to the actual economic system, because

> the actual system consists of the same basic equations as the Standard system, only in different proportions; so that once the wage is given, the rate of profits is determined for both systems regardless of the proportions of the equations in either of them.
>
> The straight-line relation between the wage and the rate of profits will

therefore hold in all cases, provided only that the wage is expressed in terms of the Standard product [P.S. § 31, p. 23].

If we are in the standard system, the linear relation is at the same time a relation between the shares of profits and wages in the standard net product *and* a relation between the rates of profits and wages (expressed in terms of the standard net product). If we are in the actual system only the second relation holds.

Reverting to our example, if in the actual system (... with $R = 20\%$) the wage is fixed in terms of the Standard net product, to $w = \frac{3}{4}$ there will correspond $r = 5\%$. But while the share of wages will be equal in value to $\frac{3}{4}$ of the Standard national income, it does not follow that the share of profits will be equivalent to the remaining $\frac{1}{4}$ of the Standard income. The share of profits will consist of whatever is left of the *actual* national income after deducting from it the equivalent of $\frac{3}{4}$ of the *Standard* national income for wages: and prices must be such as to make the value of what goes to profits equal to 5% of the value of the actual means of production of society [P.S. § 32, p. 23].

This means that the same rate of profits which in the standard system came from a ratio of *quantities* of commodities will result in the actual system from the ratio of the sums of the values of the commodities.

2.4.4 The existence and uniqueness of the standard system

Since the standard system is obtained by linear combination of all basic commodities forming the $(k - m) \times (k - m)$ indecomposable matrix $\mathbf{A}_1^1$, we must then show that $(k - m)$ non-zero multipliers exist and that the vector formed by these multipliers is uniquely defined up to a scalar multiple.

The $k - m$ multipliers are defined by the activity vector $\mathbf{q} = (q_1, q_2, \ldots, q_i, \ldots, q_{k-m})$, itself defined as the eigenvector corresponding to the dominant eigenvalue $\alpha^* = 1/(1 + R)$ of matrix $\mathbf{A}_1^1$, i.e. $\mathbf{q}\mathbf{A}_1^1 = \alpha^*\mathbf{q}$.

By the Perron–Frobenius theorem (see mathematical appendix) we know that the eigenvector $\mathbf{q}$ corresponding to the dominant eigenvalue of the indecomposable matrix $\mathbf{A}_1^1$ is unique and strictly positive. Let us briefly recall the object and the economic meaning of the Perron–Frobenius theorem. We already know that the multiplication of a row vector by a square matrix of the appropriate order gives a row vector of the same order. In this respect the eigenvectors are peculiar since the multiplication of an eigenvector by a matrix gives the same vector, up to a scalar multiple; this scalar multiple is, in fact, the eigenvalue associated with the eigenvector under consideration. In the case of a $(k \times k)$ square matrix we can have as many as k eigenvalues and eigenvectors.

The elements of the matrices characterising an economic system are necessarily positive or zero. Perron showed for matrices whose elements were all positive, and Frobenius for indecomposable matrices whose elements were positive or zero, that:

(a) a positive eigenvalue always exists

(b) a strictly positive eigenvector corresponds to the highest positive eigenvalue (α^*), also called the dominant eigenvector

(c) no other eigenvalue corresponds to this strictly positive eigenvector.

Thus the eigenvector associated with the dominant eigenvalue of an indecomposable matrix, and only this vector, is of economic interest. Furthermore, the dominant eigenvalue provides the definition of the maximum rate of profit R in the relation $R = \dfrac{1-\alpha^*}{\alpha^*}$.

We are therefore certain that when only the basic commodities are taken into account 'there cannot be more than one value of R to which there corresponds an all-positive set of values of the *qs*' (P.S. §38, p. 27).

This vector $\mathbf{q}$ corresponds to the dominant eigenvalue α^* (i.e. the greatest of all eigenvalues) and, since $\alpha^* = 1/(1+R)$, it follows that 'the value of R to which correspond all-positive prices is the *lowest* of the k possible values of R' (P.S. §42, p. 29).

In a system of single-product industries with only circulating capital, and assuming that there is at least one basic commodity, the Perron–Frobenius theorem always ensures both the existence and uniqueness of the standard system (but there are other standard commodities when rank $[\mathbf{L}, \mathbf{AL}, \ldots, \mathbf{A}^{k-1}\mathbf{L}] < k$. See T. Miyao: 'A generalisation of Sraffa's standard commodity and its complete characterisation', *International Economic Review*, Feb. 1977), which also implies that it will always be composed of positive quantities of the commodities. This problem is much more complex in the case of joint-product industries, as we shall see below.

2.5 Conditions for the existence, uniqueness, and positiveness of the prices of production . . .

2.5.1 . . . of basic commodities

Let us revert to the system characterising the basic sector:

$$(1+r)\mathbf{A}_1^1 p_1 + w\mathbf{L}_1 = \mathbf{p}_1$$

or $$\mathbf{p}_1 = w[\mathbf{I} - (1+r)\mathbf{A}_1^1]^{-1}\mathbf{L}_1$$

The wage, w, is positive, as is $\mathbf{L}_1$ the quantity vector of direct labour in the basic sector; therefore the characteristics of the price vector will only depend on the properties of matrix $[\mathbf{I}-(1+r)\mathbf{A}_1^1]^{-1}$.

We know that matrix $\mathbf{A}_1^1$ is indecomposable and semi-positive. When $0<r<R$, matrix $[\mathbf{I}-(1+r)\mathbf{A}_1^1]$ has an inverse and this inverse $[\mathbf{I}-(1+r)\mathbf{A}_1^1]^{-1}$ is positive (with $1/(1+R)=\alpha^*(\mathbf{A}_1^1)$). For all r positive and less than the maximum rate of profit R, the prices of production of basic commodities are therefore uniquely defined and necessarily positive. Moreover:

(a) for $r=0$, these prices of production are proportional to the quantities of labour directly and indirectly necessary for their production (this holds for both basics and non-basics):

$$\mathbf{p}=\mathbf{\Lambda}=[\mathbf{I}-\mathbf{A}]^{-1}\mathbf{L}$$

(b) for $r=R$, the price vector $\mathbf{p}_1$ is defined as the strictly positive eigenvector (up to the multiplication by scalars) corresponding to the dominant eigenvalue $1/(1+R)$ of the indecomposable matrix $\mathbf{A}_1^1$:

$$\mathbf{p}_1=(1+R)\mathbf{A}_1^1\mathbf{p}_1$$

Thus for all r such that $0\leq r\leq R$ the prices of production of basic commodities are uniquely defined and necessarily positive.

Moreover, it is possible to show that prices expressed in terms of the wage in the basic system (i.e. $\hat{\mathbf{p}}_1$ such that $w=1$ or $\hat{\mathbf{p}}_1=\mathbf{p}_1/w$) are increasing functions of the rate of profit.

For $r<r^*<R$ we have

$$(1+r)\mathbf{A}_1^1<(1+r^*)\mathbf{A}_1^1$$

where $(1+r)\mathbf{A}_1^1$ and $(1+r^*)\mathbf{A}_1^1$ are indecomposable semi-positive matrices whose eigenvalues $(1+r)/(1+R)$ and $(1+r^*)/(1+R)$ are less than 1. Thus we have:

$$[\mathbf{I}-(1+r)\mathbf{A}_1^1]^{-1}\leqq[\mathbf{I}-(1+r^*)\mathbf{A}_1^1]^{-1}$$

$$\hat{\mathbf{p}}_1(r)=[\mathbf{I}-(1+r)\mathbf{A}_1^1]^{-1}\mathbf{L}_1\leqq[\mathbf{I}-(1+r^*)\mathbf{A}_1^1]^{-1}\mathbf{L}_1$$

and $\hat{\mathbf{p}}_1(r)\leqq\hat{\mathbf{p}}_1(r^*)$

2.5.2 . . . of non-basic commodities

Unforeseen difficulties can, however, appear concerning 'self-reproducing non-basics'. This is Sraffa's famous 'beans' example (P.S. Appendix B, p. 90) which, as we shall see, merits some attention.

In Sraffa's terms,

> Consider a commodity which enters to an unusually large extent into the production of itself. It may be imagined to be some crop such as a species of beans or of corn the wastage on which is so great that for every 100 units sown no more than 110 are reaped. It is clear that this would not admit of a rate of profits higher than, or indeed, since other means of production must be used as well, as high as, 10%.
>
> If the product in question is a basic one there is no problem; it simply means that the maximum rate of profits of the system will have to be less than 10%.
>
> If, however, it is a non-basic product, complications arise. The way in which a non-basic is produced has, as we have seen, no influence on the general rate of profits, so that there would be nothing to prevent the Maximum rate of the system being higher than 10%: and yet the product in question is incompatible with a rate as high as 10% [P.S. Appendix B, p. 90].

The consequences of this contradictory situation manifest themselves in the behaviour of the price of the product ('beans'): when the rate of profits rises ($0 < r < R$) this price becomes negative by passing through infinity. This merits an explanation.

Consider two commodities: a basic commodity with a rate of profit (maximum) of $R = 15\%$ and a non-basic commodity, say beans, whose own surplus rate is 10%. If we admit that the basic commodity enters as an input in the production of beans in proportion a_{21}, the matrix **A** representing the system is decomposable:

$$\mathbf{A} = \begin{bmatrix} \frac{20}{23} & 0 \\ a_{21} & \frac{10}{11} \end{bmatrix}$$

The wage w is linked to the rate of profit by the following relation:

$$w = 1 - \frac{r}{R}$$

For a rate of profit r, the system giving the prices of production p_1 and p_2 of the basic product and the beans as a function of r is $(1+r)\mathbf{Ap} + w\mathbf{L} = \mathbf{p}$ that is:

$$(1+r)\begin{bmatrix} \frac{20}{23} & 0 \\ a_{21} & \frac{10}{11} \end{bmatrix} \begin{bmatrix} p_1 \\ p_2 \end{bmatrix} + w \begin{bmatrix} l_1 \\ l_2 \end{bmatrix} = \begin{bmatrix} p_1 \\ p_2 \end{bmatrix}$$

$$\Leftrightarrow \begin{cases} (1+r)\dfrac{20}{23}p_1 + wl_1 = p_1 \Leftrightarrow p_1\left[1-(1+r)\dfrac{20}{23}\right] = wl_1 \\ \\ (1+r)\left[a_{21}p_1 + \dfrac{10}{11}p_2\right] + wl_2 = p_2 \Leftrightarrow p_2\left[1-(1+r)\dfrac{10}{11}\right] = wl_2 \end{cases}$$

$$+ (1+r)a_{21}p_1$$

Thus we have

$$p_2\left[\frac{11-10-10r}{11}\right] = wl_2 + (1+r)a_{21}p_1$$

or $$p_2 = \frac{11(wl_2 + (1+r)a_{21}p_1)}{1-10r}$$

with $$p_1\left[\frac{23-20-20r}{23}\right] = \left(1 - \frac{r}{0.15}\right)l_1$$

or $$p_1 = \frac{23[0.15-r]}{0.15(3-20r)}l_1 = \frac{23}{3}l_1 > 0$$ [22]

for all r such that $0 \leq r \leq R(=0.15)$

It follows that $wl_2 + (1+r)a_{21}p_1 > 0$ since $a_{21} > 0$ and $p_1 > 0$ when $0 \leq r < 0.15$ and that

$$p_2 \begin{cases} > 0 & 0 \leq r < 0.10 \\ & \text{when} \\ < 0 & 0.10 < r \leq 0.15 \end{cases}$$

Furthermore,

$$\frac{dp_2}{dr} = \frac{11}{(1-10r)^2}\left[\left(\left(l_2 \times \frac{dw}{dr}\right) + a_{21}p_1\right)(1-10r) + 10(wl_2 + (1+r)a_{21}p_1)\right]$$

where $w = 1 - \dfrac{r}{0.15}$ and $\dfrac{dw}{dr} = -\dfrac{1}{0.15}$

$$\frac{dp_2}{dr} = \frac{11}{(1-10r)^2}\left[-\frac{l_2}{0.15} + \frac{10l_2r}{0.15} + a_{21}p_1 - 10a_{21}p_1r + 10l_2 - \frac{10l_2r}{0.15}\right.$$

$$\left. + 10a_{21}p_1 + 10ra_{21}p_1\right]$$

$$= \frac{11}{(1-10r)^2}\left[11a_{21}p_1 + \frac{l_2}{3}\right] > 0 \text{ for any } r \neq 0.10$$

and thus p_2 is an increasing function of r when $0 \leq r \leq 0.15$

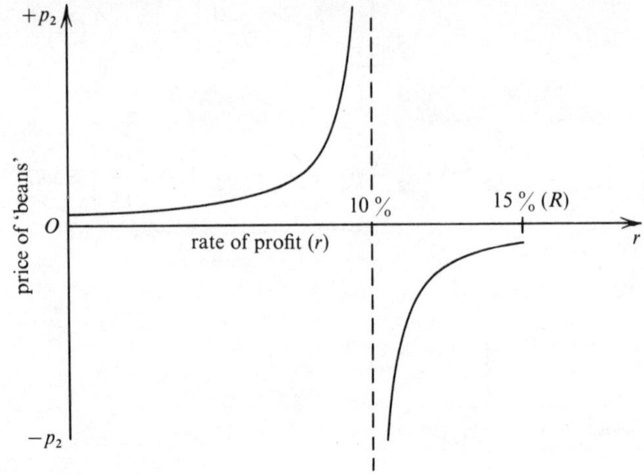

Fig. 2.2

Since $p_2(0) = 11(l_2 + a_{21}p_1) > 0$ and

$$p_2(R) = \frac{11[0 \times l_2 + 1.15a_{21}p_1]}{1 - 1.5} = -22[1.15a_{21}p_1] < 0$$

the price curve consists of *two* branches of a rectangular hyperbola which has for asymptotes the rate of profits axis and the parallel to the price-axis passing through 10%.

Despite appearances, this example is not without interest. It shows, in effect, that *although the rate of profit is determined in the basic sector,* at the same time as prices, *it is limited by the production conditions of non-basic commodities,* more precisely by the internal surplus-rate $(1 - a_{nn})/a_{nn}$ of each non-basic commodity $[\text{here } (1 - a_{22})/a_{22} = 10\%]$.

The whole range of possible values of r in the basic sector $(0 < r < R)$ cannot be realised when $[(1 - a_{nn})/a_{nn} < R]$ if we keep the assumption of a uniform rate of profits in the entire system.

Is this a problem only of theoretical interest or are there practical consequences? There are several possible consequences.

First, there is the possibility suggested by Sraffa, that the producer could sell the beans 'at a higher price than the one which, in his book-keeping, he attributes to them as means of production'. In these conditions, 'the "beans" could however, still be produced and marketed so as to show a normal profit' (P.S. Appendix B, p. 91). Other possibilities would be to stop the production of such a low-profit commodity or for the capitalists to accept a lower rate of profit in that industry or to modify the conditions of production to increase the internal surplus rate.

3

General analysis of prices: joint production, fixed capital, land and natural resources

The analysis carried out in the previous chapter was restricted to single-product industries and circulating capital. For reasons of simplification it was assumed, on the one hand, that no durable instruments of production, i.e. no machines, were required for the production of the different commodities, and, on the other, that all means of production were reproducible commodities, which meant that land had to be excluded.

As soon as these two restrictive assumptions are relaxed to take account of means of production that last for more than one year (fixed capital) or are not reproducible (land) a more general approach than that used for the analysis of single-product industries becomes necessary for the analysis of the prices of commodities and the distribution of the net product.

Systems composed of multiple-product industries, sometimes called 'joint-production systems', are necessary for this, more general, analysis.[1] Such a framework represents the most general of all possible systems since it encompasses both the single-product industries with circulating capital presented above, as well as systems that allow the treatment of both fixed capital and land. The most useful way to introduce the discussion of this framework is with a brief presentation of the analysis of economic expansion given in von Neumann's model,[2] since his analysis is at the same time more limited and more general than that proposed by P. Sraffa, which will be examined subsequently. The von Neumann model is more limited because it does not consider labour directly (even when labour is taken into account as an input the wage is not considered as paid from the surplus). At the same time it is more general because the technology matrices need not necessarily be square, while Sraffa's analysis starts from the assumption of square technological matrices.

3.1 Equilibrium prices and the rate of profit in a von Neumann model

3.1.1 Description of the model

Let us consider a von Neumann model with n goods $B_1, B_2, \ldots, B_j, \ldots,$

B_n produced by *m activities* (or *processes*) $A_1, A_2, \ldots, A_i, \ldots, A_m$. We call a *technique of production* the operation of part, or all, of the processes at given levels of activity.

Let us assume:

(i) $m \geq n$: the number of processes is at least equal to the number of goods;

(ii) we have constant returns in each activity; all commodities have the same period of production; inputs are made at the beginning of the period and outputs are obtained at the end of the same period;

(iii) joint production: changes of technique may occur (for example, to produce a good, B_j, one can use either process A_i or process A_k or a combination of both);

(iv) there is no technical progress;

(v) the system is *closed* and produces only intermediate goods in the sense that all goods consumed have been previously produced in the system and all goods produced are re-employed in the system as means of production in the following period. Let us assume initially that the system does not use labour.[3] It is therefore a system of production of commodities by means of commodities only.[4] As for capital goods, they are considered at one and the same time as both products and means of production;

(vi) there is no final consumption to be satisfied and therefore the whole surplus product is reinvested;

(vii) each good, B_j, is produced from goods, $B_1, B_2, \ldots, B_j, \ldots, B_n$ by processes, $A_1, \ldots, A_i, \ldots, A_m$, characterised by *fixed technical coefficients*.

For a finite number, m, of processes we have to introduce special notation to describe and solve the model. With the process A_i producing at the unit level we call

a_{ij} the quantity of good B_j used up in process A_i;
$\mathbf{a}_i = [a_{i1}, \ldots, a_{ij}, \ldots, a_{in}] \geq \mathbf{0}$ the input vector of process A_i;
$\mathbf{A}_{mn} = [a_{ij}]$ the input matrix of the model;
b_{ij} = the quantity of good B_j produced by process A_i;
$\mathbf{b}_i = [b_{i1}, \ldots, b_{ij}, \ldots, b_{in}] \geq \mathbf{0}$ the output vector of process A_i;
$\mathbf{B}_{mn} = [b_{ij}]$ the output matrix of the model.

Thus the process A_i is defined by the two vectors $(\mathbf{a}_i, \mathbf{b}_i)$ and the technology of the model by the two matrices $(\mathbf{A}, \mathbf{B})$.

In order for the model to reproduce itself, each good B_j must be produced by at least one process. This condition is fulfilled when the following assumption (1) holds:

given a column vector $\mathbf{p} = \begin{bmatrix} p_1 \\ \vdots \\ p_j \\ \vdots \\ p_n \end{bmatrix} \geq \mathbf{0}$, the assumption

$$\{\mathbf{p} \geq \mathbf{0} \text{ implies } \mathbf{Bp} \geq \mathbf{0}\} \tag{1}$$

is equivalent to:

$$\forall j \in \{1, 2, \ldots, n\}, \mathbf{b}^j = \begin{bmatrix} b_{1j} \\ \vdots \\ b_{kj} \\ \vdots \\ b_{mj} \end{bmatrix} \geq \mathbf{0}$$

or $b_{kj} > 0$ for at least one $k \in \{1, 2, \ldots m\}$. This assumption means that for any good B_j there exists at least one process A_k producing B_j.

Similarly, every process A_i must use up at least one good or else the system would produce goods *ex nihilo*![5] This condition is fulfilled when the following assumption (2) holds:

Given a row vector $\mathbf{q} = (q_1, \ldots, q_i, \ldots, q_m) \geq \mathbf{0}$, the assumption

$$\{\mathbf{q} \geq \mathbf{0} \text{ implies } \mathbf{qA} \geq \mathbf{0}\} \tag{2}$$

is equivalent to

$$\forall i \in \{1, 2, \ldots, m\}\ \mathbf{a}_i = (a_{i1}, \ldots, a_{ik}, \ldots, a_{in}) \geq \mathbf{0} \text{ or}$$

$a_{ik} > 0$ for at least one $k \in \{1, 2, \ldots n\}$, which means that for any process A_i there exists a good B_k used up in the process A_i.

3.1.2 Economic expansion of the system

Let p_j be the price of good B_j and $\mathbf{p} = \begin{bmatrix} p_1 \\ \vdots \\ p_j \\ \vdots \\ p_n \end{bmatrix} \geq \mathbf{0}$ be the column-vector of the prices of the n goods.

The process A_i, operating at unit level, produces a quantity b_{ij} of good B_j and thus receives as *unit income*:

$$b_{i1}p_1 + b_{i2}p_2 + \ldots + b_{ij}p_j + \ldots + b_{in}p_n = \sum_{j=1}^{n} b_{ij}p_j = \mathbf{b}_i\mathbf{p}$$

Similarly, the cost of the means of production used up when process A_i operates at unit level is

$$a_{i1}p_1 + a_{i2}p_2 + \ldots + a_{ij}p_j + \ldots + a_{in}p_n = \sum_{j=1}^{n} a_{ij}p_j = \mathbf{a}_i\mathbf{p}$$

With a rate of profit r the *total unit cost* (including profit) of process A_i is $(1+r)\mathbf{a}_i\mathbf{p}$.

If we have an economy where the rate of profit r is the same for all processes (which means that superprofit is excluded) each process must earn a non-positive superprofit such that

$$\mathbf{b}_i\mathbf{p} - (1+r)\mathbf{a}_i\mathbf{p} \leqq 0 \quad \forall i \in \{1, 2, \ldots, m\}$$

or $\quad \mathbf{Bp} \leqq (1+r)\mathbf{Ap}$

Since there must be at least one process A_i yielding a *zero* superprofit $\mathbf{b}_i\mathbf{p} - (1+r)\mathbf{a}_i\mathbf{p}$, we must therefore determine the lowest uniform rate of profit r such that $\mathbf{Bp} \leqq (1+r)\mathbf{Ap}$.

3.1.3 The system of equilibrium prices

The following theorem states that the set of numbers r satisfying the conditions

$$\begin{cases} \mathbf{Bp} \leqq (1+r)\mathbf{Ap} \\ \mathbf{p} \geq \mathbf{0} \\ r > 0 \end{cases}$$

possesses a smallest element R[6] when assumption (1) holds. R is then called the rate of profit of the model, any price vector $\mathbf{p}(R)$ associated with R is called a vector of equilibrium prices and any system $(r, \mathbf{p}(R))$ is a system of equilibrium prices.

Theorem

If assumption (1) is verified the model $(\mathbf{A}, \mathbf{B})$ has a system of equilibrium prices $[R, \mathbf{p}(R)]$.

If we consider the function $f = 1/(1+r)$ defined as

$$\mathbf{p} \geqq \mathbf{0} \rightarrow f(\mathbf{p}) = \begin{cases} \min\limits_i \dfrac{\sum\limits_j a_{ij} p_j}{\sum\limits_j b_{ij} p_j} = \min\limits_i \dfrac{\mathbf{a}_i \mathbf{p}}{\mathbf{b}_i \mathbf{p}} & \text{for } \mathbf{p} \geq \mathbf{0} \\ 0 & \text{for } \mathbf{p} = \mathbf{0} \end{cases}$$

it is sufficient to show that f has a maximum and reaches this maximum for a price vector $\mathbf{p} \geq \mathbf{0}$.

By assumption (1), when $\mathbf{p} \geq \mathbf{0}$ there exists at least one $i \in \{1, 2, \ldots m\}$ such that $\mathbf{b}_i \mathbf{p} = \sum\limits_{j=1}^{n} b_{ij} p_j > 0$; function f is defined and continuous over the entire set of real positive numbers $(\mathbf{R}^+)^n$. Since for any positive α we have $f(\alpha \mathbf{p}) = f(\mathbf{p})$ the function f is homogeneous of degree zero and we only have to find the maximum F reached by the function f in the intersection C of the unit sphere and the set of positive numbers $(\mathbf{R}^+)^n$. C being compact (closed and bounded) and f continuous over C, f reaches its maximum F for at least one $\bar{\mathbf{p}} \in C$. Since

$$\frac{1}{1 + r(\mathbf{p})} = f(\mathbf{p}), r(\mathbf{p}) = \frac{1}{f(\mathbf{p})} - 1$$

reaches its minimum $R = \dfrac{1}{F} - 1$ in $\bar{\mathbf{p}}$. Thus the vector $\bar{\mathbf{p}} \in C$ where r reaches its minimum value R is a vector of equilibrium prices $\bar{\mathbf{p}}(R)$.

Example

Von Neumann's model $(\mathbf{A}, \mathbf{B})$ where

$$\mathbf{A} = \begin{bmatrix} 8 & 1 \\ 4 & 8 \\ 4 & 3 \end{bmatrix} \quad \text{and } \mathbf{B} = \begin{bmatrix} 9 & 1 \\ 2 & 10 \\ 3 & 4 \end{bmatrix}$$

satisfies assumption (1) since matrix $\mathbf{B}$ is positive. The model has a price system defined by the rate of profit $R = 10\%$ and the price vector $\mathbf{p}(R) = \begin{bmatrix} 1 \\ 2 \end{bmatrix}$.

3.1.4 Economic goods and free goods

Good B_j is called an *economic* good when its price p_j is positive and a *free* good when p_j is zero.

Let us note that:

$\mathbf{a}_i\mathbf{p} > 0$ means that the process A_i uses at least one economic good;
$\mathbf{a}_i\mathbf{p} = 0$ means that the process A_i uses only free goods;
$\mathbf{Ap} > \mathbf{0}$ means that all processes use economic goods;
$\mathbf{b}_i\mathbf{p} > 0$ means that the process A_i produces at least one economic good;
$\mathbf{b}_i\mathbf{p} = 0$ means that the process A_i produces only free goods;
$\mathbf{Bp} > \mathbf{0}$ means that all processes produce economic goods;
supp $(\mathbf{Bp}) \subset$ supp $(\mathbf{Ap})$[7] means that a process using only free goods as inputs produces only free goods;
supp $(\mathbf{Bp}) \not\subset$ supp $(\mathbf{Ap})$ means that there is at least one process producing economic goods and using only free goods as inputs.

3.1.5 The introduction of labour in von Neumann's model

Up to this point we have considered that a process A_i produces goods $B_1, \ldots, B_j, \ldots, B_n$ exclusively from these same goods. If we suppose now that the process A_i, functioning at a unit level of activity, also employs l_i work hours, then von Neumann's model is defined by the triplet $(\mathbf{A}, \mathbf{B}, \mathbf{L})$ where the column vector $\mathbf{L} = \begin{bmatrix} l_1 \\ \vdots \\ l_i \\ \vdots \\ l_n \end{bmatrix}$ represents the labour inputs in the system.

If workers receive a basket of goods $\mathbf{d} = [d_1, \ldots, d_j, \ldots, d_n]$ as the real wage for every hour of work supplied, the process A_i, at unit level, uses quantities of goods $B_1, \ldots, B_j, \ldots, B_n$, given by vector $l_i\mathbf{d} = [l_id_1, \ldots l_id_j \ldots l_id_n]$, to produce wages for the labour employed. Since wages are advanced, the process A_i defined by $(\mathbf{a}_i, \mathbf{b}_i, l_i)$ can be represented by $(\mathbf{a}_i^*, \mathbf{b}_i)$ where $\mathbf{a}_i^* = \mathbf{a}_i + l_i\mathbf{d}$ includes all quantities of goods consumed by process A_i either as means of production or as workers' wages. The von Neumann model is represented by the couple $(\mathbf{A}^*, \mathbf{B})$ where the socio-technological matrix $\mathbf{A}^*$ is equal to $\mathbf{A} + \mathbf{Ld}$ with $a_{ij}^* = a_{ij} + l_id_j$ as the general term.

Note that if assumption (1) is verified the model $(\mathbf{A}, \mathbf{B}, \mathbf{L})$ has a system of equilibrium prices $(R', \mathbf{p}(R'))$ with R', the rate of profit of $(\mathbf{A}, \mathbf{B}, \mathbf{L})$ at most equal to R, the rate of profit of model $(\mathbf{A}, \mathbf{B})$ since part of the product is paid as wages to labour.

3.2 A system with circulating capital and joint production: Sraffa's analysis

Sraffa considers systems with circulating capital and joint production as a preliminary to the analysis of fixed capital and land and the problems they involve (P.S. Chapters 7, 8, 9). Thus, as in the case of simple production, the assumption that the methods of production use neither land nor machinery, but only circulating capital, is retained. However, for the analysis of joint production, Sraffa makes a supplementary assumption in order to be able to determine the prices:

> In Part I it has been assumed that each commodity was produced by a separate industry. We shall now suppose two of the commodities to be jointly produced by a single industry (or rather by a single process, as it will be more appropriate to call it in the present context). The conditions would no longer be sufficient to determine the prices. There would be more prices to be ascertained than there are processes; and therefore equations to determine them.
>
> In these circumstances there will be room for a second, parallel process which will produce the two commodities by a different method and, as we shall suppose at first, in different proportions. Such a parallel process will not only be possible—it will be necessary if the number of processes is to be brought to equality with the number of commodities so that the prices may be determined. We shall therefore go a step further and assume that in such cases, a second process or industry does in fact exist [P.S. § 50, p. 43].

More generally, if there are k commodities, there must be k equations of production in order to determine the k prices: 'The assumption previously made of the existence of "a second process" can now be replaced by the more general assumption that the number of processes should be equal to the number of commodities' (P.S. §50, p. 44).

Thus the framework of analysis is similar to that used by von Neumann (see Section 3.1). We will use the following notation, to investigate Sraffa's framework:

$\mathbf{A} = [a_{ij}]$ and $\mathbf{B} = [b_{ij}]$ represent respectively the $k \times k$ square, input and output matrices;[8]

$\mathbf{L}$, as in the case of simple production, represents the vector of direct labour (assumed to be homogeneous);

w and r are respectively the wage and the rate of profit.

Thus we have the following price equations:

$$(a_{11}p_1 + a_{12}p_2 + \ldots + a_{1k}p_k)(1+r) + l_1 w = b_{11}p_1 + b_{12}p_2 + \ldots + b_{1k}p_k$$
$$(a_{21}p_1 + a_{22}p_2 + \ldots + a_{2k}p_k)(1+r) + l_2 w = b_{21}p_1 + b_{22}p_2 + \ldots + b_{2k}p_k$$
$$\cdots\cdots\cdots\cdots\cdots\cdots\cdots\cdots\cdots\cdots\cdots\cdots$$
$$(a_{k1}p_1 + a_{k2}p_2 + \ldots + a_{kk}p_k)(1+r) + l_k w = b_{k1}p_1 + b_{k2}p_2 + \ldots + b_{kk}p_k$$

or

$$\mathbf{Ap}(1+r)+\mathbf{L}w=\mathbf{Bp}$$

We notice moreover (even if Sraffa mentions it only incidentally (P.S., p. 43, n. 2)) that the k processes $[\mathbf{a}_i, \mathbf{b}_i]$ must be linearly independent, that is, rank $[\mathbf{A},\mathbf{B}]=k$, $[\mathbf{A},\mathbf{B}]=[\mathbf{a}^1,\ldots,\mathbf{a}^k,\mathbf{b}^1,\ldots,\mathbf{b}^k]$ being a $k\times 2k$ matrix (this is equivalent to det $[\mathbf{B}-\mathbf{A}]\neq 0$ — matrix $[\mathbf{B}-\mathbf{A}]$ is non-singular — since rank $[\mathbf{A},\mathbf{B}]=$ rank $[\mathbf{A},\mathbf{B}-\mathbf{A}]$).

Of course, the fundamental assumption is that $(\mathbf{A},\mathbf{B})$ is capable of self-replacement. This is formally written by assuming the vector $\boldsymbol{\sigma}$ of net production to be nonnegative: $\boldsymbol{\sigma}=\mathbf{u}(\mathbf{B}-\mathbf{A})$ where $\mathbf{u}=\underbrace{[1,1,\ldots,1]}_{k}$.

The vector $\mathbf{u}$ can be interpreted as representing the assumption of unit level of activity for all processes. It is, of course, possible to use a different activity vector of the type:

$$\mathbf{q}=[q_1,\ldots,q_i,\ldots,q_k] \qquad \text{with } \mathbf{q}\geq\mathbf{0}$$

The surplus of the various commodities would then be

$$\mathbf{s}=[s_1,\ldots,s_i,\ldots,s_k]=\mathbf{q}(\mathbf{B}-\mathbf{A})\geq\mathbf{0}$$

After these preliminary remarks it is clear that prices will be uniquely defined (up to the multiplication by scalars) for a given r[9] by

$$\mathbf{p}=w[\mathbf{B}-(1+r)\mathbf{A}]^{-1}\mathbf{L}$$

provided that det $[\mathbf{B}-(1+r)\mathbf{A}]\neq 0$. The determination of the $k-1$ relative prices and the endogenous distributive variable is, of course, simultaneous.

We have again to find a standard invariant to changes in distribution. The construction of the standard system in this case will be similar to the case of single product industries. But there are difficulties due to the greater complexity of the interrelations and the disappearance of the one to one relation between products and industries. In particular we must identify the way basic commodities are to be defined.

3.2.1 Basic and non-basic commodities

In a single-product system with circulating capital each commodity was produced by a single method of production which defined the industry. Because there was a one to one correspondence between commodities and industries there was an identity between the sector of basic industries and the sector of basic commodities which was independent of the rest of the economy as far as the determination of the prices of the commodities produced in that sector and the determination of the endogenous distributive variable were concerned.

As a result, in such a system the technical autonomy of the basic sector meant that prices and the distributive variables were determined independently of the non-basic sector. To separate the basic sector from the non-basic sector we only needed to rearrange simultaneously rows and columns of the technology matrix in such a way as to obtain zeros in the upper right hand corner of the **A** matrix. Commodities entering directly or indirectly in all methods of production formed the basic sector.

Therefore, to solve an economic problem (the simultaneous determination of relative prices and distributive variables with one degree of freedom) we were able to use a technical criterion, i.e. the indecomposability of the basic sector or the participation, direct or indirect, of a commodity in the production of all commodities.

Such a criterion cannot be applied in the general case of joint production for it is now in general impossible to state that a particular means of production enters the process of any particular commodity. This is for two reasons. First, a particular commodity may be produced by several processes; and second, the contribution of any particular means of production used up in a joint process cannot be attributed to any one of the several commodities produced jointly.

In such conditions any specific attribution is impossible, except in special cases. This helps to explain the difficulties and paradoxes we meet in the case of joint production. We shall now see that economic independence is no longer equivalent to technical autonomy as was the case with simple production. The processes constitute a kind of veil over the commodities but we shall see that by resorting to the basic system we shall be able to create a certain transparency in the economic system. In general an indecomposable system is not necessarily 'basic',[10] although a basic system is always indecomposable.

(*A*) *DECOMPOSABLE AND INDECOMPOSABLE SYSTEMS*

Definition

Matrices **A** and **B** form a decomposable system if, and only if, there exists a permutation of the rows and columns such that **A** and **B** are simultaneously transformed into quasi-triangular matrices as shown below:[11]

$$\mathbf{A} = \begin{bmatrix} \mathbf{A}_1^1 & \mathbf{0} \\ \mathbf{A}_2^1 & \mathbf{A}_2^2 \end{bmatrix} \qquad \mathbf{B} = \begin{bmatrix} \mathbf{B}_1^1 & \mathbf{0} \\ \mathbf{B}_2^1 & \mathbf{B}_2^2 \end{bmatrix}$$

with $\mathbf{A}_1^1$ and $\mathbf{B}_1^1$ being square matrices of the same dimension.[12]

The system of production just described is decomposable into two groups of processes, one of them $(\mathbf{A}_1^1, \mathbf{B}_1^1)$ being technically autonomous from the rest of the economy (but with the second group dependent on the first). In these particular conditions the prices of the commodities produced and consumed by this group of processes (basic commodities) and the level of the endogenous distributive variable can be simultaneously determined independently of the prices of the other commodities.

The system of price equations is of the general form $(1 + r)\mathbf{Ap} + w\mathbf{L} = \mathbf{Bp}$ and can be written with

$$\mathbf{p} = \begin{bmatrix} \mathbf{p}_1 \\ \mathbf{p}_2 \end{bmatrix}, \quad \text{and} \quad \mathbf{L} = \begin{bmatrix} \mathbf{L}_1 \\ \mathbf{L}_2 \end{bmatrix}, \quad \text{as}$$

$$(1 + r)\begin{bmatrix} \mathbf{A}_1^1 & \mathbf{0} \\ \mathbf{A}_2^1 & \mathbf{A}_2^2 \end{bmatrix} \begin{bmatrix} \mathbf{p}_1 \\ \mathbf{p}_2 \end{bmatrix} + w\begin{bmatrix} \mathbf{L}_1 \\ \mathbf{L}_2 \end{bmatrix} = \begin{bmatrix} \mathbf{B}_1^1 & \mathbf{0} \\ \mathbf{B}_2^1 & \mathbf{B}_2^2 \end{bmatrix} \begin{bmatrix} \mathbf{p}_1 \\ \mathbf{p}_2 \end{bmatrix}$$

which produces the following two systems (assuming that the $\mathbf{p}$ and $\mathbf{L}$ vectors are of the appropriate dimension):

$$(1 + r)\mathbf{A}_1^1\mathbf{p}_1 + w\mathbf{L}_1 = \mathbf{B}_1^1\mathbf{p}_1$$

$$(1 + r)(\mathbf{A}_2^1\mathbf{p}_1 + \mathbf{A}_2^2\mathbf{p}_2) + w\mathbf{L}_2 = \mathbf{B}_2^1\mathbf{p}_1 + \mathbf{B}_2^2\mathbf{p}_2$$

The first of the two systems is sufficient to determine the vector $\mathbf{p}_1$ and one of the distributive variables given the other, and given the numeraire.

The second system allows us to find the vector $\mathbf{p}_2$, once $\mathbf{p}_1$ and the endogenous distributive variable have been determined. It thus appears as a non-basic system.

In short, when one is confronted with a decomposable system it is easy to redefine it into a basic and a non-basic sector.

But system $(\mathbf{A},\mathbf{B})$, is not, in general, decomposable. However, as we shall see, it is possible to distinguish the basic sector subject to the condition that the technology matrices have certain collinearity properties that are even less restrictive than those previously required. It is thus possible to have a non-basic system without it being decomposable.

(*B*) *BASIC AND NON-BASIC SYSTEMS*

Example

To introduce the subject, let us consider a very simple example.[13] We have an economy with two processes of joint production defined by the following positive technology matrices

$$\mathbf{A} = \begin{bmatrix} a_{11} & a_{12} \\ a_{21} & a_{22} \end{bmatrix} \qquad \mathbf{B} = \begin{bmatrix} b_{11} & b_{12} \\ b_{21} & b_{22} \end{bmatrix}$$

It is obvious that the system (**A**,**B**) is indecomposable. However, given certain assumptions of linear dependence in the system [**A**,**B**], we shall show that the system [**A**,**B**] although indecomposable is not necessarily basic.

$$[\mathbf{A},\mathbf{B}] = \begin{bmatrix} a_{11} & a_{12} & b_{11} & b_{12} \\ a_{21} & a_{22} & b_{21} & b_{22} \end{bmatrix} \text{ is a } (2 \times 4) \text{ matrix}$$

Suppose that segment (a_{12}, b_{12}) belonging to the first process is linearly dependent on the corresponding segment of the second process, in other words there exists a scalar β such that:[14]

$$[a_{12}, b_{12}] = \beta[a_{22}, b_{22}]$$

In these conditions, matrices **A** and **B** can be written as

$$\mathbf{A} = \begin{bmatrix} a_{11} & \beta a_{22} \\ a_{21} & a_{22} \end{bmatrix} \qquad \mathbf{B} = \begin{bmatrix} b_{11} & \beta b_{22} \\ b_{21} & b_{22} \end{bmatrix}$$

Thus we have the following price equations

$$(1+r)\begin{bmatrix} a_{11} & \beta a_{22} \\ a_{21} & a_{22} \end{bmatrix} \begin{bmatrix} p_1 \\ p_2 \end{bmatrix} + w\begin{bmatrix} l_1 \\ l_2 \end{bmatrix} = \begin{bmatrix} b_{11} & \beta b_{22} \\ b_{21} & b_{22} \end{bmatrix} \begin{bmatrix} p_1 \\ p_2 \end{bmatrix}$$

with $\mathbf{p} = \begin{bmatrix} p_1 \\ p_2 \end{bmatrix}$ and $\mathbf{L} = \begin{bmatrix} l_1 \\ l_2 \end{bmatrix}$

or $\quad (1+r)(a_{11}p_1 + \beta a_{22}p_2) + wl_1 = b_{11}p_1 + \beta b_{22}p_2$

$$(1+r)(a_{21}p_1 + a_{22}p_2) + wl_2 = b_{21}p_1 + b_{22}p_2$$

By using a linear combination of these two equations it is possible to find an equation with only three unknowns: p_1 and the distributive variables w and r. By multiplying the second equation by $(-\beta)$ and adding the two equations p_2 can be eliminated:

$$(1+r)(a_{11} - \beta a_{21})p_1 + w(l_1 - \beta l_2) = (b_{11} - \beta b_{21})p_1$$

This equation shows that if we chose commodity 1 as numeraire (by putting $p_1 = 1$) and assume that one of the distributive variables is given exogenously, the first commodity has every property of a basic commodity *vis-à-vis* the second commodity since we can determine the value of the endogenous distributive variable independently of p_2 (with p_1 fixed at 1). As for p_2, it can only be determined if we already know p_1 and the endogenous distributive variable.

Note that we have obtained the preceding equation, which could be considered as a basic equation, by eliminating the second commodity simultaneously from both the means of production and the quantities produced, in the first equation for prices. This elimination is only possible because of the assumption of linear dependence between the two homologous segments of the methods of production. These segments have therefore disappeared from the 'basic equation'. At the same time, it is perfectly possible for some of the 'abstract quantities' to be negative (e.g. of the type $(a_{11} - \beta a_{21}), (b_{11} - \beta b_{21}), (l_1 - \beta l_{21})$) and this, of course, cannot be related to any effective method of production. This is one of the apparent paradoxes of joint production (P.S. §56, p. 48).

It is possible to give another method of dealing with this problem, whose importance will become clear in the more general presentation given below. Let us construct a matrix (see Manara, 'Il Modello di Piero Sraffa ...')

$$\mathbf{M} = \begin{bmatrix} 1 & -\beta \\ 0 & 1 \end{bmatrix}$$

which transforms **A** and **B** in quasi-triangular matrices given the assumption of linear dependence $(a_{12}, b_{12}) = \beta(a_{22}, b_{22})$.[15]

$$\mathbf{MA} = \begin{bmatrix} 1 & -\beta \\ 0 & 1 \end{bmatrix} \begin{bmatrix} a_{11} & a_{12} \\ a_{21} & a_{22} \end{bmatrix} = \begin{bmatrix} a_{11} - \beta a_{21} & 0 \\ a_{21} & a_{22} \end{bmatrix}$$

$$\mathbf{MB} = \begin{bmatrix} 1 & -\beta \\ 0 & 1 \end{bmatrix} \begin{bmatrix} b_{11} & b_{12} \\ b_{21} & b_{22} \end{bmatrix} = \begin{bmatrix} b_{11} - \beta b_{21} & 0 \\ b_{21} & b_{22} \end{bmatrix}$$

and

$$\mathbf{ML} = \begin{bmatrix} 1 & -\beta \\ 0 & 1 \end{bmatrix} \begin{bmatrix} l_1 \\ l_2 \end{bmatrix} = \begin{bmatrix} l_1 - \beta l_2 \\ l_2 \end{bmatrix}$$

We have constructed a virtual system

$$(\bar{\mathbf{A}}_1^1, \bar{\mathbf{B}}_1^1, \bar{l}_1) = (a_{11} - \beta a_{21},\ b_{11} - \beta b_{21}, l_1 - \beta l_2)$$

which appears as a basic system. While the system $(\mathbf{A}, \mathbf{B})$ was technically indecomposable we have nonetheless been able to *create*, within the system $(\mathbf{A},\mathbf{B})$ a basic system (given the assumption of linear dependence). We can generalise this procedure without difficulty by following a method proposed by Manara.

(C) *BASIC AND NON-BASIC SYSTEMS— GENERALISATIONS*

Definition

A system $(\mathbf{A},\mathbf{B})$ is called non-basic if there exists a simultaneous permutation of the columns of $\mathbf{A}$ and $\mathbf{B}$ and a number m such that matrix $[\mathbf{A}^2,\mathbf{B}^2]$ formed of the m $(1 \leq m \leq k-1)$ last columns of $\mathbf{A}$ and $\mathbf{B}$ is at most of rank m (P.S. §60, p. 51; and Manara, *op. cit.*).

Let us suppose that such a permutation has been made. The system $(\mathbf{A},\mathbf{B})$, which is non-basic by assumption, can then be written as follows:

$k-m$ processes	$\mathbf{A}_1^1$	$\mathbf{A}_1^2$	$\mathbf{B}_1^1$	$\mathbf{B}_1^2$
m processes	$\mathbf{A}_2^1$	$\mathbf{A}_2^2$	$\mathbf{B}_2^1$	$\mathbf{B}_2^2$
	$k-m$	m	$k-m$	m

The $(k \times 2m)$ matrix $[\mathbf{A}^2,\mathbf{B}^2] = \begin{bmatrix} \mathbf{A}_1^2 & \mathbf{B}_1^2 \\ \mathbf{A}_2^2 & \mathbf{B}_2^2 \end{bmatrix}$ is at most of rank m.

It has at most m independent rows. Thus $(k-m)$ rows must be linear combinations of at most m others. If they are the first rows, we can then represent them as linear combinations of the m last rows $[\mathbf{A}_2^2,\mathbf{B}_2^2]$ taken as bases.

Let $[\mathbf{A}_1^2,\mathbf{B}_1^2] = \mathbf{H}[\mathbf{A}_2^2,\mathbf{B}_2^2]$ with $\mathbf{H}$ of dimension $(k-m, m)$.

By using Manara's procedure we can construct the matrix

$$\mathbf{M} = \begin{bmatrix} \mathbf{I}_{k-m} & -\mathbf{H} \\ \mathbf{0} & \mathbf{I}_m \end{bmatrix}$$

which transforms $\mathbf{A}$ and $\mathbf{B}$ into quasi-triangular matrices[16]

$$\mathbf{MA} = \begin{bmatrix} \mathbf{I}_{k-m} & -\mathbf{H} \\ \mathbf{0} & \mathbf{I}_m \end{bmatrix} \begin{bmatrix} \mathbf{A}_1^1 & \mathbf{A}_1^2 \\ \mathbf{A}_2^1 & \mathbf{A}_2^2 \end{bmatrix} = \begin{bmatrix} \mathbf{A}_1^1 - \mathbf{HA}_2^1 & \mathbf{0} \\ \mathbf{A}_2^1 & \mathbf{A}_2^2 \end{bmatrix}$$

$$\mathbf{MB} = \begin{bmatrix} \mathbf{I}_{k-m} & -\mathbf{H} \\ \mathbf{0} & \mathbf{I}_m \end{bmatrix} \begin{bmatrix} \mathbf{B}_1^1 & \mathbf{B}_1^2 \\ \mathbf{B}_2^1 & \mathbf{B}_2^2 \end{bmatrix} = \begin{bmatrix} \mathbf{B}_1^1 - \mathbf{HB}_2^1 & \mathbf{0} \\ \mathbf{B}_2^1 & \mathbf{B}_2^2 \end{bmatrix}$$

The smallest among the systems of the type $[(\mathbf{A}_1^1 - \mathbf{H}\mathbf{A}_2^1), (\mathbf{B}_1^1 - \mathbf{H}\mathbf{B}_2^1)]$, i.e. the system of this type to which corresponds the greatest m, is called a *basic system.* If it is identical to $(\mathbf{A},\mathbf{B})$, $(\mathbf{A},\mathbf{B})$ will be said to be a basic system.

If we multiply the initial system by $\mathbf{M}$ we have

$$(1+r)\mathbf{MAp} + \mathbf{ML}w = \mathbf{MBp}$$

and therefore we have two sub-systems of equations[17]

$$(1+r)(\mathbf{A}_1^1 - \mathbf{H}\mathbf{A}_2^1)\mathbf{p}_1 + (\mathbf{L}_1 - \mathbf{H}\mathbf{L}_2)w = (\mathbf{B}_1^1 - \mathbf{H}\mathbf{B}_2^1)\mathbf{p}_1$$

$$(1+r)(\mathbf{A}_2^1\mathbf{p}_1 + \mathbf{A}_2^2\mathbf{p}_2) + \mathbf{L}_2 w = \mathbf{B}_2^1\mathbf{p}_1 + \mathbf{B}_2^2\mathbf{p}_2$$

The first series of equations can be solved independently of the second. Of course, the two series together give the same results as the initial equations since the first are simply inferred from the second by a linear combination given by $\mathbf{M}$. Two cases can be distinguished:

– If $\mathbf{H} = \mathbf{0}$, we revert to the (technically) decomposable system in the sense previously defined. Thus the system $(\mathbf{A}_1^1, \mathbf{B}_1^1)$ is technically independent since we do not need to know the processes defined by the triplet $(\mathbf{A}_2, \mathbf{B}_2, \mathbf{L}_2)$ to determine the prices in the system $(\mathbf{A}_1^1, \mathbf{B}_1^1, \mathbf{L}_1)$.

– If $\mathbf{H} \neq \mathbf{0}$, we cannot speak of technical autonomy of a group of processes *vis-à-vis* another group. Since we have $\mathbf{A}_1^2 = \mathbf{H}\mathbf{A}_2^2$ and $\mathbf{B}_1^2 = \mathbf{H}\mathbf{B}_2^2$, it means that some commodities produced and/or used in the non-basic processes are produced and/or used as well in some basic processes. However, and although the prices of the $(k-m)$ first *commodities* are not independent of what happens in the m last *processes* of the type $(\mathbf{A}_2, \mathbf{B}_2, \mathbf{L}_2)$, we have constructed a *virtual system*:

$$(\bar{\mathbf{A}}^1, \bar{\mathbf{B}}^1, \bar{\mathbf{L}}_1) = (\mathbf{A}_1^1 - \mathbf{H}\mathbf{A}_2^1, \mathbf{B}_1^1 - \mathbf{H}\mathbf{B}_2^1, \mathbf{L}_1 - \mathbf{H}\mathbf{L}_2)$$

which determines the relative prices of the $(k-m)$ first commodities as a function of the rate of profit and independently of the prices of the m last commodities (P.S. §62).

In the case of joint production a decomposable system is only a particular case of a non-basic system whereas in the case of simple production decomposable systems and non-basic systems are equivalent.

In fact, if the system $(\mathbf{A},\mathbf{I})$ is decomposable, matrix $\mathbf{A}$ is decomposable and can be written, after permutation:

$$\mathbf{A} = \begin{bmatrix} \mathbf{A}_1^1 & \mathbf{0} \\ \mathbf{A}_2^1 & \mathbf{A}_2^2 \end{bmatrix} \text{where } \mathbf{A}_2^2 \text{ is an } (m \times m) \text{ square matrix.}$$

The $(k \times 2m)$ matrix $[\mathbf{A}^2, \mathbf{I}^2] = \begin{bmatrix} \mathbf{0} & \mathbf{0} \\ \mathbf{A}_2^2 & \mathbf{I}_m \end{bmatrix}$ is then of rank m and the system $(\mathbf{A}, \mathbf{B})$ is non-basic.

Reciprocally, if the system $(\mathbf{A}, \mathbf{I})$ is non-basic, we can perform the same permutation $\mathbf{PAP}'$ and $\mathbf{PIP}' = \mathbf{I}$ of matrices $\mathbf{A}$ and $\mathbf{I}$ such that $[\mathbf{A}^2, \mathbf{I}^2] = \begin{bmatrix} \mathbf{A}_1^2 & \mathbf{0} \\ \mathbf{A}_2^2 & \mathbf{I}_m \end{bmatrix}$ is of rank lesser or equal to m. Since $\mathbf{I}^2 = \begin{bmatrix} \mathbf{0} \\ \mathbf{I}_m \end{bmatrix}$ is of rank m, then rank $[\mathbf{A}^2, \mathbf{I}^2] = m$, which implies that $\mathbf{A}_1^2 = \mathbf{0}$ and matrix $\mathbf{A} = \begin{bmatrix} \mathbf{A}_1^1 & \mathbf{0} \\ \mathbf{A}_2^1 & \mathbf{A}_2^2 \end{bmatrix}$ as well as the system $[\mathbf{A}, \mathbf{I}]$ is decomposable.

(*D*) *TOTALLY DECOMPOSABLE SYSTEMS*

When a system $[\mathbf{A}, \mathbf{B}]$ is basic, all its goods are basic. When the system $[\mathbf{A}, \mathbf{B}]$ is non-basic we can determine a matrix $\mathbf{M} = \begin{bmatrix} \mathbf{I}_{k-m} & -\mathbf{H} \\ \mathbf{0} & \mathbf{I}_m \end{bmatrix}$ such that $\mathbf{MA} = \begin{bmatrix} \mathbf{A}_1^1 - \mathbf{HA}_2^1 & \mathbf{0} \\ \mathbf{A}_2^1 & \mathbf{A}_2^2 \end{bmatrix}$ and $\mathbf{MB} = \begin{bmatrix} \mathbf{B}_1^1 - \mathbf{HB}_2^1 & \mathbf{0} \\ \mathbf{B}_2^1 & \mathbf{B}_2^2 \end{bmatrix}$

But this does not necessarily mean that we can say whether or not there are basic goods in the system. However, if the system is totally decomposable, i.e. if there exists a square matrix $\mathbf{N}$ such that:

$$\mathbf{NMA} = \begin{bmatrix} \mathbf{A}_1^1 - \mathbf{HA}_2^1 & \mathbf{0} \\ \mathbf{0} & \mathbf{A}_2^2 \end{bmatrix} \quad \text{and } \mathbf{NMB} = \begin{bmatrix} \mathbf{B}_1^1 - \mathbf{HB}_2^1 & \mathbf{0} \\ \mathbf{0} & \mathbf{B}_2^2 \end{bmatrix}$$

then there are no basic goods since the economy can be decomposed into two independent 'sub-economies'.

Since $\det(\mathbf{B} - \mathbf{A}) \neq 0$, we note that if the matrix $[\mathbf{A}^1, \mathbf{B}^1] = \begin{bmatrix} \mathbf{A}_1^1 & \mathbf{B}_1^1 \\ \mathbf{A}_2^1 & \mathbf{B}_2^1 \end{bmatrix}$ formed by the $k - m$ first columns of matrices $\mathbf{A}$ and $\mathbf{B}$ has a rank lesser or equal to $k - m$, the system is totally decomposable. Since $\mathbf{M}$ is non-singular we have

$$\begin{aligned} 0 \neq \det(\mathbf{B} - \mathbf{A}) &= \det[\mathbf{M}(\mathbf{B} - \mathbf{A})] = \det[\mathbf{MB} - \mathbf{MA}] \\ &= \det[(\mathbf{B}_1^1 - \mathbf{HB}_2^1) - (\mathbf{A}_1^1 - \mathbf{HA}_2^1)] \det(\mathbf{B}_2^2 - \mathbf{A}_2^2) \end{aligned}$$

which implies

$$\det[(\mathbf{B}_1^1 - \mathbf{HB}_2^1) - (\mathbf{A}_1^1 - \mathbf{HA}_2^1)] \neq 0$$

or rank $[(\mathbf{B}_1^1 - \mathbf{HB}_2^1) - (\mathbf{A}_1^1 - \mathbf{HA}_2^1)] = k - m$ since the $(k-m) \times (k-m)$ square matrix $(\mathbf{B}_1^1 - \mathbf{HB}_2^1) - (\mathbf{A}_1^1 - \mathbf{HA}_2^1)$ has a non-zero determinant. Therefore we have

$$\text{rank}\,[\mathbf{A}_1^1 - \mathbf{HA}_2^1, \mathbf{B}_1^1 - \mathbf{HB}_2^1] = \text{rank}\,[\mathbf{A}_1^1 - \mathbf{HA}_2^1, (\mathbf{B}_1^1 - \mathbf{HB}_2^1) - (\mathbf{A}_1^1 - \mathbf{HA}_2^1)] = k - m$$

and if

$$\text{rank}\,[\mathbf{A}^1, \mathbf{B}^1] = \text{rank}\,[\mathbf{MA}^1, \mathbf{MB}^1] = \text{rank}\begin{bmatrix} \mathbf{A}_1^1 - \mathbf{HA}_2^1 & \mathbf{B}_1^1 - \mathbf{HB}_2^1 \\ \mathbf{A}_2^1 & \mathbf{B}_2^1 \end{bmatrix} \leq k - m$$

the vectors $[\mathbf{A}_2^1, \mathbf{B}_2^1]$ are linear combinations of the $k - m$ linearly independent vectors $[\mathbf{A}_1^1 - \mathbf{HA}_2^1, \mathbf{B}_1^1 - \mathbf{HB}_2^1]$. Then there exists a matrix $\mathbf{J}$ such that $[\mathbf{A}_2^1, \mathbf{B}_2^1] = \mathbf{J}[\mathbf{A}_1^1 - \mathbf{HA}_2^1, \mathbf{B}_1^1 - \mathbf{HB}_2^1]$ and the non-singular matrix $\mathbf{N} = \begin{bmatrix} \mathbf{I}_{k-m} & \mathbf{0} \\ -\mathbf{J} & \mathbf{I}_m \end{bmatrix}$ allows the transformation of the model $[\mathbf{MA}, \mathbf{MB}]$ into $[\mathbf{NMA}, \mathbf{NMB}]$ which is totally decomposable since.

$$\mathbf{NMA} = \begin{bmatrix} \mathbf{I}_{k-m} & \mathbf{0} \\ -\mathbf{J} & \mathbf{I}_m \end{bmatrix} \begin{bmatrix} \mathbf{A}_1^1 - \mathbf{HA}_2^1 & \mathbf{0} \\ \mathbf{A}_2^1 & \mathbf{A}_2^2 \end{bmatrix} = \begin{bmatrix} \mathbf{A}_1^1 - \mathbf{HA}_2^1 & \mathbf{0} \\ \mathbf{0} & \mathbf{A}_2^2 \end{bmatrix}$$

$$\text{and } \mathbf{NMB} = \begin{bmatrix} \mathbf{B}_1^1 - \mathbf{MB}_2^1 & \mathbf{0} \\ \mathbf{0} & \mathbf{B}_2^1 \end{bmatrix}$$

Thus, the system $[\mathbf{A}, \mathbf{B}]$ is totally decomposable.

Theorem

If matrix $\mathbf{B}$ is non-singular, the system $[\mathbf{B}^{-1}\mathbf{A}, \mathbf{I}]$ is

(i) indecomposable if, and only if, the system $[\mathbf{A}, \mathbf{B}]$ is basic

(ii) totally decomposable if, and only if, the system $[\mathbf{A}, \mathbf{B}]$ is non-basic and rank $[\mathbf{A}^1, \mathbf{B}^1] \leq k - m$. ($m$ is the highest number such that rank $[\mathbf{A}^2, \mathbf{B}^2] = m$.)

Given the result of the last paragraph, we only have to show that the system $(\mathbf{B}^{-1}\mathbf{A}, \mathbf{I})$ is decomposable if, and only if, $(\mathbf{A}, \mathbf{B})$ is non-basic. If the system $(\mathbf{A}, \mathbf{B})$ is non-basic there exist permutation matrices $\mathbf{P}$ and $\mathbf{Q}$ and a non-singular matrix $\mathbf{M}$ such that $\mathbf{MPAQ}$ and $\mathbf{MPBQ}$ are quasi-triangular. The matrix $(\mathbf{MPBQ})^{-1}\mathbf{MPAQ} = \mathbf{Q}^{-1}\mathbf{B}^{-1}\mathbf{P}^{-1}\mathbf{M}^{-1}\mathbf{MPAQ} = \mathbf{Q}^{-1}\mathbf{B}^{-1}\mathbf{AQ} = \mathbf{Q}'\mathbf{B}^{-1}\mathbf{AQ}$, product of two quasi-triangular matrices is itself quasi-triangular as is the matrix $\mathbf{Q}'\mathbf{IQ} = \mathbf{I}$ and therefore the system $(\mathbf{B}^{-1}\mathbf{A}, \mathbf{I})$ is decomposable. (Any permutation matrix $\mathbf{Q}$ is regular and has its trans-

Existence of basic goods in a system $[\mathbf{A}, \mathbf{B}]$

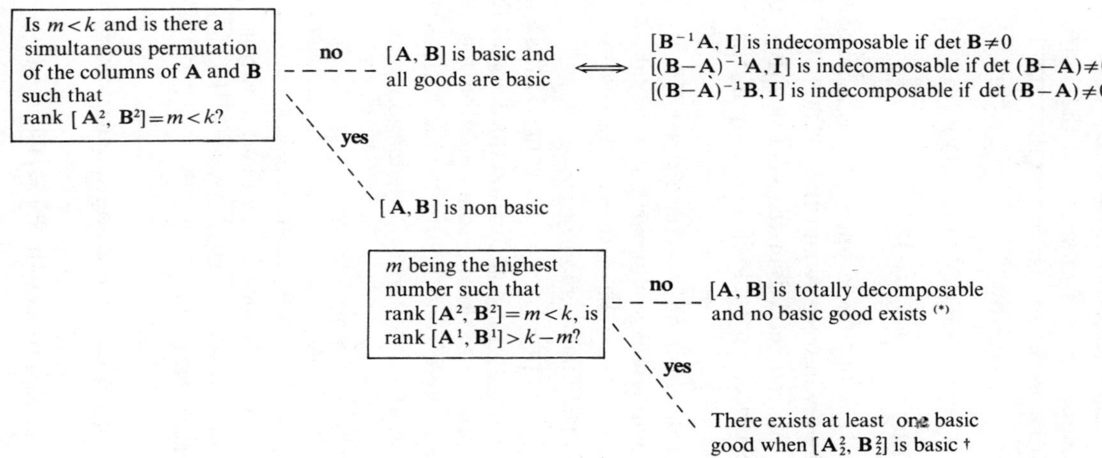

(*) if det $\mathbf{B}\neq 0$, the system $[\mathbf{B}^{-1}\mathbf{A}, \mathbf{I}]$ is totally decomposable

† when rank $[\mathbf{A}^1, \mathbf{I}^1]>k-m$ and $[\mathbf{A}_2^2, \mathbf{B}_2^2]$ is a non-basic system, there is no general rule for determining the existence of basic goods

pose $\mathbf{Q}'$ as inverse.) Reciprocally, if the system $(\mathbf{B}^{-1}\mathbf{A},\mathbf{I})$ is decomposable, there exists a permutation matrix $\mathbf{Q}$ such that the matrix $\mathbf{QB}^{-1}\mathbf{AQ}'$ is quasi-triangular. If the zero sub-matrix of $\mathbf{QB}^{-1}\mathbf{AQ}'$ is of dimension $(k-m)\times m$, we have

$$m = r[(\mathbf{QB}^{-1}\mathbf{AQ}')^2,\mathbf{I}^2] = r[\mathbf{BQ}'(\mathbf{QB}^{-1}\mathbf{AQ}')^2,(\mathbf{BQ}')\mathbf{I}^2]$$
$$= r[(\mathbf{AQ}')^2,(\mathbf{BQ}')^2] = r[\mathbf{A}^2,\mathbf{B}^2]$$

and the system $[\mathbf{A},\mathbf{B}]$ is non-basic since there is a number $m<k$ and a permutation of the columns of $\mathbf{A}$ and $\mathbf{B}$ such that $r[\mathbf{A}^2,\mathbf{B}^2]=m<k$.

In the same way we can show that the systems $[(\mathbf{B}-\mathbf{A})^{-1}\mathbf{A},\mathbf{I}]$ and $[(\mathbf{B}-\mathbf{A})^{-1}\mathbf{B},\mathbf{I}]$ are indecomposable if, and only if, the system $[\mathbf{A},\mathbf{B}]$ is non-basic and $r[\mathbf{A}^1,\mathbf{B}^1]\le k-m$.

The procedure for determining whether a system $[\mathbf{A},\mathbf{B}]$ is basic, non-basic or totally decomposable is summarised in the table on page 75. It shows clearly those cases where the existence of basic goods in the system $[\mathbf{A},\mathbf{B}]$ can be determined unambiguously.

The process by which the processes veil the commodities is now obvious. By creating a virtual system through the intermediary of the matrix $\mathbf{M}$ the Sraffa–Manara procedure throws some light on the functioning of the system. Of course, there is no reason for the various quantities (of labour, inputs, or outputs) of this virtual system to be positive.

3.2.2 The standard commodity

As in the case of simple production, and for the same reasons, the standard system must be constructed in such a way that the various commodities are produced in the same proportions as they enter the means of production. The system must be such that

$$\mathbf{qB} = (1+R)\mathbf{qA} \Leftrightarrow \alpha^*\mathbf{q} = \mathbf{qAB}^{-1} \text{ if } \mathbf{B} \text{ is non-singular and } \alpha^* = \frac{1}{1+R}.$$

(Recall that in simple production $[\mathbf{B}]=[\mathbf{B}]^{-1}=\mathbf{I}$

$\Rightarrow \mathbf{qI}=(1+R)\mathbf{qA}$, thus $\alpha^*\mathbf{q}=\mathbf{qA}$.)

Two questions arise: the first concerns the existence of a real value of α^* such that $0<\alpha^*<1$ and corresponds to the necessity of a standard ratio $R>0$; the second concerns the structure of the corresponding vector of activity $\mathbf{q}$.[18] In order to answer these two questions we must distinguish two broad series of cases.

(1) The system $[\mathbf{A},\mathbf{B}]$ is basic

By post-multiplying the matrix equation above by **A** we have

$$\alpha^*\mathbf{qA} = \mathbf{qAB}^{-1}\mathbf{A} = \mathbf{qA}(\mathbf{B}^{-1}\mathbf{A})$$

Now, we have already demonstrated (Section 3.2.1) that if the system $[\mathbf{A},\mathbf{B}]$ is basic, $(\mathbf{B}^{-1},\mathbf{A})$ is indecomposable but not necessarily non-negative. Therefore, the following sub-distinction must be made:

$$\mathbf{B}^{-1}\mathbf{A} \geq 0 \tag{1a}$$

We have just seen that $\alpha^*\mathbf{q} = \mathbf{qAB}^{-1} \Rightarrow \alpha^*\mathbf{qA} = \mathbf{qA}(\mathbf{B}^{-1}\mathbf{A})$, i.e. every eigenvalue of $(\mathbf{AB}^{-1})$ is an eigenvalue of $(\mathbf{B}^{-1}\mathbf{A})$. Since the $k \times k$ square matrix $(\mathbf{B}^{-1}\mathbf{A})$ has k eigenvalues and $(\mathbf{AB}^{-1})$, also a $k \times k$ matrix, also has k eigenvalues, they have the same set of eigenvalues.

Since $(\mathbf{B}^{-1}\mathbf{A})$ is indecomposable and semi-positive, we know by the Perron–Frobenius theorem that its dominant eigenvalue α^* is a real simple root of the characteristic equation $\det[\alpha\mathbf{I} - \mathbf{B}^{-1}\mathbf{A}] = 0$.

Therefore α^* is also a simple root of the characteristic equation of $(\mathbf{AB}^{-1})$

$$\det[\alpha\mathbf{I} - \mathbf{AB}^{-1}] = 0$$

As a consequence, the solution vector **q** of the system of homogeneous linear equations $\mathbf{q}[\alpha^*\mathbf{I} - \mathbf{AB}^{-1}] = 0$ is uniquely determined up to the multiplication by scalars since the rank of matrix $[\alpha^*\mathbf{I} - \mathbf{AB}^{-1}]$ is equal to $(k-1)$, α^* being a simple root of $\det[\alpha\mathbf{I} - \mathbf{AB}^{-1}] = 0$.

Thus **q** is uniquely determined up to the multiplication by scalars as in the case of simple production, but with the difference that there may be negative elements in the vector **q**.[19]

$$\mathbf{B}^{-1}\mathbf{A} \ngeq \mathbf{0} \tag{1b}$$

In this case α^* is not necessarily real. We can easily verify this in the simple example proposed by Manara. We have the following system $[\mathbf{A},\mathbf{B}]$

$$\mathbf{A} = \begin{bmatrix} 1 & 1.1 \\ 1.1 & 1 \end{bmatrix} \qquad \mathbf{B} = \begin{bmatrix} 1.09 & 1.144 \\ 1.144 & 0.99 \end{bmatrix}$$

The system is productive since

$$\mathbf{u}(\mathbf{B} - \mathbf{A}) = [1 \quad 1]\begin{bmatrix} 0.09 & 0.044 \\ 0.044 & -0.01 \end{bmatrix} = (0.134 \qquad 0.034) > \mathbf{0}$$

A quick calculation shows that the characteristic equation $\det[\mathbf{B} - (1+R)\mathbf{A}] = 0$ has no real root. There is no standard system in this particular case since the standard ratio is not defined.

More generally it means that there may not be any standard system when $\mathbf{B}^{-1}\mathbf{A} \ngeq \mathbf{0}$.

(2) The system $[\mathbf{A},\mathbf{B}]$ is non-basic.

We must then construct a basic system $[\bar{\mathbf{A}},\bar{\mathbf{B}}]$ whose quantities are not necessarily all positive. Therefore we make a new distinction:

(2a) $\bar{\mathbf{A}} \geq \mathbf{0}$ and $\bar{\mathbf{B}} \geq \mathbf{0}$. This is a problem similar to that of section 1 above.

(2b) $\bar{\mathbf{A}}$ and/or $\bar{\mathbf{B}} \ngeq \mathbf{0}$. α^* and $\mathbf{q}$ still stand for the system of homogeneous linear equations $\mathbf{q}[\alpha^*\bar{\mathbf{B}} - \bar{\mathbf{A}}] = 0$. The number α^* is the solution of the equation of the $(k-m)$th degree $\det[\alpha\bar{\mathbf{B}} - \bar{\mathbf{A}}] = 0$. In these conditions nothing can be said about the existence and uniqueness of $\mathbf{q}$. In particular if the equation

$$\det[\alpha\bar{\mathbf{B}} - \bar{\mathbf{A}}] = 0$$

has no real solutions, α, then $\mathbf{q}$, and therefore the standard system, do not exist. If $\det[\alpha\bar{\mathbf{B}} - \bar{\mathbf{A}}]$ has at least one real root, α, the uniqueness of the standard system is not certain.[20] And in any case, there may be negative elements in the vector $\mathbf{q}$ (if it exists).

If the standard system exists, we can follow the same procedure to construct the standard commodity as in the case of simple production. Manara (*op. cit.*) makes the following remark on this point: 'It does not seem that Sraffa had the least doubt concerning the possibility that the existence of a standard commodity could be shown, while, on the contrary, this is not always possible'.

The aim of the preceding section was simply to show the truth of Manara's remark.[21]

Let us return to Sraffa's analysis. When the standard system exists, the system of basic equations 'differ however from the original system, not only for excluding non-basics, but in two other respects. In the first place a basic equation does not in general represent a productive process– it is merely the result of combining the equations of a number of processes. In the second place it may contain negative quantities as well as positive ones' (P.S. §62, pp. 52–3).

Sraffa had previously noted that in this case 'it becomes impossible to visualise the Standard system as a conceivable re-arrangement of the actual processes. We must therefore in the case of joint-products be content with the system of abstract equations, transformed by appropriate multipliers, without trying to think of it as having a bodily existence' (P.S. §56, p. 48).

But, in fact, it does not matter.

> The *raison d'être* of the Standard system, however, is to provide a Standard commodity. And in the case of the latter there is fortunately no insuperable difficulty in conceiving as real the negative quantities[22] that are liable to occur among its components. These can be interpreted, by analogy with the accounting concept, as liabilities or debts while the positive components will be regarded as assets [P.S. §56, p. 48].

Therefore, we should not be concerned by the positive or negative character of the standard commodity which is only an analytical auxiliary (see P.S. §43, pp. 31–2). This standard commodity is again, *at least generally*, the standard of prices and wages we were looking for.

By expressing prices and wages in terms of this standard we *generally* have the famous relation between r and w_s. The system of equations of prices of production is written

$$\mathbf{Ap}_s(1+r)+\mathbf{L}w_s=\mathbf{Bp}_s$$

Thus $r\mathbf{Ap}_s+\mathbf{L}w_s=(\mathbf{B}-\mathbf{A})\mathbf{p}_s$

Let $1=\mathbf{q}(\mathbf{B}-\mathbf{A})\mathbf{p}_s=r\mathbf{qAp}_s+\mathbf{qL}w_s=\dfrac{r}{R}\mathbf{q}R\mathbf{Ap}_s+(\mathbf{qL})w_s$

But $\mathbf{q}R\mathbf{A}=\mathbf{q}(\mathbf{B}-\mathbf{A})$; if we can normalise the vector $\mathbf{q}$ such that $\mathbf{qL}=1$, it immediately follows:

$$1=\frac{r}{R}+w_s \Leftrightarrow r=R(1-w_s)$$

Let us recall that this relation, if it exists, is true not only in the standard system, but also in the actual system, 'provided only that the wage is expressed in terms of the Standard product' (P.S. §31, p. 22).

The decreasing linear relation between r and w_s can obviously only be true if the standard commodity exists. But this is only a necessary condition, and not in any way a sufficient condition. We know that, if the standard system exists, negative components can exist in vector $\mathbf{q}$ in various cases and therefore it may be impossible to have $\mathbf{qL}=1$. For example if

$$\mathbf{q}=[1;-3] \text{ and } \mathbf{L}=\begin{bmatrix}0.75\\0.25\end{bmatrix}$$

We have $\mathbf{qL}=0$

In this case it is obviously impossible to show the decreasing linear relation between r and w_s.

We are thus led to the conclusion that the analytical construction thought out by Sraffa has more limited implications in the case of joint production:

(a) the existence of the standard system and of the standard commodity is not guaranteed,

(b) even if the standard system exists, the uniqueness is not always certain,

(c) when the standard system (and therefore the standard commodity) exists and is unique, it is not always possible to establish the decreasing linear relationship between the rate of profits and the wage expressed in terms of the standard commodity.

3.2.3 Prices and the standard ratio in joint production

We have already seen above that in the case of joint production the standard system does not necessarily exist, in particular because there may not be a standard ratio. Such a situation is excluded in the case of simple production as long as the system is productive. We know that in the latter case the prices $\hat{\mathbf{p}} = \mathbf{p}/w$ expressed in terms of wage of the basic commodities are on one hand positive for all r between 0 and R, and an increasing function of r on the other. We have also pointed out that peculiarities can occur in determining the prices of non-basic commodities used in their own reproduction (the case of 'beans').

Multiple product systems also show some peculiarities even if the analysis is limited to basic commodities. First, because the existence of a maximum rate of profit is not certain, and second, because the prices of basic commodities in terms of wage goods can themselves become negative; the first peculiarity explains the second. The occurrence of negative prices in a way indicates the limit of the economic viability of the system, which means that in the case of joint production this limit can be expressed either in the existence of a maximum rate of profit or in the appearance of negative prices.

The following theorem will help to make these various points more precise.

Schefold's theorem

A basic system $(\mathbf{A}, \mathbf{B}, \mathbf{L})$ where $\mathbf{A} \geq \mathbf{0}$ and $\mathbf{B} \geq \mathbf{0}$ has one of the three following properties:

– either a maximum rate of profit exists and thus a standard system exists

– or the vector of prices in terms of wages $\hat{\mathbf{p}}(r) = \dfrac{\mathbf{p}(r)}{w}$ is not semi-positive for all r

– or there exists a maximum rate of profit (and thus a standard system) and the vector of prices in terms of wages $\hat{\mathbf{p}}(r)$ is not semi-positive for all r.[23]

Let us assume that $\hat{\mathbf{p}}(r) = [\mathbf{B} - (1+r)\mathbf{A}]^{-1}\mathbf{L} \geq \mathbf{0}$ for all $r \geq r_0 \geq 0$ with, of course, $\det[\mathbf{B} - (1+r)\mathbf{A}] \neq 0$. Since $\mathbf{u}_{(1,k)}$ is the row vector $[1, 1, \ldots, 1]$, we have $\mathbf{uA} > \mathbf{0}, \mathbf{uB} = \mathbf{u}$ (normalisation conditions) and $\mathbf{u}(\mathbf{B} - \mathbf{A}) \geq \mathbf{0}$.

We can write $\mathbf{uA} = \gamma\mathbf{u} + \mathbf{v}$ with $\mathbf{v} \geq 0$ and $0 < \gamma < 1$ and for all $r \geq r_0 > 0$, we have

$$[\mathbf{B} - (1+r)\mathbf{A}]\hat{\mathbf{p}}(r) = \mathbf{L}$$

or $$\mathbf{B}\hat{\mathbf{p}}(r) - (1+r)\mathbf{A}\hat{\mathbf{p}}(r) = \mathbf{L}$$

By premultiplying by $\mathbf{u}$, we have

$$\mathbf{uB}\hat{\mathbf{p}}(r) - (1+r)\mathbf{uA}\hat{\mathbf{p}}(r) = \mathbf{uL}$$

or by normalising $\mathbf{L}$ by $\mathbf{uL} = 1$

$$\mathbf{u}\hat{\mathbf{p}}(r) - (1+r)(\gamma\mathbf{u} + \mathbf{v})\hat{\mathbf{p}}(r) = 1$$

or $$\mathbf{u}\hat{\mathbf{p}}(r)[1 - (1+r)\gamma] - (1+r)\mathbf{v}\hat{\mathbf{p}}(r) = 1$$

Since by assumption $\hat{\mathbf{p}}(r) \geq \mathbf{0}$ we have

$$\mathbf{u}\hat{\mathbf{p}}(r) > \mathbf{0} \text{ and } \mathbf{v}\hat{\mathbf{p}}(r) \geq \mathbf{0}$$

and thus the quantity $\mathbf{u}\hat{\mathbf{p}}(r)[1 - (1+r)\gamma] - (1+r)\mathbf{v}\hat{\mathbf{p}}(r)$ is negative (and therefore cannot be equal to 1) when $1 - (1+r)\gamma < 0$ or $r > \frac{1}{\gamma} - 1$. Thus at least one of the two assumptions $\hat{\mathbf{p}}(r) \geq \mathbf{0}$ for $r \geq r_0 \geq 0$

$$r > \frac{1}{\gamma} - 1.$$

cannot be true, since if we simultaneously use the two assumptions we are led to the contradiction seen above. So we must exclude either one of the two assumptions, or both.

(i) If we exclude the second assumption, $r > (1/\gamma) - 1$, we have $r < (1/\gamma) - 1$ which means that r is bounded by $(1/\gamma) - 1$.
Therefore there is a maximum rate of profit (and a standard system).

(ii) If we exclude the first assumption: $\hat{\mathbf{p}}(r) \geq \mathbf{0}$ for $r \geq r_0 > 0$ the vector $\hat{\mathbf{p}}(r)$ is not semi-positive for all r.

(iii) If we exclude both assumptions simultaneously, there is a maximum rate of profit and the vector $\hat{\mathbf{p}}(r)$ is not semi-positive.

Remark

In some cases of joint production (**A**, **B**, **L**) the existence of the standard ratio is assured. This occurs when $(\mathbf{B}-\mathbf{A})^{-1}>0$ and in the cases seen in Section 4.4.

3.3 Fixed capital

3.3.1 Fixed capital as a special case of joint production

> The interest of Joint Products does not lie so much in the familiar examples of wool and mutton, or wheat and straw, as in its being the genus of which Fixed Capital is the leading species. And it is mainly as an introduction to the subject of fixed capital that the preceding chapters devoted to the intricacies of joint products find their place.
>
> We shall regard durable instruments of production as part of the annual intake of a process, on the same footing as such means of production (e.g. raw materials) as are entirely used up in the course of a year; while what is left of them at the end of the year will be treated as a portion of the annual joint product of the industry, of which the more conspicuous part consists of the marketable commodity that is the primary object of the process.
>
> For example, a knitting-machine enters the means of production at the beginning of the year, along with the yarn, the fuel, etc., with which it is employed; and at the end of the year the partly worn-out, older machine which emerges from the process will be regarded as a joint product with the year's output of stockings [P.S. §73, p. 63].

This approach to fixed capital, attributed by Sraffa to Torrens (P.S., Appendix D, pp. 93–5), could be called the Sraffa–von Neumann approach. We shall later examine the problem in detail and we shall see more particularly how the required price equation may be formed. First, however, we should point out that in the following arguments only systems with *pure* fixed capital will be considered. All problems associated with the traditional definition of joint production[24] are therefore, for analytical reasons that shall be seen below, excluded.

3.3.2 Value of machines with constant efficiency in time

Sraffa's approach to fixed capital

> implies that the same machine, at different ages, should be treated as so many different products, each with its own price. In order to determine these prices, an equal number of additional equations (and therefore of processes) is required.
>
> Accordingly, an industry which employs a durable instrument must be regarded as being subdivided into as many separate processes as are the years

of the total life of the instrument in question. Each of these processes is distinguished by the fact that it uses an instrument of a different age; and each of them 'produces', jointly with a quantity of a marketable commodity, an instrument a year older than the one which it uses—with the exception of the process using the expiring instrument in its last year, which produces singly the marketable commodity [P.S. §74, pp. 63–4].

Let us take the simple example of a single machine used during T years producing only one particular commodity.[25] The proposed method is based on the equations of separate processes corresponding to the successive ages of the machine $M_0, M_1, \dots, M_{T-1}$ producing the same commodity, i.e. the same final good b_g of price p_g. We call $p_{m,0}, p_{m,1}, \dots p_{m,T-1}$ the respective prices, or book-values, of $M_0, M_1, \dots M_{T-1}$; $\mathbf{a}_h$ the inputs of the $(h+1)$th process and $\mathbf{p}$ the price vector of inputs.[26] We have T equations:

$$\begin{cases} (1+r)[\mathbf{a}_0\mathbf{p} + M_0 p_{m,0}] + wl_0 = b_{0,g}p_g + M_1 p_{m,1} \\ (1+r)[\mathbf{a}_1\mathbf{p} + M_1 p_{m,1}] + wl_1 = b_{1,g}p_g + M_2 p_{m,2} \\ \text{-------------------------------} \\ (1+r)[\mathbf{a}_{T-1}\mathbf{p} + M_{T-1} p_{m,T-1}] + wl_{T-1} = b_{T-1,g}p_g \end{cases}$$

If we adopt Sraffa's simplifying assumption that the machine works with constant efficiency throughout its life, we have

$$b_{0,g} = b_{1,g} = \dots = b_{T-1,g} = \text{constant}$$

$$\mathbf{a}_0 = \mathbf{a}_1 = \dots \mathbf{a}_{T-1} = \text{constant}$$

$$l_0 = l_1 = \dots l_{T-1} = \text{constant}$$

Thus the price equation of the $(h+1)$th process corresponding to the $(h+1)$th utilisation period of the machine is $(1+r)(\mathbf{a}_h\mathbf{p} + p_{m,h}) + wl_h = b_g p_g + p_{m,h+1}$.[27]

This price equation can be written as a function of the allowance for depreciation during period h which is calculated as the difference $p_{m,h} - p_{m,h+1}$ from the definition of the machine's book-value. In fact, in order to write the price equations correctly we must take into account the total charge for the machine for each period, F_h, which includes the allowance for depreciation previously defined, as well as the profit allocated to the machine calculated on the value of invested capital, $rp_{m,h}$. The total charge for the period $(h+1)$ is thus $F_h = (p_{m,h} - p_{m,h+1}) + rp_{m,h} = (1+r)p_{m,h} - p_{m,h+1}$. The price equation of the $(h+1)$th process thus becomes $(1+r)\mathbf{a}_h\mathbf{p} + F_h + wl_h = b_g p_g$.

Since the price, p_g, of the final commodity must be the same irrespective of the process used and since we have made the simplifying assumption of constant efficiency of machines of whatever age $h(0 \leq h \leq T-1)$, the provision F_h must be constant and the preceding equation must be true for all conceivable h. Thus we have

$$F = F_h = (1+r)p_{m,h} - p_{m,h+1} \qquad h = 0, \ldots, T-1$$

We can easily find the total annual charge F by multiplying the two sides of each relation of the preceding type by $(1+r)^{T-h-1}$ and by adding up the relations so obtained:

$$\begin{cases} F(1+r)^{T-1} = (1+r)^T p_{m,0} - (1+r)^{T-1} p_{m,1} \\ F(1+r)^{T-2} = (1+r)^{T-1} p_{m,1} - (1+r)^{T-2} p_{m,2} \\ \cdots\cdots\cdots\cdots\cdots\cdots \\ F(1+r)^{T-h-1} = (1+r)^{T-h} p_{m,h} - (1+r)^{T-h-1} p_{m,h+1} \\ \cdots\cdots\cdots\cdots\cdots\cdots \\ F = (1+r)p_{m,T-1} \\ \hline F \sum_{t=1}^{T} (1+r)^{T-t} = (1+r)^T p_{m,0} \end{cases}$$

or $$(1+r)^T p_{m,0} = F \frac{(1+r)^T - 1}{r}$$ [28]

$$F = \frac{r(1+r)^T}{(1+r)^T - 1} p_{m,0}$$

This result expresses the constant annual charge for the machine and appears in the price equations of the h processes.

We could have reached this result, which is well known in the financial theory of the firm, by 'the usual way of calculating the depreciation and interest on a fixed capital asset' (P.S. §74, p. 64). But such a method cannot be generalised: 'While the two methods give the same result in the extremely simplified case of constant efficiency to which both can be applied, the advantage of the joint-production-equations method is that it is not restricted to that case but has general validity' (P.S. §77, p. 66).

First, this method can be used without difficulty when we remove Sraffa's simplifying assumption of constant efficiency of the machine throughout its lifetime. The system of equations of prices of production initially presented was, in fact, perfectly general and, in that case, 'the charge will in general not be constant but changing, and probably falling, with the ageing of the instrument or asset' (P.S. §77, p. 66).[29]

Secondly, this method can be applied in economically more complex cases because 'The same type of machine (e.g. a lorry) may be used in several industries and it may be subject to greater wear and tear when employed in one than in the other' (P.S. §78, p. 66). (If a single machine were to be used in k industries and had a specific working life, T_i, or different conditions of use in each industry it would have $\sum_1^k T_i$ different values.)

Let us revert to our previous example which has the advantage of being simple. Once the constant annual charge of the machine is known, it is easy to find the successive prices of the machine (or the prices of the worn-out machines) as a function of the distribution and of its initial price $p_{m,0}$ (the case of variable efficiency is dealt with in Section 3.3.4, below). We have already shown (see note 28) that

$$F\sum_{t=1}^{T-h}(1+r)^{T-h-t}=(1+r)^{T-h}p_{m,h}$$

that is: $F\dfrac{(1+r)^{T-h}-1}{r}=(1+r)^{T-h}p_{m,h}$

which, given F, can be written

$$\frac{r(1+r)^T}{(1+r)^T-1}p_{m,0}\frac{(1+r)^{T-h}-1}{r}=(1+r)^{T-h}p_{m,h}$$

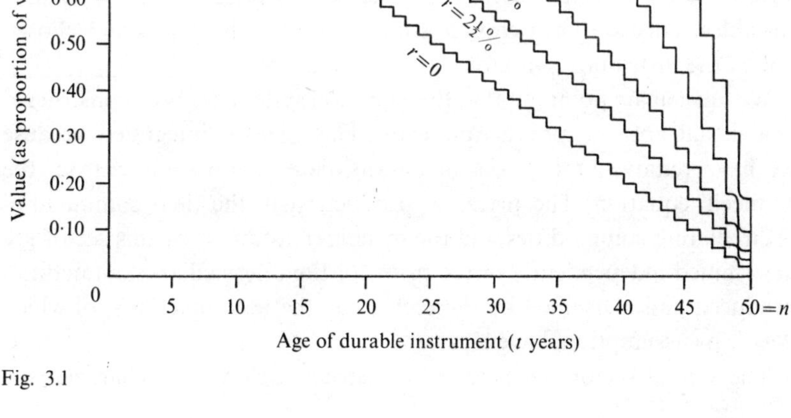

Fig. 3.1

$$\text{or} \quad p_{m,h} = \frac{(1+r)^T - (1+r)^h}{(1+r)^T - 1} p_{m,0}$$

The prices of the worn-out machines are therefore determined (or if one prefers, the successive prices $p_{m,h}$ of a machine of initial price $p_{m,0}$ and of lifetime T) as a function of the distribution of income, or, more exactly, of the rate of profit.[30] Sraffa's diagram gives a good representation of how the ratio $\frac{p_{m,h}}{p_{m,0}}$ for a machine having a total life of 50 years varies when r is varied.[31]

3.3.3 The notion of an integrated sector

The assumptions of constant efficiency for the single machine producing commodity g, and uniformity of the price of g, produce the following single equation for the entire series of equations of prices of production

$$(1+r)\mathbf{a}_h\mathbf{p} + F + wl_h = b_g p_g.$$

By replacing F with its expression as a function of the initial price of the machine and the rate of profit, we have *the 'reduced equation' of the production branch g*:

$$(1+r)\mathbf{a}_h\mathbf{p} + \frac{r(1+r)^T}{(1+r)^T - 1} p_{m,0} + wl_h = b_g p_g$$

Let us assume that all means of production, direct and indirect, of commodity g, are produced without using fixed capital.[32] We have a system of $(k+1)$ equations, k production equations corresponding to the means of production of commodity g and the already derived reduced equation. With the usual mathematical conditions (e.g. the system must have rank $k+1$) we can solve the system ($k+1$ prices and 2 distributive variables) once we have chosen a numeraire for the prices and chosen one of the distributive variables as exogenous.

We must again point out that this equation system has been constructed as a virtual, abstract, production sector. This sector is 'integrated' because we have removed the prices of intermediate commodities[33] from the 'reduced' equation. The prices of production of the final commodities (k circulating commodities and the machine) produced by this sector are determined independently of the prices of the intermediate commodities produced and consumed by the sector (i.e. the used machines, of which $T-1$, by assumption, have a price).

The virtual sector we have just constructed shows the characteristic property of a basic system relative to the production system formed of $(k + T - 1)$ production processes required for commodity g.

Of course, a reduced equation does not represent a real production process any more than a basic equation, but rather the result of combining the equations of a certain number of processes. However, there are two differences to be noted between an integrated system and a basic system. First, the coefficients used for combining the integrated system are variable.[34] They are powers of $(1 + r)$ and therefore are functions of the distribution of income and time. Second, while there can be negative as well as positive quantities in the basic system, there can only be positive quantities in the integrated system. (Recall that joint production is still excluded.) Thus in these conditions our search for a standard commodity will not lead to the apparent paradoxes previously encountered.

3.3.4 Efficiency and obsolescence

We can examine the problems related to the obsolescence of fixed capital using the price equation for the $(h + 1)$th period of the machine utilisation under the general assumption of variable efficiency.

Thus $(1 + r)(\mathbf{a}_h\mathbf{p} + p_{m,h}) + wl_h = b^g_h p_g + p_{m,h+1}$

from which we have

$$F_h = b^g_h p_g - (1 + r)\mathbf{a}_h\mathbf{p} - wl_h$$

Since, by definition, $F_h = (1 + r)p_{m,h} - p_{m,h+1}$,

F_h represents the total charge of the machine (i.e. the allowance for depreciation plus the profit allocated to the machine at the uniform rate of profit, r). In this case, the total charge is variable since the efficiency is no longer supposed to be constant. In this new formulation of the price equation it is obvious that the evolution of F_h through time is linked to the assumption made about changes in efficiency over time. w, r, p_g and $\mathbf{p}$ are here exogenous and can be considered as fixed (with $\mathbf{p}$ and $p_g > 0$). As a result we can distinguish three cases:

constant efficiency:

$$\left\{\begin{array}{l} \mathbf{a}_0 = \ldots = \mathbf{a}_h = \ldots = \mathbf{a}_{T-1} \\ \\ l_0 = \ldots = l_h = \ldots = l_{T-1} \\ b_0 = \ldots = b_h = \ldots = b_{T-1} \end{array}\right\} \Leftrightarrow \left\{\begin{array}{l} F_h \text{ constant and strictly} \\ \quad \text{positive} \\ F_h = (1 + r)p_{m,h} - p_{m,h+1} \\ \quad \text{with } F_{T-1} = (1 + r)p_{m,T-1} \\ \quad\quad (p_{m,T} = 0) \end{array}\right\}$$

increasing efficiency:

$$\left\{\begin{array}{l} \mathbf{a}_0 \geqq \ldots \geqq \mathbf{a}_h \ldots \geqq \mathbf{a}_{T-1} \\ l_0 \geq \ldots \geq l_h \ \ldots \geq l_{T-1} \\ b_0 \leq \ldots \leq b_h \ldots \leq b_{T-1} \end{array}\right\} \Leftrightarrow F_0 \leq \ldots \leq F_h \ldots \leq F_{T-1}$$

decreasing efficiency:

$$\left\{\begin{array}{l} \mathbf{a}_0 \leqq \ldots \leqq \mathbf{a}_h \ldots \leqq \mathbf{a}_{T-1} \\ l_0 \leq \ldots \leq l_h \ \ldots \leq l_{T-1} \\ b_0 \geq \ldots \geq b_h \ldots \geq b_{T-1} \end{array}\right\} \Leftrightarrow F_0 \geq \ldots \geq F_h \ldots \geq F_{T-1}$$

We notice in passing that constant efficiency implies a uniform annual charge ($F_h = F$) on the machines whatever their age, and moreover, that increasing efficiency implies that the charge increases with the utilisation period of the machine. In the case of decreasing efficiency the annual charge also decreases and does not necessarily remain positive after a certain period of utilisation.

At the same time we can add some precision to the determination of the prices of 'older machines'. Since, by definition, we have

$$F_h = (1 + r)p_{m,h} - p_{m,h+1}$$

then $p_{m,h} = \dfrac{1}{1+r}(F_h + p_{m,h+1})$

Therefore *the prices of used machines are always positive when we assume constant or increasing efficiency but they can become negative or zero*[35] *in the case of decreasing efficiency.*

This important result needs more explanation than the mathematical demonstration given above. The prices of machines with increasing efficiency are always positive. This is true even for those among them (the oldest) which do not seem to produce a profit (for example if $F_0 < 0$, $F_1 < 0, \ldots$ etc.). On the contrary machines with decreasing efficiency can lose their value, or even take a negative value, after they pass a certain age. This means that, for a given r, they receive subsidies if they are kept functioning during their physical lifetime.

Let us note that to analyse fixed capital as a particular case of joint production we have implicitly and paradoxically used the traditional method of valuing assets according to their discounted value of expected net returns.

Since by definition $F_H = (1 + r)p_{m,h} - p_{m,h+1}$, we have, multiplying the different values of $p_{m,h}, p_{m,h+1}, p_{m,T-1}$ successively by $\frac{1}{1+r}, \frac{1}{(1+r)^2}, \ldots,$ $\frac{1}{(1+r)^{T-h-1}}$

$$\begin{cases} p_{m,h} = \dfrac{F_h}{1+r} + \dfrac{p_{m,h+1}}{1+r} \\[2ex] \dfrac{p_{m,h+1}}{1+r} = \dfrac{F_{h+1}}{(1+r)^2} + \dfrac{p_{m,h+2}}{(1+r)^2} \\ \cdots\cdots\cdots\cdots\cdots\cdots\cdots\cdots\cdots \\ \dfrac{p_{m,T-1}}{(1+r)^{T-h-1}} = \dfrac{F_{T-1}}{(1+r)^{T-h}} \qquad \text{since } p_{m,T} = 0 \end{cases}$$

$$p_{m,h} = \sum_{i=h}^{i=T-1} \frac{F_i}{(1+r)^{i-h+1}}$$

This result means that the price of a used machine of age h is the sum of the expected net returns for each period, discounted by the rate of interest, r.

These net returns are of the form:

$$F_i = b_i^g p_g - (1+r)\mathbf{a}_i\mathbf{p} - wl_i$$

We have thus shown in passing that the traditional method of valuing capital goods is a particular case of the more general analysis in terms of joint production. We can then determine the prices of old and new machines either in terms of prices of production or of discounted net returns (since $F_0 = b_0^g p_g - (1+r)\mathbf{a}_0\mathbf{p} - wl_0$; see Schefold, 'Theorie der Kuppelproduktion').

At the same time we can explain situations of increasing and decreasing efficiency of machines. The case of increasing efficiency, apparently exceptional, corresponds mainly to the case of learning by doing and 'work in progress'—the extreme case could be represented by the installation of a plant, or the building of a dam, over several years. During the building process no production occurs, net returns are negative during the τ first years ($F_h < 0$ for $h \leq \tau$) but if there is no alternative, that is, if the final product cannot be produced in any better way, then the dam in construction will be assigned a positive value, i.e. the net returns expected in the future will be implicitly discounted. Of course, it is not very likely for a machine to have an ever-increasing efficiency; in fact, after a certain number of periods the efficiency will decrease. The concept of increasing efficiency then has only analytical importance.

The case of decreasing efficiency is different. While prices cannot become negative in the case of increasing efficiency because the old machines are indispensable, in the case of decreasing efficiency prices can become negative because the old machines are not indispensable. The net product of the whole system can be maintained at the same level by increasing the number of new machines and by decreasing the economic life of old machines. By doing this, we should have a system where all prices are positive (subject of course to the fulfilment of the basic condition $\mathbf{u}(\mathbf{B}-\mathbf{A}) \geq \mathbf{0}$ or else the system would not be economically viable).

At the same time we realise that the maximum lifetime of a machine is eventually determined by economic considerations and that the notion of a fixed lifetime determined by physical wear and tear is a simplification.[36] Obsolescence is in reality determined by economic considerations and is affected by the distribution of income.

3.3.5 Construction of the standard commodity

We shall use a simple example to show that, in the general case of fixed capital, it will be generally possible 'for the Standard system to be constructed by means of exclusively positive multipliers' (P.S. §84, p. 73). (As in the case considered above, the only effect of the machine is on the productivity of the system which remains a single-product system and thus has a standard.)

We have the following configuration:

Inputs A					Outputs B			
Wheat	M_0	M_1	M_2	L	Wheat	M_0	M_1	M_2
a_1				l_1		1		
a_2	1			l_2	b_2		1	
a_3		1		l_3	b_3			1
a_4			1	l_4	b_4			

We assume that there are only two types of goods: wheat (meant to represent circulating capital) and the machine with a lifetime of three years. The new machine (M_0) is produced from 'wheat' and, of course, labour (l_1).[37] The second process, using the new machine, a quantity of wheat (a_2) and, evidently, direct labour (l_2) produces at the same time a quantity b_2 of wheat and a used machine M_1. The third process using the used machine M_1, a quantity of wheat (a_3) and direct labour (l_3) produces (b_3) of wheat and the used machine M_2. The final process uses this machine with direct labour (l_4) and wheat (a_4) to produce wheat and a used machine M_3 which does not appear in the example since by assumption it is not used again. The machine is considered as a product, never as a means of production, therefore it is necessarily a non-basic product and it cannot in any way be included in the standard commodity whose composition we are trying to determine.

We know that the standard system must be constructed in such a way that it produces the various commodities in the same proportions as they enter the aggregate of the means of production. With R as the standard ratio (unknown) and $\mathbf{q} = [q_1, q_2, q_3, q_4]$ the utilisation vector of the various activities, we have

$$(1+R)\mathbf{qA} = \mathbf{qB}$$

or

$$\begin{cases} (q_1a_1 + q_2a_2 + q_3a_3 + q_4a_4)(1+R) = q_2b_2 + q_3b_3 + q_4b_4 \\ q_2(1+R) = q_1 \\ q_3(1+R) = q_2 \\ q_4(1+R) = q_3 \end{cases}$$

First, it is obvious that $\dfrac{q_1}{q_2} = \dfrac{q_2}{q_3} = \dfrac{q_3}{q_4} = \ldots = \dfrac{q_i}{q_{i+1}} = 1 + R$

This verifies Sraffa's assertion that 'Durable instruments, if basics,[38] will have to be represented in the Standard commodity by specimens of the various ages in their due proportions' (P.S. §84, p. 72). Sraffa assumes a standard ratio of 10%, it is therefore easy to show that

> The three processes employing machines of 0, 1 and 2 years of age will receive such multipliers as to result in the machines' entering the aggregate of the means of production of the three processes in the proportions of 100 two-year-old machines, 110 one-year-old ones and 121 new ones:[39] hence, at the end of the year, the number of each age-group found in the product will exceed by 10% the number of the same age that had been included in the means of production at the beginning of the year [P.S. §84, pp. 72–3].

Second, we must determine whether or not the standard ratio exists. The equation system used above can be summed up in the equation

$$a_1(1+R)^4 + a_2(1+R)^3 + (a_3 - b_2)(1+R)^2 + (a_4 - b_3)(1+R) - b_4 = 0$$

for which we require a solution $R > 0$, given that:

$\sum_{i=1}^{4} a_i - \sum_{i=2}^{4} b_i < 0$ because there is less wheat consumed than is produced,

and $a_1 > 0$, because the production of the new machine requires wheat.

Let us consider the function f defined by

$$r \rightarrow f(r) = a_1(1+r)^4 + a_2(1+r)^3 + (a_3 - b_2)(1+r)^2 + (a_4 - b_3)(1+r) - b_4$$

f is continuous and defined such that

$$f(0) = \sum_{i=1}^{4} a_i - \sum_{i=2}^{4} b_i < 0$$

$$f(r) \rightarrow \infty \quad \text{when} \quad r \rightarrow \infty$$

takes the value $f(R) = 0$ in at least one point

$$R \in [0 \ \infty[.$$

3.3.6 Special cases: everlasting machines

We shall call 'everlasting' those machines whose lifetime is physically unlimited, i.e. infinite, as long as they are properly maintained.

Mathematically, this means that the columns $\mathbf{a}^e\mathbf{b}^e$ representing the (everlasting) machine e in a joint production system $(\mathbf{A}, \mathbf{B})$ are characterised by equal elements in the same row, in the same production process (for example $a_i^e = b_i^e$) except in the kth process for which $a_k^e = 0, b_k^e > 0$.

This means that the machine considered is produced by a process (the kth) and reappears later in the same form in all processes in which it has been used.

Thus it has the following characteristics:

$$\begin{cases} a_1^e = b_1^e = 0 = \ldots = a_{k-1}^e = b_{k-1}^e = 0 \\ a_k^e = 0, b_k^e > 0 \\ a_h^e = b_h^e > 0 \text{ for } h > k \text{ if } a_h^e > 0 \end{cases}$$

Machines of this type are at the frontier between fixed capital and land for they earn a sort of quasi-rent, which is why they are accorded particular attention.

In the case given above (see Section 3.3.2) of a machine with constant efficiency throughout its lifetime T, the reduced equation can be written as

$$\frac{r(1+r)^T}{(1+r)^T - 1} p_{m,0} + (1+r)\mathbf{a}_h\mathbf{p} + wl_h = b_g p_g$$

When T tends to infinity, the expression $\frac{r(1+r)^T}{(1+r)^T - 1}$ tends towards r and for a machine with constant efficiency and a very long lifetime, we have the following equation

$$rp_{m,0} + (1+r)\mathbf{a}_h\mathbf{p} + wl_h = b_g p_g$$

An equivalent to this equation can be written as:

$$(1+r)(p_{m,0} + \mathbf{a}_h\mathbf{p}) + wl_h = b_g p_g + p_{m,0}$$

Now, it is clear that the machine leaves the process of production in the same condition as it entered the process and therefore the price of the 'produced', 'used' commodity is the same as the price of the new one. The second equation is probably a better expression of the phenomenon of joint production, but the first allows more detailed and interesting analysis. We can, in fact, interpret $\rho_e = rp_{m,0}$ (for $r \neq 0$) as a use-price, a sort of quasi-rent, allocated to its owner. The preceding equation becomes

$$\rho_e + (1+r)\mathbf{a}_h\mathbf{p} + wl_h = b_g p_g \qquad \text{with} \quad \rho_e = rp_{m,0}.$$

We shall see below that a relation exists between this equation and that we shall establish for land. It is now clear that the everlasting machine is a limiting case between fixed capital and land. The analysis is made more interesting by the fact that here again the everlasting machine belongs much more to an analytical category than to a particular class of machines defined by their intrinsic characteristics. In fact, the frontier between a machine with a limited lifetime and a machine with an unlimited lifetime (with possibly very high permanent maintenance costs) is very imprecise: a railway line has an infinite lifespan because its rails are periodically replaced. But[40] this is also true of a knife whose blade is replaced every two months and whose handle is replaced every six months (see Schefold, *op.cit.* p. 79).

Thus the 'everlasting machines' have a much greater importance as an analytical category than as a real category. They appear as intermediate elements between fixed capital and land because they involve quasi-rents. Because they are not just exceptional cases, but represent a method of treating the whole of fixed capital, they provide a justification for the similar analysis of fixed capital and land in terms of joint production.

3.4 Land and natural resources

All natural resources used in production which enable their owners to obtain a rent because they are scarce will be included in this category (see P.S. §85, p. 74). These commodities are exactly the same at both the end and the beginning of each process of production and they are not themselves produced by any other process. (It is this later characteristic which distinguishes 'land' from an 'everlasting' machine.)

Commodity k can be defined as 'land' if, and only if,

$$\mathbf{a}^k = \mathbf{b}^k = \begin{bmatrix} T_1^k \\ \vdots \\ T_i^k \\ \vdots \\ T_n^k \end{bmatrix}$$

where T_i^k expresses the quantity (i.e. the surface) of land of quality k used in the ith process. We shall allow as many as m different qualities of land, that is m column-vectors of the type defined above $(0 < k \leq m)$. In order to simplify the analysis temporarily we shall assume a single quality of land $(k = 1)$ and call p_T (not to be confused with rent) the price of a unit of land (an acre for example). The equation of the ith process then becomes

$$(1 + r)(\mathbf{a}_i\mathbf{p} + T_i p_T) + wl_i = b_i^j p_j + T_i p_T$$

where $\mathbf{a}_i$ is an input vector and b_i^j the crop produced.

We can write this equation in a more usual form which does not, moreover, presuppose that the quality of land is unaffected by the type of productive process considered:

$$(1 + r)\mathbf{a}_i\mathbf{p} + T_i\rho + wl_i = b_i^j p_j$$

$\rho = rp_T$ is the rent (per acre) received by the landowner.

Thus, rent exists whether the land is the object of exchange or not. If there is exchange, the price of the land is determined by the rent discounted at the current interest rate.[41] This is the price that appears in the first form of the equation characterising the ith process.

Since land is evaluated by discounting its rent (as shown above) we can stress either its evaluation as a commodity or the calculation of the income that its use brings to the landowner. The second aspect is the one normally chosen.

But the income of this type of ownership is not, in fact, directly linked to the ownership of land since it can be zero even when all land is owned. This paradox is only apparent and can be explained by the fact that 'the scarcity of land…provides the background from which rent arises'

(P.S. §88, p. 76). Scarcity is thus at the centre of the phenomenon of rent, or even better, of the different types of rent.

3.4.1 Various types of rents

One consequence of scarcity of land relative to the desired production of wheat is the cultivation of less fertile land (this is the classical assumption). But another, less obvious, consequence is the simultaneous occurrence of two methods of production on land with uniform productive qualities. We shall successively consider these two usual forms of rent, the more general cases being simply a combination of the two cases.

(A) The first (classical) case establishes the principle of differential rent (see P.S. §86, p. 74). Assume there is only one product, corn, growing on m plots of land of different quality. Production of corn will then require m different methods. Therefore we have m production equations of the following type:

$$(1+r)\mathbf{a}_i\mathbf{p} + T_i\rho_i + wl_i = b_i^j p_j$$

In addition, we shall assume that one of the plots of land does not yield any rent i.e. $\rho_1\rho_2\ldots\rho_m = 0$

Thus we have $m+1$ supplementary equations corresponding to a similar number of variables representing the rent of the m qualities of land and the price of corn.

Let us suppose, arbitrarily, that the land which does not yield any rent is the first one: $\rho_1 = 0$. This assumption yields the following system of m equations:

$$\begin{aligned}
(1+r)\mathbf{a}_1\mathbf{p} + wl_1 \qquad\quad &= b_1^j p_j \\
(1+r)\mathbf{a}_2\mathbf{p} + T_2\rho_2 + wl_2 &= b_2^j p_j \\
\cdots\cdots\cdots\cdots\cdots\cdots\cdots\cdots\cdots & \\
(1+r)\mathbf{a}_m\mathbf{p} + T_m\rho_m + wl_m &= b_m^j p_j
\end{aligned}$$

Only the first of these equations is necessary to determine the price of corn: the others determine, independently, the $(m-1)$ rents.

The price of corn is given on the less fertile land, the land that does not pay any rent to its owner. We shall distinguish two cases according as whether corn is a basic or a non-basic good.

(a) if corn is a basic good, its price is determined, for a given wage level w, at the same time as the prices of the basic goods and the rate of profit, r. The problem is to determine which of the m possible methods of production of corn enters the basic system.

Montani[42] suggests the calculation, given the wage level w, of the rate of profit for each of the m systems formed by the sector producing industrial goods and one of the m methods for producing corn. The quality of land yielding the highest rate of profit is the first chosen. If it provides the entire output required, there is no rent. If it does not produce enough to satisfy the demand for corn, the quality of land with the next highest rate of profit (r_2) is then brought into cultivation. In this case, the first plot of land receives a rent and the second is marginal if it is only partially used. In this way Montani determines what he calls the order of fertility of land.

(b) if corn is a non-basic good the rate of profit and the price of industrial goods are determined by the basic system for a given wage level.

The cost of production per unit produced can be defined for each of the (m) methods of production of corn:

$$k_i = \frac{(1+r)\mathbf{a}_i\mathbf{p} + wl_i}{b_i^j}$$

The smallest k_i will thus indicate the least fertile land, the next highest k_i, the next most fertile land, and so on.

It should not be forgotten that in both cases the order of fertility of land has been determined for a given level of wages, w. Obviously there is no reason why the order of fertility should remain the same if a different wage level were chosen. The immediate, and important, consequence of this is that there is no natural order of fertility; no particular plot of land is *intrinsically* more fertile than another, as Sraffa points out in the following terms: 'the order of fertility... is not defined independently of the rents; that order, as well as the magnitude of the rents themselves, may vary with the variations of r and w' (P.S. §86, p. 75).

Moreover, Montani has shown ('La Teoria Ricardiana', pp. 240–1) that the order of fertility does not necessarily coincide with the order of rentals. This means that if plot 1 is more fertile than plot 2, which is more fertile than plot 3 it is, nonetheless, possible for the rent (ρ_2) obtained from producing on plot 2 to be greater than the rent (ρ_1) obtained from plot 1; although, if plot 2 is the *marginal* land then it must be true that $\rho_1 > \rho_2 = 0$.

(B) The second type of rent appears when all the land available for cultivation must be used to achieve the output required.

Let us suppose that the available surface is limited and that there is only one quality of land: 'this by itself makes it possible for two different processes or methods of cultivation to be used consistently side by side on similar lands determining a uniform rent per acre' (P.S. §87, p. 75).

The rent ρ and the price of corn are jointly determined by the two following methods used simultaneously:

$$(1+r)\mathbf{a}_1\mathbf{p} + T_1\rho + wl_1 = b_1^j p_j$$
$$(1+r)\mathbf{a}_2\mathbf{p} + T_2\rho + wl_2 = b_2^j p_j$$

To simplify, suppose good j, corn, to be non-basic so that it does not directly enter its own production.[43] We can normalise the system by putting $b_1^j = b_2^j = 1$. Define $k_i = (1+r)\mathbf{a}_i\mathbf{p} + wl_i$ as the cost per unit of output (T_i = area required per unit of output). Thus

$$\begin{cases} k_1 + T_1\rho = p_j \\ k_2 + T_2\rho = p_j \end{cases}$$

and $\rho = \dfrac{k_1 - k_2}{T_2 - T_1}$

Therefore, $\rho > 0$ if, and only if, $k_i < k_j$ implies $T_j < T_i$ (i and $j = 1, 2$) 'which implies that the method that produces more corn per acre' (that is, uses less acres to produce a given quantity of corn, $T_j < T_i$) 'should show a higher cost per unit of product ($k_j > k_i$), the cost being calculated at the ruling levels of the rate of profits, wages and prices' (P.S. §87, p. 76).

It is interesting to note that in conditions of constant returns to scale, production is progressively increased by gradually extending the method with the highest unit cost of production of corn or, in other words (since there is equivalence), the method using land more intensively.

Let Q be the total production of corn and T the total surface (by assumption, fully used). For activity levels q_1 and q_2, we have

$$\begin{cases} q_1 T_1 + q_2 T_2 = T \\ q_1 + q_2 = Q \end{cases}$$

If Q increases, there is a parallel shift of the straight-line $q_1 + q_2 = Q$ and the technique using land more intensively (that is, with the lowest T_i, i.e. technique 2 in the figure) is extended to a larger proportion of the available land. Since a relatively low T_i corresponds to a relatively high k_i (a necessary condition for a positive rent) this means that agricultural production expands by increasing the utilisation of the technique with the relatively higher unit cost.

Sraffa notes that 'While the case of lands of different qualities will be readily recognised as the outcome of a process of "extensive" diminishing returns, it may be less obvious that a similar connection exists between the employment of two methods of producing corn on land of a single

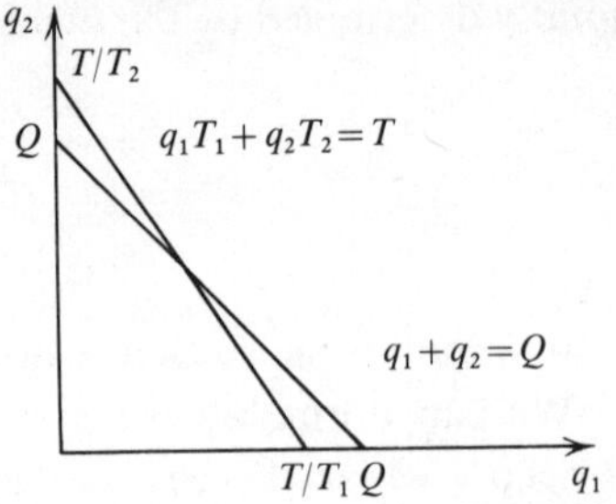

Fig. 3.2

quality and a process of "intensive" diminishing returns' (P.S. §88, p. 76).

This is the case shown in the figure (taken from Schefold *op.cit.*, p. 84). Rent and price can only rise when the two initial methods are completely superseded by 'a third method which produces still more corn at a still higher cost... Thus the stage is set for a new phase of increase in production through the gradual extension of the third method at the expense of the intermediate one' (P.S. §88, p. 76). Sraffa concludes by pointing out the exact role of scarcity: 'While the scarcity of land thus provides the background from which rent arises, the only evidence of this scarcity to be found in the process of production is the duality of methods: if there were no scarcity, only one method, the cheapest would be used on the land and there could be no rent' (P.S. §88, p. 76).[44]

3.4.2 Specialisation of land

We can use the two well-known, already discussed, cases as the starting point for the analyses of more general cases (excluding, for reasons of simplicity, the possibility of multiple products, except for land itself). As Sraffa points out 'The main type of complication arises from the multiplicity of agricultural products' (P.S. §89, p. 76) and later 'What is required in any case is that the number of separate processes should be equal to the number of qualities of land plus the number of products concerned' (*ibid.*, p. 77). We shall show that the necessity of a uniform rent and a uniform rate of profit for a given quality of land leads, in the case of simple production, to a specific use of the land. We thus assume that k commodities are produced on m qualities of land.

Let us first consider a generalisation of the first case, that is, the case where a particular plot of land does not yield any rent to its owner. Suppose, moreover, that all of the k agricultural products are grown on this land. In these conditions *only a single type of product will generally*[45] *be cultivated on each of the lands yielding rent.* There are k products and m plots of land, one of which, by assumption, does not pay any rent. Therefore, there are k prices to determine and m-1 rental payments, i.e. $k+m-1$ unknowns. Since, by assumption, the k agricultural products are all grown on the land which does not yield any rent, and since, again by assumption, there is no joint production (with the exception of land) it follows that all k processes co-exist on the no-rent land. These k types of cultivation determine the k price unknowns. We still have to determine the $m-1$ unknowns, i.e. the $m-1$ rents with the $m-1$ processes of production used on the remaining $m-1$ plots of land. Cases of joint production excluded, the value of the rent for each remaining plot will be determined by each of the $m-1$ processes: thus there will be only one process, one type of cultivation, for each of the $m-1$ rent-paying plots of land. Therefore, each plot of land is specialised in the production of one type of product when all agricultural products are grown on the no-rent land.

But we can also generalise the second case and assume that all qualities of land pay a rent to their owner.[46] If we suppose that all products are grown on a particular type of land, then *one single type of product will be cultivated on each of the remaining plots of land.* We now have $k+m$ unknowns (k prices and m rents) and therefore we need $k+m$ independent equations, i.e. $k+m$ different cultivation processes. But if all products are grown on a particular plot, one of them being produced by two distinct processes, we already have $k+1$ distinct equations of production (joint production is excluded by assumption). For the solution of the system[47] we must have one process producing one good on each of the $(m-1)$ remaining plots, and this means that there will be absolute specialisation on $m-1$ plots of land.[48]

3.4.3 'Land' and the standard system

Natural resources 'can be said to occupy among means of production a position equivalent to that of "non-basics" among products. Being employed in production, but not themselves produced, they are the converse of commodities which, although produced, are not used in production' (P.S. §85, p. 74). Natural resources are thus included in the broader definition of non-basics as land if, and only if, $\mathbf{a}^l = \mathbf{b}^l$. Thus, if we join two m vectors of the type $\mathbf{a}^l, \mathbf{b}^l$, they form a $(k \times 2m)$ matrix of the type $[\mathbf{A}^2, \mathbf{B}^2]$ which is at most of rank m, i.e. there are at most m independent vectors since for any $l(0 \leq l \leq m)$ we have $\mathbf{a}^l = \mathbf{b}^l$. Therefore 'The similarity of rent-earning natural resources with non-basic products shows itself at once in the impossibility of their being counted among the components of the Standard product' (P.S. §85, p. 74).

In order to clarify further some propositions made by Sraffa (P.S. §90, p. 77) about the notion of a system we must go back to the construction of the standard system in the case of joint production with non-basic products. We have previously shown that in a non-basic system (**A**, **B**) it is possible for negative quantities to exist in the components of the standard commodity.

> Now this possibility of negative components is the characteristic feature of what we have called the 'multiple-product system' and is also the chief cause of its limited usefulness as a conception in contrast with the system of 'single-product industries'. It is therefore disconcerting to see it appear in a case where each of the processes produces a single commodity.
>
> The fact is that the introduction of means of production which are not themselves produced, by rendering possible a multiplicity of processes producing the same commodity even though each process has no more than one product, has disrupted our distinction between the two types of system, making its reconstruction necessary.
>
> To effect such reconstruction we must in the first place redefine a 'system' as a set of industries, or methods of production, equal in number, not as formerly to the different products, but to the different things that are produced and/or used as means of production. Besides, the properties which we had attributed to the system of 'single-product industries' must be transferred to a system in which each commodity is produced by *not more than one* method

(this means that the output matrix **B** is diagonal) as in the case of simple production. Similarly, 'the properties of the system of "multiple-product" industries must be transferred to a system in which at least one commodity is produced by *more than one* method, even though all industries were single-product industries' (P.S. §90, pp. 77–8) (here matrix **B** cannot be diagonal).

The standard commodity (without land of any sort) is composed of positive quantities of commodities (the assumption of no joint production is maintained) when each commodity is produced by not more than one method; when corn, for example, is grown only on one quality of land. But there is a second case in which the standard commodity is also composed of non-negative quantities of commodities even though matrix **B** is not diagonal, i.e. even though a commodity is produced by more than one method.

This happens when one of the plots of land, being a free good, does not pay any rent to its owner. Under such an assumption, the production system for corn (the analysis is easily extended to the case of any number of products) takes the following form:

$$(\mathbf{A},\mathbf{B}) = \begin{bmatrix} a_1 & 0\ldots 0 & \ldots 0 & \ldots 0 & b_1^j & 0\ldots 0 & \ldots 0 & \ldots 0 \\ a_2 & 0\ldots T_2 & \ldots 0 & \ldots 0 & b_2^j & 0\ldots T_2 & \ldots 0 & \ldots\ 0 \\ \vdots & & & & \vdots & & & \\ a_i & 0\ldots 0 & \ldots T_i & \ldots 0 & b_i^j & 0\ldots 0 & \ldots T_i & \ldots 0 \\ \vdots & & & & \vdots & & & \\ a_m & 0\ldots 0 & \ldots 0 & \ldots T_m & b_m^j & 0\ldots 0 & \ldots\ 0 & \ldots T_m \end{bmatrix}$$

It is obvious that this system is decomposable (the **H** matrix is zero). Therefore, a basic system exists[49] (in this case the cultivation of corn on the no-rent land) which appears directly and thus does not need to be reconstructed. When the land is a free good no negative quantities can appear among the components of the standard commodity.

3.4.4 Some particular cases

Sraffa considers the particular case of 'Machines of an obsolete type which are still in use ... [as] similar to land in so far as they are employed as means of production, although not currently produced. The quasi-rent ... which is received for those fixed capital items which, having been in active use in the past, have now been superseded but are worth employing for what they can get, is determined precisely in the same way as the rent of land (P.S. §91, p. 78).[50] Thus we have a type of machine whose return takes the form of a quasi-rent, in Sraffa's terminology. This type of fixed capital is treated in a way that is similar to that used for land.

We would like to consider a second particular case, that of exhaustible resources. They can be analysed as a particular case of 'land' with a limited period of utilisation due to their fixed quantity. During the entire period of utilisation rent is paid to their owners and the selling price of this natural resource is obtained by discounting the expected income (at the current rate r) until the fixed quantity of the resource is exhausted. The only difference in relation to traditional rent is that in the traditional case we have an infinite horizon, while for exhaustible resources the horizon is finite.

But it would be more interesting to analyse the exhaustible resource as a symmetric case to that of the 'everlasting' machine. Assuming constant efficiency in both cases, we can compare their characteristics as follows:

'Everlasting' machine 'e'		*Exhaustible resource 'g'*	
$a_1^e = b_1^e = 0 = \ldots = a_{k-1}^e = b_{k-1}^e = 0$		$a_1^g = b_1^g = \ldots = a_{k-1}^g = b_{k-1}^g > 0$	
$a_k^e = 0$	$b_k^e > 0$	$a_k^g > 0$	$b_k^g = 0$
$a_h^e = b_h^e = \text{constant} > 0$		$a_h^g = b_h^g = 0$	for all $h > k$
for all $h > k$ if $a_h^e > 0$			

There is also symmetry in the comparison of the incomes received by the owners of the two types of assets. The owner of the everlasting machine normally receives a use-price or rental ρ_e calculated by applying the current rate of profit r to the price of the 'everlasting' machine $p_{mo}: \rho_e = rp_{mo}$.[51] The owner of the exhaustible resource receives a rent ρ_g as indicated above but this time the total income of the exhaustible resource determines its selling price, calculated by the traditional discounting formula. We note that if the natural resource is inexhaustible, its selling price will be $p_g = \dfrac{\rho_g}{r}$ which, in its mathematical formulation, is identical to the relation we would have in the (limit) case of an obsolete machine (i.e. no longer the product of a production process) with an infinite working life. Of course there is not much practical interest in a particular category restricted to everlasting, but obsolete, machines.

3.5 Determination of prices and values: a summing-up

3.5.1 Price determination

From the preceding discussion it is possible to sketch a general picture of the various methods of determining equilibrium prices. Equilibrium prices are the same prices as in the analyses given above, but we stress here that we are concerned with the determination of *equilibrium* prices to avoid any ambiguity. We are not concerned with the level of prices in a disequilibrium situation characterised by deficient or excess supply or demand, but by prices in conditions where wage levels and the rate of profit are fixed and uniform in the whole economy and where technology, defined by the square matrices **A** and **B** and the vector **L**, does not change. We are therefore in J. Robinson's 'state of tranquillity'. Assuming constant returns to scale, we want to single out the elements influencing the formation of normal, long-period prices.

In what follows, the conditions of production are considered in their broader sense including purely technical conditions of production (defined by the square matrices **A** and **B** and vector **L**) as well as the level of the exogenous distributive variable. The rate of profit will be considered as an independent variable. We still have one degree of freedom which could be removed by choosing the price of any of the commodities, or of Sraffa's standard commodity, as numeraire. For our purposes, we have chosen the wage as numeraire by setting $w = 1$. This allows us to carry out our analysis with prices defined in terms of wages, for short, wage-prices of the type $\hat{p}_i = p_i/w$.

As we know, *these conditions of production are sufficient to determine the wage-prices in a system of simple production.* Samuelson and Koopmans among others[52] have shown that when there is no joint production, a variation in the final demand has no influence on prices (assuming constant returns to scale). This appears very clearly since we have shown that the prices of all basic commodities are simultaneously determined by the technical conditions of production and the exogenous level of the rate of profit without the intervention of demand. Neither does demand intervene in the determination of non-basic commodities' prices. These prices, as seen previously, are determined by their own conditions of production, by the exogenous level of the rate of profit, and of course by the prices of basic commodities. All this does not mean that demand has no influence in the system. In fact, its role is to determine the quantities of commodities of various types to be produced by the system, but not to fix their prices.

The case of *land and natural resources, exhaustible or not, as well as obsolete machines* is, one might say, just the opposite. *The prices of these commodities* which have never been produced for the former, and have ceased to be produced for the latter, are *exclusively determined by their expected conditions of utilisation*, that is, their rents or quasi-rents, as the case may be, are determined by the series of their expected net returns discounted at the current rate of interest, r.

These two types of situation are, in a sense, extremes representing the exclusive role of the conditions of production in the former and exclusive role of the conditions of utilisation in the latter. But we must also examine the intermediate case of *fixed capital*. In the case of new *and* old machines *conditions of production and of utilisation have an equivalent role.* We have shown that the prices of the machines could be determined by using either the production equations or the usual technique of capitalisation of the expected net returns at the ruling rate of profit r (see section 3.3, above). In the first method, the conditions of use play no role, while they play an exclusive role in the second method. The result is, however, identical.

This equivalence, which we have already demonstrated, is easily explained. One can say that in any economic system there are three categories of goods. The first is made up of non-basic goods and basic goods other than machines. These goods have been produced by the system but either they are not required for the production of other goods (the case of the non-basic goods), or they are only used during one period (this is the definition of circulating capital). Consequently, their prices are determined by the conditions of production; the prices of the circulating basic goods are, moreover, simultaneously determined because they are at the same time produced and used. The second category is made of goods that have never been produced (land and natural resources, exhaustible or not) or have ceased to be produced ('obsolete' machines). Their price can only be determined by the conditions in which they are used in the system. Finally fixed capital, i.e. machines of varying age, makes up a separate category because it has been produced (and is still being produced) and because it is used by the system for several periods. Consequently, its price can be determined either by the technical conditions of production in the system or by the conditions in which it is used in that same system.

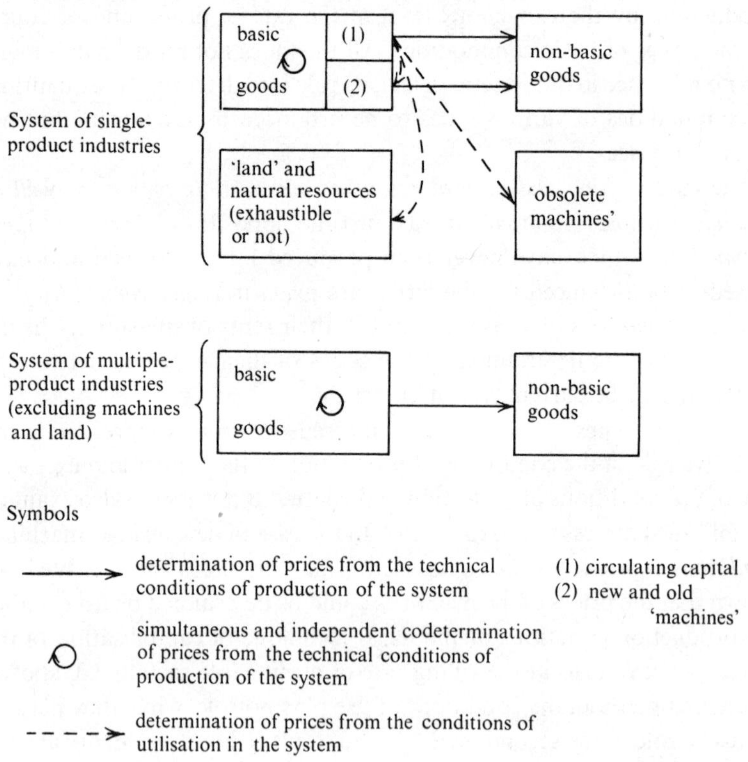

Let us go back to the various ways of determining prices in the case of joint production. Suppose there are k processes, or production methods, for k goods (this is the case considered by Sraffa). The solution of this system presents no difficulty. The $n(=k)$ prices are only determined by the conditions of production after the distinction between basic and non-basic products has been made with the help of the Sraffa–Manara procedure[53] as represented in the table on page 104.

3.5.2 Determination of values in Marx's sense

The accompanying table, as well as the analysis it summarises, has been drawn up for any exogenous level of the rate of profit $(0 \leq r \leq R)$. Thus the conclusions drawn from the table can be applied to the particular case where $r = 0$, that is, to the case corresponding to Marx's theory of labour-values. We shall take this opportunity to investigate more closely the determinants of the value of various commodities in terms of labour.

In the case of a system with single-product industries, the results already obtained concerning the measure of value can be verified easily. We shall only point out that the distinction between basic and non-basic commodities is still relevant here. The values of basic commodities are simultaneously determined, $\mathbf{\Lambda} = (\mathbf{I} - \mathbf{A})^{-1}\mathbf{L}$, and they are then used to determine the values of non-basic commodities together with the conditions of production of the latter. Of course the quantity of commodities produced is fixed by demand and a commodity is produced only if it answers a social need. But once a commodity is produced, its value is independent of the level of demand.[54] 'Nothing can have value, without being an object of utility' (Marx, *Capital*, Vol. I, p. 41). Once an object 'is' value, the measure of this value is given by the quantity of abstract labour, direct and indirect, contained in the commodity. We can also verify that all commodities which are not products of labour cannot have any value and we can generalise Marx's analysis to the aggregate of natural resources, exhaustible or not, to show that land, which is not the product of labour, therefore has no value.

The assumption of joint production which Marx does not seem to have taken into account merits some attention. We have seen that in the case of joint production, the prices of production $\mathbf{p}(0)$ corresponding to a zero rate of profit can be written as:

$$\mathbf{Bp}(0) = (1 + 0)\,\mathbf{Ap}(0) + \mathbf{L}.1$$

or

$$(\mathbf{B} - \mathbf{A})\,\mathbf{p}(0) = \mathbf{L}$$

and if $\det(\mathbf{B} - \mathbf{A}) \neq 0$

we have $\mathbf{p}(0) = (\mathbf{B} - \mathbf{A})^{-1}\mathbf{L}$

In the absence of a very restrictive assumption such as $(\mathbf{B} - \mathbf{A})^{-1} > \mathbf{0}$ the occurrence of negative components in the vector $\mathbf{p}(0)$ is not excluded. In this case, can we continue to equate prices $\mathbf{p}(0)$ with values $\mathbf{\Lambda}$ as we did in the case of simple production?

In the case of simple production it is easy to grasp the meaning of labour-value, i.e. the labour contained in any commodity when this commodity is the only output of a process, which transmits to its product the totality of the direct and indirect labour necessary to its production. The values of such commodities are necessarily positive given the usual productivity conditions, that is $(\mathbf{I} - \mathbf{A})^{-1} > 0$ or, equivalently, $\alpha^*(\mathbf{A}) < 1$. Commodities thus appear directly as 'value-bearers', embodiments of abstract labour.

In the case of joint production the system is no longer transparent since the labour incorporated in a process must be distributed among the various commodities it produces. There is thus a problem of imputation which can be avoided only by finding the quantity of labour directly and indirectly necessary to produce a unit of each commodity.

We can employ the following procedure for this purpose.[55] To produce a net surplus of commodities $\mathbf{d} = [d_1, \dots, d_i, \dots, d_k]$ we must use the vector of activity levels $\mathbf{\Omega}$ such that $\mathbf{\Omega B} = \mathbf{\Omega A} + \mathbf{d}$

In particular, to produce a unit of the ith good, i.e. the net surplus vector $\mathbf{d}_i = [0, \dots, 1, 0]$ whose elements are zero except the ith which is equal to 1, we must use the vector $\mathbf{\Omega}_i$ such that

$$\mathbf{\Omega}_i\mathbf{B} = \mathbf{\Omega}_i\mathbf{A} + \mathbf{d}_i \qquad \text{or} \quad \mathbf{\Omega}_i(\mathbf{B} - \mathbf{A}) = \mathbf{d}_i$$

$$\text{or} \quad \mathbf{\Omega}_i = \mathbf{d}_i(\mathbf{B} - \mathbf{A})^{-1} \qquad \text{if} \quad \det(\mathbf{B} - \mathbf{A}) \neq 0.$$

The quantity of labour used by the system is given by $\mathbf{\Omega}_i\mathbf{L} = \mathbf{d}_i(\mathbf{B} - \mathbf{A})^{-1}\mathbf{L}$ which represents the quantity of labour directly or indirectly necessary to produce a unit of the ith good, that is the *labour-value* λ_i of this good. Thus we have:

$$\lambda_i = \mathbf{\Omega}_i\mathbf{L} = \mathbf{d}_i(\mathbf{B} - \mathbf{A})^{-1}\mathbf{L}$$

and

$$\mathbf{\Lambda} = \begin{bmatrix} \lambda_1 \\ \vdots \\ \lambda_i \\ \vdots \\ \lambda_k \end{bmatrix} = \begin{bmatrix} \mathbf{d}_1 \\ \vdots \\ \mathbf{d}_i \\ \vdots \\ \mathbf{d}_k \end{bmatrix} (\mathbf{B} - \mathbf{A})^{-1}\mathbf{L} = (\mathbf{B} - \mathbf{A})^{-1}\mathbf{L}$$

since

$$\begin{bmatrix} \mathbf{d}_1 \\ \vdots \\ \mathbf{d}_i \\ \vdots \\ \mathbf{d}_k \end{bmatrix} = \begin{bmatrix} 1 & 0 & \dots & 0 \\ 0 & 1 & & 0 \\ \vdots & & \ddots & \\ \vdots & & 1 & 0 \\ & & & \ddots \\ 0 & 0 & 0 & 1 \end{bmatrix} = \mathbf{I}$$

Thus this method provides us with a way of determining the direct or indirect labour content of a commodity and shows that it is always possible to calculate values as a particular case of the calculation of prices of production ($r = 0$) since:

$$\mathbf{Bp}(0) = (1 + 0)\mathbf{Ap}(0) + \mathbf{L} \text{ implies } \mathbf{p}(0) = (\mathbf{B} - \mathbf{A})^{-1}\mathbf{L} = \mathbf{\Lambda}$$

This method allows us to understand how negative components can appear in the vector $\mathbf{\Lambda}$ of values and can represent, in spite of all common sense, negative labour quantities!

In fact, we may have to operate processes at a negative level[56] in order to get a net surplus of the *i*th (and only of the *i*th) good.

The possibility of a commodity with a negative value in joint production, i.e. which had to be produced by a *negative* quantity of labour, did not escape Sraffa's attention:

> [it] is not merely that, e.g. in the remote contingency of the rate of profits falling to zero, the price of such a commodity would, if other things remained equal, have to become negative; but that we are driven to the conclusion that in the actual situation, with profits at the perfectly normal rate of, say, 6%, that commodity is in fact produced by a *negative* quantity of labour.
>
> This looks at first as if it were a freak result of abstraction-mongering that can have no correspondence in reality. But if... we suppose that the quantity of such a commodity entering the net product of the system is *increased* (the other components being kept unchanged), we shall find that as a result the aggregate quantity of labour employed by society has indeed been *diminished*.
>
> Nevertheless, since the change in production is carried out while the ruling rate of profits is, as in the above example, at 6% and the system of prices is the one appropriate to that rate, nothing abnormal will be noticeable: in effect the diminution in the expense for labour will be more than balanced by an increased charge for profits, so that the addition to net output will entail a positive addition to cost of production.
>
> What happens is that in order to effect the required change in the net product, one of the two joint-production processes must be expanded while the other is contracted: and in the case under consideration the expansion

of the former process employs ... a quantity of labour which is smaller, but means of production which at the prices appropriate to the given rate of profits are of greater value, and therefore attract a heavier charge for profits, than does ... the contraction of the latter process (P.S. §70, p. 60].[57]

Let us note that any process A_i producing and/or consuming a commodity B_j is defined by the triplet $(\mathbf{a}_i, \mathbf{b}_i, l_i)$ where $\mathbf{a}_i = (a_{i1}, \ldots, a_{ij}, \ldots, a_{ik})$ and $\mathbf{b}_i = (b_{i1}, \ldots, b_{ij}, \ldots, b_{ik})$. If good B_j has a negative value λ_j, it is equivalent to defining each process A_i producing and/or consuming it by the triplet $(\tilde{\mathbf{a}}_i, \tilde{\mathbf{b}}_i, \tilde{l}_i)$ where $\tilde{\mathbf{a}}_i = (a_{i1}, \ldots, b_{ij}, \ldots, a_{ik})$ and $\tilde{\mathbf{b}}_i = (b_{i1}, \ldots, a_{ij}, \ldots, b_{ik})$ and to attribute to good B_j the positive value $\tilde{\lambda}_j = -\lambda_j$.

More generally, if the production system $(\mathbf{A}, \mathbf{B}, \mathbf{L})$ produces and/or consumes some commodities B_l having a negative value λ_l, it can be defined in an equivalent way by the system $(\tilde{\mathbf{A}}, \tilde{\mathbf{B}}, \mathbf{L})$ where matrices $\tilde{\mathbf{A}}$ and $\tilde{\mathbf{B}}$ are obtained by substituting the columns $\mathbf{a}^l$ of $\mathbf{A}$ for the columns $\mathbf{b}^l$ of $\mathbf{B}$ and replacing the columns $\mathbf{b}^l$ of $\mathbf{B}$ by the columns $\mathbf{a}^l$ of $\mathbf{A}$. Then we attribute to goods B_j the positive values $\tilde{\lambda}_l = -\lambda_l$ and all goods produced by the constructed system $(\tilde{\mathbf{A}}, \tilde{\mathbf{B}}, \mathbf{L})$ have a positive value.

For Sraffa, the interest of joint production essentially lies 'in its being the genus of which Fixed Capital is the leading species' (P.S. §73 p. 63) and therefore it may be interesting to see if similar paradoxes could occur in the case of fixed capital. It is clear that the value of machines can be determined either from the technical conditions of production or by discounting the net expected 'returns' (with $r = 0$) (as is well known, discounting at a zero rate is equivalent to adding up).

The simplest case is evidently that of constant efficiency of the machine throughout its working life. We have previously shown (Section 3.3.2) that in this case, for $r = 0$, we have

$$p_{m,h} = \left(1 - \frac{h}{T}\right) p_{m,0}$$

or

$$\lambda_{m,h} = \left(1 - \frac{h}{T}\right) \lambda_{m,0}$$

During each period it is used, a fraction $1/T$ of the initial value of the machine is transmitted to the new commodity produced, so that after T periods the machine ceases to be used at the same time as its value reaches zero. In this case, constant capital transmits to the produced commodities only the value created during a previous period.[58] There is no particular difficulty either in the case of increasing efficiency since the 'value of used machines always remains positive (see Section 3.3.2, above) or in the particular case of an 'everlasting' machine.[59]

Used machines with constant or increasing efficiency do not produce any problems of negative 'value' since we have already shown that their price of production remains positive (for all r such that $0 \leq r \leq R$). But we know that the price of machines of decreasing efficiency can become negative. We are not interested here in the possibility that the price of production of some used machines may become negative (this simply means that the processes using these machines must therefore be abandoned, hence the link between the rate of profit and the economic working-life of machines). Here we are interested in the possibility that the prices of production of the machine $p_m(r)$ remain positive while the value of the machine becomes negative in a given period. Let us once again (see Section 3.3.5, above) use the very simple example of a 'machine', produced by 'corn' and labour, used during three periods to produce 'corn' from inputs of corn and direct labour. We call λ the value of a unit of corn and $\lambda_{m,0}, \lambda_{m,1}, \lambda_{m,2}$ respectively the values of the new and aged machines. The value equations are written:

$$\begin{cases} a_1\lambda \qquad\qquad + l_1 = \lambda_{m,0} \\ a_2\lambda + \lambda_{m,0} + l_2 = \lambda_{m,1} + b_2\lambda \\ a_3\lambda + \lambda_{m,1} + l_3 = \lambda_{m,2} + b_3\lambda \\ a_4\lambda + \lambda_{m,2} + l_4 = \qquad\quad b_4\lambda \end{cases}$$

By stating

$$\mathbf{A} = \begin{bmatrix} a_1 & 0 & 0 & 0 \\ a_2 & 1 & 0 & 0 \\ a_3 & 0 & 1 & 0 \\ a_4 & 0 & 0 & 1 \end{bmatrix}, \mathbf{B} = \begin{bmatrix} 0 & 1 & 0 & 0 \\ b_2 & 0 & 1 & 0 \\ b_3 & 0 & 0 & 1 \\ b_4 & 0 & 0 & 0 \end{bmatrix}, \mathbf{\Lambda} = \begin{bmatrix} \lambda \\ \lambda_{m,0} \\ \lambda_{m,1} \\ \lambda_{m,2} \end{bmatrix} \text{ and } \mathbf{L} = \begin{bmatrix} l_1 \\ l_2 \\ l_3 \\ l_4 \end{bmatrix}$$

the system of value equations can be written:

$$\mathbf{A\Lambda} + \mathbf{L} = \mathbf{B\Lambda} \quad \text{or} \quad (\mathbf{B} - \mathbf{A})\mathbf{\Lambda} = \mathbf{L}$$

If $\det(\mathbf{B} - \mathbf{A}) = \sum_{i=1}^{4} (b_i - a_i) \neq 0$, by setting $b_1 = 0$, matrix $(\mathbf{B} - \mathbf{A})$ is non-singular and we have

$\mathbf{\Lambda} = (\mathbf{B} - \mathbf{A})^{-1}\mathbf{L}$ or

$$\mathbf{\Lambda} = \frac{1}{\sum_{i=1}^{4}(b_i - a_i)}$$

$$\times \begin{bmatrix} 1 & 1 & 1 & 1 \\ \sum_{i=2}^{4}(b_i - a_i) & a_1 & a_1 & a_1 \\ \sum_{i=3}^{4}(b_i - a_i) & \sum_{i=3}^{4}(b_i - a_i) & -\sum_{i=1}^{2}(b_i - a_i) & -\sum_{i=1}^{2}(b_i - a_i) \\ b_4 - a_4 & b_4 - a_4 & b_4 - a_4 & -\sum_{i=1}^{3}(b_i - a_i) \end{bmatrix} \begin{bmatrix} l_1 \\ l_2 \\ l_3 \\ l_4 \end{bmatrix}$$

and in particular

$$\lambda = \frac{\sum_{i=1}^{4} l_i}{\sum_{i=1}^{4}(b_i - a_i)}$$

$$\lambda_{m,0} = \frac{1}{\sum_{i=1}^{4}(b_i - a_i)}\left[l_1 \sum_{i=2}^{4}(b_i - a_i) + a_1 \sum_{i=2}^{4} l_i\right]$$

We note that the value of a unit of corn and of the new machine are positive subject to the single condition that in all processes more corn is produced than consumed.

Moreover, if the value of the used machine becomes negative, which *can* happen in the case of decreasing efficiency, we can construct the system $(\tilde{\mathbf{A}}, \tilde{\mathbf{B}}, \mathbf{L})$, previously defined, in order to investigate this possibility. Let us assume, for example, that the value $\lambda_{m,2}$ of the machine M_2 is negative. Then system $(\mathbf{A}, \mathbf{B}, \mathbf{L})$ is equivalent to system $(\tilde{\mathbf{A}}, \tilde{\mathbf{B}}, \mathbf{L})$, where

$$\tilde{\mathbf{A}} = \begin{bmatrix} a_1 & 0 & 0 & 0 \\ a_2 & 1 & 0 & 0 \\ a_3 & 0 & 1 & 1 \\ a_4 & 0 & 0 & 0 \end{bmatrix} \quad \text{and} \quad \tilde{\mathbf{B}} = \begin{bmatrix} 0 & 1 & 0 & 0 \\ b_2 & 0 & 1 & 0 \\ b_3 & 0 & 0 & 0 \\ b_4 & 0 & 0 & 1 \end{bmatrix}$$

are obtained by exchanging the fourth columns $\mathbf{a}^4$ and $\mathbf{b}^4$ of $\mathbf{A}$ and $\mathbf{B}$. If we observe system $(\tilde{\mathbf{A}}, \tilde{\mathbf{B}}, \mathbf{L})$ we note that the used machine M_2 (now with a positive value $\tilde{\lambda}_{m,2} = -\lambda_{m,2}$) is 'virtually' produced by the fourth process and used by the third one which seems to use machines M_1 and M_2 without producing any older machine.

The case of a machine still used but no longer produced (an 'obsolete' machine) because a 'new' machine has been introduced in the system following an innovation can also be analysed.[60] The 'obsolete' machine, being the result of human labour, has a value, but since it is not produced anymore, its value cannot be determined by its conditions of production. Consequently its value will be determined by its conditions of utilisation in the system which we shall try to clarify. This 'obsolete' machine has been replaced by a 'new' machine producing the same commodity and transmitting to this commodity during each period of utilisation a fraction of its value. The conditions of utilisation (and thus of production) of the 'new' machine will in some way reflect back on to the value of the 'obsolete' machine. This value will be determined by adding-up (for the remaining working life) the values transmitted during each period by the 'new' machine.

4

Proportional growth–duality

Chapter 3 dealt with von Neumann's model of balanced expansion. It demonstrated that in von Neumann's model a system of equilibrium prices $(R, \mathbf{p}(R))$ exists when:

(assumption (1)) each good B_j is produced by at least one process A_i.

The present chapter analyses the process of technological expansion of this model. We shall show that an optimal technique of production $\mathbf{y}(G)$ exists which produces proportional growth at the maximum rate G when:

(assumption (2)) each process A_i uses at least one good B_j.

When assumptions (1) and (2) are simultaneously fulfilled von Neumann has shown that the rate of profit, R, and the rate of growth, G, are equal if matrix $\mathbf{A}+\mathbf{B}$ is (strictly) positive. This result has been generalised by D. Gale[1] and S. M. Robinson[2] when the model $(\mathbf{A}, \mathbf{B})$ is technologically or economically indecomposable. We thus require a definition of decomposable and indecomposable models in order to state the sufficient conditions for $R = G$.

First, we shall present methods of calculating R, $\mathbf{p}(R)$, G and $\mathbf{y}(G)$ when matrices $\mathbf{A}$ and $\mathbf{B}$ are square, non-singular and subject to certain conditions of positiveness. Then we discuss the generality of the analysis and point out dual relationships among the parameters and variables.[3]

4.1 Technological expansion of the system

Let $y_{i,t}$ be the activity level of process A_i during period t and $\mathbf{y}_t = (y_{1,t}, y_{2,t}, \ldots, y_{i,t}, \ldots, y_{m,t}) \geq 0$ be the row-vector representing the technique of production during period t.

The quantity

$$\mathbf{y}_t\mathbf{a}^j = y_{1,t}a_{1j} + y_{2,t}a_{2j} + \ldots + y_{i,t}a_{ij} + \ldots + y_{m,t}a_{mj}$$

$$= \sum_{i=1}^{m} y_{i,t}a_{ij}$$

is the input $x_{j,t}$ of good B_j required by the system during period t while

$$\mathbf{y}_t\mathbf{b}^j = y_{1,t}b_{1j} + y_{2,t}b_{2j} + \ldots + y_{i,t}b_{ij} + \ldots + y_{m,t}b_{mj}$$
$$= \sum_{i=1}^{m} y_{i,t}b_{ij}$$

is the output $X_{j,t}$ of good B_j obtained at period $t+1$ since each process of production is of unit time duration.

If we want the rate of growth of the economy to be g the output $X_{j,t}$ of any good B_j at each period t must at least be equal to the input $x_{j,t}$ plus the accumulation $gx_{j,t}$ of this good. Thus we must have

$$\mathbf{y}_t\mathbf{b}^j \geqq (1+g)\mathbf{y}_t\mathbf{a}^j \quad \text{for any } j \in \{1, 2, \ldots, n\}$$

or $\quad \mathbf{y}_t\mathbf{B} \geqq (1+g)\mathbf{y}_t\mathbf{A}$

Since von Neumann's model is a model of production and since there is no final consumption there cannot be any surplus for at least one good B_j, i.e. its output $\mathbf{y}_t\mathbf{b}^j$ must be equal to $(1+g)\mathbf{y}_t\mathbf{a}^j$. Thus we must determine the highest rate of growth g such that $\mathbf{y}_t\mathbf{B} \geqq (1+g)\mathbf{y}_t\mathbf{A}$.

PROPORTIONAL GROWTH

A production system defined by the techniques of production $\{\mathbf{y}_0, \mathbf{y}_1, \ldots, \mathbf{y}_t, \ldots\}$ is said to produce proportional growth at the rate g if

$$\mathbf{y}_{t+1} = (1+g)\mathbf{y}_t \text{ for all } t \in \{0, 1, 2, \ldots\}.$$

Thus we have:

$\mathbf{X}_{t+1} = \mathbf{y}_{t+1}\mathbf{B} = (1+g)\mathbf{y}_t\mathbf{B} = (1+g)\mathbf{X}_t$ for all t i.e. the relative increase $(\mathbf{X}_{t+1} - \mathbf{X}_t)/\mathbf{X}_t = g$ of the output from one period to the other is constant and equal to g. The sequence of vectors $\{\mathbf{X}_1, \mathbf{X}_2, \ldots, \mathbf{X}_t, \ldots\}$ where $\mathbf{X}_{t+1} = (1+g)\mathbf{X}_t$ for all t is called a growth path of rate g.

SYSTEM OF OPTIMAL PROPORTIONAL GROWTH

In a system of proportional growth the structure of the technique of production $\mathbf{y}_t$ at t is independent of t since we have $\mathbf{y}_{t+1} = (1+g)\mathbf{y}_t$ for all t.

It follows that the maximum rate of growth g such that $\mathbf{y}_{t+1}\mathbf{B} \geqq (1+g)\mathbf{y}_{t+1}\mathbf{A}$ is the same as the rate fulfilling $\mathbf{y}_t\mathbf{B} \geqq (1+g)\mathbf{y}_t\mathbf{A}$. And thus we only have to determine the maximum rate of growth g such that $\mathbf{yB} \geqq (1+g)\mathbf{yA}$ where $\mathbf{y}$ defines the structure of vectors $\mathbf{y}_t$.

In the following theorem we shall show that the set of numbers g

satisfying the conditions

$$\begin{cases} \mathbf{yB} \geqq (1+g)\mathbf{yA} \\ \mathbf{y} \geq \mathbf{0} \\ g > 0 \end{cases}$$

has a maximum element G when assumption (2) is satisfied. G is then said to be the optimal rate of growth of the system, any vector of activity levels $\mathbf{y}(G)$ associated with G is said to be an optimal technique of production[4] and any system $(G, \mathbf{y}(G))$ is called a system of optimal proportional growth.

Note that if the initial stock of commodities is given by the vector $\mathbf{c}_0$ it necessarily follows that $\mathbf{y}_0\mathbf{A} \leq \mathbf{c}_0$, i.e. the technique of production $\mathbf{y}_0$ at period 0 is defined by

$$\begin{cases} \mathbf{y}_0 \quad = \beta \mathbf{y} \\ \mathbf{y}_0\mathbf{A} \leq \mathbf{c}_0 \end{cases}$$

Theorem

If assumption (2) is satisfied, model $(\mathbf{A}, \mathbf{B})$ contains a system of optimal proportional growth $(G, \mathbf{y}(G))$.

Let us consider a function $h = 1 + g$ defined by

$$\mathbf{y} \geqq \mathbf{0} \rightarrow h(\mathbf{y}) = \begin{cases} \min\limits_j \dfrac{\sum\limits_i y_i b_{ij}}{\sum\limits_i y_i a_{ij}} = \min\limits_j \dfrac{\mathbf{yb}^j}{\mathbf{ya}^j} & \text{for } \mathbf{y} \geq 0 \\ 0 & \text{for } \mathbf{y} = 0 \end{cases}$$

We only have to show that function h has a maximum that it reaches for a vector of activity levels $\mathbf{y}$.

Assumption (2) implies that when $\mathbf{y} \geq \mathbf{0}, \mathbf{yA} \geq \mathbf{0}$, i.e. there exists at least one $j \in \{1, 2, \ldots, n\}$ such that $\mathbf{ya}^j = \sum\limits_i y_i a_{ij} > 0$ and h is defined and continuous in the positive orthant $(\mathbf{R}^+)^m$. Since for any scalar α we have $h(\alpha\mathbf{y}) = h(\mathbf{y})$, h is homogeneous of degree zero. It is sufficient to find the maximum value H of h in the intersection C of the unit-sphere and $(\mathbf{R}^+)^m$. The set C being compact (closed and bounded), function h, continuous on C, takes on its maximum value for at least one value $\bar{\mathbf{y}} \in C$. Since $g = h - 1$, g assumes its maximum value $G = H - 1$ for $\bar{\mathbf{y}} \in C$. Thus an optimal technique $\mathbf{y}(G)$ compatible with the initial stock $\mathbf{c}_0$ is such that $\mathbf{y}_0\mathbf{A} \leq \mathbf{c}_0$; since it must be proportional to $\mathbf{y}$ we have $\mathbf{y}(G) = \beta\mathbf{y}$ where β

$= \sup \{\beta \geq 0 | \beta \mathbf{y}_0 \mathbf{A} \leqq \mathbf{c}_0\}$.[5] Note that the socio-technological matrix $\mathbf{A}^*$ (see Section 3.1) which takes labour into account satisfies assumption (2) if matrix $\mathbf{A}$ does. Then model $(\mathbf{A}^*, \mathbf{B})$ has a system of optimal proportional growth $(G', \mathbf{y}(G'))$ whose rate of growth G' is less than rate G of model $(\mathbf{A}, \mathbf{B})$ since in that case workers consume part of the output $\mathbf{X}_t$.

VON NEUMANN'S RAY

Let $(G,\mathbf{y}(G))$ be a system of optimal proportional growth in a von Neumann model. We have

$$\mathbf{y}(G)\mathbf{B} \geqq (1+G)\,\mathbf{y}(G)\mathbf{A}$$

or $\quad \mathbf{y}(G)\mathbf{b}^j \geqq (1+G)\,\mathbf{y}(G)\mathbf{a}^j \quad \text{for all } j \in \{1, 2, \ldots, n\}.$

We can separate the n goods $B_1, B_2, \ldots, B_j, \ldots, B_n$ into two categories:

- those satisfying $\mathbf{y}(G)\mathbf{b}^j > (1+G)\mathbf{y}(G)\mathbf{a}^j$, which are therefore in excess supply. Their prices are zero and they are called free goods;
- those satisfying $\mathbf{y}(G)\mathbf{b}^j = (1+G)\mathbf{y}(G)\mathbf{a}^j$ whose production increases at the rate of growth G of the economy. Their prices are positive and they are called economic goods.

A path of optimal growth $\{(\mathbf{x}_t, \mathbf{X}_t) | \mathbf{X}_t = (1+G)\mathbf{x}_t \ \forall t\}$ is called a von Neumann ray. The input $\mathbf{x}_t$ and output $\mathbf{X}_t$ vectors only comprise economic goods since they are the only ones to increase at the rate G. And thus, if $\mathbf{B}_l$ is a free good the components $x_{l,t}$ and $X_{l,t}$ of the vectors $\mathbf{x}_t$ and $\mathbf{X}_t$ are zeros for all t.

Examples

(1) Von Neumann's model $(\mathbf{A}, \mathbf{B})$ already seen in Section 3.1.3, where:

$$\mathbf{A} = \begin{bmatrix} 8 & 1 \\ 4 & 8 \\ 4 & 3 \end{bmatrix} \qquad \text{and } \mathbf{B} = \begin{bmatrix} 9 & 1 \\ 2 & 10 \\ 3 & 4 \end{bmatrix}$$

satisfies assumption (2) since matrix $\mathbf{A}$ is positive. An optimal technique of production $\mathbf{y}(G) = (y_1, y_2, y_3)$ must be such that

$$\mathbf{y}(G)\mathbf{B} \geqq (1+G)\mathbf{y}(G)\mathbf{A}$$

or $\quad \mathbf{y}(G)[\mathbf{B} - (1+G)\mathbf{A}] \geqq \mathbf{0}$

Since the rate of growth of the model is $G = R = 10\%$ (see Sections 3.1.3

and 4.3) we have

$$\mathbf{B} - (1+G)\mathbf{A} = \mathbf{B} - (1.1)\mathbf{A} = \begin{bmatrix} 0.2 & -0.1 \\ -2.4 & 1.2 \\ -1.4 & 0.7 \end{bmatrix}$$

and the components y_1, y_2 and y_3 of an optimal vector $\mathbf{y}(G)$ satisfy the system of inequalities:

$$\begin{cases} 0.2y_1 - 2.4y_2 - 1.4y_3 \geq 0 \\ -0.1y_1 + 1.2y_2 + 0.7y_3 \geq 0 \end{cases}$$

which imply $0.2y_1 - 2.4y_2 - 1.4y_3 = 0$ or

$$y_1 - 12y_2 - 7y_3 \quad = 0$$

The two vectors (12, 1, 0) and (7, 0, 1) are semi-positive and their components satisfy $y_1 - 12y_2 - 7y_3 = 0$. It follows that all vectors

$$\begin{aligned} \mathbf{y}_v(G) &= v(12,1,0) + (1-v)(7,0,1) \\ &= (7+5v, v, 1-v) \end{aligned}$$

where $0 \leq v \leq 1$ are optimal techniques of production for this von Neumann model with proportional growth of 10%.

Note that we can have *two independent* optimal techniques of production. Any linear combination of these two techniques are then optimal techniques of production. This explains why we have an optimal technique of production

(i) either using only the first two processes with the proportions 12 and 1;

(ii) or using only the first and the third processes with the proportions 7 and 1;

(iii) or using the three processes with the proportions $7+5v, v$, and $1-v$ where $0 < v < 1$.

Generally speaking, whenever there are at least two independent optimal techniques of production in a von Neumann model $(\mathbf{A}, \mathbf{B})$ we can obtain an *infinity* of optimal techniques of production which are linear combinations of the independent techniques.

Let us note that whatever the technique of production $\mathbf{y}_v(G) = (7+5v, v, 1-v)$ where $0 < v < 1$ we have $\mathbf{y}_v(G)\mathbf{B} - (1+G)\mathbf{y}_v\mathbf{A} = \mathbf{y}_v(G)\,[\mathbf{B} - (1.1)\mathbf{A}] = (0,0)$, i.e. the two goods have exactly $G = 10\%$ as their rate of growth. The von Neumann ray is $(\mathbf{x}_t, \mathbf{X}_t)$ where $\mathbf{x}_t = \mathbf{y}_t\mathbf{A}$, $\mathbf{X}_t = \mathbf{y}_t\mathbf{B}$ and $\mathbf{y}_t = (1+G)^t\mathbf{y}_v = (1.1)^t\mathbf{y}_v$ thus we have $\mathbf{X}_t = (1+G)\mathbf{x}_t = (1.1)\mathbf{x}_t$.

since $\mathbf{X}_t = \mathbf{y}_t\mathbf{B} = (1.1)^t\,(66 + 44v, 11 + 11v)$ and $\mathbf{x}_t = \mathbf{y}_t\mathbf{A} = (1.1)^t\,(60 + 40v, 10 + 10v)$

(2) Let us consider a von Neumann model $(\mathbf{A}, \mathbf{B})$ where

$$\mathbf{A} = \begin{bmatrix} 8 & 1 \\ 4 & 8 \\ 4 & 3 \end{bmatrix} \qquad \text{and } \mathbf{B} = \begin{bmatrix} 9 & 1 \\ 2 & 10 \\ 3 & 3.5 \end{bmatrix}$$

we still have $G = R = 10\%$ and $\mathbf{p} = \begin{bmatrix} 1 \\ 2 \end{bmatrix}$

The only difference from the model in example (1) is the last element of **B** which is 3.5 instead of 4.

$$\text{Then we have } \mathbf{B} - (1.1)\mathbf{A} \begin{bmatrix} 0.2 & -0.1 \\ -2.4 & 1.2 \\ 1.4 & 0.2 \end{bmatrix}$$

and the components y_1, y_2, y_3 of an optimal vector $\mathbf{y}(G)$ satisfy the system of inequalities:

$$\begin{cases} 0.2y_1 - 2.4y_2 + 1.4y_3 \geq 0 \\ -0.1y_1 + 1.2y_2 + 0.2y_3 \geq 0 \end{cases}$$

and since $\mathbf{y}(G) \geq 0$, we have $y_3 = 0$ and $0.2y_1 - 2.4y_2 = 0$ or $y_1 = 12y_2$.

In this model we only have one optimal technique of production $\mathbf{y}(G) = (12, 1, 0)$. The third process which realises a profit:

$\mathbf{b}^3\mathbf{p} - (1.1)\mathbf{a}^3\mathbf{p} = 10 - (1.1) \times 10 = -1 < \mathbf{0}$ is not used.

Von Neumann's ray is $\{(\mathbf{x}_t, \mathbf{X}_t)\}$ where since

$\mathbf{X}_t = \mathbf{y}_t\mathbf{B} = (1.1)^t\,(110, 22)$ and
$\mathbf{x}_t = \mathbf{y}_t\mathbf{A} = (1.1)^t\,(100, 20)$ we have
$\mathbf{X}_t = (1.1)\mathbf{x}_t$

GOODS PRODUCED AND USED UP BY A TECHNIQUE OF PRODUCTION

When processes $A_1, \ldots, A_i, \ldots, A_m$ are employed at activity levels $y_1, \ldots, y_i, \ldots, y_m$, the technique of production $\mathbf{y} = (y_1, \ldots, y_i, \ldots, y_m)$ uses up and produces quantities $\mathbf{ya}^j$ and $\mathbf{yb}^j$ of good B_j.

Note that:

$\mathbf{ya}^j > 0$ means that B_j is an input of the technique of production $\mathbf{y}$;
$\mathbf{ya}^j = 0$ means that B_j is not an input of technique $\mathbf{y}$;
$\mathbf{yA} > \mathbf{0}$ means that all goods enter technique $\mathbf{y}$;
$\mathbf{yb}^j > 0$ means that B_j is an output of technique $\mathbf{y}$;
$\mathbf{yb}^j = 0$ means that B_j is not an output of technique $\mathbf{y}$;
$\mathbf{yB} > \mathbf{0}$ means that all goods are produced by technique $\mathbf{y}$;
$\text{supp}\,(\mathbf{yA}) \subset \text{supp}\,(\mathbf{yB})$ means that every good consumed is produced;
$\text{supp}\,(\mathbf{yA}) \not\subset \text{supp}\,(\mathbf{yB})$ means that at least one good consumed is not produced.

4.2 Decomposable and indecomposable models

Suppose a von Neumann model $(\mathbf{A}, \mathbf{B})$ where matrices $\mathbf{A}$ and $\mathbf{B}$ are $m \times n$. If $\mathbf{P}$ and $\mathbf{Q}$ are m and n permutation matrices, matrices $\mathbf{PAQ}$ and $\mathbf{PBQ}$ are obtained by simultaneously permuting some rows and some columns in both matrices $\mathbf{A}$ and $\mathbf{B}$. Thus, the von Neumann model $(\mathbf{PAQ}, \mathbf{PBQ})$ is identical to model $(\mathbf{A}, \mathbf{B})$.

We shall now define the notions of technological decomposability and indecomposability which enable us to distinguish between von Neumann models $(\mathbf{A}, \mathbf{B})$, using only a part, v, of the n goods to reproduce themselves, and those models which need to use all n goods. By symmetry we define economic decomposability and indecomposability to distinguish models where some processes produce free goods from those where all processes produce economic goods.

It is often convenient to group the v goods produced by the system without using any of the $n - v$ other goods as inputs or to group the μ processes producing only free goods. It is sufficient to rearrange certain processes or certain goods, i.e. to replace model $(\mathbf{A}, \mathbf{B})$ by an identical model $(\mathbf{PAQ}, \mathbf{PBQ})$ which produces these permutations.

4.2.1 Technological decomposability

Definition

The von Neumann model $(\mathbf{A}, \mathbf{B})$ is said to be technologically decomposable if there exist permutation matrices $\mathbf{P}$ and $\mathbf{Q}$ such that matrices $\mathbf{PAQ}$

and **PBQ** are of the following form:

$$\mathbf{PAQ} = \begin{array}{c|c|c|} & v & n-v \\ \hline \mu & \mathbf{A}_1^1 & 0 \\ \hline m-\mu & \mathbf{A}_2^1 & \mathbf{A}_2^2 \\ \hline \end{array} \qquad \mathbf{PBQ} = \begin{array}{c|c|c|} & v & n-v \\ \hline \mu & \mathbf{B}_1^1 & \mathbf{B}_1^2 \\ \hline m-\mu & \mathbf{B}_2^1 & \mathbf{B}_2^2 \\ \hline \end{array}$$

where each column of matrix $\mathbf{B}_1^1$ has at least one positive element.

Property

If a model $(\mathbf{A}, \mathbf{B})$ is technologically decomposable, there exists at least one vector of activity levels, $\mathbf{y} \geq \mathbf{0}$ such that supp $(\mathbf{yA}) \subset$ supp $(\mathbf{yB})$ with $\mathbf{yA} \not> \mathbf{0}$.[6]

If model $(\mathbf{A}, \mathbf{B})$ is technologically decomposable, any technique of production $\bar{\mathbf{y}} = (y_1, \ldots, y_i, \ldots, y_\mu, 0, \ldots, 0)$ when $y_i > 0$ for any $i \in \{1, 2, \ldots, \mu\}$ is such that

$\bar{\mathbf{y}}\mathbf{PAQ} = (x_1, \ldots, x_j, \ldots, x_v, 0, \ldots, 0) \not> \mathbf{0}$ and

$\bar{\mathbf{y}}\mathbf{PBQ} = (X_1, \ldots, X_j, \ldots, X_v, \ldots, X_n)$ where $X_j > 0$ for any $j \in \{1, 2, \ldots, v\}$. Thus vector $\mathbf{y} = \bar{\mathbf{y}}\mathbf{P} \geq \mathbf{0}$ is such that supp $(\mathbf{yA}) \subset$ supp $(\mathbf{yB})$ with $\mathbf{yA} \not> 0$.

This property expresses the fact that it is possible to produce a sub-set of v goods $(v < n)$ without consuming any of the other $n - v$ goods.

Note that:

– when matrix $\mathbf{A}_2^1 = \mathbf{0}$ and each column of matrix $\mathbf{B}_2^2$ has at least one positive element, von Neumann's model $(\mathbf{A}, \mathbf{B})$ is *totally technologically decomposable* in the sense that it can be decomposed into two sub-economies: the first is formed of the first μ processes (after permutation of **A** and **B**) which only consume the first v goods in their production and the second is formed of the processes which only use the last $n - v$ goods in their production.

– when **A** and **B** are square matrices and $\mathbf{B}_1^2 = \mathbf{0}$, $(\mathbf{A}, \mathbf{B})$ is decomposable in the Sraffa–Manara sense (see Section 3.2). The first v goods are basic goods and the $n - v$ others are non-basic.

TECHNOLOGICAL INDECOMPOSABILITY

Definition:

A model $(\mathbf{A}, \mathbf{B})$ not technologically decomposable is said to be technologically indecomposable.

Property
If a model $(\mathbf{A}, \mathbf{B})$ is technologically indecomposable for all $\mathbf{y} \geq 0$ such that $\text{supp}(\mathbf{yA}) \subset \text{supp}(\mathbf{yB})$, we have $\mathbf{yA} > \mathbf{0}$ (or $\text{supp}(\mathbf{yA}) = \{1,2,\ldots,n\}$).

This property means that only the techniques of production $\mathbf{y} \geq \mathbf{0}$ using – and thus producing – *all n* goods can produce the inputs entering their production processes.

Note that:

– when matrix $\mathbf{A}$ is (strictly) positive, $(\mathbf{A}, \mathbf{B})$ is technologically indecomposable since for all $\mathbf{y} \geq \mathbf{0}$ we have $\mathbf{yA} > \mathbf{0}$;

– any technologically indecomposable model $(\mathbf{A}, \mathbf{B})$ satisfies assumption (2) because if there was a vector $\mathbf{y} \geq \mathbf{0}$ such that $\mathbf{yA} = \mathbf{0}$, we would have $\text{supp}(\mathbf{yA}) = \phi \subset \text{supp}(\mathbf{yB})$ without having $\mathbf{yA} > \mathbf{0}$ and this contradicts the assumption that the model is technologically indecomposable;

– the simple production model $(\mathbf{A}, \mathbf{I})$ is technologically decomposable or indecomposable according to whether the semi-positive square matrix $\mathbf{A}$ is decomposable or indecomposable;

– the multiple production model $(\mathbf{I}, \mathbf{B})$ where each process uses only one good is technologically decomposable.

4.2.2 Economic decomposability

Von Neumann's model $(\mathbf{A}, \mathbf{B})$ is said to be economically decomposable when there exist permutation matrices $\mathbf{P}$ and $\mathbf{Q}$ such that matrices $\mathbf{PAQ}$ and $\mathbf{PBQ}$ have the following forms:

$$\mathbf{PAQ} = \begin{array}{c|c|c|} & v & n-v \\ \hline \mu & \mathbf{A}_1^1 & \mathbf{A}_1^2 \\ \hline m-\mu & \mathbf{A}_2^1 & \mathbf{A}_2^2 \\ \hline \end{array} \quad \text{and } \mathbf{PBQ} = \begin{array}{c|c|c|} & v & n-v \\ \hline \mu & \mathbf{B}_1^1 & \mathbf{B}_1^2 \\ \hline m-\mu & \mathbf{0} & \mathbf{B}_2^2 \\ \hline \end{array}$$

where each row of matrix $\mathbf{A}_1^1$ has at least one positive element.

Property
If a model $(\mathbf{A}, \mathbf{B})$ is economically decomposable, there exists at least one price vector $\mathbf{p} \geq \mathbf{0}$ such that $\text{supp}\,(\mathbf{Bp}) \subset \text{supp}\,(\mathbf{Ap})$ with $\mathbf{Bp} \not> \mathbf{0}$.

If $(\mathbf{A}, \mathbf{B})$ is economically decomposable any price vector

$$\bar{\mathbf{p}} = \begin{bmatrix} p_1 \\ \vdots \\ p_j \\ \vdots \\ p_v \\ 0 \\ \vdots \\ 0 \end{bmatrix}$$

where $p_j > 0$ for any $j \in \{1, 2, \ldots, v\}$ is such that

$$\mathbf{PAQ}\bar{\mathbf{p}} = \begin{bmatrix} \alpha_1 \\ \vdots \\ \alpha_i \\ \vdots \\ \alpha_\mu \\ \alpha_{\mu+1} \\ \vdots \\ \alpha_n \end{bmatrix} \quad \text{where } \alpha_i > 0 \text{ for all } i \in \{1, 2, \ldots, \mu\}$$

$$\text{and } \mathbf{PBQ}\bar{\mathbf{p}} = \begin{bmatrix} \beta_1 \\ \vdots \\ \beta_i \\ \vdots \\ \beta_\mu \\ 0 \\ \vdots \\ 0 \end{bmatrix} \not> \mathbf{0}$$

And thus the price vector $\mathbf{p} = \mathbf{Q}\bar{\mathbf{p}}$ is such that $\text{supp}(\mathbf{Bp}) \subset \text{supp}(\mathbf{Ap})$ with $\mathbf{Bp} \not> \mathbf{0}$.

This property means that if every process producing economic goods consumes economic goods, then there exist $m - \mu$ processes, when $\mu < m$, producing only free goods.

ECONOMIC INDECOMPOSABILITY

Definition

A model $(\mathbf{A},\mathbf{B})$ not economically decomposable is said to be economically indecomposable.

Property

If a model $(\mathbf{A},\mathbf{B})$ is economically indecomposable for all price vectors $\mathbf{p} \geq \mathbf{0}$ such that supp $(\mathbf{Bp}) \subset$ supp $(\mathbf{Ap})$ we have $\mathbf{Bp} > \mathbf{0}$ (or supp $(\mathbf{Bp}) = \{1,2,\ldots,m\}$.

This property means that if a price vector $\mathbf{p}$ is such that no process can produce economic goods from free goods, then *all* processes produce and consume economic goods.

Note that:

– when matrix $\mathbf{B}$ is (strictly) positive, $(\mathbf{A},\mathbf{B})$ is economically indecomposable since for $\mathbf{p} \geq \mathbf{0}$ we have $\mathbf{Bp} > \mathbf{0}$;

– any economically indecomposable model $(\mathbf{A},\mathbf{B})$ satisfies assumption (1) because if there existed a vector $\mathbf{p} \geq \mathbf{0}$ such that $\mathbf{Bp} = \mathbf{0}$ we would have $\text{supp}(\mathbf{Bp}) = \phi \subset \text{supp}(\mathbf{Ap})$ without $\mathbf{Bp} > \mathbf{0}$. And this contradicts the assumption that model $(\mathbf{A},\mathbf{B})$ is economically indecomposable;

– the simple production model $(\mathbf{A},\mathbf{I})$ is economically decomposable;

– model $(\mathbf{I},\mathbf{B})$ is economically decomposable or indecomposable according to whether the semi-positive square matrix $\mathbf{B}$ is decomposable or indecomposable.

Remarks

Technological and economic indecomposability are independent properties in the sense that a von Neumann model $(\mathbf{A},\mathbf{B})$ can have one property without necessarily having the other.

For example, model $(\mathbf{A},\mathbf{B})$ where:

$$\mathbf{A} = \begin{bmatrix} 1 & 1 \\ 2 & 1 \\ 1 & 2 \end{bmatrix} \qquad \text{and } \mathbf{B} = \begin{bmatrix} 3 & 4 \\ 7 & 5 \\ 5 & 6 \end{bmatrix}$$

is technologically and economically indecomposable;

$$\mathbf{A} = \begin{bmatrix} 4 & 0 \\ 1 & 2 \\ 2 & 1 \end{bmatrix} \qquad \text{and } \mathbf{B} = \begin{bmatrix} 5 & 2 \\ 2 & 3 \\ 4 & 2 \end{bmatrix}$$

is technologically decomposable and economically indecomposable;

$$\mathbf{A} = \begin{bmatrix} 2 & 1 \\ 1 & 2 \\ 3 & 1 \end{bmatrix} \qquad \text{and } \mathbf{B} = \begin{bmatrix} 5 & 2 \\ 0 & 5 \\ 0 & 7 \end{bmatrix}$$

is technologically indecomposable and economically decomposable;

$$\mathbf{A} = \begin{bmatrix} 4 & 0 \\ 1 & 2 \\ 3 & 1 \end{bmatrix} \qquad \text{and } \mathbf{B} = \begin{bmatrix} 5 & 2 \\ 0 & 5 \\ 0 & 7 \end{bmatrix}$$

is technologically and economically decomposable.

4.3 Comparison of the rate of growth G and the rate of profit R

We shall show that in a von Neumann model $(\mathbf{A}, \mathbf{B})$ satisfying assumptions (1) and (2) the technological or economic indecomposability is sufficient for the rate of growth G to be equal to the rate of profit R.

Lemma

If von Neumann's model $(\mathbf{A}, \mathbf{B})$ *satisfies assumptions* (1) *and* (2) *we have* $R \leq G$.

We have shown (Sections 3.1 and 4.1) that

– if assumption (1) is fulfilled there exists an equilibrium price system $(R, \mathbf{p}(R))$ where R is the lowest r such that $\mathbf{Bp} \leqq (1+r)\mathbf{Ap}$ and $\mathbf{p} \geq \mathbf{0}$;

– if assumption (2) is fulfilled there exists an optimal proportional growth system $(G, \mathbf{y}(G))$ where G is the highest g such that $\mathbf{yB} \geqq (1+g)\mathbf{yA}$ and $\mathbf{y} \geq \mathbf{0}$.

Let us consider matrix $\mathbf{C} = \mathbf{B} - (1+G)\mathbf{A}$. The inequality of $\mathbf{yC} > \mathbf{0}$ does not have a nonnegative solution because if $\mathbf{y}_0 \geq \mathbf{0}$ were a solution of $\mathbf{y}_0\mathbf{C} > \mathbf{0}$ we would have $\mathbf{y}_0\mathbf{B} > (1+G)\mathbf{y}_0\mathbf{A}$ and it would be possible to find a small enough $\varepsilon > 0$ such that $\mathbf{y}_0\mathbf{B} \geqq (1+G+\varepsilon)\mathbf{y}_0\mathbf{A}$. This contradicts the fact that G is the highest g such that $\mathbf{yB} \geqq (1+G)\mathbf{yA}$. Since $\mathbf{yC} > \mathbf{0}$ does not have a nonnegative solution there exists a vector $\mathbf{p} \geq \mathbf{0}$ such that $\mathbf{Cp} \leqq \mathbf{0}$[7] or $[\mathbf{B} - (1+G)\mathbf{A}]\mathbf{p} \leqq \mathbf{0}$.

Thus we have $\mathbf{Bp} \leqq (1+G)\mathbf{Ap}$ and this implies $R \leq G$ since by definition R is the lowest r such that $\mathbf{Bp} \leqq (1+r)\mathbf{Ap}$.

Theorem 1

If a von Neumann model $(\mathbf{A}, \mathbf{B})$ *satisfies assumption* (1) *and is technologically indecomposable, we have* $G = R$.

Since the model is technologically indecomposable it also satisfies assumption (2) and by the preceding lemma we have $R \leq G$. It is thus sufficient to show that $G \leq R$.

The vectors of optimum activity levels $\mathbf{y} = \mathbf{y}(G)$ and of optimum prices $\mathbf{p} = \mathbf{p}(R)$ are such that $\mathbf{yB} \geqq (1+G)\,\mathbf{yA}$ and $\mathbf{Bp} \leqq (1+R)\mathbf{Ap}$. And since $\mathbf{y} \geq \mathbf{0}$ and $\mathbf{p} \geq \mathbf{0}$ it follows that $\mathbf{yBp} \geq (1+G)\mathbf{yAp}$ and $\mathbf{yBp} \leq (1+R)\ \mathbf{yAp}$ or $(1+G)\mathbf{yAp} \leq \mathbf{yBp} \leq (1+R)\mathbf{yAp}$ and we have $(1+G)\mathbf{yAp} \leq (1+R)\mathbf{yAp}$.

Moreover, $\mathbf{yB} \geqq (1+G)\mathbf{yA}$ implies $\text{supp}\,(\mathbf{yA}) \subset \text{supp}\,(\mathbf{yB})$; since the model is technologically indecomposable we have $\mathbf{yA} > \mathbf{0}$ and since $\mathbf{p} \geq \mathbf{0}$, we have $\mathbf{yAp} > \mathbf{0}$ and the inequality $(1+G)\mathbf{yAp} \leq (1+R)\mathbf{yAp}$ implies $1+G \leq 1+R$ or $G \leq R$ and thus we have $G = R$.

Theorem 2

If a von Neumann model $(\mathbf{A}, \mathbf{B})$ *satisfies assumption* (2) *and is economically indecomposable, we have* $G = R$.

Since the model is economically indecomposable, it also satisfies assumption (1) and by the preceding lemma we have $R \leq G$. We only have to show that $G \leq R$ knowing that $(1+G)\mathbf{yAp} \leq (1+R)\mathbf{yAp}$. The relation $\mathbf{Bp} \leqq (1+R)\mathbf{Ap}$ implies that $\text{supp}\,(\mathbf{Bp}) \subset \text{supp}\,(\mathbf{Ap})$. Since the model is economically indecomposable we have $\mathbf{Bp} > \mathbf{0}$ and consequently $\mathbf{Ap} > \mathbf{0}$. Since $\mathbf{y} \geq \mathbf{0}$ we have $\mathbf{yAp} > 0$ and it follows from the inequality $(1+G)\mathbf{yAp} \leq (1+R)\mathbf{yAp}$ that $G \leq R$ and we have $G = R$.

Remark

From the two preceding theorems we conclude that it is *sufficient* for a von Neumann model to be:

(i) technologically and economically indecomposable or
(ii) technologically indecomposable and satisfying assumption (1) or
(iii) economically indecomposable and satisfying assumption (2) for the rate of profit R to be equal to the rate of growth G of the model.

More generally, to have $R = G$, it is sufficient that

for all $\mathbf{y} \geq \mathbf{0}$ such that $\text{supp}\,(\mathbf{yA}) \subset \text{supp}\,(\mathbf{yB})$ and
for all $\mathbf{p} \geq \mathbf{0}$ such that $\text{supp}\,(\mathbf{Bp}) \subset \text{supp}\,(\mathbf{Ap})$

we have $\mathbf{yBp} > 0$ or equivalently $\mathbf{yAp} > 0$.

4.4 Determination of R, $\mathbf{p}(R)$, G and $\mathbf{y}(G)$ when $m = n$

When m, the number of processes is equal to n, the number of goods, matrices $\mathbf{A}$ and $\mathbf{B}$ are square. If we state $m = n = k$, $\mathbf{A}$ and $\mathbf{B}$ are square matrices of order k. For some square matrices $\mathbf{A}$ and $\mathbf{B}$ we only have to find their eigenvalues and eigenvectors to determine the numbers R and G and the vectors $\mathbf{p}(R)$ and $\mathbf{y}(G)$.

We shall successively consider the cases where:

(i) the square matrix $\mathbf{B}$ is diagonal and has an inverse;
(ii) the square matrix $\mathbf{B}$ has an inverse and $\mathbf{B}^{-1}\mathbf{A} \geq \mathbf{0}$ and/or $\mathbf{AB}^{-1} \geq \mathbf{0}$;
(iii) the square matrix $\mathbf{A}$ is diagonal and has an inverse;
(iv) the square matrix $\mathbf{A}$ has an inverse and $\mathbf{A}^{-1}\mathbf{B} \geq \mathbf{0}$ and/or $\mathbf{BA}^{-1} \geq \mathbf{0}$.

The last two cases are not very 'realistic'. They are considered because they allow us to observe their symmetry with the two other cases.

4.4.1 Matrix B is diagonal and has an inverse

When matrix $\mathbf{B}$ is diagonal the von Neumann model $(\mathbf{A}, \mathbf{B})$ is a model of simple production and the square matrix $\mathbf{B}^{-1}$ is diagonal and semi-positive.

From $[\mathbf{B} - (1+r)\mathbf{A}]\mathbf{p} \leqq 0$ and since $\mathbf{B}^{-1} \geq \mathbf{0}$ we have

$$\mathbf{B}^{-1}[\mathbf{B} - (1+r)\mathbf{A}]\mathbf{p} \leqq \mathbf{0} \quad \text{or} \quad [\mathbf{I} - (1+r)\mathbf{B}^{-1}\mathbf{A}]\mathbf{p} \leqq \mathbf{0}$$

If $(\mathbf{A}, \mathbf{B})$ is technologically indecomposable, the square matrix $\mathbf{A}$ is indecomposable and since $\mathbf{B}^{-1} \geq \mathbf{0}$ the square matrix $\mathbf{B}^{-1}\mathbf{A}$ is semi-positive and indecomposable. By Frobenius' Theorem (see mathematical appendix) the dominant eigenvalue $1/(1+R)$ of $\mathbf{B}^{-1}\mathbf{A}$ is positive and the associated eigenvector on the right $\mathbf{p}(R)$ is positive. Any number r such that $[\mathbf{I} - (1+r)\mathbf{B}^{-1}\mathbf{A}]\mathbf{p} \leqq \mathbf{0}$ satisfies $[1/(1+r)]\mathbf{p} \leqq \mathbf{B}^{-1}\mathbf{A}\mathbf{p}$ where $1/(1+r) > 0$ and $\mathbf{p} \geqq \mathbf{0}$. By lemma 5 (of the mathematical appendix) we have $1/(1+r) \leq 1/(1+R)$ and the lowest r such that $[\mathbf{I} - (1+r)\mathbf{B}^{-1}\mathbf{A}]\mathbf{p} \leqq \mathbf{0}$ is the number r satisfying the equality

$$\frac{1}{1+r} = \frac{1}{1+R} \qquad \text{or} \quad r = R$$

It follows that the lowest r satisfying the inequality $[\mathbf{B} - (1+r)\mathbf{A}]\mathbf{p} \leqq \mathbf{0}$ is the number R, where $1/(1+R)$ is the dominant eigenvalue of $\mathbf{B}^{-1}\mathbf{A}$. Thus the equilibrium price vector $\mathbf{p}(R)$ is the eigenvector on the right of matrix $\mathbf{B}^{-1}\mathbf{A}$ associated with the dominant eigenvalue $1/(1+R)$.

Similarly, from the inequality $\mathbf{y}[\mathbf{B} - (1+g)\mathbf{A}] \geqq \mathbf{0}$ and since $\mathbf{B}^{-1} \geq \mathbf{0}$, we have

$$\mathbf{y}[\mathbf{B} - (1+g)\mathbf{A}]\mathbf{B}^{-1} \geqq \mathbf{0}$$

$$\text{or} \quad \mathbf{y}[\mathbf{I} - (1+g)\mathbf{AB}^{-1}] \geqq \mathbf{0}$$

If the von Neumann model $(\mathbf{A},\mathbf{B})$ is technologically indecomposable, matrix $\mathbf{AB}^{-1}$ is semi-positive and indecomposable. The dominant eigenvalue $1/(1+G)$ of $\mathbf{AB}^{-1}$ is equal to the dominant eigenvalue $1/(1+R)$ of matrix $\mathbf{B}^{-1}\mathbf{A}$ and thus we have $G=R$. Any number g satisfying the inequality $\mathbf{y}[\mathbf{I}-(1+g)\mathbf{AB}^{-1}]\geqq\mathbf{0}$ satisfies $1/(1+g)\mathbf{y}\geqq\mathbf{yAB}^{-1}$ where $1/(1+g)>0$ and $\mathbf{y}\geq 0$. By lemma 5 we have $1/(1+g)\geq 1/(1+G)$ and the greatest g such that $\mathbf{y}[\mathbf{I}-(1+g)\mathbf{AB}^{-1}]\geqq\mathbf{0}$ is the number g satisfying the equality

$$\frac{1}{1+g}=\frac{1}{1+G} \quad \text{or} \quad g=G.$$

Therefore, the greatest g satisfying the inequality $\mathbf{y}[\mathbf{B}-(1+g)\mathbf{A}]\geqq\mathbf{0}$ is the number G where $1/(1+G)$ is the dominant eigenvalue of $\mathbf{AB}^{-1}$; thus the optimal technique of production $\mathbf{y}(G)$ is the eigenvector on the left of matrix $\mathbf{AB}^{-1}$ associated with the dominant eigenvalue $1/(1+G)$.

To sum up, if von Neumann's model $(\mathbf{A},\mathbf{B})$ is *technologically indecomposable* the rate of growth of the model G is equal to the rate of profit R and $1/(1+R)=1/(1+G)$ is the dominant eigenvalue of the indecomposable matrices $\mathbf{B}^{-1}\mathbf{A}$ and $\mathbf{AB}^{-1}$. The system $(R, \mathbf{p}(R))$, where $\mathbf{p}(R)$ is an eigenvector on the right of $\mathbf{B}^{-1}\mathbf{A}$ associated to $1/(1+R)$, is an equilibrium price system of the model and system $(G, \mathbf{y}(G))$, where $\mathbf{y}(G)$ is an eigenvector on the left of $\mathbf{AB}^{-1}$ associated to $1/(1+G)$, is an optimal proportional growth system of the von Neumann model $(\mathbf{A},\mathbf{B})$.

Example

Suppose a von Neumann model $(\mathbf{A},\mathbf{B})$ where

$$\mathbf{A}=\begin{bmatrix}45 & 10\\ 23 & 54\end{bmatrix} \quad \text{and } \mathbf{B}=\begin{bmatrix}54 & 0\\ 0 & 108\end{bmatrix}$$

$$\mathbf{B}^{-1}\mathbf{A}=\begin{bmatrix}\frac{1}{54} & 0\\ 0 & \frac{1}{108}\end{bmatrix}\begin{bmatrix}45 & 10\\ 23 & 54\end{bmatrix}=\begin{bmatrix}\frac{5}{6} & \frac{5}{27}\\ \frac{23}{108} & \frac{1}{2}\end{bmatrix}$$

The characteristic equation is $\alpha^2-(4/3)\alpha+(275/729)=0$, its dominant eigenvalue is $(25/27)$ and the second eigenvalue is $(11/27)$. The rate of profit R of the model such that $1/(1+R)=(25/27)$ is equal to $(2/25)=0.08$ or 8%. Since the vector $\begin{bmatrix}2\\ 1\end{bmatrix}$ is an eigenvector on the right of matrix $\mathbf{B}^{-1}\mathbf{A}$

associated to the dominant eigenvalue (25/27), the system ($R = 0.08$, $\mathbf{p}(R) = \begin{bmatrix} 2 \\ 1 \end{bmatrix}$) is an equilibrium price system of model $(\mathbf{A}, \mathbf{B})$.

We know that matrix

$$\mathbf{AB}^{-1} = \begin{bmatrix} 45 & 10 \\ 23 & 54 \end{bmatrix} \begin{bmatrix} \frac{1}{54} & 0 \\ 0 & \frac{1}{108} \end{bmatrix} = \begin{bmatrix} \frac{5}{6} & \frac{5}{54} \\ \frac{23}{54} & \frac{1}{2} \end{bmatrix}$$

has the same eigenvalues as matrix $\mathbf{B}^{-1}\mathbf{A}$. Thus its dominant eigenvalue is (25/27) and the rate of growth G of the model is also equal to 8%. Since the vector [23, 5] is an eigenvector on the left of matrix $\mathbf{AB}^{-1}$ associated with the dominant eigenvalue (25/27), the system ($G = 0.08$, $\mathbf{y}(G) = [23, 5]$) is an optimal proportional growth system of model $(\mathbf{A}, \mathbf{B})$.

Note that since matrix $\mathbf{B}$ is diagonal, model $(\mathbf{A}, \mathbf{B})$ is not economically indecomposable; if it is not technologically indecomposable as well, we have $R < G$.

Consider a von Neumann model $(\mathbf{A}, \mathbf{B})$ where

$$\mathbf{A} = \begin{bmatrix} 4 & 0 \\ 1 & 9 \end{bmatrix} \qquad \text{and } \mathbf{B} = \begin{bmatrix} 5 & 0 \\ 0 & 10 \end{bmatrix}$$

The rate of growth of this model is $G = \frac{1}{4}$ and the rate of profit $R = \frac{1}{9} < G$. The vector $\begin{bmatrix} 0 \\ 1 \end{bmatrix}$ is an equilibrium price vector and the vector [1,0] is an optimal technique of production. The first good in the equilibrium price vector is a free good and the second process is not used in the optimal technique of production (cf. Sraffa's 'beans', Chapter 2, above).

However, we can have $R = G$ although $(\mathbf{A}, \mathbf{B})$ is neither technologically or economically indecomposable. Consider a von Neumann model $(\mathbf{A}, \mathbf{B})$ where

$$\mathbf{A} = \begin{bmatrix} 10 & 0 \\ 2 & 7 \end{bmatrix} \qquad \text{and} \quad \mathbf{B} = \begin{bmatrix} 11 & 0 \\ 0 & 10 \end{bmatrix}$$

the rate of profit R and the rate of growth G of this model are both equal to 10%. The vector $\begin{bmatrix} 23 \\ 22 \end{bmatrix}$ is an equilibrium price vector and the vector [1,0] is an optimal technique of production.

4.4.2 Matrix B has an inverse and $\mathbf{B}^{-1}\mathbf{A} \geq \mathbf{0}$

The matrix inequality $[\mathbf{I}-(1+r)\mathbf{B}^{-1}\mathbf{A}]\mathbf{p} \leqq \mathbf{0}$ implies $[\mathbf{B}-(1+r)\mathbf{A}]\mathbf{p} \leqq \mathbf{0}$ *since* $\mathbf{B} \geq \mathbf{0}$.

Similarly, the matrix inequality $\mathbf{y}[\mathbf{I}-(1+g)\mathbf{A}\mathbf{B}^{-1}] \geqq \mathbf{0}$ implies $\mathbf{y}[\mathbf{B}-(1+g)\mathbf{A}] \geqq \mathbf{0}$.

If we call

r_1 the lowest r such that $[\mathbf{I}-(1+r)\mathbf{B}^{-1}\mathbf{A}]\mathbf{p} \leqq \mathbf{0}$ where $\mathbf{p} \geq \mathbf{0}$;
R the lowest r such that $[\mathbf{B}-(1+r)\mathbf{A}]\mathbf{p} \leqq \mathbf{0}$ where $\mathbf{p} \geq \mathbf{0}$;
g_1 the highest g such that $\mathbf{y}[\mathbf{I}-(1+g)\mathbf{A}\mathbf{B}^{-1}] \geqq \mathbf{0}$ where $\mathbf{y} \geq \mathbf{0}$;
G the highest g such that $\mathbf{y}[\mathbf{B}-(1+g)\mathbf{A}] \geqq \mathbf{0}$ where $\mathbf{y} \geq \mathbf{0}$ we have $R \leq r_1$ and $g_1 \leq G$.

If the semi-positive matrix $\mathbf{B}^{-1}\mathbf{A}$ is indecomposable we can show, as in the preceding paragraph, that $1/(1+r_1)$ is the dominant eigenvalue of $\mathbf{B}^{-1}\mathbf{A}$. When the semi-positive matrix $\mathbf{B}^{-1}\mathbf{A}$ is decomposable and has a (strictly) positive eigenvector on the left, $1/(1+r_1)$ is the dominant eigenvalue of $\mathbf{B}^{-1}\mathbf{A}$. (See mathematical appendix, Section A.7, Theorem 3.)

Similarly, when the square matrix $\mathbf{A}\mathbf{B}^{-1}$ is semi-positive, $1/(1+g_1)$ is the dominant eigenvalue of $\mathbf{A}\mathbf{B}^{-1}$ if $\mathbf{A}\mathbf{B}^{-1}$ is indecomposable or if it is decomposable and has a (strictly) positive eigenvector on the right.

We can distinguish the following cases:

– Both matrices $\mathbf{B}^{-1}\mathbf{A}$ and $\mathbf{A}\mathbf{B}^{-1}$ are semi-positive and at least one of them is indecomposable: we have $R = r_1 = g_1 = G$ and $\mathbf{p}(R) > \mathbf{0}$ and $\mathbf{y}(G) \geq \mathbf{0}$ (or $\mathbf{p}(R) \geq \mathbf{0}$ and $\mathbf{y}(G) > \mathbf{0}$) are respectively the eigenvector on the right of $\mathbf{B}^{-1}\mathbf{A}$ and the eigenvector on the left of $\mathbf{A}\mathbf{B}^{-1}$ associated with the dominant eigenvalue $1/(1+r_1) = 1/(1+g_1)$.

– Both matrices $\mathbf{B}^{-1}\mathbf{A}$ and $\mathbf{A}\mathbf{B}^{-1}$ are semi-positive and decomposable: if the first matrix has a (strictly) positive eigenvector on the left and the second has a (strictly) positive eigenvector on the right, we have $R = r_1 = g_1 = G$ and the vectors $\mathbf{p}(R) \geq \mathbf{0}$ and $\mathbf{y}(G) \geq \mathbf{0}$ are respectively the eigenvector on the right of $\mathbf{B}^{-1}\mathbf{A}$ and the eigenvector on the left of $\mathbf{A}\mathbf{B}^{-1}$ associated with the dominant eigenvalue $1/(1+r_1) = 1/(1+g_1)$.

– Matrix $\mathbf{A}\mathbf{B}^{-1}$ is not semi-positive and $\mathbf{y} \ngeq \mathbf{0}$ where $\mathbf{y}$ is the eigenvector on the left of $\mathbf{A}\mathbf{B}^{-1}$ corresponding to the dominant eigenvalue $1/(1+g_1) = 1/(1+r_1)$; in this case if $R = G$ we have $R < r_1$.

If $\mathbf{A}\mathbf{B}^{-1} \geq \mathbf{0}$ but $\mathbf{B}^{-1}\mathbf{A}$ is not semi-positive and $\mathbf{p} \ngeq \mathbf{0}$ where $\mathbf{p}$ is the eigenvector on the right of $\mathbf{B}^{-1}\mathbf{A}$ associated with the dominant eigenvalue $1/(1+r_1) = 1/(1+g_1)$: in this case if $R = G$, we have $G > g_1$.

Remark

If for all $i \in \{1, 2, \ldots, k\}$ we have

$$\frac{b_{ii}}{a_{ii}} > \alpha > \begin{cases} \dfrac{b_{ij}}{a_{ij}} & \text{for all } j \neq i\,^{8} \\ \dfrac{b_{ji}}{a_{ji}} & \text{for all } j \neq i \end{cases}$$

when one of the two square matrices $\mathbf{B}^{-1}\mathbf{A}$ and $\mathbf{AB}^{-1}$ is semi-positive, we have $R = G$ where $1/(1+R) = 1/(1+G)$ is the dominant eigenvalue of matrices $\mathbf{B}^{-1}\mathbf{A}$ and $\mathbf{AB}^{-1}$.

Example

Suppose a von Neumann model $(\mathbf{A}, \mathbf{B})$ where

$$\mathbf{A} = \begin{bmatrix} 8 & 1 \\ 4 & 8 \end{bmatrix} \qquad \text{and } \mathbf{B} = \begin{bmatrix} 9 & 1 \\ 2 & 10 \end{bmatrix}.$$

Matrix $\mathbf{B}$ has an inverse and

$$\mathbf{B}^{-1}\mathbf{A} = \frac{1}{88}\begin{bmatrix} 10 & -1 \\ -2 & 9 \end{bmatrix}\begin{bmatrix} 8 & 1 \\ 4 & 8 \end{bmatrix} = \frac{1}{88}\begin{bmatrix} 76 & 2 \\ 20 & 70 \end{bmatrix} > \mathbf{0}$$

is indecomposable. The characteristic equation of $\mathbf{B}^{-1}\mathbf{A}$ is $\alpha^2 - \frac{73}{44}\alpha + \frac{15}{22} = 0$. Its dominant eigenvalue is (10/11), the second eigenvalue is $\frac{3}{4}$. The rate of profit R of the model such that $\dfrac{1}{1+R} = \dfrac{10}{11}$ is equal to 0.1 or 10%. Since the vector $\begin{bmatrix} 1 \\ 2 \end{bmatrix}$ is an eigenvector on the right of $\mathbf{B}^{-1}\mathbf{A}$ corresponding to the dominant eigenvalue (10/11), the system $\left(R = 0.10, \mathbf{p}(R) = \begin{bmatrix} 1 \\ 2 \end{bmatrix}\right)$ is an equilibrium price system of the model $(\mathbf{A}, \mathbf{B})$.

We know that matrix

$$\mathbf{AB}^{-1} = \begin{bmatrix} 8 & 1 \\ 4 & 8 \end{bmatrix}\frac{1}{88}\begin{bmatrix} 10 & -1 \\ -2 & 9 \end{bmatrix} = \frac{1}{88}\begin{bmatrix} 78 & 1 \\ 24 & 68 \end{bmatrix} > \mathbf{0}$$

has the same eigenvalues as matrix $\mathbf{B}^{-1}\mathbf{A}$. Thus its dominant eigenvalue is equal to (10/11) and the rate of growth G of the model is also 10%. Since the vector [12, 1] is an eigenvector on the left side of matrix $\mathbf{AB}^{-1}$ corresponding to the dominant eigenvalue (10/11), the system $(G = 0.10, \mathbf{y}(G) = [12, 1])$ is an optimal proportional growth system of model $(\mathbf{A}, \mathbf{B})$.

4.4.3 Matrix A is diagonal and has an inverse

When matrix $\mathbf{A}$ is diagonal the von Neumann model $(\mathbf{A}, \mathbf{B})$ is a model of 'simple consumption' in the sense that each process uses one good and only one. The square matrix $\mathbf{A}^{-1}$ is diagonal and semi-positive.

From the inequality $[\mathbf{B}-(1+r)\mathbf{A}]\mathbf{p} \leqq \mathbf{0}$ we have $\mathbf{A}^{-1}[\mathbf{B}-(1+r)\mathbf{A}]\mathbf{p} \leqq 0$ or $[\mathbf{A}^{-1}\mathbf{B}-(1+r)\mathbf{I}]\mathbf{p} \leqq \mathbf{0}$ since $\mathbf{A}^{-1} \geq 0$.

When model $(\mathbf{A}, \mathbf{B})$ is economically indecomposable the square matrix $\mathbf{B}$ is indecomposable and since $\mathbf{A}^{-1} \geq \mathbf{0}$ the square matrix $\mathbf{A}^{-1}\mathbf{B}$ is semi-positive and indecomposable. By Frobenius' theorem the dominant eigenvalue $1+R$ of $\mathbf{A}^{-1}\mathbf{B}$ is positive and the associated eigenvector on the right $\mathbf{p}(R)$ is positive. Any number r such that $[\mathbf{A}^{-1}\mathbf{B}-(1+r)\mathbf{I}]\mathbf{p} \leqq \mathbf{0}$ satisfies $(1+r)\mathbf{p} \geqq \mathbf{A}^{-1}\mathbf{B}\mathbf{p}$ where $1+r>0$ and $\mathbf{p} \geq \mathbf{0}$. By lemma 5 we have $1+r \geq 1+R$ and the lowest r such that $[\mathbf{A}^{-1}\mathbf{B}-(1+r)\mathbf{I}]\mathbf{p} \leqq \mathbf{0}$ is the number r satisfying $1+r=1+R$ or $r=R$. Thus the lowest r such that $[\mathbf{B}-(1+r)\mathbf{A}]\mathbf{p} \leqq \mathbf{0}$ is the number R where $1+R$ is the dominant eigenvalue of $\mathbf{A}^{-1}\mathbf{B}$. The equilibrium price vector $\mathbf{p}(R)$ is therefore the eigenvector on the right of matrix $\mathbf{A}^{-1}\mathbf{B}$ corresponding to the dominant eigenvalue $1+R$.

Similarly, from the inequality $\mathbf{y}[\mathbf{B}-(1+g)\mathbf{A}] \geqq \mathbf{0}$ we have, since $\mathbf{A}^{-1} \geq \mathbf{0}, \mathbf{y}[\mathbf{B}-(1+g)\mathbf{A}]\mathbf{A}^{-1} \geqq \mathbf{0}$ or $\mathbf{y}[\mathbf{B}\mathbf{A}^{-1}-(1+g)\mathbf{I}] \geqq \mathbf{0}$.

If von Neumann's model $(\mathbf{A}, \mathbf{B})$ is economically indecomposable, matrix $\mathbf{B}\mathbf{A}^{-1}$ is semi-positive and indecomposable, the dominant eigenvalue $1+G$ of $\mathbf{B}\mathbf{A}^{-1}$ is equal to the dominant eigenvalue $1+R$ of matrix $\mathbf{A}^{-1}\mathbf{B}$ and thus we have $G=R$. Any number g such that $\mathbf{y}[\mathbf{B}\mathbf{A}^{-1}-(1+g)\mathbf{I}] \geqq \mathbf{0}$ satisfies $(1+g)\mathbf{y} \leqq \mathbf{y}\mathbf{B}\mathbf{A}^{-1}$ where $1+g>0$ and $\mathbf{y} \geq \mathbf{0}$. By lemma 5 we have $1+g \leq 1+G$ and the greatest g such that $\mathbf{y}[\mathbf{B}\mathbf{A}^{-1}-(1+g)\mathbf{I}] \geqq 0$ is the number satisfying the equality $1+g=1+G$ or $g=G$. Thus the greatest g such that $\mathbf{y}[\mathbf{B}-(1+g)\mathbf{A}] \geqq \mathbf{0}$ is the number G where $1+G$ is the dominant eigenvalue of matrix $\mathbf{B}\mathbf{A}^{-1}$. The optimal technique of production $\mathbf{y}(G)$ is then the eigenvector on the left of matrix $\mathbf{B}\mathbf{A}^{-1}$ associated with the dominant eigenvalue $1+G$.

To sum up, if the von Neumann model $(\mathbf{A}, \mathbf{B})$ is economically indecomposable the rate of growth G of the model is equal to the rate of profit R and $1+R=1+G$ is the dominant eigenvalue of the indecomposable matrices $\mathbf{A}^{-1}\mathbf{B}$ and $\mathbf{B}\mathbf{A}^{-1}$. The system $(R, \mathbf{p}(R))$ where $\mathbf{p}(R)$ is an eigenvector on the right of matrix $\mathbf{A}^{-1}\mathbf{B}$ corresponding to $1+R$ is an equilibrium price system of the model, and the system $(G, \mathbf{y}(G))$ where $\mathbf{y}(G)$ is an eigenvector on the left of matrix $\mathbf{B}\mathbf{A}^{-1}$ associated with $1+G$ is an optimal proportional growth system of the von Neumann model $(\mathbf{A}, \mathbf{B})$.

Example

Consider the von Neumann model $(\mathbf{A}, \mathbf{B})$ where

$$\mathbf{A} = \begin{bmatrix} 50 & 0 \\ 0 & 200 \end{bmatrix} \qquad \text{and } \mathbf{B} = \begin{bmatrix} 53 & 1 \\ 15 & 208 \end{bmatrix}$$

$$\mathbf{A}^{-1}\mathbf{B} = \begin{bmatrix} \frac{1}{50} & 0 \\ 0 & \frac{1}{200} \end{bmatrix} \begin{bmatrix} 53 & 1 \\ 15 & 208 \end{bmatrix} = \begin{bmatrix} 1.06 & 0.02 \\ \frac{3}{40} & 1.04 \end{bmatrix}$$

The characteristic equation of $\mathbf{A}^{-1}\mathbf{B}$ is $\alpha^2 - 2.1\alpha + 1.1009 = 0$. Its dominant eigenvalue is 1.09 and the second eigenvalue is 1.01. The rate of profit R such that $1 + R = 1.09$ is equal to 0.09 or 9%. Since the vector $\begin{bmatrix} 2 \\ 3 \end{bmatrix}$ is an eigenvector on the right of matrix $\mathbf{A}^{-1}\mathbf{B}$ associated with the dominant eigenvalue 1.09, the system ($R = 0.09$, $\mathbf{p}(R) = \begin{bmatrix} 2 \\ 3 \end{bmatrix}$) is an equilibrium price system of the model $(\mathbf{A}, \mathbf{B})$.

We know that matrix

$$\mathbf{BA}^{-1} = \begin{bmatrix} 53 & 1 \\ 15 & 208 \end{bmatrix} \begin{bmatrix} \frac{1}{50} & 0 \\ 0 & \frac{1}{200} \end{bmatrix} = \begin{bmatrix} 1.06 & 0.005 \\ 0.3 & 1.04 \end{bmatrix}$$

has the same eigenvalues as matrix $\mathbf{A}^{-1}\mathbf{B}$. Thus its dominant eigenvalue is equal to 1.09 and the rate of growth G of the model is also 9%. Since the vector [10, 1] is an eigenvector on the left of matrix $\mathbf{BA}^{-1}$ associated with the dominant eigenvalue 1.09, the system ($G = 0.09$, $\mathbf{y}(G) = [10, 1]$) is an optimal proportional growth system of the model $(\mathbf{A}, \mathbf{B})$.

Note that since the square matrix $\mathbf{A}$ is diagonal the model $(\mathbf{A}, \mathbf{B})$ is not technologically indecomposable. If moreover, it is not economically indecomposable, we have $R < G$. Consider a von Neumann model $(\mathbf{A}, \mathbf{B})$ where

$$\mathbf{A} = \begin{bmatrix} 8 & 0 \\ 0 & 10 \end{bmatrix} \qquad \text{and } \mathbf{B} = \begin{bmatrix} 9 & 0 \\ 1 & 11 \end{bmatrix}$$

Its rate of growth is $G = \frac{1}{8} = 12.5\%$ and its rate of profit $R = 10\% < G$. The vector $\begin{bmatrix} 0 \\ 1 \end{bmatrix}$ is an equilibrium price vector and the vector [1, 0] is an optimal technique of production.

4.4.4 Matrix A has an inverse and $\mathbf{A}^{-1}\mathbf{B} \geq \mathbf{0}$

The matrix inequality $[\mathbf{A}^{-1}\mathbf{B} - (1+r)\mathbf{I}]\mathbf{p} \leqq \mathbf{0}$ *implies*

$$[\mathbf{B} - (1+r)\mathbf{A}]\mathbf{p} \leqq \mathbf{0}, \text{ since } \mathbf{A} \geq \mathbf{0}.$$

Similarly, the matrix inequality $\mathbf{y}[\mathbf{B}\mathbf{A}^{-1} - (1+g)\mathbf{I}] \geqq \mathbf{0}$ *implies*

$$\mathbf{y}[\mathbf{B} - (1+g)\mathbf{A}] \geqq \mathbf{0}.$$

If we call:

r_1 the lowest r such that $[\mathbf{A}^{-1}\mathbf{B} - (1+r)\mathbf{I}]\mathbf{p} \leqq \mathbf{0}$ with $\mathbf{p} \geq \mathbf{0}$;
R the lowest r such that $[\mathbf{B} - (1+r)\mathbf{A}]\mathbf{p} \leqq \mathbf{0}$ with $\mathbf{p} \geq \mathbf{0}$;
g_1 the highest g such that $\mathbf{y}[\mathbf{B}^{-1}\mathbf{A} - (1+g)\mathbf{I}] \geqq \mathbf{0}$ with $\mathbf{y} \geq \mathbf{0}$;
G the highest g such that $\mathbf{y}[\mathbf{B} - (1+g)\mathbf{A}] \geqq \mathbf{0}$ with $\mathbf{y} \geq \mathbf{0}$,

we have $R \leq r_1$ and $g_1 \leq G$.

If the square semi-positive matrix $\mathbf{A}^{-1}\mathbf{B}$ is indecomposable, we can show, as in the preceding paragraph, that $1 + r_1$ is the dominant eigenvalue of $\mathbf{A}^{-1}\mathbf{B}$. When the semi-positive matrix $\mathbf{A}^{-1}\mathbf{B}$ is decomposable and has a (strictly) positive eigenvector on the left, $1 + r_1$ is the dominant eigenvalue of $\mathbf{A}^{-1}\mathbf{B}$.

Similarly, when the square matrix $\mathbf{B}\mathbf{A}^{-1}$ is semi-positive $1 + g_1$ is the dominant eigenvalue of $\mathbf{B}\mathbf{A}^{-1}$ if $\mathbf{B}\mathbf{A}^{-1}$ is indecomposable or if it is decomposable and has a (strictly) positive eigenvector on the right.

We can distinguish the following cases:

– both matrices $\mathbf{A}^{-1}\mathbf{B}$ and $\mathbf{B}\mathbf{A}^{-1}$ are semi-positive and at least one of them is indecomposable: we have $R = r_1 = g_1 = G$; $\mathbf{p}(R) > \mathbf{0}$ and $\mathbf{y}(G) \geq \mathbf{0}$ (or $\mathbf{p}(R) \geq \mathbf{0}$ and $\mathbf{y}(G) > \mathbf{0}$) are respectively the eigenvector on the right of $\mathbf{A}^{-1}\mathbf{B}$ and the eigenvector on the left of $\mathbf{B}\mathbf{A}^{-1}$ associated with the dominant eigenvalue $1 + r_1 = 1 + g_1$.

– both matrices $\mathbf{A}^{-1}\mathbf{B}$ and $\mathbf{B}\mathbf{A}^{-1}$ are semi-positive and decomposable: if the first matrix has a (strictly) positive eigenvector on the left and the second has a (strictly) positive eigenvector on the right, we have $R = r_1 = g_1 = G$ and $\mathbf{p}(R) \geq \mathbf{0}$ and $\mathbf{y}(G) \geq \mathbf{0}$ are respectively the eigenvector on the right of $\mathbf{A}^{-1}\mathbf{B}$ and the eigenvector on the left of $\mathbf{B}\mathbf{A}^{-1}$ associated with the dominant eigenvalues $1 + r_1 = 1 + g_1$.

– matrix $\mathbf{B}\mathbf{A}^{-1}$ is not semi-positive and $\mathbf{y} \ngeq \mathbf{0}$ where $\mathbf{y}$ is the eigenvector on the left of $\mathbf{B}\mathbf{A}^{-1}$ associated with the dominant eigenvalue $1 + g_1 = 1 + r_1$. In this case if $R = G$ we have $R < r_1$. If $\mathbf{B}\mathbf{A}^{-1} \geq \mathbf{0}$ but $\mathbf{A}^{-1}\mathbf{B}$ is not semi-positive and $\mathbf{p} \ngeq \mathbf{0}$ where $\mathbf{p}$ is the eigenvector on the right of $\mathbf{A}^{-1}\mathbf{B}$ corresponding to the dominant eigenvalue $1 + r_1 = 1 + g_1$; and if $R = G$, we have $G > g_1$.

Remark

If for all $i \in \{1, 2, \ldots, k\}$ we have

$$\frac{b_{ii}}{a_{ii}} < \alpha < \begin{cases} \dfrac{b_{ij}}{a_{ij}} & \text{for all } j \neq i \\[2ex] \dfrac{b_{ji}}{a_{ji}} & \text{for all } j \neq i \end{cases}$$

when one of the two square matrices $\mathbf{A}^{-1}\mathbf{B}$ and $\mathbf{BA}^{-1}$ is semi-positive, we have $R = G$ where $1/(1+R) = 1/(1+G)$ is the dominant eigenvalue of $\mathbf{A}^{-1}\mathbf{B}$ and $\mathbf{BA}^{-1}$.

Example

Consider a von Neumann model $(\mathbf{A}, \mathbf{B})$ where

$$\mathbf{A} = \begin{bmatrix} 16 & 8 \\ 1 & 13 \end{bmatrix} \qquad \text{and } \mathbf{B} = \begin{bmatrix} 18 & 9 \\ 3 & 14 \end{bmatrix}$$

matrix $\mathbf{A}$ has an inverse and matrix

$$\mathbf{A}^{-1}\mathbf{B} = \frac{1}{200}\begin{bmatrix} 13 & -8 \\ -1 & 16 \end{bmatrix}\begin{bmatrix} 18 & 9 \\ 3 & 14 \end{bmatrix} = \frac{1}{40}\begin{bmatrix} 42 & 1 \\ 6 & 43 \end{bmatrix}$$

is positive and indecomposable. Its characteristic equation is $\alpha^2 - (17/8)\alpha + (9/8) = 0$ and the dominant eigenvalue is $(9/8)$ while the second eigenvalue is 1. The rate of profit R such that $1 + R = (9/8)$ is equal to $(1/8)$ or 12.5%. Since the vector $\begin{bmatrix} 1 \\ 3 \end{bmatrix}$ is an eigenvector on the right of matrix $\mathbf{A}^{-1}\mathbf{B}$ associated with the dominant eigenvalue $(9/8)$, the system $\left(R = 12.5\%, \mathbf{p}(R) = \begin{bmatrix} 1 \\ 3 \end{bmatrix}\right)$ is an equilibrium price system of the model.

Since the model $(\mathbf{A}, \mathbf{B})$ is technologically and economically indecomposable the rate of growth G of the model is equal to R, i.e. 12.5%. Any optimal technique of production $\mathbf{y}(G) \geq \mathbf{0}$ is the solution of the matrix inequality $\mathbf{y}(G)[\mathbf{B} - (1+G)\mathbf{A}] \geqq \mathbf{0}$ or $\mathbf{y}(G)[\mathbf{B} - (9/8)\mathbf{A}] \geqq \mathbf{0}$.

Since $\mathbf{B} - \frac{9}{8}\mathbf{A} = \begin{bmatrix} 0 & 0 \\ \frac{15}{8} & -\frac{5}{8} \end{bmatrix}$ the components y_1 and y_2 of $\mathbf{y}(G)$

satisfy the system of inequalities.

$$[y_1 \quad y_2]\begin{bmatrix} 0 & 0 \\ \frac{15}{8} & -\frac{5}{8} \end{bmatrix} \geqq \mathbf{0} \quad \text{or} \quad \begin{bmatrix} \frac{15}{8}y_1 \geq 0 \\ -\frac{5}{8}y_2 \geq 0 \end{bmatrix}$$

This implies that $y_2 = 0$ and that y_1 can take any value. Since the components y_1 and y_2 of $\mathbf{y}(G)$ must be non-negative the techniques of production $\mathbf{y}(G) = \lambda[1,0]$ where $\lambda > 0$ are optimal. The system $(G = 12.5\%$, $\mathbf{y}(G) = [1,0]$ is an optimal proportional growth system.

Note that matrix $\mathbf{BA}^{-1} = \frac{1}{8}\begin{bmatrix} 9 & 0 \\ 1 & 8 \end{bmatrix}$ is semi-positive but is not indecomposable. However, it has the same eigenvalues, (9/8) and 1, as matrix $\mathbf{A}^{-1}\mathbf{B}$ and any eigenvector on the left of $\mathbf{BA}^{-1}$ associated with the dominant eigenvalue (9/8) which is proportional to $[1,0]$ is an optimal technique of production.

Remark

When neither matrices $\mathbf{A}^{-1}\mathbf{B}$ nor $\mathbf{BA}^{-1}$ are nonnegative it is possible that they may have a common positive eigenvalue α such that both the eigenvector $\mathbf{p}$ on the right of $\mathbf{A}^{-1}\mathbf{B}$ and the eigenvector $\mathbf{y}$ on the left of $\mathbf{BA}^{-1}$, are nonnegative.

In this case, for a von Neumann model $(\mathbf{A},\mathbf{B})$ we have $R = G = \alpha - 1$, $\mathbf{p}(R) = \mathbf{p}$ and $\mathbf{y}(G) = \mathbf{y}$.

Thus for a model $(\mathbf{A},\mathbf{B})$ where

$$\mathbf{A} = \begin{bmatrix} 8 & 1 \\ 4 & 3 \end{bmatrix} \quad \text{and} \quad \mathbf{B} = \begin{bmatrix} 9 & 1 \\ 3 & 4 \end{bmatrix}$$

we have

$$\mathbf{A}^{-1}\mathbf{B} = \frac{1}{20}\begin{bmatrix} 24 & -1 \\ -12 & 28 \end{bmatrix} \quad \text{and } \mathbf{BA}^{-1} = \frac{1}{20}\begin{bmatrix} 23 & -1 \\ -7 & 29 \end{bmatrix}$$

Both matrices $\mathbf{A}^{-1}\mathbf{B}$ and $\mathbf{BA}^{-1}$ have the same characteristic equation $\alpha^2 - (26/10)\alpha + (33/20) = 0$ and their eigenvalues are $\alpha_1 = 1.5$ and $\alpha_2 = 1.1$.

To the eigenvalue $\alpha_2 = 1.1$ correspond the eigenvector $\mathbf{p} = \begin{bmatrix} 1 \\ 2 \end{bmatrix}$ on the right of $\mathbf{A}^{-1}\mathbf{B}$ and the eigenvector $\mathbf{y} = [7, 1]$ on the left of $\mathbf{BA}^{-1}$ and we have $R = G = 1.1 - 1 = 0.1 = 10\%, \mathbf{p}(R) = \begin{bmatrix} 1 \\ 2 \end{bmatrix}$ and $\mathbf{y}(G) = [7, 1]$.

Therefore the system $\left(R = 0.1, \mathbf{p}(R) = \begin{bmatrix} 1 \\ 2 \end{bmatrix} \right)$ is an equilibrium price system of the model $(\mathbf{A}, \mathbf{B})$ and the system $(G = 0.1, \mathbf{y}(G) = [7, 1])$ is an optimal proportional growth system of this model.

Note that the conditions given in the remark in Section 4.4.2 are fulfilled, the number α is greater than 1 and less than (9/8).

4.5 Exclusion relations

We have shown that when assumptions (1) and (2) are satisfied we have $R \leq G$. In these conditions, $\mathbf{y} = \mathbf{y}(G)$ is the vector of optimum activity levels and $\mathbf{p} = \mathbf{p}(R)$ the vector of optimum prices, so that

$$\mathbf{yB} \geqq (1 + G)\mathbf{yA} \quad \text{and} \quad \mathbf{Bp} \leqq (1 + R)\mathbf{Ap} \leqq (1 + G)\mathbf{Ap}$$

Since the vectors $\mathbf{y}$ and $\mathbf{p}$ are semi-positive, we have

$$\mathbf{yBp} \geq (1 + G)\mathbf{yAp} \quad \text{and} \quad \mathbf{yBp} \leq (1 + G)\mathbf{yAp}$$

and thus

$$\mathbf{yBp} = (1 + G)\mathbf{yAp} \quad \text{or} \quad \mathbf{y}[\mathbf{B} - (1 + G)\mathbf{A}]\mathbf{p} = \mathbf{0}$$

From the relations

$$\begin{cases} \mathbf{yB} \geqq (1 + G)\mathbf{yA} \\ [\mathbf{yB} - (1 + G)\mathbf{yA}]\mathbf{p} = \mathbf{0} \end{cases} \text{or} \begin{cases} \mathbf{yb}^j \geq (1 + G)\mathbf{ya}^j \\ \sum_{j=1}^{n} [\mathbf{yb}^j - (1 + G)\mathbf{ya}^j]p_j = 0 \end{cases}$$

it follows that if $\mathbf{yb}^j > (1 + G)\mathbf{ya}^j$ we have $p_j = 0$, i.e. any good with a rate of growth greater than the rate of growth G of the model is a *free* good. Thus it is necessary that all goods have the same rate of growth G to be economic goods.

Similarly, from the relations

$$\begin{cases} \mathbf{Bp} \leqq (1 + G)\mathbf{Ap} \\ \mathbf{y}[\mathbf{Bp} - (1 + G)\mathbf{Ap}] = 0 \end{cases} \text{or} \begin{cases} \mathbf{b}_i\mathbf{p} \leq (1 + G)\mathbf{a}_i\mathbf{p} \\ \sum_{i=1}^{m} y_i[\mathbf{b}_i\mathbf{p} - (1 + G)\mathbf{a}_i\mathbf{p}] = 0 \end{cases}$$

it follows that if $\mathbf{b}_i\mathbf{p} < (1 + G)\mathbf{a}_i\mathbf{p}$ we have $y_i = 0$, i.e. any process realising a negative superprofit is not used. Therefore, all processes must have a zero superprofit to be used.

It is useful to point out the symmetry existing between:

(i) goods and processes;
(ii) prices and activity levels, each playing the role of a weighting system for the goods and processes;
(iii) rate of growth, G and rate of profit, R;
(iv) growth of goods and profits of processes;
(v) economic goods and used processes;
(vi) free goods and non-used processes;
(vii) equilibrium price system $(R, \mathbf{p}(R))$ and optimal proportional growth system $(G, \mathbf{y}(G))$;
(viii) technological decomposability (indecomposability) and economic decomposability (indecomposability).

5

Accumulation, conflicts and quasi-duality

Von Neumann's system of proportional growth is a far cry from the real world process of capital accumulation in which the entire 'surplus' is not always directly controlled by the capitalists and conflicts of interest occur among workers, capitalists and owners of natural resources. These conflicts among the various social interest groups are not the only ones. In addition to those conflicts concerning the distribution of the surplus there is also a second kind of conflict concerning its utilisation. This second conflict between the tempo of accumulation and the level of consumption involves problems that highlight the question of the effect of variations in the level of consumption on the rate of growth and on levels of activity. The investigation of this question will involve a transposition of Sraffa's analysis to construct a 'standard commodity for activity levels' as well as an analysis of the particular role played by what we shall call 'anti-basic' activities. This will allow us to identify a duality property, as in von Neumann, when the system is indecomposable as well as a 'quasi-duality' property which holds when the system is decomposable.

However, it is not possible to resolve the two main types of conflicts outlined above by treating them independently one from the other. This is obvious from the well-known relation between the rate of profit and the rate of growth which depends directly on the capitalists' propensity to save or on the financing decisions of firms. The possibility of what we shall call 'conflicts of objectives' will clearly appear in the case of changes in techniques.

5.1 Social conflicts and the 'trade-off' between the distributive variables

5.1.1 The relation between the rate of profit and the wage

The relation between the rate of profit and the wage is linear when prices and the wage are expressed in terms of Sraffa's standard commodity (see Chapters 2 and 3, above) but takes a very different shape when a particular commodity is chosen as the standard. Let us first consider the case where there is only one basic good. The analysis can then be generalised without difficulty.

(*A*) *ONE BASIC GOOD*

Consider the very simple case of an economy with circulating capital and two productive processes. The first produces a machine (with a working life of one year) using this same machine and labour. The second produces wheat with the same machine (thus it is a sort of universal machine tool) and labour. Since wheat is a non-basic commodity there is only one basic good in this system. We would then have the following technology matrix:

$$\mathbf{A} = \begin{bmatrix} a_{11} & 0 \\ a_{21} & 0 \end{bmatrix}$$

with p_1, p_2 the prices of the machine and wheat,
l_1, l_2 the quantities of direct labour in the two processes,
w and r the wage and the rate of profit.
The equations of prices of production can be written

$$(1+r)a_{11}p_1 + wl_1 = p_1$$

$$(1+r)a_{21}p_1 + wl_2 = p_2$$

Thus we have a two equation system with four unknowns: two prices and two distributive variables. If we choose one good as numeraire (wheat, for example) we have a two-equation system with three unknowns: one price (here the price of the machine in terms of wheat), the rate of profit and the wage level (expressed in wheat):

$$(1+r)a_{11}p_1 + wl_1 = p_1$$

$$(1+r)a_{21}p_1 + wl_2 = 1 \qquad (\text{since } p_2 = 1)$$

By substituting the value of p_1 calculated from the first equation into the second equation we have

$$p_1 = [1-(1+r)a_{11}]^{-1}wl_1$$

$$1 = (1+r)a_{21}[1-(1+r)a_{11}]^{-1}wl_1 + wl_2$$

$$1 = w\left[l_2 + (1+r)\frac{a_{21}l_1}{1-(1+r)a_{11}}\right]$$

or, calling Δ the determinant of matrix

$$\begin{bmatrix} a_{11} & l_1 \\ a_{21} & l_2 \end{bmatrix}$$

i.e. $\Delta = a_{11}l_2 - a_{21}l_1$

we have the equivalent implicit relation between w and r.

$$1 = (1+r)a_{11} + wl_2 - (1+r)w\Delta$$

This is the fundamental relation between the rate of profit and the wage which produces the traditional diagram. The intersection of the curve with the x and y axes give the maximum rate of profit and the maximum wage level for the technique in use as

$$w_{max} = \frac{1-a_{11}}{l_2 - \Delta} \text{ for } r = 0$$

$$r_{max} = R = \frac{1-a_{11}}{a_{11}} \text{ for } w = 0$$

We can also show that the implicit relation between w and r is necessarily of negative slope[1] but that the exact shape of the curve depends on the value of Δ, i.e. on the relative degree of mechanisation in the two sectors.

There are three possible cases to be distinguished:

(1) $\Delta = l_2a_{11} - l_1a_{21} = 0$

This means[2] that the degree of mechanisation is the same in both sectors

$$\frac{a_{11}}{l_1} = \frac{a_{21}}{l_2}$$

and the wage–profit relation is linear:

$$(1+r)a_{11} + wl_2 = 1$$

(2) $\Delta = l_2a_{11} - l_1a_{21} < 0$

or $\quad \dfrac{a_{21}}{l_2} > \dfrac{a_{11}}{l_1}$

The sector of consumption goods, wheat in the example, is more mechanised than the machine good sector. The wage–profit curve is convex to

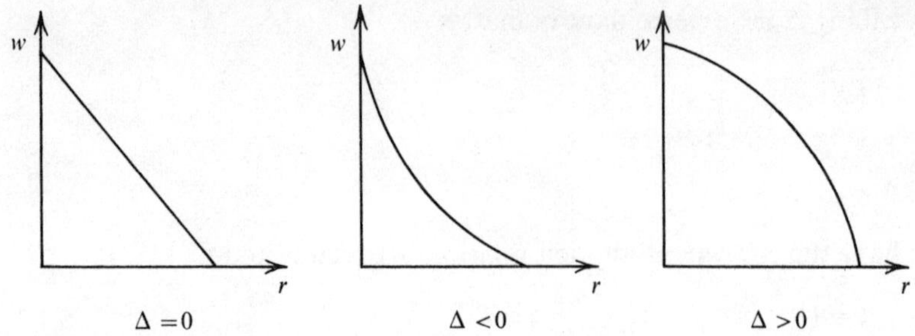

Fig. 5.1

the origin since

$$\frac{d^2w}{dr^2} > 0$$

(3) $\Delta = l_2 a_{11} - l_1 a_{21} > 0$ or $\dfrac{a_{21}}{l_2} < \dfrac{a_{11}}{l_1}$

the consumption sector is less mechanised than the machine good sector. The wage–profit curve is concave to the origin since

$$\frac{d^2w}{dr^2} < 0$$

The diagrams above give the three possible shapes of the implicit relation between w and r that is obtained from the price equations by taking one of the goods as numeraire and thus eliminating the price of the second. We note that the curve takes on a particularly simple shape when only one basic commodity exists in the system.[3] As in the traditional derivation of the relation either r or w may be considered as exogenously determined, but when one of the distributive variables is determined the second becomes endogenous.

(B) *THE CASE OF TWO BASIC GOODS*

The technology matrix in this case is

$$\mathbf{A} = \begin{bmatrix} a_{11} & a_{12} \\ a_{21} & a_{22} \end{bmatrix}$$

and the price system can be written

$$p_1 = (1 + r)(a_{11}p_1 + a_{12}p_2) + wl_1$$

$$p_2 = (1 + r)(a_{21}p_1 + a_{22}p_2) + wl_2$$

with $p_2 = 1$, we have

$$\begin{cases} [1-(1+r)a_{11}]p_1 = (1+r)a_{12} + wl_1 \Rightarrow p_1 = \dfrac{(1+r)a_{12}+wl_1}{1-(1+r)a_{11}} \\ 1 = (1+r)a_{21}p_1 + (1+r)a_{22} + wl_2 \end{cases}$$

thus

$$1 = (1+r)a_{21}\left[\frac{(1+r)a_{12}+wl_1}{1-(1+r)a_{11}}\right] + (1+r)a_{22} + wl_2$$

or

$$1 = w\left\{\frac{(1+r)a_{21}l_1}{1-(1+r)a_{11}} + l_2\right\} + (1+r)a_{22} + \frac{(1+r)^2a_{21}a_{12}}{1-(1+r)a_{11}}$$

and

$$w = \frac{1-(1+r)a_{22}-(1+r)^2a_{21}a_{12}[1-(1+r)a_{11}]^{-1}}{[1-(1+r)a_{11}]^{-1}(1+r)a_{21}l_1 + l_2}$$

Since $[1-(1+r)a_{11}]^{-1}$ is an increasing function of r, the numerator is a decreasing function of r and the denominator is an increasing function of r; therefore w is a decreasing function of r.

(C) *THE GENERAL CASE: THE SYSTEM PRODUCES k GOODS*

If the system produces k goods we can write the square matrix of order k as:

$$\left[\begin{array}{c|c} \mathbf{A} & \mathbf{a}^n \\ (k-1, k-1) & \\ \hline \mathbf{a}_n & a_{nn} \end{array}\right]$$

We call $\mathbf{p}$ the vector of the $(k-1)$ basic prices and p_n the price of the last good, which is taken as the standard.

We then have the following price equations:

$$\begin{cases} \mathbf{p} = (1+r)(\mathbf{A}\mathbf{p} + \mathbf{a}^n p_n) + w\mathbf{L} \\ p_n = (1+r)[\mathbf{a}_n\mathbf{p} + a_{nn}p_n] + wl_n \end{cases}$$

Note that if $\mathbf{a}^n = \mathbf{0}$ the last good is not basic.

With $p_n = 1$, we have

$$[\mathbf{I} - (1 + r)\mathbf{A}]\mathbf{p} = (1 + r)\mathbf{a}^n + w\mathbf{L}$$

or $$\mathbf{p} = [\mathbf{I} - (1 + r)\mathbf{A}]^{-1}(w\mathbf{L} + (1 + r)\mathbf{a}_n)$$

and $$1 = (1 + r)\mathbf{a}_n\mathbf{p} + (1 + r)a_{nn} + wl_n$$

Hence

$$1 = (1 + r)\mathbf{a}_n[\mathbf{I} - (1 + r)\mathbf{A}]^{-1}w\mathbf{L} + (1 + r)^2\mathbf{a}_n[\mathbf{I} - (1 + r)\mathbf{A}]^{-1}\mathbf{a}^n + (1 + r)a_{nn} + wl_n$$

and

$$1 = w\{l_n + (1 + r)\mathbf{a}_n[\mathbf{I} - (1 + r)\mathbf{A}]^{-1}\mathbf{L}\} + (1 + r)^2\mathbf{a}_n[\mathbf{I} - (1 + r)\mathbf{A}]^{-1}\mathbf{a}^n + (1 + r)a_{nn}$$

or $$w = \frac{1 - (1 + r)^2\mathbf{a}_n[\mathbf{I} - (1 + r)\mathbf{A}]^{-1}\mathbf{a}^n - (1 + r)a_{nn}}{l_n + (1 + r)\mathbf{a}_n[\mathbf{I} - (1 + r)\mathbf{A}]^{-1}\mathbf{L}}$$

Since $[\mathbf{I} - (1 + r)\mathbf{A}]^{-1}$ is an increasing function of r, the numerator of the expression is a decreasing function of r while the denominator is an increasing function of r; thus w is a decreasing function of r.

(*D*) *THE CASE OF A PART OF THE WAGE PAID IN ADVANCE*

Up to now we have assumed, as did Sraffa, that the entire wage was deducted from the surplus after it has been produced. But we know that the 'classical' economists, in particular Marx, considered the wage as being 'advanced' to labour. We shall examine an intermediate situation where the wage is composed of two parts. The first part (w_0) is fixed, 'advanced' by capitalists, and determined by physiological and socio-historical considerations. The second part (w') is variable, deducted from the surplus, and depends directly on social relations ($w = w' + w_0$).

Let us go back to the example already introduced of an economy producing two commodities, machines and wheat. The technology matrix **A** was

$$\mathbf{A} = \begin{bmatrix} a_{11} & 0 \\ a_{21} & 0 \end{bmatrix}$$

Suppose now that part of the wage is advanced. We have the vector of real wages per hour, $\mathbf{d} = [0, d_2]$. The socio-technological matrix $\mathbf{A}^*$

becomes

$$\mathbf{A}^* = \mathbf{A} + \mathbf{Ld} = \begin{bmatrix} a_{11} & 0 \\ a_{21} & 0 \end{bmatrix} + \begin{bmatrix} l_1 \\ l_2 \end{bmatrix} [0 \quad d_2]$$

or $$\mathbf{A}^* = \begin{bmatrix} a_{11} & 0 \\ a_{21} & 0 \end{bmatrix} + \begin{bmatrix} 0 & l_1 d_2 \\ 0 & l_2 d_2 \end{bmatrix} = \begin{bmatrix} a_{11} & l_1 d_2 \\ a_{21} & l_2 d_2 \end{bmatrix}^4$$

The form of the implicit relation between the rate of profit and the wage level remains the same but now the minimum level of the wage is fixed at $w_0 = \mathbf{dp}$ and constitutes an inviolable limit. As a consequence the maximum rate of profit, R^*, for the system is less (or equal in certain cases) than the maximum rate of profit, R, in the case of the wage paid *post factum.*

We can distinguish two limiting cases for the general expression[5] $w = w_0 + w' = \mathbf{dp} + w'$

– the wage is totally advanced $w' = 0 \Rightarrow w = w_0$: the wage–profit curve is reduced to one point. There is no 'trade off' between the wage and the rate of profit and the rate of profit is determined by the level of $w_0 = \mathbf{dp}$ and the technological conditions.

– the wage is totally paid from the surplus $w_0 = 0 \Rightarrow w = w'$: the wage–profit curve is defined for all values of $w = w'$ corresponding to $0 \leq w \leq 1$.

In the general case where $w' \neq 0$ and $w_0 \neq 0$ the 'generalised' prices of production are

$$\mathbf{p} = (1 + r)\mathbf{A}^*\mathbf{p} + w'\mathbf{L} \qquad \text{with } w = w_0 + w' = \mathbf{dp} + w'$$

and $\mathbf{A}^* = \mathbf{A} + \mathbf{Ld}$

5.1.2 The relation between the rate of profit, wages and rent

(A) *THE WAGE–RENT–RATE-OF-PROFIT SURFACE*

When natural resources (land, oil, etc...) are taken into account, it becomes impossible to characterised a method of production only by the implicit relation existing between the wage and the rate of profit. When the owner of the natural resource receives an income, i.e. a rent, there is an implicit relation between the wage, the rate of profit and rent which determines not a curve in a plane, but a surface in a three-dimensional space.[6]

We shall consider 'land' of uniform quality yielding rent, and we shall assume that there is no joint production (except for land). Two processes produce two commodities, wheat and a machine. The machine is the only basic commodity (cf. the example of 5.1.1).

With the usual notation and assuming that the two processes use, respectively quantities T_1 and T_2 of land, we have the following equations for the prices of production

$$\begin{cases} (1+r)a_{11}p_1 + wl_1 + \rho T_1 = p_1 \\ (1+r)a_{21}p_1 + wl_2 + \rho T_2 = p_2 \end{cases}$$

From the first equation we have

$$[1-(1+r)a_{11}]p_1 = wl_1 + \rho T_1$$

By introducing the expression for p_1 in the second equation and taking the price of 'wheat' as numeraire we have

$$\begin{aligned} 1 &= (1+r)a_{21}p_1 + wl_2 + \rho T_2 \\ &= (1+r)a_{21}\frac{wl_1 + \rho T_1}{1-(1+r)a_{11}} + wl_2 + \rho T_2 \end{aligned}$$

$$1 = w\left[l_2 + (1+r)\frac{a_{21}l_1}{1-(1+r)a_{11}}\right] + \rho\left[T_2 + (1+r)\frac{a_{21}T_1}{1-(1+r)a_{11}}\right]$$

This implicit relation between w, r and ρ determines the analogue of the wage–rate-of-profit curve; in this case a surface in the space w, r and ρ. The shape of this surface can be easily determined.

First we note that the relation between w and ρ is decreasing and linear (for a given r, this relation is of the form $w = a - b\rho$ where a and b are positive numbers and both functions of r). We can easily find the intersection of this surface with the planes (w,ρ), (ρ,r) and (r,w).

$$r = 0 \rightarrow w\left[l_2 + \frac{a_{21}l_1}{1-a_{11}}\right] + \rho\left[T_2 + \frac{a_{21}T_1}{1-a_{11}}\right] = 1$$

$$w = 0 \rightarrow \rho\left[T_2 + (1+r)\frac{a_{21}T_1}{1-(1+r)a_{11}}\right] = 1$$

$$\rho = 0 \rightarrow w\left[l_2 + (1+r)\frac{a_{21}l_1}{1-(1+r)a_{11}}\right] = 1$$

Both relations (ρ,r) and (w,r) are decreasing, their exact shape depending on the characteristics of the methods of production. As an illustrative example, they could take the following forms:

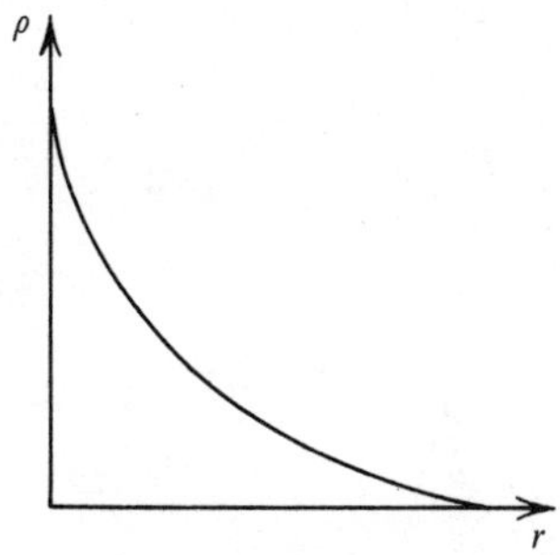

Fig. 5.2 (a)

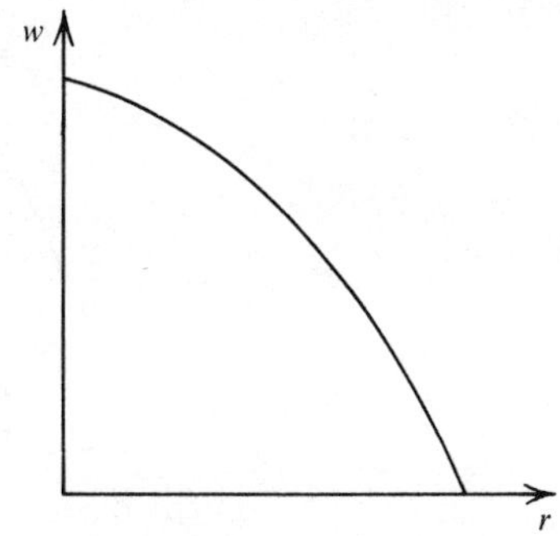

Fig. 5.2 (b)

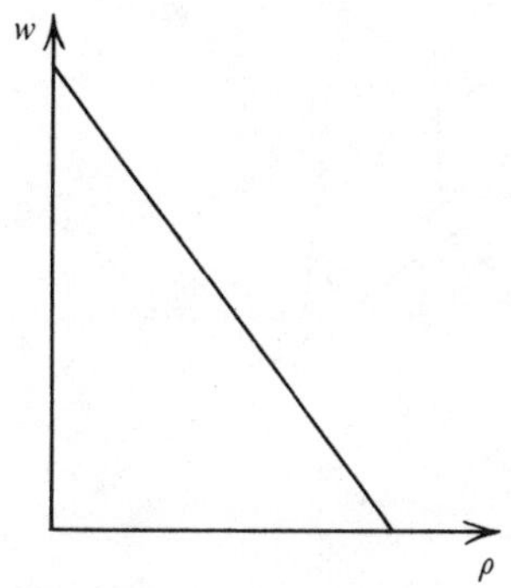

Fig 5.2 (c)

The relation (w, ρ) is always linear.

Therefore, we can draw the surface rent–rate-of-profit–wage in the three dimensional space as in Fig. 5.3.[7]

Note that in this case we have two degrees of freedom, two independent variables (for example, rent and the rate of profit) which determine the third variable (wage). If we fix rent at an arbitrary level ρ_1, we can draw a wage–profit curve (w_1, r_1) (the dotted lines on the figure). It is obvious that, the higher the wage level and the rate of profit, the lower the possible level of rent.

Similarly, if we fix arbitrarily the rate of profit at r_2 we can show a possibility of a 'trade off' between wages and rent (w_2, ρ_2). Of course, when the rate of profit reaches its maximum, R, $\det[\mathbf{I} - (1 + R)\mathbf{A}] = 0$ and thus both the real wage and rent are zero. When the rate of profit decreases, wage and rent take increasing values (to finite maxima).

It is clear that if $r = 0$ the relation $(w - \rho)$ describes the confrontation between landowners and workers in a pre-capitalistic economy. On the contrary, if we assume that the wage is totally advanced, we can interpret

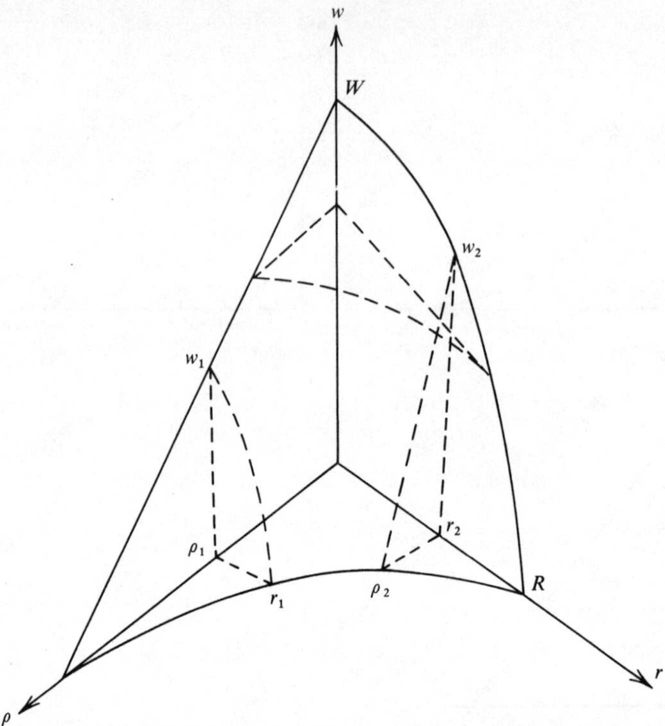

Fig. 5.3

the curve (ρ,r) drawn in the horizontal plane (or in a parallel plane) as exhibiting the conflict between landowners and capitalists when the wage is fixed at the minimum level of subsistence.

Another possible interpretation concerns international trade theory. Since ρ represents the 'tribute' paid to the landowner or the owner of a 'scarce' natural resource, the analysis can be extended beyond the national level; ρ can be interpreted as that part of a country's output required to pay foreign energy suppliers (oil, raw materials). An increase of ρ can only reduce the 'standard of living' of the national economy as can be seen in the projection of the wage–profit curve on the plane (w,r).

(B) A LINEAR RELATIONSHIP BETWEEN THE WAGE, RENT AND THE RATE OF PROFIT AND THE ROLE OF THE STANDARD COMMODITY

It is possible to imagine very special technological cases where the surface representing the possible arbitrage between the three distributive variables is a plane. For example, in the case already seen of two commodities (one of which is basic) produced by two methods each using a certain quantity of land, the capital–labour ratio and the land–labour ratio must be identical in the two processes. In this case, the implicit relation between w, r and ρ becomes

$$1 = (1+r)a_{11} + wl_2 + \rho T_2$$

i.e. $\dfrac{a_{11}}{l_1} = \dfrac{a_{21}}{l_2}$

and $\dfrac{a_{11}}{T_1} = \dfrac{a_{21}}{T_2}$

It is easy to verify that this is the equation of a plane.

It is more interesting to show that, whatever the technology, the relation (w, r, ρ) is necessarily linear (the surface showing this relation is therefore a plane) provided that we choose a particular commodity to express the wage and rent. In the same way as Sraffa demonstrated that the wage–rate-of-profit relation was necessarily linear provided that the wage was expressed in terms of 'the' standard commodity, Metcalfe and Steedman ('Reswitching') have shown that the wage–rent–rate-of-profit relation will necessarily be linear when an appropriate standard commodity is chosen.

Steedman's analysis is undertaken on the basis of single-product industries with circulating capital. Using the usual notation, the vector of prices of production is written:

$$(1+r)\mathbf{Ap} + w\mathbf{L} + \rho\mathbf{T} = \mathbf{p} \tag{1}$$

where $\mathbf{T}$ is a column vector representing the utilisation of 'land' by each activity.

The standard commodity is constructed in the usual way. Its composition is given by the vector $\mathbf{q}$ such that

$$(1+r)\mathbf{qA} = \mathbf{q} \tag{2}$$

with

$$\mathbf{q} > 0 \quad \text{and} \quad \mathbf{qL} = 1 \tag{3}$$

The net product of the standard system $\mathbf{q}(\mathbf{I}-\mathbf{A})$ is by assumption such that $\mathbf{q}(\mathbf{I}-\mathbf{A})\mathbf{p} = 1$

Note also[8] that we have $\mathbf{q}(\mathbf{I}-\mathbf{A}) = \mathbf{q}\dfrac{R}{1+R}$ (4)

Multiplying equation (1) by $\mathbf{q}$ and using (2), (3) and (4) we have

$$(1+r)\mathbf{qAp} + w\mathbf{qL} + \rho\mathbf{qT} = \mathbf{qp}$$

or

$$\frac{1+r}{1+R}\mathbf{qp} + w + \rho(\mathbf{qT}) = \mathbf{qp}$$

thus

$$w + \rho(\mathbf{qT}) = \frac{R-r}{1+R}\mathbf{qp} = \frac{(R-r)}{R}\mathbf{q}(\mathbf{I}-\mathbf{A})\mathbf{p}$$

If now we define w_s and ρ_s respectively as the wage and rent in terms of the standard commodity: $w_s = \dfrac{w}{\mathbf{q}(\mathbf{I}-\mathbf{A})\mathbf{p}}$ and $\rho_s = \dfrac{\rho}{\mathbf{q}(\mathbf{I}-\mathbf{A})\mathbf{p}}$ the equation above becomes

$$w_s + \rho_s(\mathbf{qT}) = \frac{R-r}{R} \Leftrightarrow w_s + (\mathbf{qT})\rho_s + \frac{r}{R} = 1$$

Thus, the relation between the rate of profit, wages and rent expressed in terms of the standard commodity is linear and the surface that graphically describes this relation is a plane.

This shows again, very clearly, the abstract character of the standard commodity. The coefficient $\mathbf{qT}$ is a weighted average of the T_i by the q_i expressing $\left(\text{since } \mathbf{qL} = 1 \text{ implies } \mathbf{qT} = \dfrac{\mathbf{qT}}{\mathbf{qL}}\right)$ the global land–labour ratio 'virtually' implied in the production of the standard commodity. Virtually because it may not be possible to actually produce the standard commodity. This would be the case for example if $\mathbf{qT}$ (with $\mathbf{qL} = 1$) were greater than the available quantity of land.

When no rent is paid for the land or when no land is used in the process of production ($\rho = 0$ or $T = 0$) Sraffa's original case applies. The generalisation to the case of land of various qualities or to the case of multiple natural resources is obvious.

To sum up, *the relation* $(r, w, \rho_1, \ldots, \rho_i, \ldots, \rho_n)$ *between the rate of profit, wages and rent paid to the owners of the n natural resources is linear if prices, wages and rent are expressed in terms of the standard commodity* whose composition is determined by the vector $\mathbf{q}$ such that

$$\mathbf{q} = (1+R)\mathbf{qA} \quad \text{with} \quad \mathbf{qL} = 1$$

5.2 Conflicts between accumulation and consumption and quasi-duality

5.2.1 The 'trade off' between the rate of growth and the level of consumption

We now consider the problem of the conflict between accumulation and consumption; for this we will use the simple case of two commodities, 'machines' and 'wheat', produced by two, single-product, industries. The technology matrix **A** is assumed to be indecomposable and the technology is invariant. Moreover, we assume that the wage is completely paid *post factum* from the produced surplus (cf. Section 5.1.1 (*B*)).

Let the technology matrix $\mathbf{A} = \begin{bmatrix} a_{11} & a_{12} \\ a_{21} & a_{22} \end{bmatrix} > 0$

$\mathbf{y} = (y_1, y_2)$ is the activity level in the two industries considered, g is the rate of accumulation, i.e. the rate of growth of the means of production, assumed to be uniform. Since **A** is strictly positive, both goods are considered as means of production.

The structure of consumption $\boldsymbol{\delta} = (\delta_1, \delta_2) > 0$ is assumed to be known. Thus we assume that both goods enter into consumption as well as being means of production. Vector $\boldsymbol{\delta}$ is defined up to the multiplication by scalars and thus can be normalised by setting $\delta_1 p_1 + \delta_2 p_2 = 1$, supposing prices and income distribution to be given. ξ, the consumption level, is a scalar which multiplies the consumption vector $\boldsymbol{\delta}$. The assumption of a proportional increase (or decrease) in consumption implies income elasticities equal to 1 for all goods in consumption.

With these definitions the system of equations for activity levels can be written in matrix form as follows:

$$\mathbf{y} = (1+g)\mathbf{y}\mathbf{A} + \xi\boldsymbol{\delta}$$

or

$$\begin{cases} y_1 = (1+g)(y_1 a_{11} + y_2 a_{21}) + \xi\delta_1 \\ y_2 = (1+g)(y_1 a_{12} + y_2 a_{22}) + \xi\delta_2 \end{cases}$$

The vector of activity levels, defined up to the multiplication by scalars, can be normalised in any number of ways. We shall, arbitrarily, set $y_2 = 1$. Hence we have

$$\begin{cases} y_1 = (1+g)(y_1 a_{11} + a_{21}) + \xi\delta_1 \\ 1 \;= (1+g)(y_1 a_{12} + a_{22}) + \xi\delta_2 \end{cases}$$

From the first equation we have

$$y_1[1-(1+g)a_{11}] = (1+g)a_{21} + \xi\delta_1$$

We can introduce this expression of y_1 as a function of g and ξ into the second equation. Thus

$$1 = (1+g)a_{12}\frac{(1+g)a_{21} + \xi\delta_1}{1-(1+g)a_{11}} + (1+g)a_{22} + \xi\delta_2$$

or

$$1 = \xi\left\{\frac{(1+g)a_{12}\delta_1}{1-(1+g)a_{11}} + \delta_2\right\} + (1+g)a_{22} + \frac{(1+g)^2 a_{12}a_{21}}{1-(1+g)a_{11}}$$

This gives us *an implicit relation between the level of consumption ξ and the rate of growth of the means of production g.*

It can easily be shown that the relation (ξ, g) is decreasing and produces a curve in the plane (ξ, g), which will normally be different from the curve established for (w, r). Since there is symmetry with the analysis of the problem of income distribution in the system, we could define a trade-off surface between the possible uses of the national income. For example, if we introduced a third use (e.g. collective consumption or exports) in addition to the two already considered (accumulation, expressed by g and consumption expressed by ξ) we could define a surface in $\mathbf{R}^3$ or a hyper-surface in $\mathbf{R}^n$ if we considered $(n-2)$ supplementary uses. Of course, the available labour, land and natural resources play the role of constraints.

The preceding analysis evidently has a limited scope, first because it only considers the simple case of two commodities produced by two single-product industries, and second because, although it points out the implicit relation between the rate of growth and the level of consumption, it does not take into account variations in the activity levels. We shall look more closely at this problem in the following paragraphs.

5.2.2 Effects of changes in the level of consumption on the rate of growth and the activity levels

This is a dual problem to that examined by Sraffa concerning the search for an invariant standard of prices. Our concern is not 'to observe the effect of changes in the wage on the rate of profits and on the prices of individual commodities, on the assumption that the methods of production remain unchanged' (P.S. §13, p. 12) but to observe the effects of changes in consumption on the rate of growth and on the activity levels of the various processes. Once again we assume that the methods of production remain invariant. This means that we replace the wage, as considered by Sraffa, with consumption; the rate of profits with the rate of growth; and prices with activity levels.

We shall limit our analysis to a single-product system with circulating capital. Let

- $\mathbf{y}$ be the vector of activity levels,
- g be the (uniform) rate of growth of the means of production,
- $\boldsymbol{\delta} = (\delta_1, \delta_2, \ldots, \delta_k)$ be the structure of consumption, defined up to the multiplication by scalars; we thus have, in addition, $\boldsymbol{\delta}\mathbf{p} = 1$
- ξ be the consumption level.

(Note the symmetry with Sraffa's analysis Section 2.2, above, where w represented the wage level and $\mathbf{L}$ the vector of direct labour.)

With these definitions the equations for the levels of activity can be written

$$\mathbf{y} = (1 + g)\mathbf{y}\mathbf{A} + \xi\boldsymbol{\delta}$$

We have a system of k equations with $k + 2$ unknowns, i.e. the k activity levels, the rate of growth g and the level of consumption ξ. If we choose to analyse the changes in activity levels as a function of consumption assumed to be exogenously given, we still have one degree of freedom. (Again, symmetrically, the rate of growth could have been exogenous.)

We thus normalise the activity levels using the following equation:

$$y_1\left[1 - \sum_j a_{1j}\right] + \ldots + y_i\left[1 - \sum_j a_{ij}\right] + \ldots + y_k\left[1 - \sum_j a_{kj}\right] = 1$$

Note that the left side of this equation represents the national product of a system that replaces what it has used up in production since this national product is made up of the aggregate of the commodities[9] that remain when from the gross national product we have removed item by item the articles which go to replace the means of production used up in all the industries. This is equivalent to normalising the activity levels in such a way that the activity levels (or the levels of production) of type y_i, weighted by the net surplus obtained for each commodity $\left[1 - \sum_j a_{ij}\right]$, sum to unity. This is the definition of the standard in which the level of consumption and the k activity levels are expressed.

Consequently it is possible to find the level of each of the $k + 1$ variables as functions of the various (assumed exogenous) consumption levels. Let us first consider two particular cases:

(i) Suppose that the whole net product is consumed, i.e. $g = 0$ and $\xi = 1$. The corresponding activity levels are

$$\mathbf{y} = \mathbf{y}\mathbf{A}(\mathbf{I} + 0) + \boldsymbol{\delta} \quad \text{or} \quad \mathbf{y}[\mathbf{I} - \mathbf{A}] = \boldsymbol{\delta}$$

and

$$\mathbf{y} = \boldsymbol{\delta}[\mathbf{I} - \mathbf{A}]^{-1} \text{ provided that } [\mathbf{I} - \mathbf{A}] \text{ is non-singular.}^{10}$$

(ii) Suppose, conversely, that the whole net product is invested, i.e. $\xi = 0$ and $g = G$, the maximum rate of growth of the system. The equations for the activity levels are then

$$\mathbf{y}\mathbf{A}(1 + G) = \mathbf{y} \Leftrightarrow \mathbf{y}\mathbf{A} = \frac{1}{1 + G}\mathbf{y} = \alpha^*\mathbf{y}$$

with $\alpha^* = \dfrac{1}{1 + G}$

It is obvious that the maximum rate of growth G is positive if, and only if, α^*, the dominant eigenvalue of matrix $\mathbf{A}$, is such that $0 < \alpha^* < 1$. Moreover, we know that $\mathbf{y}$ the eigenvector (on the left) associated with the dominant eigenvalue α^* of $\mathbf{A}$ is strictly positive when matrix $\mathbf{A}$ is indecomposable. If $\mathbf{A}$ is decomposable, $\mathbf{y}$ is semi-positive, i.e. some processes may not be used.

Having considered these two particular cases we can proceed to the analysis of the effect of a change in the level of consumption on the levels of activity. Let us start from a situation in which the whole net product is consumed ($g = 0$) and assume a decrease in consumption, which implies at the same time that the rate of growth becomes positive ($g > 0$ with $g < G$).

The key to the variation in the activity levels produced by a change in the level of consumption lies in the inequality of the proportions in which the various commodities produced are allocated between consumption and investment respectively. It is obvious that if this proportion were the same for all commodities, no change in the activity level would appear, whatever the diversity of the processes using the various commodities as means of production, because for each commodity a uniform fall in the consumption level would release exactly those commodities required as means of production for a uniform rate of growth to appear without any modification to existing activity levels.

However, there is no reason for this proportion to be identical for all commodities. Consequently, in order to maintain a uniform rate of growth of the means of production in the whole system, some changes in the activity levels will have to occur when there are variations in the levels of consumption. First, the activity levels of the processes producing commodities used in relatively high proportion for consumption will have to fall, those producing commodities entering consumption in a relatively low proportion will have to rise and, finally, the activity levels of the processes producing 'average' commodities characterised by a 'critical proportion' of consumption/means of production will remain constant whatever the consumption levels and the rate of growth.

Consider the case of a commodity used in relatively high proportion for consumption. In the first instance a decrease in the share of consumption in the total net product will normally involve a decrease in the activity level of the process producing this good. In this way the share of the commodity will decrease so as to eliminate its excess production, thus allowing the rate of growth of the means of production, assumed to be unique, to be re-established.

Such a conclusion can only be provisional. Suppose now that the processes using the commodity under consideration, b_1, produce a commodity, b_2, itself consumed in a lower proportion than the critical proportion. This could mean that the activity level of the process producing b_1 would have to increase to compensate the rise in the quantity of commodity b_1 necessary to produce the higher quantity of b_2.

It is therefore impossible to formulate general conclusions about the reactions of the activity levels to changes in the consumption level when the commodities are *used* in proportions other than the critical proportion. The only certain result is negative: no process, except those producing the 'average' commodities in the critical proportion, can remain at an invariant level during any sequence, long or short, of variations in consumption (cf. P.S. §19, pp. 14–15).

At the same time, it is easy to see that for a commodity to have the 'critical proportion' it is absolutely necessary that this proportion should hold for all commodities which are required, directly or indirectly, in the production of the commodity considered. This is, therefore, a *condition of downstream recurrence* analogous to the condition noted by Sraffa which we could call a *condition of upstream recurrence.* A commodity used in such conditions ('downstream recurrence') presents all the requisite properties of a *standard of measure of activity levels* since the activity level of the process producing this commodity is necessarily invariant to modifications in the level of consumption or in the rate of growth. This commodity can thus be used as a standard, for example, to compare changes in activity levels of the processes producing the various goods in the system. Since it is not very likely that such a commodity exists, it will be necessary to construct a '*virtual commodity*' possessing all the requisite properties; this will be the '*standard commodity*' *for activity levels* '*dual of the standard commodity for prices constructed by Sraffa.*

It is important to refer to the definition of the 'critical proportion' or 'equilibrium proportion', again adapting Sraffa's price analysis to activity levels.

Let us suppose that the rate of growth of the means of production is uniform for the aggregate of commodities and depends only on the level of consumption; then the quantity ratio of the net surplus to the means of production is in general different according to the commodity considered as standard and most often depends on the particular circumstances of its utilisation. In fact, the equation representing the activity level of the process producing the jth commodity is written

$$y_j = \mathbf{y}\mathbf{a}^j(1+g) + \xi\delta_j$$

where $\mathbf{a}^j$ is the column vector of intermediate consumption and δ_j the final consumption of the jth commodity. Hence the expression of the ratio of the net product of the jth commodity $(y_j - \mathbf{y}\mathbf{a}^j)$ to the intermediate consumption $(\mathbf{y}\mathbf{a}^j)$

$$\frac{y_j - \mathbf{y}\mathbf{a}^j}{\mathbf{y}\mathbf{a}^j} = g + \xi\frac{\delta_j}{\mathbf{y}\mathbf{a}^j}$$

is a ratio which differs according to the commodity considered.

However, there is an exception. Suppose that consumption is zero and that the whole net product goes to enlarge the means of production. In this particular case the quantity ratio of net product to intermediate consumption necessarily coincides with the average rate of growth. The quantity ratios can differ widely for other consumption levels, but for this particular level they are equal for all commodities. For $\xi = 0$ we have $g = G$, the maximum rate of growth, such that

$$\mathbf{y}\mathbf{A}(1+G) = \mathbf{y} \text{ or equivalently } \frac{y_j - \mathbf{y}\mathbf{a}^j}{\mathbf{y}\mathbf{a}^j} = G = a \text{ constant.}$$

We thus reach a symmetrical, *dual* conclusion to Sraffa's (cf. P.S., pp. 16–17): the quantity ratio which is equal to the rate of growth corresponding to a zero level of consumption is the only one invariant to changes in the level of consumption and is thus the equilibrium or 'critical' ratio.

5.2.3 Construction of the standard commodity for activity levels

Why do we need a particular standard of measure? Once again the need to express a given activity level in terms of another, arbitrarily chosen as a standard of comparison, makes the study of the movements in activity levels produced by changes in the distribution of the national product more difficult. It is impossible to determine whether a change in a given activity level results from a characteristic of the process under consideration or from a change in the standard used. The characteristics under investigation could include such a simple fact as the inequality of the production of consumption to means of production in the 'successive uses' i.e. the direct and indirect uses of the commodity considered. Because of this inequality a change in the level of consumption necessarily involves a change in the net quantity produced of a given commodity relative to intermediate consumption.

The 'equilibrium' commodity identified above does not present any peculiarity of this kind since it enters all its 'uses' in the same proportions. It is true that when consumption falls the activity level of the process producing such a commodity may rise or fall relatively to another activity level, just as for any other commodity. Yet, we would be certain that all such variations are caused exclusively by the conditions of 'use' of the commodity produced by the other process, and not from its own conditions of 'use'.

It is not very likely that such a *simple* commodity satisfying even approximately the requisite conditions can be found. Therefore, we shall have to construct a combination of commodities, a virtual commodity, in such a way that the critical proportion between the value of the net product and the value of its uses destined for accumulation is respected. The critical proportion has been previously defined as the dominant eigenvalue of the technology matrix **A**. The prices compatible with the critical proportion are defined by the vector $\bar{\mathbf{p}}$, the eigenvector on the right associated with the dominant eigenvalue of matrix $\mathbf{A}:\mathbf{A}\bar{\mathbf{p}} = \alpha^*\bar{\mathbf{p}} = [1/(1+G)]\bar{\mathbf{p}}$. Such a system satisfies by construction the critical proportion between the value of the net product and the value of the productive uses.

Once again, the question is to find out whether such a commodity can be constructed. Let us go back to the concrete system proposed by Sraffa for the construction of a standard commodity for prices. As we have already seen this is a basic system and can be presented in the following way:

Inputs			Outputs		
Iron(t)	Coal(t)	Wheat(qr)	Iron(t)	Coal(t)	Wheat(qr)
90	120	60	180		
50	125	150		450	
40	40	200			480

or, alternatively:

$$\mathbf{A} = \begin{bmatrix} \frac{1}{2} & \frac{12}{45} & \frac{1}{8} \\ \frac{5}{18} & \frac{5}{18} & \frac{5}{16} \\ \frac{2}{9} & \frac{4}{45} & \frac{5}{12} \end{bmatrix} \quad \text{and } \mathbf{B} = \begin{bmatrix} 1 & 0 & 0 \\ 0 & 1 & 0 \\ 0 & 0 & 1 \end{bmatrix}$$

Starting from this concrete system we want to find a system of a different scale fulfilling the requisite properties. Let us recall that in Sraffa's example the scale and the structure of the system were determined by the *structure of production* of the commodities (vector **q**) while in our case, and for the reasons indicated above, they will be determined by the *structure of values* of these same commodities.[11]

This structure of values can be obtained from the eigenvector $\bar{\mathbf{p}}$ (on the right) associated with the dominant eigenvalue α^* of matrix **A**

$$\mathbf{A}\bar{\mathbf{p}} = \alpha^*\bar{\mathbf{p}} = \frac{1}{1+G}\bar{\mathbf{p}}$$

$\bar{\mathbf{p}}$ is therefore defined up to the multiplication by scalars as $\bar{\mathbf{p}} = \begin{bmatrix} 11 \\ 10 \\ 8 \end{bmatrix}$.

Because of the units adopted this vector does not give us directly the desired structure of values. The components 11, 10, 8 simply show that if 180 tons of iron cost 11, 450 tons of coal cost 10, and 480 quarters of wheat cost 8 (see mathematical appendix). But we require a price structure defined per unit of commodity. Since the price vector is defined up to the multiplication by scalars the desired vector can be obtained without difficulty: a ton of iron costs 11/6, a ton of coal 10/15 and a quarter of wheat 8/16 ($=\frac{1}{2}$).

Thus the structure of prices becomes

$$\bar{\mathbf{p}}_u = \begin{bmatrix} 11 \\ 4 \\ 3 \end{bmatrix}$$

On the basis of this structure the system reconstructed with the requisite proportions can be obtained by valuing the commodity iron at 11, the commodity coal at 4 and the commodity wheat at 3. The resulting system is as follows:

Value of the inputs			Value of the outputs		
Iron	Coal	Wheat	Iron	Coal	Wheat
990	480	180	1980		
550	500	450		1800	
440	160	600			1440

The relative proportions of the values of the three outputs (1980/1800/1440) are identical to those of the values of the inputs of the processes for each of the three commodities (1650/1500/1200).[12] The 'virtual' commodity is therefore characterised by the following proportions:

$$\begin{bmatrix} 11 \\ 10 \\ 8 \end{bmatrix}$$

This virtual commodity is the dual to Sraffa's 'composite' commodity which was characterised by a structure of commodities used as inputs (1 ton of iron/1.5 tons of coal/2 quarters of wheat). Similarly, we will call the set of value equations (or commodities) in the proportions producing the standard commodity the *dual standard system*.

In this system we can also state that it is possible to identify the standard system that is implicit in any concrete economic system. Furthermore, just as in the determination of the invariable standard of price, it will generally be useful to set $\boldsymbol{\delta}\bar{\mathbf{p}} = 1$.

The fact that in the dual standard system the values of the quantities produced by the various processes are in the same proportions as the values of the quantities consumed by these processes implies that the percentage of the excess of the produced value over the consumed value is the same in each of them. In the preceding example the rate is 20% for each process as can be seen by rearranging the numbers so that the sum of the inputs in the process considered corresponds to the value of its outputs.

$$(990+480+180)(1+20/100)=1980$$
$$(550+500+450)(1+20/100)=1800$$
$$(440+160+600)(1+20/100)=1440$$

Obviously the proportion applied to each process is also the proportion in which the value of the total product of the standard system exceeds the value of its means of production, i.e. the ratio of the value of the net product to the value of the means of production. This ratio will be called the *dual standard ratio.* (Note that in the example, the matrix is *indecomposable* and thus $R=G$; this means that *in this case the dual standard ratio is identical to the 'primal' standard ratio*).

This result would not be affected if we were to multiply the various processes of the standard system by their activity levels. Thus, in the standard system, the ratio between the value of the net product and the value of the means of production would remain unchanged whatever the variations in the division of the net surplus between consumption and accumulation and whatever the resulting changes in the activity levels:

$$\mathbf{y}\bar{\mathbf{p}}=(1+G)\mathbf{y}\mathbf{A}\bar{\mathbf{p}} \Leftrightarrow G=\frac{\mathbf{y}\bar{\mathbf{p}}-\mathbf{y}\mathbf{A}\bar{\mathbf{p}}}{\mathbf{y}\mathbf{A}\bar{\mathbf{p}}} \text{ for any } \mathbf{y}$$

To sum up, the problem of the construction of the standard commodity for activity levels can be solved by finding the eigenvector on the right $\bar{\mathbf{p}}$ associated with the dominant eigenvalue of matrix $\mathbf{A}$

$$\mathbf{A}\bar{\mathbf{p}}=\frac{1}{1+G}\bar{\mathbf{p}}$$

the ratio, G, the maximum rate of growth occurring in the system is called the dual standard ratio. Since the vector $\bar{\mathbf{p}}$ is defined up to the multiplication by scalars we have the additional equation $\boldsymbol{\delta}\bar{\mathbf{p}}=1$. Thus we have $(k+1)$ equations to determine the k 'multipliers' and G.

By applying the k 'multipliers' to the equations of the real system we can transform it into a 'dual' standard system written as follows:

$$[\mathbf{y}\mathbf{A}(1+g)+\zeta\,\boldsymbol{\delta}]\overset{\circ}{\bar{\mathbf{p}}}=\mathbf{y}\overset{\circ}{\mathbf{p}}$$

$$\text{where } \overset{\circ}{\bar{\mathbf{p}}}=\begin{bmatrix}\bar{\mathbf{p}}_1 & 0 & 0 \ldots 0\\ 0 & \bar{\mathbf{p}}_2 & 0 \ldots 0\\ 0 & 0 & \bar{\mathbf{p}}_3 \ldots 0\\ \ldots & \ldots & \ldots\\ 0 & 0 & 0 \ldots \bar{\mathbf{p}}_k\end{bmatrix}$$

We have, moreover, the normalisation equation on the **y**s: $\mathbf{y}[\mathbf{I}-\mathbf{A}]\bar{\mathbf{p}}=1$ which means that the net product (in value) of all processes or the net product of the dual standard system is set equal to one. This 'virtual' commodity is the standard of activity levels and of consumption that is required.

Sraffa has pointed out that there is a decreasing linear relation between the rate of profits and the wage provided that the wage is expressed in terms of the standard commodity. Symmetrically, we shall show that there exists a decreasing linear relation between the rate of growth and consumption provided that the latter is expressed in terms of the net product of the dual standard system. We have the following system of equations of activity levels:

$$\mathbf{yA}(1+g)+\xi\boldsymbol{\delta}=\mathbf{y} \qquad \text{or} \quad g\mathbf{yA}+\xi\boldsymbol{\delta}=\mathbf{y}(\mathbf{I}-\mathbf{A})$$

multiplying (on the right) by $\bar{\mathbf{p}}$, we have $g\mathbf{yA}\bar{\mathbf{p}}+\xi\boldsymbol{\delta}\bar{\mathbf{p}}=\mathbf{y}(\mathbf{I}-\mathbf{A})\bar{\mathbf{p}}$. From the normalisation conditions $\boldsymbol{\delta}\bar{\mathbf{p}}=1$ and the definition of the dual standard ratio $G=\mathbf{y}(\mathbf{I}-\mathbf{A})\bar{\mathbf{p}}/\mathbf{yA}\bar{\mathbf{p}}$, it follows that $g[\mathbf{y}(\mathbf{I}-\mathbf{A})\bar{\mathbf{p}}/G]+\xi=\mathbf{y}(\mathbf{I}-\mathbf{A})\bar{\mathbf{p}}$

or $$\frac{g}{G}+\frac{\xi}{\mathbf{y}(\mathbf{I}-\mathbf{A})\bar{\mathbf{p}}}=1$$

Calling $\xi_s=\left(\dfrac{\xi}{\mathbf{y}(\mathbf{I}-\mathbf{A})\bar{\mathbf{p}}}\right)$ the share of the net product allocated to consumption or equivalently the level of consumption expressed in terms of standard net product, we have

$$1=\frac{g}{G}+\xi_s \Leftrightarrow g=G(1-\xi_s)$$

This relation is represented graphically as a straight line (Fig. 5.4).

It can easily be shown[13] that the scope of this relation is not limited to

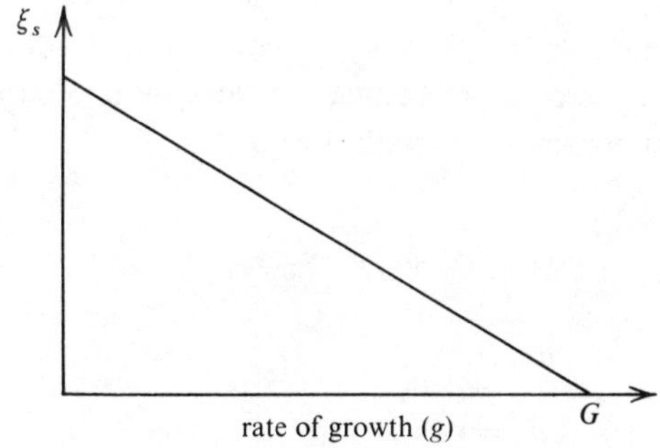

Fig. 5.4

the imaginary standard system but can be extended to the real economic system. The linear relation between consumption and the rate of growth holds in all cases where consumption is expressed in terms of the standard net product. The proof of the existence and uniqueness of the standard commodity can also be extended to the present analysis. In the same manner as we have shown the existence, uniqueness and positiveness of the prices of the basic commodities, the existence, uniqueness and positiveness of the activity levels can similarly be demonstrated in the case of an indecomposable matrix. Finally, extending Sraffa's proof to the remaining analysis we can show that the activity levels in terms of the level of consumption (i.e. the $\hat{\mathbf{y}}$s such that $\xi = 1$ or $\hat{y}_i = y_i/\xi$) are increasing functions of the rate of growth g in the same manner as prices in terms of wage (i.e. the $\hat{\mathbf{p}}$s such that $w = 1$ or $\hat{p}_i = p_i/w$) are increasing functions of the rate of profit. Moreover all activity levels are always strictly positive: all processes are used.

All these results have been established under the assumption that matrix $\mathbf{A}$ is indecomposable, i.e. $R = G$. We must now examine more closely the case where the $\mathbf{A}$ matrix is decomposable.

5.2.4 Antibasic and non-antibasic processes

When the $\mathbf{A}$ matrix is decomposable, not all processes play an equivalent role.

We know (see Chapter 2 and mathematical appendix) that in the case of a decomposable matrix it is possible to obtain the following configuration:

$$\mathbf{A} = \underset{(k-m)\quad\ (m)}{\begin{bmatrix} \mathbf{A}_1^1 & \mathbf{0} \\ \mathbf{A}_2^1 & \mathbf{A}_2^2 \end{bmatrix}} \begin{matrix} (k-m) \\ (m) \end{matrix}$$

Now we can distinguish $\mathbf{y}_1$ and $\mathbf{y}_2$, the vectors of activity levels respectively producing the $(k-m)$ first and the (m) last commodities with $\mathbf{y} = (\mathbf{y}_1, \mathbf{y}_2)$. Similarly, $\boldsymbol{\delta}_1$ and $\boldsymbol{\delta}_2$ are the respective consumption vectors of the $(k-m)$ first and (m) last commodities with $\boldsymbol{\delta} = (\boldsymbol{\delta}_1, \boldsymbol{\delta}_2)$.

$$(1+g)(\mathbf{y}_1, \mathbf{y}_2)\begin{bmatrix} \mathbf{A}_1^1 & 0 \\ \mathbf{A}_2^1 & \mathbf{A}_2^2 \end{bmatrix} + \xi(\boldsymbol{\delta}_1, \boldsymbol{\delta}_2) = (\mathbf{y}_1, \mathbf{y}_2)$$

Thus we have two systems of equations

$$\begin{cases} (1+g)(\mathbf{y}_1\mathbf{A}_1^1 + \mathbf{y}_2\mathbf{A}_2^1) + \xi\boldsymbol{\delta}_1 = \mathbf{y}_1 \\ (1+g)(\mathbf{y}_2\mathbf{A}_2^2) + \xi\boldsymbol{\delta}_2 = \mathbf{y}_2 \end{cases}$$

The *second* system of m equations determines simultaneously the (m) activity levels, the rate of growth g and the level of consumption ξ. Provided we choose an adequate standard, there is one degree of freedom and we only have to fix one of the unknowns to determine the others. In this case, therefore, the rate of growth is determined by the system of m equations for any level ξ of consumption (if the exogenous variable is the level of consumption). The processes forming the m last rows after permutation (i.e. $\mathbf{A}_2$) are then 'basic' processes, as far as the determination of the rate of growth of the activity levels and of the consumption level is concerned, while commodities forming the $(k-m)$ first columns (i.e. $\mathbf{A}^1$) were 'basic' for the determination of the rate of profit, prices and the wage. To avoid any ambiguity, we call the processes forming $\mathbf{A}_2$ '*anti-basic*'. We shall see later that they will not in general correspond to the processes producing luxury goods, that is, non-basic goods.

The *first* of the two systems of equations just identified (of $(k-m)$ equations) gives the activity levels of what we shall call non-antibasic processes as a function of the activity levels of the antibasic processes and of the rate of growth as determined by the antibasic system.

Let us look more closely at the distinction between antibasic and non-antibasic processes to clarify the characteristics of an antibasic process. Sraffa defines a *basic good as a good entering, directly or indirectly, the production of all goods. Similarly, a process will be called antibasic if it uses all goods directly or indirectly.*[14] If this condition is not fulfilled, the process is said to be *non-antibasic*.

Because only those processes using all goods directly or indirectly, i.e. the antibasic processes, can belong to the 'dual' standard system previously defined, it is necessary to give a precise definition of antibasic processes. Careful definition is further necessary because antibasic processes do not necessarily coincide with those producing non-basic goods and, symmetrically, non-antibasic processes do not always correspond to those producing basic goods. There are several cases that may be distinguished.

(1) *The* **A** *matrix is indecomposable: all processes are anti-basic and all goods are basic.*

(2) *The* **A** *matrix is decomposable.*

(2.1) **A** *is totally decomposable*: the economy can be considered as a juxtaposition of independent 'sub-economies' without any link between them. Then there is *no antibasic process and no basic good.*

(2.2) *A is not totally decomposable* ($\mathbf{A}_2^1$ is not entirely formed of zeros) $\mathbf{A}_1^1$ and $\mathbf{A}_2^2$ being indecomposable.

There are four possible configurations for **A**.

(2.2.1) there are m antibasic processes and $(k-m)$ non-antibasic processes. In this case (which has already been considered at the beginning of this section) all non-basic goods are produced by antibasic processes and all basic goods are produced by non-antibasic processes.

$$\begin{array}{|c|c|l}
\hline
\mathbf{A}_1^1 & \mathbf{0} & (k-m) \\
\hline
\mathbf{A}_2^1 & \mathbf{A}_2^2 & (m) \\
\hline
\multicolumn{1}{c}{(k-m)} & \multicolumn{1}{c}{(m)} &
\end{array}$$

(2.2.2)

$$\begin{array}{|c|c|c|l}
\hline
\mathbf{A}_1^1 & \mathbf{0} & \mathbf{0} & k-(m_1+m_2) \\
\hline
\mathbf{A}_2^1 & \mathbf{A}_2^2 & \mathbf{0} & m_2 \\
\hline
\mathbf{A}_3^1 & \mathbf{A}_3^2 & \mathbf{A}_3^3 & m_1 \\
\hline
\multicolumn{1}{c}{k-(m_1+m_2)} & \multicolumn{1}{c}{(m_2)} & \multicolumn{1}{c}{(m_1)} &
\end{array}$$

with $\mathbf{A}_2^1$ and $\mathbf{A}_3^2$ not entirely composed of zeros.[15]

In this case there are: $k-(m_1+m_2)$ basic goods

m_1 antibasic processes

m_1+m_2 non-basic goods

$k-m_1$ non-antibasic processes

(2.2.3)

$$\begin{array}{|c|c|c|l}
\hline
\mathbf{A}_1^1 & \mathbf{0} & \mathbf{0} & k-(m_1+m_2) \\
\hline
\mathbf{A}_2^1 & \mathbf{A}_2^2 & \mathbf{0} & (m_2) \\
\hline
\mathbf{A}_3^1 & \mathbf{0} & \mathbf{A}_3^3 & (m_1) \\
\hline
\multicolumn{1}{c}{k-(m_1+m_2)} & \multicolumn{1}{c}{m_2} & \multicolumn{1}{c}{m_1} &
\end{array}$$

with $\mathbf{A}_2^1$ and $\mathbf{A}_3^1$ not entirely composed of zeros.
In this case there are: $k-(m_1+m_2)$ basic goods

m_1+m_2 non-basic goods

Note that in this configuration there are no antibasic processes.

(2.2.4)

$$\begin{array}{|c|c|c|l} \hline \mathbf{A}_1^1 & \mathbf{0} & \mathbf{0} & k-(m_1+m_2) \\ \hline \mathbf{0} & \mathbf{A}_2^2 & \mathbf{0} & m_2 \\ \hline \mathbf{A}_3^1 & \mathbf{A}_3^2 & \mathbf{A}_3^3 & m_1 \\ \hline k-(m_1+m_2) & m_2 & m_1 & \end{array}$$

with $\mathbf{A}_3^1$ and $\mathbf{A}_3^2$ not entirely composed of zeros.

In this case there are m_1 antibasic processes
$k - m_1$ non-antibasic processes
and no basic good.

We know (Section 3.2) that the necessary condition for a system $(\mathbf{A},\mathbf{I})$ to have at least one basic process is for the rank of matrix $(\mathbf{A}^1,\mathbf{I}^1)$ made up of the $[k-(m_1+m_2)]$ first columns of $\mathbf{A}$ and $\mathbf{I}$ to be greater than $[k-(m_1+m_2)]$.[16] Similarly, we form matrix $\begin{bmatrix}\mathbf{A}_3\\ \mathbf{I}_3\end{bmatrix}$ from the m_1 last rows of $\mathbf{A}$ and $\mathbf{I}$. The necessary condition for the existence of at least one antibasic process can be written as

$$\text{rank}\begin{bmatrix}\mathbf{A}_3\\ \mathbf{I}_3\end{bmatrix} > m_1$$

Once again it must be pointed out that this is only a necessary condition and not in any way a sufficient one.

$$\text{rank}\begin{bmatrix}\mathbf{A}_3\\ \mathbf{I}_3\end{bmatrix} \leq m_1 \Rightarrow \text{there is no antibasic process}$$

$$\text{rank}\begin{bmatrix}\mathbf{A}_3\\ \mathbf{I}_3\end{bmatrix} > m_1 \Rightarrow \text{an antibasic process may exist}$$

The table on page 165 gives the various possible cases for joint-production systems.

Sraffa's 'beans' paradox (cf. Section 2.5, above) can now easily be explained using the preceding notation: when matrix $\mathbf{A}$ is decomposable the rate of profit is determined for a wage level (w) given by $\mathbf{A}_1^1$ (with $0 \leq r \leq R$) while the rate of growth of the means of production is determined for a level of consumption given by $\mathbf{A}_3^3$ (with $0 \leq g \leq G$). If $R > G$ the price of the beans becomes negative passing through infinity as soon as

$r > G$; this means that the rate of profit, uniform by assumption, is determined by the conditions of production of the basic commodities ($\mathbf{A}_1^1$) and the exogenous wage level, but that it is bounded by the maximum rate of growth (and of profit) determined by the sector of non-antibasic processes. (This holds when $\mathbf{A}_2^2$ has a dominant eigenvalue less than those of $\mathbf{A}_1^1$ and $\mathbf{A}_3^3$. In the opposite case there are additional constraints on r and/or g.)

If $R < G$ we have already seen that the price of the non-basic commodities can be found easily but a paradox symmetric to that of the 'beans' occurs for the activity levels; as soon as $g > R$ the non-antibasic activity levels would become negative passing through infinity. The rate of growth of the means of production, uniform by assumption, is thus determined by an exogenous level ξ of consumption simultaneously with the antibasic activity levels ($\mathbf{A}_3^3$), but it is bounded by the maximum rate of profit (and of growth) determined by the sector of basic commodities. When matrix $\mathbf{A}$ is indecomposable, it would be of interest, in the context of development policy, to estimate the nature and importance of the repercussions that the various sectors might have on the economy as a whole. The 'classic' distinction between 'backward linkage' and 'forward linkage' can be related to the distinction we have made between 'basic commodities' and 'antibasic processes'.[17]

Concerning prices and activity levels, the notion of duality used by von Neumann in the case of an indecomposable system must be replaced by that of *quasi-duality*.

In effect we have seen that for a salary level w fixed exogenously, the rate of profit r and basic goods prices $\mathbf{p}_1$ are determined simultaneously in the basic sector ($\mathbf{A}_1^1$,$\mathbf{I}$), then the prices of the other goods follow.

In the same way, for a fixed level of consumption ξ, the rate of growth g and the levels $\mathbf{y}_3$ of antibasic activities are simultaneously determined in the antibasic sector ($\mathbf{A}_3^3$,$\mathbf{I}$), then the levels of the other activities follow. One can say then that the vectors $\mathbf{p}_1$ and $\mathbf{y}_3$ and by extension $\mathbf{p}$ and $\mathbf{y}$, are quasi-duals.

5.3 Commodity prices and activity levels–dual norms

In recent years the 'wage–profit relation', although occasionally under a different label,[18] has been the object of numerous controversies. Indeed, it is only for convenience that we speak of 'the' wage–profit relation, of 'the' wage–profit curve, for the exact shape of the curve depends on the choice of the numeraire, the wage being measured in terms of a 'simple or composite commodity'. In fact, since the wage and the rate of profit

Existence of basic goods and antibasic processes in a system [**A**, **B**]

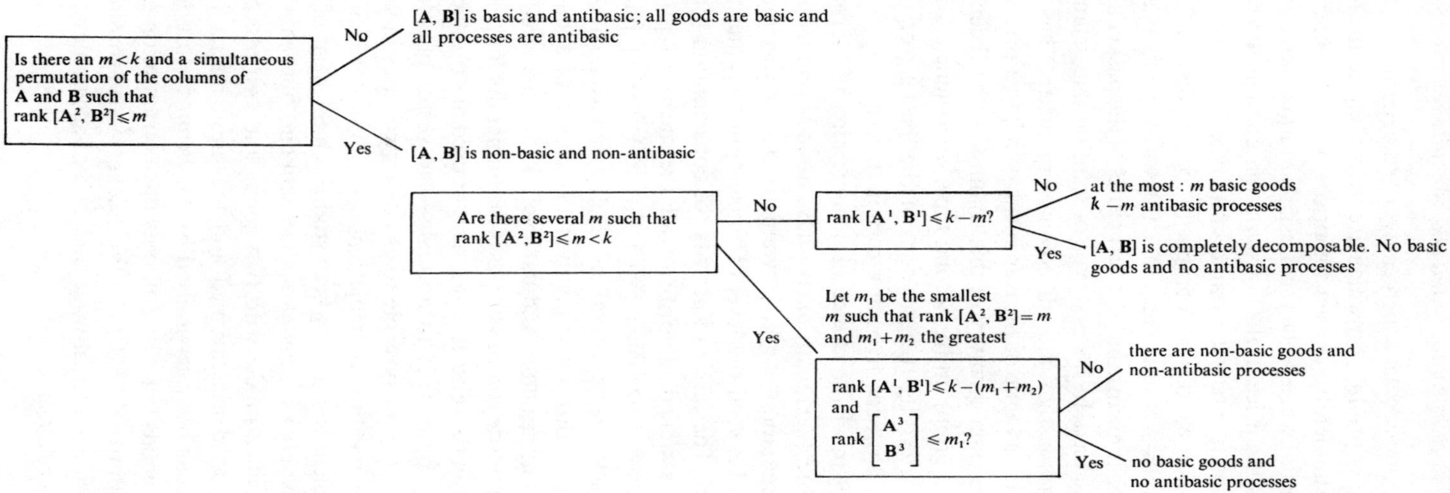

(the latter expressed as a percentage) are determined by the equations of the prices of production which are defined up to the multiplication by scalars, the numeraire chosen for prices is at the same time the unit of measurement of wages. The most usual solutions are of two types: either one chooses the price of the consumption good as the unit (this is particularly adequate when the frame of analysis is a two good, two sector model); or one chooses a 'composite' commodity, a 'basket' of goods, which in Sraffa's case is such that the wage–profit relation is linear.[19] In both cases it means that the 'structure' of the basket and thus its 'level' have been defined. In the first type of solution the assumption that $p_i = 1$ not only means that the ith commodity (wheat) has been chosen as numeraire, i.e. as unit of measurement of relative prices and wages, but also that a certain quantity of this commodity has been specified (a ton, 17 kilos, or a gram). In the second type, we assume additionally that the vector characterising the structure of the 'basket', or of the composite commodity, has been fixed at a certain 'level'.

The problem of the choice of a numeraire, of 'normalisation' is not limited to 'the' (w, r) relation. We have already pointed out the existence of an 'accumulation conflict', symmetric to the distribution conflict, in the relation between the level of consumption (ξ) and the rate of accumulation (g). The levels of activity, of consumption (ξ) and the rate of growth (g), assumed uniform for all the means of production, are all simultaneously determined given the structure of final consumption. But of course the vector of activity levels is defined up to the multiplication by scalars and this again involves the choice of a numeraire and the definition of its structure and its 'level'. The numeraire for activity levels is not a 'composite commodity' as is the numeraire for prices, but a 'virtual commodity' in the sense that it is neither used nor produced by the system and its only purpose is to normalise the vector of activity levels. This being said, it is now possible to examine two cases in which the rate-of-profit–wage and the accumulation–consumption relations are identical.

This problem has already been studied on the basis of rather particular assumptions: Hicks (*Capital and Growth*) and Spaventa[20] have analysed a very simplified model with two goods and two processes, where only the second good is consumed and the input matrix is decomposable. The model has been generalised by M. Bruno[21] to a larger number of production goods but with still only one consumption good and decomposable input matrix. C.C. von Weizsäcker[22] also considered the identity of the rate-of-profit–real-wage and rate-of-accumulation–consumption-per-capita relations.

Let us investigate the general case of an economy with k processes and k commodities. This means that we do not consider the problems of choice or of changes of techniques, which are presumed to be solved.

The analysis is limited to the case of single-product systems, but the results obtained can be extended without any difficulty to production systems using machines, i.e. fixed capital, provided that the Sraffa–von Neumann method (see Chapter 3) is applied to the latter. The problem to be resolved within this general framework is one of 'dual normalisation', i.e. what are the normalisation conditions for the price system on the one hand, and the activity levels on the other, which allow the wage–profit (w,r) and consumption–accumulation (ξ,g) relations to be identical?

5.3.1 Price equations and the rate-of-profit–wage curves

The price equations are written, in matrix notation

$$\mathbf{p} = (1+r)\mathbf{Ap} + w\mathbf{L}$$

where r is the rate of profit assumed to be equal in all branches of production and w is the uniform wage.

We have k equations and $k+2$ unknowns: k prices $p_1,\dots,p_i,\dots,p_k$, the wage, w, and the rate of profit, r.

Since, in fact, we are interested in the *relative* prices of the commodities, we have to choose a *numeraire*, which can be one of the k goods or a composite commodity made up from these k goods. Let the structure of the composite commodity be $\mathbf{u} = (u_1,\dots,u_i,\dots,u_k)$. We are free to choose the 'quantity' of this commodity which we shall use as a standard for prices, that is, we set $\beta\mathbf{up} = 1$, where β is a positive scalar which can be fixed arbitrarily.

For all given $r \in \left[0, \dfrac{1-\alpha}{\alpha}\right]$ (with α the dominant eigenvalue of the input matrix $\mathbf{A}$) we have

$$\mathbf{p} - (1+r)\mathbf{Ap} = w\mathbf{L} \quad \text{or} \quad \mathbf{p}(r) = w(r)[\mathbf{I} - (1+r)\mathbf{A}]^{-1}\mathbf{L}$$

where $[\mathbf{I} - (1+r)\mathbf{A}]^{-1} > \mathbf{0}$. From the numeraire chosen for prices $\mathbf{U} = \beta\mathbf{u}$ we can construct a relation

$$1 = \mathbf{Up}(r) = \beta\mathbf{up}(r) = w(r)\beta\mathbf{u}[\mathbf{I} - (1+r)\mathbf{A}]^{-1}\mathbf{L}$$

$$\text{or} \qquad w_u(r) = \frac{1}{\beta\mathbf{u}[\mathbf{I} - (1+r)\mathbf{A}]^{-1}\mathbf{L}}$$

which shows directly the dependence of $w(r)$ on the numeraire chosen.

Since the scalar β can be arbitrarily fixed we can choose it such that the *wage* of a labour unit *when the whole surplus goes to labour* ($r=0$) is equal to 1, that is,

$$1 = w_U(0) = \frac{1}{\beta\mathbf{u}[\mathbf{I}-\mathbf{A}]^{-1}\mathbf{L}}$$

Thus we have $\beta\mathbf{u}[\mathbf{I}-\mathbf{A}]^{-1}\mathbf{L}=1$ or $\beta = \dfrac{1}{\mathbf{u}[\mathbf{I}-\mathbf{A}]^{-1}\mathbf{L}}$

For every numeraire of prices $\mathbf{U}=\beta\mathbf{u}$ there is an associated rate-of-profit–wage relation

$$r \multimap w_U(r) = \frac{1}{\mathbf{U}[\mathbf{I}-(1+r)\mathbf{A}]^{-1}\mathbf{L}}$$

which is a decreasing function of r in the interval $[0,(1-\alpha)/\alpha[$ —since $[\mathbf{I}-(1+r)\mathbf{A}]^{-1}$ is an increasing function of r in the same interval—and its graphic representation is a curve passing through the points ($r=0$, $w=1$) and ($r=(1-\alpha)/\alpha$, $w=0$).

When matrix $\mathbf{A}$ is *indecomposable* we note that

(a) if $\mathbf{L}$ is an eigenvector on the right of matrix $\mathbf{A}$ corresponding to the dominant eigenvalue α we have

$$[\mathbf{I}-(1+r)\mathbf{A}]^{-1}\mathbf{L} = \frac{\mathbf{L}}{1-\alpha(1+r)} \quad \text{and}$$

$$w_U(r) = \frac{1}{\mathbf{U}[\mathbf{I}-(1+r)\mathbf{A}]^{-1}\mathbf{L}} = \frac{1-\alpha(1+r)}{\mathbf{UL}} = -\frac{\alpha}{\mathbf{UL}}r + \frac{1-\alpha}{\mathbf{UL}}$$

$$= -\frac{\alpha}{1-\alpha}r+1$$

since $\mathbf{UL}=1-\alpha$, that is, for any chosen numeraire $\mathbf{U}$, the curve representing the function $r \multimap w_U(r)$ is a straight line of slope $-\alpha/(1-\alpha)$ intersecting the axis at the point ($r=0$, $w=1$).

(b) if $\mathbf{U}$, the numeraire of prices, is an eigenvector on the left of matrix $\mathbf{A}$ associated with the dominant eigenvalue α, we have

$$\mathbf{U}[\mathbf{I}-(1+r)\mathbf{A}]^{-1} = \frac{\mathbf{U}}{1-\alpha(1+r)} \quad \text{and}$$

$$w_U(r) = \frac{1}{\mathbf{U}[\mathbf{I}-(1+r)\mathbf{A}]^{-1}\mathbf{L}} = \frac{1-\alpha(1+r)}{\mathbf{UL}} = -\frac{\alpha}{1-\alpha}r+1$$

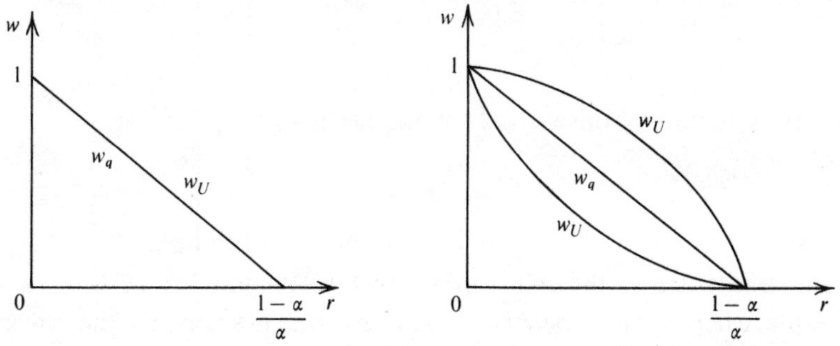

L is an eigenvector of **A**

Fig. 5.5(a)

L is not an eigenvector of **A**

Fig. 5.5(b)

This means that whatever the vector of labour **L**, there exists a numeraire[23] of prices $\mathbf{U} = \mathbf{q}$ such that the curve $r \multimap w_q(r)$ is a straight line of slope $-\alpha(1-\alpha)$ intersecting the axis at the point $(r = 0, w = 1)$.

To sum up, in a model defined by $[\mathbf{A}, \mathbf{I}, \mathbf{L}]$ and the condition $w(0) = 1$, any rate-of-profit–wage curve $r \multimap w_U(\mathrm{r})$ passes through the points $(r = 0, w = 1)$ and $(r = (1-\alpha)/\alpha, w = 0)$. There exists at least one numeraire **q** such that the curve $r \rightarrow w_q(r)$ is a straight line. In what follows we shall call any row vector $\mathbf{U} \geq \mathbf{0}$ such that $\mathbf{U}[\mathbf{I} - \mathbf{A}]^{-1}\mathbf{L} = 1$ the normalisation vector of prices.

5.3.2 Equations of activity levels and accumulation–consumption curves

The k equations of activity levels are written in matrix notation $\mathbf{y} = (1+g)\mathbf{y}\mathbf{A} + \xi\boldsymbol{\delta}$ where g is the rate of growth of means of production, assumed to be equal for all commodities and ξ is the level of consumption.

We have k equations and $k+2$ unknowns given by the k activity levels $y_1, \dots y_i, \dots, y_k$, the level of consumption ξ and the rate of accumulation g.

Let $\mathbf{y}\mathbf{V} = 1$, since we are in fact interested in the relative activity levels of the k processes. This means that we assume the quantity of a commodity **V** produced (or used) by the system to be equal to unity. Then we can assume:

(i) either $\mathbf{y}\mathbf{A}^i = 1$, i.e. we normalise vector **y** by the column vector $\mathbf{A}^i$ representing the use of the ith commodity

(ii) or $\mathbf{y}\mathbf{B}^i = 1$, i.e. we normalise vector **y** by the vector $\mathbf{B}^i$ representing the production of the ith commodity. Note that since we have a single-product system we have $\mathbf{B} = \mathbf{I}$ and $\mathbf{y}\mathbf{B}^i = y_i$, thus $y_i = 1$

(iii) or $\mathbf{y}\mathbf{V} = 1$ where this time **V** represents the production (or use) of a 'virtual' commodity.

If the structure of this virtual commodity is $\mathbf{v} = \begin{bmatrix} v_1 \\ \vdots \\ v_i \\ \vdots \\ v_k \end{bmatrix}$

we are free to choose the unit of measure of this commodity, i.e. we assume $\mathbf{V} = \beta'\mathbf{v}$ where β' is a positive scalar depending solely on the chosen unit for the virtual commodity.

But for all $g \in [0,(1-\alpha)/\alpha[$ we have $\mathbf{y} - (1+g)\mathbf{y}\mathbf{A} = \xi\boldsymbol{\delta}$

or $\mathbf{y}(g) = \xi(g)\boldsymbol{\delta}[\mathbf{I} - (1+g)\mathbf{A}]^{-1}$ where $[\mathbf{I} - (1+g)\mathbf{A}]^{-1} > \mathbf{0}$

The normalisation vector $\mathbf{V} = \beta'\mathbf{v}$ is related to

$$1 = \mathbf{y}(g)\mathbf{V} = \xi(g)\boldsymbol{\delta}[\mathbf{I} - (1+g)\mathbf{A}]^{-1}\beta'\mathbf{v}$$

or

$$\xi_v(g) = \frac{1}{\beta'\boldsymbol{\delta}[\mathbf{I} - (1+g)\mathbf{A}]^{-1}\mathbf{v}}$$

which means that the level of consumption $\xi(g)$ is a function of the chosen normalisation vector. Since the scalar β' can be arbitrarily fixed we can choose it such that the maximum level of consumption associated with $g = 0$ is equal to 1. We have

$$1 = \xi_v(0) = \frac{1}{\boldsymbol{\delta}[\mathbf{I} - \mathbf{A}]^{-1}\mathbf{V}} \quad \text{and thus}$$

$$\boldsymbol{\delta}[\mathbf{I} - \mathbf{A}]^{-1}\mathbf{V} = 1 \quad \text{or} \quad \boldsymbol{\delta}[\mathbf{I} - \mathbf{A}]^{-1}\beta'\mathbf{v} = 1$$

or $$\beta' = \frac{1}{\boldsymbol{\delta}[\mathbf{I} - \mathbf{A}]^{-1}\mathbf{v}}$$

The rate-of-accumulation–level-of-consumption relation

$$g \multimap \xi_v(g) = \frac{1}{\boldsymbol{\delta}[\mathbf{I} - (1+g)\mathbf{A}]^{-1}\mathbf{V}}$$

is a decreasing function of g in the interval $[0,(1-\alpha)/\alpha[$ and the curve representing it intersects the axes at $(g = 0, \xi = 1)$ and $(g = (1-\alpha)/\alpha, \xi = 0)$.

Since the **A** matrix is indecomposable we note in particular that if

(a) $\boldsymbol{\delta}$ is an eigenvector on the left of matrix **A** associated with the dominant eigenvalue α, we have

$$\boldsymbol{\delta}[\mathbf{I}-(1+g)\mathbf{A}]^{-1}=\frac{\boldsymbol{\delta}}{1-\alpha(1+g)} \qquad \text{and}$$

$$\xi_V(g)=\frac{1}{\boldsymbol{\delta}[\mathbf{I}-(1+g)\mathbf{A}]^{-1}\mathbf{V}}=\frac{1-\alpha(1+g)}{\boldsymbol{\delta}\mathbf{V}}=-\frac{\alpha}{\boldsymbol{\delta}\mathbf{V}}g+\frac{1-\alpha}{\boldsymbol{\delta}\mathbf{V}}$$

$$=-\frac{\alpha}{1-\alpha}g+1 \qquad \text{since} \quad \boldsymbol{\delta}\mathbf{V}=1-\alpha$$

i.e. whatever the normalisation vector **V** chosen for the activity levels the curve representing the function $g \to \xi_V(g)$ is a straight line of slope $-\alpha/(1-\alpha)$ intersecting the axis at the point $(g=0, \xi=1)$.

(b) the normalisation vector **V** of the activity levels is the eigenvector on the right of matrix **A** associated with the dominant eigenvalue α, we have

$$[\mathbf{I}-(1+g)\mathbf{A}]^{-1}\mathbf{V}=\frac{\mathbf{V}}{1-\alpha(1+g)} \qquad \text{and}$$

$$\xi_V(g)=\frac{1}{\boldsymbol{\delta}[\mathbf{I}-(1+g)\mathbf{A}]^{-1}\mathbf{V}}=\frac{1-\alpha(1+g)}{\boldsymbol{\delta}\mathbf{V}}=-\frac{\alpha}{1-\alpha}g+1$$

i.e. whatever the vector of final consumption $\boldsymbol{\delta}$ there exists a normalisation vector $\mathbf{V}$[24] of the activity levels $\mathbf{V}=\bar{\mathbf{p}}$ such that the curve $g \multimap \xi_{\bar{\mathbf{p}}}(g)$ is a straight line of slope $-\alpha/(1-\alpha)$ intersecting the axis at the point $(g=0, \xi=1)$.

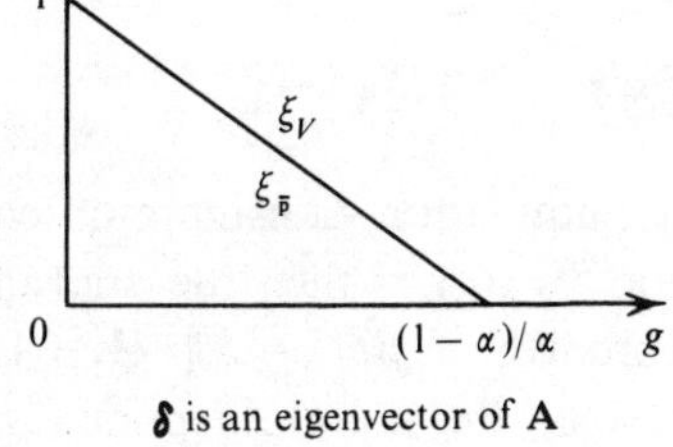

Fig. 5.6(a)

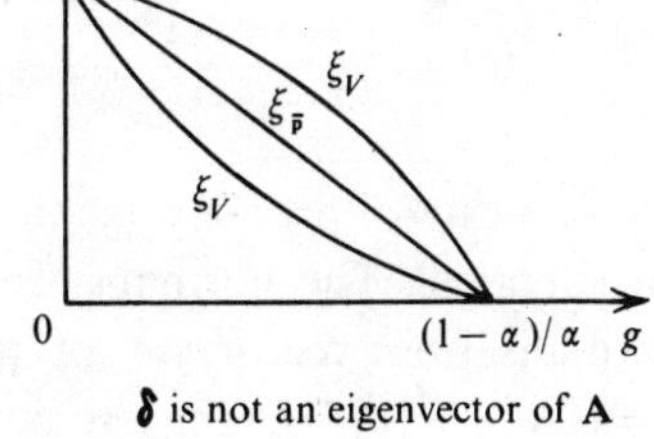

Fig. 5.6(b)

5.3.3 Equivalence of the rate-of-profit–wage curve and the accumulation–consumption curve

In a model $[\mathbf{A}, \mathbf{I}, \mathbf{L}, \boldsymbol{\delta}]$ where we assume $w(0) = 1$ and $\xi(0) = 1$ there is a rate-of-profit–wage curve

$$r \multimap w_U(r) = \frac{1}{\mathbf{U}[\mathbf{I} - (1+r)\mathbf{A}]^{-1}\mathbf{L}}$$

associated to each normalisation vector $\mathbf{U}$ of prices $\mathbf{p}$ and there is an accumulation–consumption curve

$$g \multimap \xi_V(g) = \frac{1}{\boldsymbol{\delta}[\mathbf{I} - (1+g)\mathbf{A}]^{-1}\mathbf{V}}$$

associated to each normalisation vector $\mathbf{V}$ of the activity levels $\mathbf{y}$.

Every curve $r \multimap w_U(r)$ intersects the axes $(0r, 0w)$ at the points $(0, 1)$ and $((1-\alpha)/\alpha, 0)$ and every curve $g \multimap \xi_V(g)$ intersects the axes $(0g, 0\xi)$ at the points $(0, 1)$ and $((1-\alpha)/\alpha, 0)$.

We shall show that a normalisation vector $\mathbf{V}$ of $\mathbf{y}$ such that the curves $r \multimap w_U(r)$ and $g \multimap \xi_V(g)$ are identical can be associated with some normalisation vectors $\mathbf{U}$ of $\mathbf{p}$. $\mathbf{U}$ and $\mathbf{V}$ will then be said to be *dual* normalisation vectors.

PARTICULAR DUAL NORMALISATION VECTORS

(a) If we consider the two expressions

$$w_U(r) = \frac{1}{\mathbf{U}[\mathbf{I} - (1+r)\mathbf{A}]^{-1}\mathbf{L}} \quad \text{and} \quad \xi_V(g) = \frac{1}{\boldsymbol{\delta}[\mathbf{I} - (1+g)\mathbf{A}]^{-1}\mathbf{V}}$$

we note that if we choose the normalisation vectors[25] $\mathbf{U} = \beta\boldsymbol{\delta}$ and $\mathbf{V} = \beta\mathbf{L}$ where β is a positive scalar, we have

$$w_U(r) = \frac{1}{\beta\boldsymbol{\delta}[\mathbf{I} - (1+r)\mathbf{A}]^{-1}\mathbf{L}} \quad \text{and}$$

$$\xi_V(g) = \frac{1}{\boldsymbol{\delta}[\mathbf{I} - (1+g)\mathbf{A}]^{-1}\beta\mathbf{L}} = \frac{1}{\beta\boldsymbol{\delta}[\mathbf{I} - (1+g)\mathbf{A}]^{-1}\mathbf{L}}$$

and the rate-of-profit–wage and the accumulation–consumption curves are identical. The normalisation vector $\beta\mathbf{L}$ of $\mathbf{y}$ is then the dual of the normalisation vector $\beta\boldsymbol{\delta}$ of $\mathbf{p}$.[26] Moreover if $\beta\boldsymbol{\delta}[\mathbf{I} - \mathbf{A}]^{-1}\mathbf{L} = 1$, i.e. $\beta = (1/\boldsymbol{\delta}[\mathbf{I} - \mathbf{A}]^{-1}\mathbf{L})$ the two curves intersect the axis at the point $(0, 1)$.

(b) Let $\mathbf{q}$ be the eigenvector on the left of $\mathbf{A}$ associated with the dominant eigenvalue α such that $\mathbf{q}[\mathbf{I}-\mathbf{A}]^{-1}\mathbf{L}=1$ or $\mathbf{qL}=1-\alpha$ and let $\bar{\mathbf{p}}$ be the eigenvector on the right of $\mathbf{A}$ corresponding to α such that $\boldsymbol{\delta}[\mathbf{I}-\mathbf{A}]^{-1}\bar{\mathbf{p}}=1$ or $\boldsymbol{\delta}\bar{\mathbf{p}}=1-\alpha$. If we choose the normalisation vectors $\mathbf{U}=\mathbf{q}$ and $\mathbf{V}=\bar{\mathbf{p}}$ we have

$$w_U(r)=\frac{1}{\mathbf{q}[\mathbf{I}-(1+r)\mathbf{A}]^{-1}\mathbf{L}}=\frac{1-\alpha(1+r)}{\mathbf{qL}}=-\frac{\alpha}{1-\alpha}r+1 \quad \text{since}$$

$$\mathbf{qL}=1-\alpha$$

and

$$\xi_V(g)=\frac{1}{\boldsymbol{\delta}[\mathbf{I}-(1+g)\mathbf{A}]^{-1}\bar{\mathbf{p}}}=\frac{1-\alpha(1+g)}{\boldsymbol{\delta}\bar{\mathbf{p}}}=-\frac{\alpha}{1-\alpha}g+1 \qquad \text{since}$$

$$\boldsymbol{\delta}\bar{\mathbf{p}}=1.$$

The rate-of-profit–wage curve and the accumulation–consumption curve are therefore identical straight lines of slope $-\alpha/(1-\alpha)$ intersecting the axis at the point $(0,1)$ and the normalisation vector $\bar{\mathbf{p}}$ of $\mathbf{y}$ is dual of the normalisation vector $\mathbf{q}$ of $\mathbf{p}$.[27]

These two dual normalisation vectors always exist in the case of a decomposable matrix; the normalisation vectors ensure the linearity (and identity) of the curves (w,r) and (ξ,g) since they are the eigenvectors on the left and on the right associated with the dominant eigenvalue of matrix $\mathbf{A}$. Moreover, we note that the normalisation vector $\mathbf{q}_1$ associated with the strictly positive eigenvector on the left of matrix $\mathbf{A}_1^1$ gives a linear relation between w and r of slope $-(1/R)$ while the 'quasi-dual' normalisation vector $\bar{\mathbf{p}}_3$, strictly positive eigenvector on the right of $\mathbf{A}_3^3$ shows a linear relation between ξ and g of slope $-(1/G)$.

5.4 Interdependence of the 'trade offs'

In the preceding sections we have identified a double conflict, the first concerning the distribution of national income (schematically represented by the relation (w,r)), the second concerning the use of the national product (represented by the relation (ξ,g)). Thus, there are two sets of choices, two types of 'trade off':

(i) the trade off between w and r, with w or r exogenously determined

(ii) the trade off between ξ and g, with ξ or g exogenously determined.

The problem is now to see if these two sets of choices can be made independently. We shall show that this is not possible and that the two are interdependent. As soon as we come (at last!) to the question of markets and of demand, the fundamental link between the rate of profit and rate of growth, given by the capitalists' propensity to save, becomes evident.

5.4.1 First case: workers consume the whole of their wages

To maintain a steady state it is not enough for goods to be produced, they still have to be sold in markets. We shall show that the same conditions apply to both the sale of capital equipment and consumption goods. Let us consider a system with circulating capital. The analysis can be easily extended to the case of fixed capital, with machines being used during several periods, by using the Sraffa–von Neumann procedure previously examined (see Section 3.3).

Assuming the rate of growth g of all means of production to be uniform, the quantity of *capital equipment*, or more generally of *means of production*, produced during each period can be written very simply as ($g\mathbf{yA}$). This means that ($g\mathbf{yAp}$) represents the value of the new means of production, or of the net investment in the system in the absence of technical progress or change in the methods of production.

The demand for new means of production can only come from the capitalists, since, by assumption, workers only consume consumption goods, and also by assumption, they use the whole of their incomes for this purpose. Now, since we have assumed that the aggregate of the means of production earn profits at a uniform rate r, the total profits, π, received by capitalists, can be expressed as $\pi = r\mathbf{yAp}$.

Let us call s_c the capitalists' average propensity to save from their profits. When $s_c < 1$ part of these, i.e. $s_c\pi$, is saved, and the rest, i.e. $(1 - s_c)\pi$, is used to buy consumption goods.

Thus, in order for the new means of production produced to be sold on the market the equality between supply and demand must be satisfied. This can be written as (note that $\mathbf{p}$ is determined as a price of production):

$$g(\mathbf{yAp}) = s_c\pi = s_c r(\mathbf{yAp})$$

or since ($\mathbf{yAp}$) is a non zero scalar

$$g = s_c r \quad \text{or} \quad r = \frac{g}{s_c} \quad \text{or} \quad g - rs_c = 0$$

The three formulations are equivalent:

(i) in the first one, $g = s_c r$, the rate of growth appears as dependent variable; the rate of growth of the means of production is equal to the product of the rate of profit, the independent variable, and the capitalists' propensity to save out of their profits.

(ii) in the second one, $r = g/s_c$, is the formulation favoured by the neo-Cambridge school; the rate of profit is equal to the ratio of the rate of growth of the means of production, the independent variable, to the capitalists' propensity to save out of their profits.

(iii) in the third formulation $g - rs_c = 0$, an implicit relation between r and g appears through the intermediary of s_c. This is the most adequate formulation for our analysis. It underlines the interdependence of the two sets of choices. In fact, this relation shows that there is only one degree of freedom overall, the exogenous determination of r or g (by choice) implying the determination of g or r and ξ and w being determined through the implicit relations (ξ, g) and (w, r).

It can now easily be shown that the same relation must be satisfied to ensure the sale of *consumption goods.*

The quantity of consumption goods produced is determined by the quantity equations.

From $\mathbf{y} = (1 + g)\mathbf{yA} + \xi\boldsymbol{\delta}$

we have $\xi\boldsymbol{\delta} = \mathbf{y}(\mathbf{I} - \mathbf{A}) - g\mathbf{yA}$

and thus the value of the consumption goods produced $\xi\boldsymbol{\delta}\mathbf{p} = \mathbf{y}(\mathbf{I} - \mathbf{A})\mathbf{p} - g(\mathbf{yAp})$.

As for the demand for consumption goods, it comes from two sources:

– from the workers who, by assumption, devote the whole of their wages to consumption, i.e. $(\mathbf{yL})w$

– from the capitalists who devote to consumption a part $(1 - s_c)$ of their profits, i.e. $(1 - s_c)\pi = (1 - s_c)r(\mathbf{yAp})$.

Now from the price equations $\mathbf{p} = (1 + r)\mathbf{Ap} + \mathbf{L}w$ we get

$$\mathbf{yp} = \mathbf{yAp} + r(\mathbf{yAp}) + \mathbf{yL}w$$

or $$\mathbf{y}(\mathbf{I} - \mathbf{A})\mathbf{p} = r(\mathbf{yAp}) + (\mathbf{yL})w$$

and the demand for consumption goods can be written

$$\begin{aligned}(1 - s_c)r(\mathbf{yAp}) + (\mathbf{yL})w &= r(\mathbf{yAp}) - s_c(\mathbf{yAp}) + (\mathbf{yL})w \\ &= \mathbf{y}(\mathbf{I} - \mathbf{A})\mathbf{p} - s_c r(\mathbf{yAp})\end{aligned}$$

using the relation obtained from the price equations.

Thus the condition of equilibrium on the consumption goods market can be written:

$$\mathbf{y}[\mathbf{I} - \mathbf{A}]\mathbf{p} - g(\mathbf{yAp}) = \mathbf{y}(\mathbf{I} - \mathbf{A})\mathbf{p} - s_c r(\mathbf{yAp}) \qquad \text{or}$$

$$s_c r(\mathbf{yAp}) = g(\mathbf{yAp})$$

and we have

$$g = rs_c \quad \text{or} \quad r = \frac{g}{s_c} \quad \text{or} \quad g - rs_c = 0$$

This fundamental relation between r and g requires some preliminary remarks. Under the form $r = g/s_c$ it throws some light on Kalecki's paradox that says that the 'workers spend what they get, and the capitalists get what they spend'. We can see that for a given g, when s_c is lower, r is higher ($r \leq R$). But we must specify the restrictive character of the assumption behind this paradox, namely, that g is an independent variable and that the form of the relation is always $r = \phi(g)$ and never $g = \psi(r)$. If we admit this latter form ($g = s_c r$) we can conclude that for a given r, g is a direct function of the propensity to save of the capitalists (with $g \leq G$).

In the particular case where capitalists save their entire profits ($s_c = 1$) we have $r = g$, the rate of growth of the means of production is equal to the rate of profit, as in von Neumann's model. Note that this model is particular in two respects; first because it assumes that capitalists save the whole of their profits (hence $r = g$) and, second, because it rests on the assumption that the rate of growth is maximum ($g = G$) and the rate of profit is maximum ($r = R$), hence $R = G$ if the system $[\mathbf{A}, \mathbf{B}]$ is indecomposable. It is, indeed, not very realistic to assume that the wage and the level of consumption are zero (as $r = R$ and $g = G$ imply). We can refer to matrix $\mathbf{A}^*$ which, as we know, includes the basket of goods necessary to the subsistence of workers. The wage w can then be decomposed into two parts, the first one (w_0) is fixed and 'advanced' by capitalists, the second one (w') is variable and paid *post factum* from the surplus. Thus $w = w_0 + w'$. In the same way, we can distinguish two parts for the level of consumption ξ, one ξ_0 being the irreducible consumption necessary for the reproduction of labour power, the other ξ' which is variable and a charge on the surplus. Thus the dominant eigenvalue of matrix $\mathbf{A}^*$ determines the maximum rate of growth $G^* < G$ and the maximum rate of profit $R^* < R$ for the level of consumption and wage corresponding, not to zero, but to the fixed levels, i.e. $w = w_0$ with $w' = 0$ and $\xi = \xi_0$ with $\xi' = 0$.

Finally, we notice that these relations allow us to analyse the problem examined by Marx under the title of 'realisation of the surplus value'. For profit to appear, workers must be exploited; but as Marx well knew this is a necessary but not sufficient condition. It is necessary, moreover, that commodities should be sold, or else the workers would have been exploited in vain, for the capitalists could not realise the surplus-value due to lack of demand.

5.4.2 Second case: workers save part of their wages

The previous case may seem meaningless; indeed, there is no reason to believe *a priori* that in the framework of contemporary capitalist systems the saving of the workers should necessarily be zero. We shall therefore generalise the preceding analysis using the Kaldor–Pasinetti theorem[28] which allows the determination of a simple link between the rate of profit and the rate of growth without the propensity to save of the workers playing any role *in this regard*.

Let us recall the various assumptions. The first one is related to the behaviour of workers: they are supposed to save, during their working life, a certain part of their income. Thus there is a *demand for financial assets* by the active workers who, in view of their retirement, save part of their income. It does not matter if this demand for financial assets is direct or indirect, for example, passing through the intermediary of pensions funds or insurance companies. We assume that as a consequence of the increase of the population and of the standard of living the saving of the active workers exceeds the dis-saving of the retired workers by an amount which can be expressed as a fraction, s_w, $(0 \leq s_w < 1)$ of total wages ($w\mathbf{yL}$). Thus the net saving of the workers $s_w(w\mathbf{yL})$, assumed to be net of investment in housing, appears as a net demand for securities.

As for the *supply of securities*, it comes from two sources.

First there is a *supply of new assets* coming from new issues of securities (to fund investment) by corporations. We assume, on one hand, that corporations keep a fraction, s_c, of their profits, π, and issue new securities equal to a fraction, $i (0 \leq i \leq 1)$, of their investment expenditures $g(\mathbf{yAp})$, on the other. To this component of the supply of securities we must add a second component, made up of second-hand securities, which is dependent on shareholders' behaviour. We shall assume that all current income received in the form of dividends is spent, i.e. $(1 - s_c)\pi$, as well as a fraction, c, of capital gains, E.

Capital gains, E, represent the variations in the market values of shares. They can be estimated as follows. The market value of corporations is given by the product of the number of outstanding shares, N, by their prices, ω, e.g. ωN. Given the value of capital goods ($\mathbf{yAp}$) we can define the ratio of the market value of securities to the value of capital goods by

$$V = \frac{\omega N}{\mathbf{yAp}} = \text{a constant, hence } V(\mathbf{yAp}) = \omega N$$

By differentiating the preceding expression, we have

$$V \frac{d}{dt}(\mathbf{yAp}) = \omega \frac{dN}{dt} + N \frac{d\omega}{dt}$$

Since we have

$$\frac{d}{dt}(\mathbf{yAp}) = g\mathbf{yAp} \text{ (growth of the means of production at a rate } g)$$

$$\omega\frac{d(N)}{dt} = ig\mathbf{yAp} \text{ (the issue of new securities is a fraction } i \text{ of the growth of the means of production),}$$

$$N\frac{d\omega}{dt} = E \text{(by definition),}$$

then

$$Vg(\mathbf{yAp}) = ig(\mathbf{yAp}) + E$$

or $$E = (V - i)g(\mathbf{yAp})$$

The *equilibrium in the securities market* will have to be such that the net demand for securities (by wage-earners) is equal to the supply composed of the new issues by the firms and of offers for sale by shareholders wishing to spend in excess of their current income. Thus

$$s_w(w\mathbf{yL}) = ig(\mathbf{yAp}) + cE$$

From the expression derived above for E we can write

$$s_w(w\mathbf{yL}) - c(V - i)g(\mathbf{yAp}) = ig(\mathbf{yAp}) \tag{a}$$

There will be *equilibrium in the goods market* if the supply of the new means of production in value terms (i.e. $g(\mathbf{yAp})$ is equal to the demand for them composed of the savings by wage-earners ($s_w(w\mathbf{yL})$) plus saving by corporations ($s_c r(\mathbf{yAp})$) less any consumption by shareholders from capital gains cE):

$$s_w(w\mathbf{yL}) - c(V - i)g\mathbf{yAp} + s_c r(\mathbf{yAp}) = g(\mathbf{yAp}) \tag{b}$$

Considering (a) and (b) together we have

$$g = r\frac{s_c}{1-i} \quad \text{or} \quad r = g\frac{1-i}{s_c} \quad \text{or} \quad g - r\frac{s_c}{1-i} = 0$$

(If $i = 0$ these formulations reduce to those of Section 5.4.1.)

and

$$V = \frac{1}{c}\left\{s_w\frac{\mathbf{y[I - A]p}}{g(\mathbf{yAp})} - \frac{s_w}{s_c}(1 - i) - i(1 - c)\right\}$$

The first set of equivalences demonstrates a *simple relation between the rate of profit and the rate of growth* based on the decisions of the corporations concerning the retention of profits ($0 \leq s_c \leq 1$) and the financing of investment ($0 \leq i \leq 1$) without any influence from the propensity to save of wage-earners. The exogenous determination of r or g implies the determination of the remaining variable which again demonstrates the interdependence of the 'trade offs'.

The more complex expression for V requires some further explanation. From the formulation that has been presented here it could be deduced that, given the propensities to consume (s_w, s_c, c) and the financing policy of the corporations, there is a particular value of V *for any given* g such that household savings are sufficient to purchase the corporations' new issues of securities (see equation (a)). Household savings are here defined as the savings out of wages (assumed positive) less any consumption out of capital gains by shareholders. Some specific examples may help to clarify this point.

In the absence of new issues ($i = 0$) the securities market will establish a price level at which the purchase of securities by wage-earners (savings) will equal the sale of titles by the shareholders (dis-savings) and net savings by households will be zero.

The issue of new securities will normally reduce prices, i.e. E. This will reduce the sale of securities and thus the amount of dis-saving until net savings are again equal to the amount of the new issues. That V plays an equilibrating role in this process can be more clearly seen by considering the very special case where corporations are net buyers of securities from the households ($i < 0$). In this case V would rise until the net dis-savings of the household sector were just equal to the sale of securities to the corporations.

However, it must be remembered that *if the relation between the rate of profit and the rate of growth is indeed independent of the wage-earners' saving propensity it is not necessarily true that the consumption–savings behaviour of wage-earners has no influence on the rate of profit or the rate of growth.* The expression given above for V shows clearly that V depends on s_w and that an implicit relation exists between either V and g or V and r, depending on whether r or g is given exogenously. In fact, there are two independent implicit relations between the three variables V, g and r, with the direct influence of s_w visible in the implicit relation between V and g (or V and r).

5.4.3 The influence of the behaviour of the owners of natural resources

The preceding analysis can be generalised to cover the use of the rents received by the owners of land and natural resources. Let us suppose that there is only one category of scarce 'land'. The quantity of land in use is then $\mathbf{yT}$ where $\mathbf{T} = \begin{bmatrix} T_1 \\ \vdots \\ T_k \end{bmatrix}$ and the total of rents received by landowners will be $\rho\mathbf{yT}$, with a part $s_p(\rho\mathbf{yT})$ saved. The saving propensity of landowners is $s_p(0 \leq s_p \leq 1)$.

It is then simple to introduce $s_p(\rho\mathbf{yT})$ into the framework used above as an additional component of the demand for securities. The new *equilibrium conditions in the securities market and the goods market* would then be:

(a′) $s_w(w\mathbf{yL}) + s_p(\rho\mathbf{yT}) - c(V' - i)g(\mathbf{yAp}) = ig(\mathbf{yAp})$

(b′) $s_w(w\mathbf{yL}) + s_p(\rho\mathbf{yT}) - c(V' - i)g(\mathbf{yAp}) + s_c r(\mathbf{yAp}) = g(\mathbf{yAp})$

From which

$$ig(\mathbf{yAp}) + s_c r(\mathbf{yAp}) = g(\mathbf{yAp})$$

Simplifying ($\mathbf{yAp}$ is a non-zero scalar)

$$g = r\frac{s_c}{1-i} \quad \text{or} \quad r = g\frac{1-i}{s_c} \quad \text{or} \quad g - r\frac{s_c}{1-i} = 0$$

The conclusion is clear: *the relation between the rate of profit and the rate of growth is independent of the consumption behaviour of the owners of natural resources* just as it was independent of the wage-earners' propensity to save.

But the expenditure decisions of these groups will not be without influence on the price of securities which will be expressed through the influence of the ratio of the market value of securities and the book-value of the corporations. If we call this ratio V' when landowners save and are thus net demanders of securities we can deduce it from the definition of V in the following way:

$$V' = V + \frac{s_p}{c}\frac{\rho\mathbf{yT}}{g(\mathbf{yAp})} \rightarrow V' = V \quad \text{if} \quad \rho = 0$$

or since $\rho = rp_T$ by definition (see Section 3.3) (p_T is the price of land)

$$\frac{\rho\mathbf{yT}}{g(\mathbf{yAp})} = \frac{r\mathbf{yT}p_T}{g(\mathbf{yAp})} = \frac{(1-i)\mathbf{yT}p_T}{s_c\mathbf{yAp}}$$

Thus $V' = V + \dfrac{s_p(1-i)}{cs_c}\dfrac{\mathbf{yT}p_T}{\mathbf{yAp}}$

Here again it should be noted that if the relation (r, g) is independent of the behaviour of landowners (and of wage-earners), it cannot be deduced that the rate of profit and the rate of growth are independent of the behaviour of these groups.

5.5 Changes of technique and conflicts of objectives

Up to this point we have assumed that there was only one method of production for each commodity in a system of single-product industries. We are now going to consider the more realistic assumption that there is the possibility of choosing between two alternative methods of production for at least one of the commodities.

Sraffa has shown (P.S. Part III) that the methods of production chosen could vary with the distribution of income. From this point of view the choice of the method of production is determined by factors related to the analysis of the distribution of national income (and of prices). But it is also possible to show that the superior methods of production can be determined by factors associated with the 'dual' analysis of the levels of activity (or equivalently with the quantity analysis in the absence of joint production). Changes in the use of the national output and in the 'trade off' between consumption and the rate of growth can also be viewed as determinants of the choice of production methods. The presentation of the different types of criteria for the choice of methods of production allows us to see that they do not all lead to the same result (except in particular cases). This highlights the risks involved in different objectives of analysis. The nature and the degree of these risks require further discussion.

By way of introduction recall that a 'technique' is the combination of methods of production used at a given point in time. In the preceding analyses there was only a single 'technique' (composed of k methods to produce the k commodities). From now on the existence of several techniques will be considered. Two techniques are different when there is one commodity produced by different method of production in each technique; while the $k-1$ other methods may be identical.

5.5.1 The choice of the technique of production

(*A*) *USE OF THE WAGE–PROFIT RELATION*

It is thus assumed that there are several available techniques of production in the economy, each producing the same consumption good, or the same consumption basket, and therefore capable of fulfilling the same needs even though they use different methods of production.

Up to this point it has been implicitly supposed that the economy only had one available technique (i.e. if there are k commodities, there must be at least k methods of production in order to determine the k prices) represented by its technology matrix and a vector of direct labour. From now on we will assume that the economy has several available techniques 1, 2, 3, 4 each characterised by a series of specific parameters. There will then be several wage–profit curves, the wage measured in terms of the same numeraire **U** for each of them.

The problem is then to determine which of the available techniques will be chosen when it is recognised that not all the available techniques need to be employed simultaneously. Here again there is an interaction between distribution and technology, with the technique chosen varying with the ruling wage or rate of profit. The technique chosen will differ for different combinations of the wage and the rate of profit (i.e. 'switching').

It should be noted that this refers to a change in the choice of the technique to be used, from all the existing techniques which are assumed given and known from the start (i.e. it is not a change of techniques of production resulting from innovation and technical progress but simply the choice of a different technique among those already in existence).

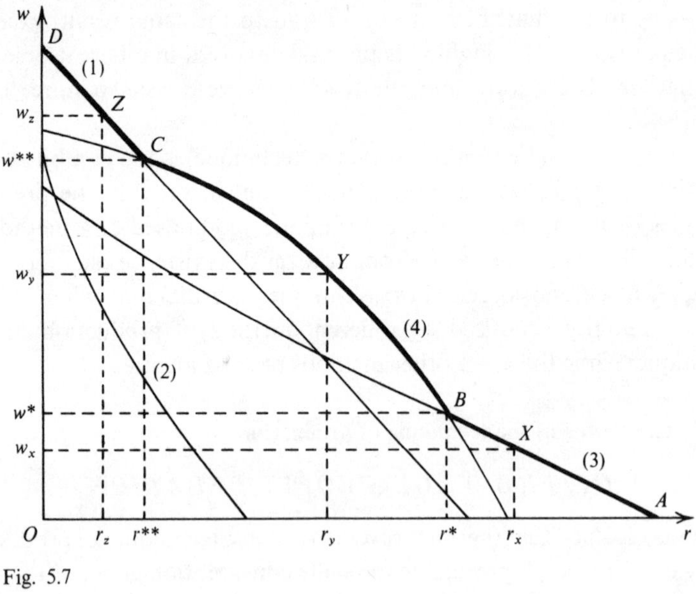

Fig. 5.7

To continue our examination of the choice of technique in the simplest case we will suppose

(a) there are 4 techniques, 1, 2, 3, 4 that satisfy the consumption requirements of the economy. The wage–profit curves for these techniques are given in Fig. 5.7.

(b) the four techniques are equally available in three different countries X, Y, Z. The wage is considered given at a very low level in X, an intermediate level in Y, and at a very high level in Z.

It is clear that technique (2) will not be used in any of the three economies for, whatever the wage rate, it is always possible to obtain a higher rate of profit by using one of the other techniques. The actual choice is thus between 1, 3, and 4, not 1, 2, 3 and 4. In fact, the technique chosen in each country will be different.

In country X where the wage rate is low (say at $w_X < w^*$) technique (3) would be chosen because techniques 1 and 4, and obviously 2, although possible choices, all imply a lower rate of profit.

In country Z where the wage rate is high (say $w_Z > w^{**}$) technique (1) will be chosen because it yields the highest rate of profit for that wage, indeed, there is no other technique which could be used at such high wage rates.

In country Y with its intermediate wage rate ($w^{**} > w_Y > w^*$) technique (4) is chosen on the same grounds.

The wage–profit relation is no longer represented by a continuous curve, but rather by an envelope of the wage–profit curves associated with each technique, i.e. by the heavy discontinuous line ABCD in the diagram. Points B and C are called the points of change in technique (switch points). They represent situations in which distribution is such that producers in the same economy would be indifferent between two techniques (3 and 4 for B, 1 and 3 for C).

It should be stressed that this analysis does not refer to actual changes in technique. Given the wage, w_Z, in country Z technique (1) would be chosen and would produce a rate of profit, r_Z, while in country Y with wage, w_Y, technique (4) would be used to earn a rate of profit, r_Y. It would not be true to deduce from this that if country Z reduced its wage rate (from w_Z to w_Y) a rise in the rate of profit (from r_Z to r_Y) would result.

It is an analysis of comparison of steady state conditions which should not be confused with the analysis of changes which would require concepts and tools of a different kind.

Let us now consider a different configuration of wage–profit curves. To simplify the analysis we will suppose that there are only two available

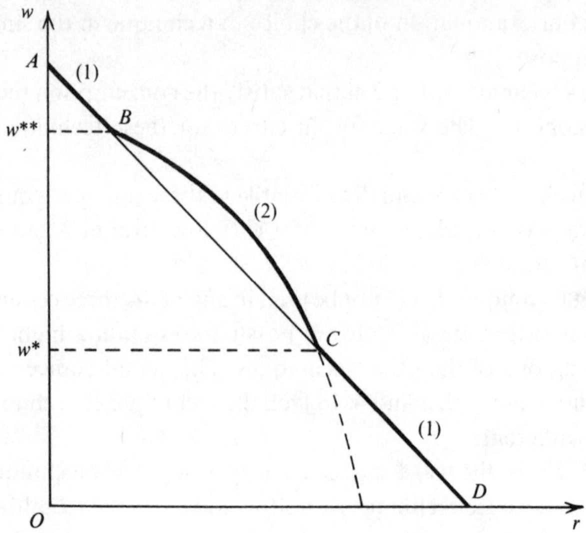

Fig. 5.8

techniques, (1) and (2). The wage–profit curve for (1) is linear (because $\mathbf{U} = \mathbf{q}(\mathbf{I} - \mathbf{A})$), while (2) is concave to the origin (it could just as easily be convex). The important point is that now there are two points of intersection between the two curves, which did not occur in the preceding figure where no two curves intersected more than once. (The argument is analogous for the case of convexity.)

In this case there is a 'reswitching of technique', for one technique ((1) in the figure used here) is the most profitable for two different ranges of profit rates. The wage–profit relation is still represented by the curve ABCD in which the sections AB and CD both refer to technique (1) (in difference to the previous curve where each technique composed only one segment of the envelope). This implies that the same technique will be most profitable and will thus be chosen in both low wage ($w < w^*$) and in high wage ($w > w^{**}$) countries.

This evidently contradicts the generally accepted idea that the technique of production chosen when the wage rate is low will be very different from that chosen when wages are high. It should be pointed out, however, that there is no reason to consider that this case should be of more or less frequent occurrence than the preceding case which was presented first simply for reasons of ease of exposition.

There is however one (very special) case where 'reswitching' is absolutely excluded. This is when the wage–profit curves for all the available techniques are linear. Two straight lines cannot, in fact, intersect more than

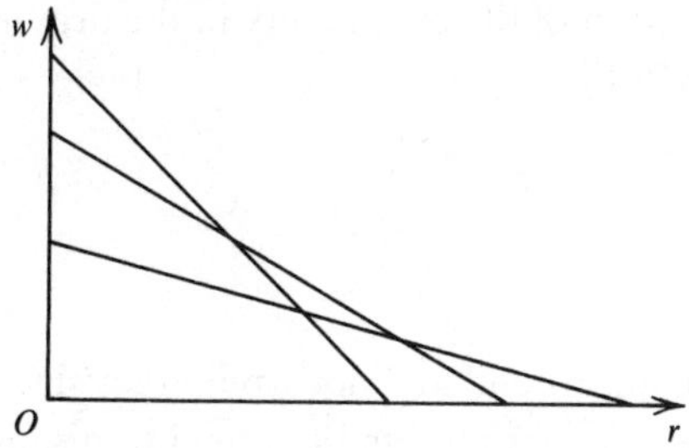

Fig. 5.9

once and in this case the reswitching is evidently impossible. But this can only represent a very special case.

The real paradox is not to be found in 'reswitching' but in admitting only the special case which excludes reswitching *a priori.*

(*B*) *DIFFERENTIAL QUASI-RENTS*

It is clear that the preceding discussion in terms of the $(w - r)$ curves is not meant to be a realistic representation of economic decision making but is simply an analytical construction. Since the economic agents do not, and cannot, know the wage–profit curves the question is to find out how and why switching of techniques appears necessary and desirable to them.

The discussion of this problem will be limited to some brief comments. Technical progress is assumed to be exogenous (i.e. the problem of the generation of technical progress is not discussed) and the problem of the actual introduction of the new technique will not be treated here.

The point that we would like to emphasise is that the appearance of a superior technique leads to temporary 'quasi-rents' for those who introduce it, which lead economic agents to adopt it.

Let $(\mathbf{A},\mathbf{I},\mathbf{L})$ be the characteristics of the existing technique with $\mathbf{U}$ the numeraire. Then

$$\begin{cases} \mathbf{p} = (1 + r)\mathbf{A}\mathbf{p} + w\mathbf{L} \\ \mathbf{U}\mathbf{p} = 1 \end{cases}$$

Suppose that a technical advance appears which improves production methods for the *i*th commodity, but that the improvement is introduced in only one firm such that the commodity is produced in the economy by two different methods at the same time. The price, p_i, determined by the initial method of production $(\mathbf{a}_i, l_i)$ thus allows a 'quasi-rent' or a superprofit to be earned on the production of the commodity in the firm using the superior method $(\tilde{\mathbf{a}}_i, \tilde{l}_i)$. Thus both

$$p_i = (1+r)\mathbf{a}_i\mathbf{p} + wl_i$$
$$p_i = (1+r)\tilde{\mathbf{a}}_i\mathbf{p} + w\tilde{l}_i + \rho$$

hold simultaneously.

The amount ρ is considered a 'quasi-rent' and not a pure rent since the superiority of the new technique is temporary and destined to disappear (except for cases of monopoly, patents, barriers to entry, etc.) as the new technique is introduced by other producers. When this process is complete and all the output of commodity i is produced with the new method there will no longer be two techniques in use and the 'quasi-rent' will disappear. For a given level of wages, w, the prices of production and the uniform rate of profit will then be determined simultaneously by the new production conditions characterised by the change in the ith line. Obviously the rate of profit will not be affected unless the change in the conditions of production has occurred in the basic sector.

The preceding analysis can be linked to a number of concepts treated by Marx. We know that, given the characteristics of the initial technique $(\mathbf{A}, \mathbf{I}, \mathbf{L})$ the value system can be written

$$\mathbf{\Lambda} = \mathbf{A\Lambda} + \mathbf{L} = \mathbf{A\Lambda} + \mathbf{L}(1+e)\mathbf{d\Lambda}$$

Suppose, as above, that two methods of production exist for the production of the ith commodity whose value λ_i is determined by the least productive method:

$$\lambda_i = \mathbf{a}_i\mathbf{\Lambda} + l_i = \mathbf{a}_i\mathbf{\Lambda} + l_i\mathbf{d\Lambda} + el_i\mathbf{d\Lambda}$$

In the case of simple commodity production where commodities exchange at their values there is an 'extra' surplus-value ρ_λ which accrues to the superior method of production defined as

$$\lambda_i = \tilde{\mathbf{a}}_i\mathbf{\Lambda} + \tilde{l}_i + \rho_\lambda = \tilde{\mathbf{a}}_i\mathbf{\Lambda} + \tilde{l}_i\mathbf{d\Lambda} + e\tilde{l}_i\mathbf{d\Lambda} + \rho_\lambda$$

and $\rho_\lambda = (\mathbf{a}_i - \hat{\mathbf{a}}_i)\mathbf{\Lambda} + l_i - \tilde{l}_i$

This concept of 'extra' surplus-value is defined by Marx in the following terms:

> the capitalist who applies the improved method of production, appropriates to surplus-labour a greater portion of the working-day, than the other capitalists in the same trade. He does individually, what the whole body of capitalists engaged in producing relative surplus-value, do collectively.... however, this extra surplus-value vanishes, so soon as the new method of production

> has become general, and has consequently caused the difference between the individual value of the cheapened commodity and its social value to vanish [*Capital*, I, pp. 318–19].

In the capitalist mode of production commodities do not exchange at their values and Marx's analysis is thus carried out in the following terms: 'A capitalist working with improved but not as yet generally adopted methods of production sells below the market price, but above his individual price of production; his rate of profit rises until competition levels it out' (*Capital*, I, p. 226).

Finally we can point out that in this case the level of demand intervenes to determine the values and also the prices (of production). It is clear that in the preceding examples the simultaneous use of two methods of production for the *i*th commodity is subject to demand being sufficient, otherwise only the superior method would be used. If the *i*th commodity is non-basic its price of production and its value are determined with reference to the conditions of production of the 'inferior' plant or of the 'least efficient' activity. If it is a basic good the problem is more complicated because of the interdependence, already cited, which results when the prices of other commodities are indirectly determined by the level of demand for the *i*th commodity. The same applies for its value. But this was clearly seen by Marx in Volume III of *Capital*;[29] one cannot abstract from demand either in the determination of labour-values on the one-hand or prices of production on the other.

(C) ON SOME SPECIAL DIFFICULTIES OF MULTIPLE-PRODUCT SYSTEMS

The problem of the choice of techniques becomes more complex in systems where at least one commodity is produced by more than one method.

> With single-product industries, each process or method of production is identified by the commodity which it produces, so that when an additional, $(k+1)$th, method is introduced there is no doubt as to which of the pre-existing methods it is an alternative to.
>
> When, however, each process or method produces several commodities, and each commodity is produced by several methods, this criterion fails. *And the problem arises of how to identify among the pre-existing methods the one to which the new method is an alternative* [italics added].

In order to resolve the problem Sraffa indicates that after having determined

> that rate of profits at which *each* of the k commodities is produced, whether by the new method or by the old ones, at the same prices ... Our problem is to spot the method that will be superseded when the rate of profits rises beyond that point.
>
> In doing this we proceed in a somewhat roundabout way. We begin by turning our attention away from the individual methods of joint-production and concentrate upon the possible systems which are respectively defined by the *absence* of one of the methods from among their components. With $k+1$ methods (or processes) we can form k different systems of k processes, all of the systems including the new method and each of them omitting in turn one of the k old methods.
>
> Suppose now that the rate of profits is raised by a very small fraction ... For all the k systems the resulting wage will be lower than before: but it will be different for each of the systems (although expressed in the same standard). Consider the system which at the newly given rate of profits allows of the highest wage ... Now this system is distinguished by the *absence* from among its constituents of one particular method of production, which is present in all the other systems. That particular method is thus shown to be the least profitable to employ in the new circumstances, and is therefore the one that will be superseded by the new method [P.S. §96, pp. 86–7].

Sraffa also shows that if we assume wages rather than the rate of profits to be given, the same system will be found to be the most profitable in the sense that it will have a higher rate of profits than any other system (*ibid.*)

(D) *THE CONSUMPTION–GROWTH RELATION AND THE CHOICE OF TECHNIQUES*

It is also possible to study the problem of the choice of techniques on the basis of the (ξ,g) relation, now supposing that the objective of the society is, for example, to maximise the level of consumption for a given g. By following the same procedure used in the case of the (w,r) relation it can be shown that, when several techniques are available, the (ξ,g) relation is no longer a single continuous curve but an envelope of the (ξ,g) curves associated with the available techniques. The most profitable technique will then be that which yields the highest g given ξ or the highest level of ξ given g.

The results already achieved for prices and distribution can be directly applied. Evidently the apparent paradox of the return of techniques will also be found and the same technique may be the most 'advantageous' for different values of g. In the case represented in Figure 5.10 technique (2)

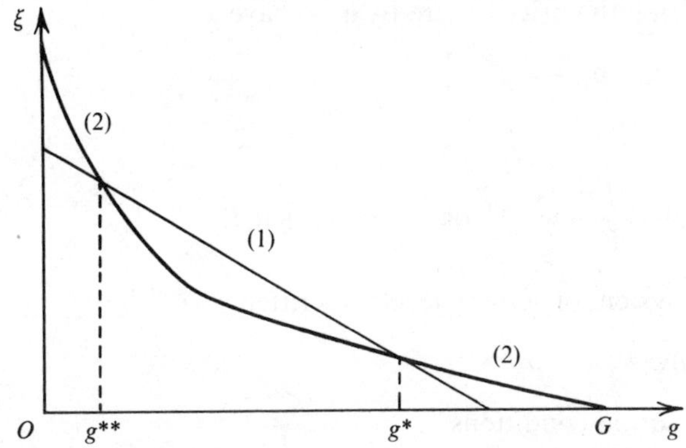

Fig. 5.10

will be chosen both when the rate of growth is very high ($g^* < g < G$) and when it is very low ($0 < g < g^{**}$).

5.5.2 Conflicts of objectives and the wage–consumption relation

In the case where the system $(\mathbf{A},\mathbf{B})$ is decomposable, it has already been showed that the level of wages and the rate of profit were defined within the basic system $(\mathbf{A}_1^1,\mathbf{B}_1^1)$ while the level of consumption and the rate of growth were defined within the antibasic system $(\mathbf{A}_3^3,\mathbf{B}_3^3)$. We are now going to specify the relation between the level of wages and the level of consumption for the simple case of single-product industries and circulating capital,[30] wages and consumption being defined in terms of the *standard of prices* for wages and of the *standard of activity levels* for consumption. Thus we must keep in mind that w_s will represent both the level of wages and the share of wages in the standard net product (of prices), and, in the same way, ξ_s is both the level of consumption and the share of consumption in the net product of the standard system of activity levels, the dual of the standard used by Sraffa. It is this relation (w_s, ξ_s) that we shall now try to specify.

The price system of basic goods is written:

$$\mathbf{p}_1 = (1+r)\mathbf{A}_1^1\mathbf{p}_1 + w_s\mathbf{L}_1$$

with the normalisation conditions

$$\mathbf{q}\mathbf{L}_1 = 1 \qquad \mathbf{q}(\mathbf{I}-\mathbf{A}_1^1)\mathbf{p}_1 = 1 \qquad \text{and} \qquad \mathbf{q} = (1+R)\mathbf{q}\mathbf{A}_1^1$$

from which $\quad \mathbf{q}(\mathbf{I}-\mathbf{A}_1^1)\mathbf{p}_1 = 1 = R\mathbf{q}\mathbf{A}_1^1\mathbf{p}_1$

and $\quad \mathbf{q}\mathbf{p}_1 = \mathbf{q}\mathbf{A}_1^1\mathbf{p}_1 + R\mathbf{q}\mathbf{A}_1^1\mathbf{p}_1 = (1+R)\mathbf{q}\mathbf{A}_1^1\mathbf{p}_1 = \dfrac{1+R}{R}$

By premultiplying the price system by $\mathbf{q}$ we have

$$\mathbf{q}\mathbf{p}_1 = (1+r)\mathbf{q}\mathbf{A}_1^1\mathbf{p}_1 + w_s\mathbf{q}\mathbf{L}_1$$

thus

$$\frac{1+R}{R} = (1+r)\frac{1}{R} + w_s \qquad \text{or} \qquad R = r + w_s R$$

The antibasic system of activity levels is written

$$\mathbf{y}_3 = (1+g)\mathbf{y}_3\mathbf{A}_3^3 + \xi_s\boldsymbol{\delta}_3$$

with the normalisation conditions

$$\boldsymbol{\delta}_3\bar{\mathbf{p}} = 1 \qquad \mathbf{y}_3(\mathbf{I}-\mathbf{A}_3^3)\bar{\mathbf{p}} = 1 \qquad \text{and} \qquad \bar{\mathbf{p}} = (1+G)\mathbf{A}_3^3\bar{\mathbf{p}}$$

From which $\mathbf{y}_3(\mathbf{I}-\mathbf{A}_3^3)\bar{\mathbf{p}} = 1 = G\mathbf{y}_3\mathbf{A}_3^3\bar{\mathbf{p}}$

and $\mathbf{y}_3\bar{\mathbf{p}} = \mathbf{y}_3\mathbf{A}_3^3\bar{\mathbf{p}} + G\mathbf{y}_3\mathbf{A}_3^3\bar{\mathbf{p}} = (1+G)\mathbf{y}_3\mathbf{A}_3^3\bar{\mathbf{p}} = \dfrac{1+G}{G}$

By post-multiplying the system of activity levels by $\bar{\mathbf{p}}$ we have

$$\mathbf{y}_3\bar{\mathbf{p}} = (1+g)\mathbf{y}_3\mathbf{A}_3^3\bar{\mathbf{p}} + \xi_s\boldsymbol{\delta}_3\bar{\mathbf{p}}$$

Thus $\dfrac{1+G}{G} = (1+g)\dfrac{1}{G} + \xi_s \qquad \text{or} \qquad G = g + \xi_s G$

To derive the (w_s, ξ_s) relation it is sufficient to refer to the relation already established between the rate of profit, r, and the rate of growth, g (i.e. $r = g/s_c$ in the case where workers consume all their wages[31]). We thus have

$$\begin{cases} G = g + \xi_s G \\ R = r + w_s R \\ g = r s_c \end{cases}$$

By substituting we find the desired relation between ξ_s and w_s

$$\frac{1-\xi_s}{1-w_s} = s_c\frac{R}{G} \qquad \left(= \frac{R}{G} \quad \text{if} \quad s_c = 1\right)$$

that can be represented as in Fig. 5.11 when $G < R$ and

$$G = 20\% \qquad R = 25\% \qquad s_c = \frac{1}{2} \text{ and } s_c = 1$$

An analogous relation could be drawn in the case of $G > R$.

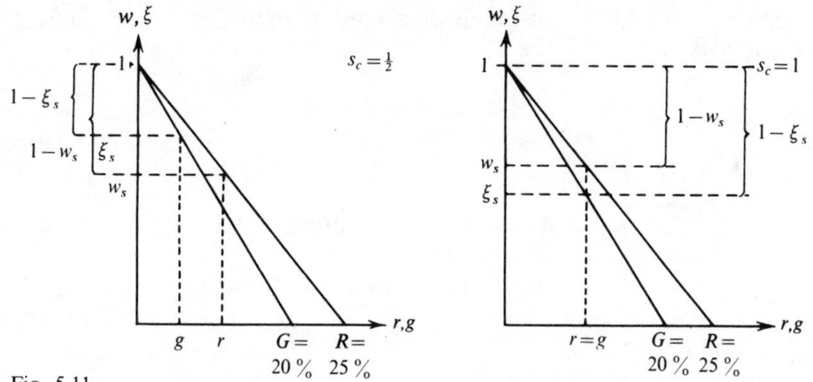

Fig. 5.11

In the case where the matrix is indecomposable $R = G$ and, further, if we assume that $\mathbf{y}(\mathbf{I} - \mathbf{A})\bar{\mathbf{p}} = 1 = \mathbf{q}(\mathbf{I} - \mathbf{A})\mathbf{p}$ the two linear relations (w_s, r) and (ξ_s, g) are combined[32] and the relation is written

$$\frac{1 - \xi_s}{1 - w_s} = s_c \qquad \text{and} \qquad \xi_s = w_s \qquad \text{if } s_c = 1$$

With $G = R = 25\%$ we have the relation represented in Fig. 5.12.

Finally, it should be noted that, excepting very special cases, a major portion of the curves expressing the relations (w_s, r) and (ξ_s, g) remain 'virtual', and as a result should be drawn as dotted lines, whether or not the system is decomposable. The constraints on g and on r which can be written, we recall, $g \leq G, r \leq R$ should also take into account the relation between r and g of the form $g = rs_c$. Thus there are two series of constraints:

$$g \leq \min(G, s_c R) \qquad\qquad r \leq \min\left(R, \frac{G}{s_c}\right)$$

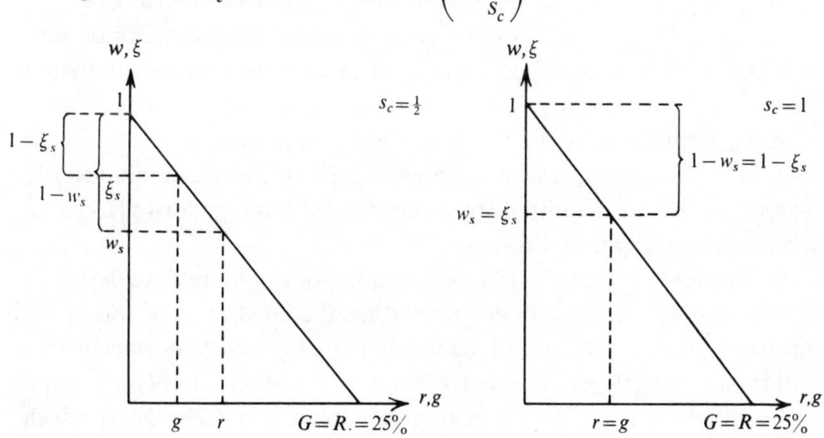

Fig. 5.12

Several cases can be distinguished according to the respective values of s_c and G/R

$$s_c < \frac{G}{R} \Leftrightarrow \begin{cases} s_c R < G \Rightarrow & \text{constraint on } g \\ \dfrac{G}{s_c} > R \Rightarrow & \text{no constraint on } r \end{cases}$$

$$s_c > \frac{G}{R} \Leftrightarrow \begin{cases} s_c R > G \Rightarrow & \text{no constraint on } g \\ \dfrac{G}{s_c} < R \Rightarrow & \text{constraint on } r \end{cases}$$

$$s_c = \frac{G}{R} \Leftrightarrow \begin{cases} s_c R = G \Rightarrow & \text{no constraint on } g \\ \dfrac{G}{s_c} = R \Rightarrow & \text{no constraint on } r \end{cases}$$

Let us return to the previous example above where $G = 20\%$ and $R = 25\%$.

– If $s_c = \frac{1}{2}$ we are in the first series of cases ($s_c = \frac{1}{2} < (G/R) = \frac{4}{5}$), i.e. there is no additional constraint on r which can vary from 0 to 25% while g must remain below $s_c R = \frac{1}{2} 25\% = 12.5\%$.

– If $s_c = 1$ we are in the second series of cases ($s_c = 1 > (G/R) = \frac{4}{5}$), i.e. g is free to vary between 0 and 25% but r must be inferior to $G/s_c = 20\%$.

– If $s_c = \frac{4}{5}$ there is no constraint on either r or g which may take values $0 \leq g \leq G$ and $0 \leq r \leq R$. It should be noted that if the system is indecomposable ($R = G$) savings behaviour is such that there is no additional constraint for either r or g, so that $s_c = G/R = G/G = 1$.

In the general case where the system is decomposable:

(a) the rate of profit, level of wages and relative prices are simultaneously determined by the conditions of production of basic goods ($\mathbf{A}_1^1$), one of the variables being fixed exogenously;

(b) the rate of growth, level of consumption and relative levels of activity are simultaneously determined by the conditions of use of the antibasic activities ($\mathbf{A}_3^3$) one of the variables being fixed exogenously.

It is thus perfectly possible that a change in the conditions of production of basic goods is produced (within $\mathbf{A}_1^1$) (switch of techniques) which modifies, for a given w, the relative prices and the rate of profit ($R' > R$)

without modifying the conditions of utilisation (in $\mathbf{A}_3^3$). Inversely, it is perfectly possible that a change in the conditions of use of antibasic activities is produced (in $\mathbf{A}_3^3$) which modifies, ξ given, the levels of activity and the rate of growth ($G' > G$) without any change in the conditions of production ($\mathbf{A}_1^1$). There will, however, be an indirect impact by means of the relation between g and r.

In these conditions it is not impossible that a change in technique that increases the rate of profit which (for a given level of wages) brings about (s_c supposed to be fixed) an increase in the rate of growth should be translated into a reduction of the level of consumption. Thus the conflict of objectives for the maximisation of the rate of profit can in certain cases produce a decrease in the level of consumption.

It should be noted that such a 'conflict of objectives' can appear even when the system is indecomposable. Let the system $(\mathbf{A},\mathbf{I},\mathbf{L},\boldsymbol{\delta})$ be indecomposable. The (w,r) and (ξ,g) curves can be made identical by means of a normalisation procedure as already seen above. Let us further suppose without restricting the generality of the analysis which follows, that the numeraire $\mathbf{U}$ of prices and $\mathbf{V}$ of the activity levels have been chosen such that the (w,r) and (ξ,g) curves are coincident straight lines.

Let there be a change in technique such that the new system is indecomposable. To have a common base which allows the comparison of the two systems $\mathbf{U}$ and $\mathbf{V}$ will continue as the norms for prices and activity levels. It is clear that the new curves need not be either linear or coincident.

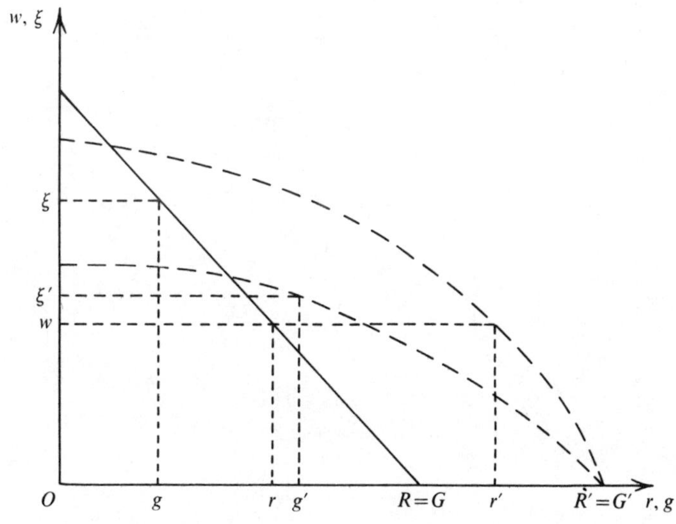

Fig. 5.13

In the case represented in Fig. 5.13 (where the new curves are drawn with broken lines) it seems clear that at the wage rate w the new technique of production will be adopted since it allows a higher rate of profit r' for the given wage. For a fixed propensity to save s_c a higher rate of growth g' will result and, in this case, a lower level of consumption. It is thus perfectly possible for a change in technique to bring about both a higher rate of return and a lower level of consumption. Obviously, results other than those represented in the diagram are possible.

6

Value: duality and 'transformation'

The relation between Marxian theory and the concept of duality is not as paradoxical as it may at first appear. In the very first lines of the *Critique of Political Economy*, Marx clearly indicates the duality of his analysis in terms of both values and quantities: 'Every commodity, however, has a two-fold aspect—*use-value* and *exchange-value*' (C, p. 27). This theme also appears in *Capital*: 'Every useful thing, as iron, paper, etc., may be looked at from the two points of view of quality and quantity' (I, p. 35) with the clarification that 'When treating of use-value, we always assume to be dealing with definite quantities, such as dozens of watches, yards of linen or tons of iron' (I, p. 36).

Marx insists frequently on the 'two-fold nature of the labour contained in commodities' (I, p. 41) and on the importance of his discovery: 'I was the first to point out and to examine critically this two-fold nature of the labour contained in commodities' (I, p. 41); 'The best points in my book are: (1) *the two-fold character of labour*, according to whether it is expressed in use-value or exchange-value ... It is emphasised immediately, in the *first* chapter' (Marx and Engels: *Selected Correspondence*, letter n. 93, [London] 24 August, 1867).

There is thus a duality between exchange-values and use-values, between values and quantities (in the present context between values and activity levels). But, as pointed out in Chapter 1, two approaches to the value of the commodities exist in Marx's analysis, one in terms of exchange-values and the other in terms of prices of production. Therefore it is necessary to make clear whether our discussion of duality is situated in value space or prices of production space.

At this point it is opportune to point out that we are not here concerned with the possible historical significance of the process of the 'transformation' of values into prices but rather with its logical and theoretical relevance.[1] Althusser says clearly: 'The object of Marx's study is therefore contemporary bourgeois society, which is thought as a historical *result*:

but the understanding of this society, far from being obtained from the theory of the genesis of this result, is on the contrary, obtained exclusively from the theory of the "body", i.e., of the *contemporary structure of society*, without its genesis intervening in any way whatsoever' (*Reading Capital* p. 65). This idea is rigorously expressed by Marx in *The Poverty of Philosophy*: 'How, indeed, could the single logical formula of movement, of sequence, of time, explain the body of society, in which all relations coexist simultaneously [gleichzeitig] and support one another' (pp. 110–11) and again in *A Contribution to the Critique of Political Economy*: 'It is not a matter of the connexion established historically between the economic relations in the succession of different forms of society. Still less their order of succession "in the idea" ... But of their articulated combination [gliederung] within modern bourgeois society' (Grundrisse p. 28).

The distinction between values and prices of production in a system of capitalist production led us (see Chapter 1) to rigorous definition of the fundamental Marxian theorem in terms of the necessary and sufficient condition for the existence of a positive uniform rate of profit in all industries, i.e. the exploitation of labour ($R > 0 \Leftrightarrow e > 0$). Symmetrically it can be shown that the necessary and sufficient condition for the existence of a positive uniform rate of growth for the means of production of all commodities is, again, the exploitation of labour ($G > 0 \Leftrightarrow e > 0$).

It should not be surprising that the analysis of accumulation in a capitalist production system should lead us to emphasise the relevance (at least analytically) of growth by means of a Marx–von Neumann system in which capitalists save the whole of their surplus (or surplus-value) and where all sectors have the same growth rate. We shall show, in particular, how the 'transformation' of global surplus-value into global profit and of values into prices of production is then ensured in this case. In the general case where capitalists consume part of the surplus-value, we shall show how Marx's formulations can be corrected by means of the standard system built from matrix $\mathbf{A}^*$.

The relation between the rate of profit (R) and the rate of exploitation (e) can be understood more easily through the intermediary of the concept of the organic composition of the standard commodity of the system $[\mathbf{A}^*, \mathbf{I}]$.

Marx's proposition that the rate of profit is linked to the rate of exploitation through the average organic composition is true in at least two particular cases: (a) the labour vector is an eigenvector on the right of matrix $\mathbf{A}$ (this is equivalent to the assumption of uniform organic composition), and (b) the vector of activity levels is an eigenvector on the left of **A** (this is equivalent to the assumption that capitalists save the whole surplus-value).

6.1 Accumulation in the capitalist production system

First we shall rapidly detail the way Marx proceeds in *Capital* because the analysis of the development and the accumulation in a capitalist production system given there is carried out on a number of different theoretical levels and with various degrees of abstraction.

In Volume I, Part VII is dedicated, as its title indicates, to the study of 'The Accumulation of Capital' in an economic system considered at the highest level of aggregation. The aggregation of the various commodities is in terms of values. Since the theory of prices of production is developed later in *Capital*, at this stage the framework of the analysis is the value system. Yet, this does not mean that we have a system of simple commodity production represented by commodities–money–commodities (C–M–C′). Rather we have a system of capitalist commodity production: money–commodities–money (M–C–M′) with M′ > M, production of exchange-values (and not of use-values), and the accent on the quantitative aspect (and not on the qualitative aspect) of the circulation process. The capitalist uses his money as capital, he transforms it on the market into labour power and production goods so as to obtain a surplus-value. But this analysis of the fundamental mechanisms of the accumulation of capital is highly aggregated and extremely abstract.

In Volume II Marx disaggregates the analysis and considers the 'process of circulation of capital', a project very different from that of Volume I where 'the process of capitalist production was analysed as an individual act as well as a process of reproduction: the production of surplus-value and the production of capital itself. The changes of form and substance experienced by capital in the sphere of circulation were assumed without dwelling upon them' (II, p. 356). This sphere of circulation is the object of Volume II where the first part deals with 'the metamorphoses of capital and their circuits' and the second with 'the turnover of capital'. This shows that the specificity of the various capital goods is at the centre of Marx's preoccupations. This analysis is carried out in more detail in Part III of Volume II entitled 'Reproduction and Circulation of the Aggregate Social Capital' where Marx attempts to answer the question he raises at the beginning of *Capital* 'The question that confronts us directly is this: How is the *capital* consumed in production *replaced in value*[2] out of the annual product and how does the movement of this replacement intertwine with the consumption of the surplus-value by the capitalists and of the wages by the labourers?' (II, p. 397). This analysis of sectoral interdependence is carried out by means of the schemes of reproduction[3] which are based on the assumption that there is no 'realisation problem'. It is only in Volume III (particularly in Part III) that Marx demonstrates the contradictions of the system. Until this point in his analysis he has always assumed, implicitly or explicitly, that the surplus-value extracted from the workers through exploitation was effectively transformed into profit, but 'the condition of direct exploitation, and those of realising it, are not identical' (II, p. 239).

In fact, Marx clearly warns the reader of this simplifying assumption: 'The first condition of accumulation is that the capitalist must have contrived to sell his commodities, and to reconvert into capital the greater part of the money so received. In the following pages we shall assume that capital circulates in its normal way. The detailed analysis of the process will be found in Book II' (I, p. 564). Marx found it necessary to simplify the analysis because 'The simple fundamental form of the process of accumulation is obscured by the incident of the circulation which brings it about, and by the splitting-up of surplus-value. An exact analysis of the process, therefore, demands that we should, for a time, disregard all phenomena that hide the play of its inner mechanism' (I, p. 565).

The analysis of 'simple reproduction' does not bring about any difficulty. Marx gives the following clarification: 'The conditions of production are also those of reproduction. No society can go on producing, in other words, no society can reproduce, unless it constantly reconverts a part of its products into means of production, or elements of fresh products' (I, p. 566).

With the usual notation, $\mathbf{\Lambda}$, the vector of values, can be written:

$$\mathbf{\Lambda} = \mathbf{A\Lambda} + \mathbf{L} = \mathbf{A\Lambda} + \mathbf{L}(1+e)\mathbf{d\Lambda}$$

If the economy under consideration produces, at any moment of time, t, commodities whose physical quantities are $(y_{1,t}, \ldots, y_{i,t}, \ldots, y_{n,t})$ we have

$$\mathbf{y}_t = (y_{1,t} \cdots y_{i,t} \cdots y_{n,t})$$

the total value of the commodities can be written

$$\begin{aligned}\mathbf{y}_t\mathbf{\Lambda} &= \mathbf{y}_t\mathbf{A\Lambda} + \mathbf{y}_t\mathbf{L} = \mathbf{y}_t\mathbf{A\Lambda} + \mathbf{y}_t\mathbf{L}(1+e)\mathbf{d\Lambda} \\ &= \mathbf{y}_t\mathbf{A\Lambda} + \mathbf{y}_t\mathbf{Ld\Lambda} + e\mathbf{y}_t\mathbf{Ld\Lambda}\end{aligned}$$

In order to maintain the productivity of the system at a constant level, given Marx's explicit assumption that commodities are sold at their values, it is necessary to replace

(a) the 'values', i.e. the value of constant capital used up, $\mathbf{y}_t\mathbf{A}\boldsymbol{\Lambda}$ and the value of the employed labour force $\mathbf{y}_t\mathbf{Ld}\boldsymbol{\Lambda}$;

(b) the quantities

– of means of production (constant capital) $\mathbf{y}_t\mathbf{A}$

– of means of subsistence for the labour force $\mathbf{y}_t\mathbf{Ld}$.

It follows that if the surplus-value ($e\mathbf{y}_t\mathbf{Ld}\boldsymbol{\Lambda}$) is integrally consumed by the capitalists who own the means of production, there is simple reproduction or replacement production (i.e. without an increase of productive capacity). Obviously this reproduction process of social capital is also a process of reproduction (and thus perpetuation) of social relationships: 'Capitalist production, therefore, of itself reproduces the separation between labour-power and the means of labour. It thereby reproduces and perpetuates the condition for exploiting the labourer. It incessantly forces him to sell his labour-power in order to live, and enables the capitalist to purchase labour-power in order that he may enrich himself' (I, p. 577).

However, this analysis of simple reproduction is only an introduction; Marx goes on to show that the normal situation of a system of capitalist production is not replacement or simple reproduction at all but rather 'enlarged' reproduction through accumulation and transformation of surplus-value into capital.

The phenomenon of capitalism as a dynamic system must now be explained. The exploitation of workers is indeed a necessary condition for the existence of a 'surplus' but not a sufficient one. Exploitation gives the possibility for expansion, but it can remain simply 'virtual' if surplus-value is completely consumed. Surplus-value appears as the product of capital, as the result of the process of capitalist production characterised by exploitation. 'Hitherto, we have investigated how surplus-value emanates from capital; we have now to see how capital arises from surplus-value' (I, p. 579). Given the existence of surplus-value, the problem becomes the allocation of the surplus: 'Employing surplus-value as capital, reconverting it into capital, is called accumulation of capital' (I, p. 579). Marx adds some humorous detail on this process a few pages later: 'Nor does it matter if simple reproduction is replaced by reproduction on an extended scale, by accumulation. In the former case the capitalist squanders the whole surplus-value in dissipation, in the latter he demonstrates his bourgeois virtue by consuming only a portion of it and converting the rest into money' (I, p. 586).

Thus there are only two possible utilisations or allocations of surplus-value; it is either consumed or saved. 'it is by the owner of the surplus-value, by the capitalist, alone, that the division is made... That part of the tribute exacted by him which he accumulates, is said to be saved by him, because he does not eat it' (I, p. 591).

In other words, at the most aggregate level, we have a total surplus-value $e\mathbf{y}_t\mathbf{L}\mathbf{d}\mathbf{\Lambda}$. A fraction ($\gamma$) is saved and used as an accumulation fund by the capitalist, while the rest ($1-\gamma$) is consumed. But for Marx, 'it is not values in use and the enjoyment of them, but exchange-value and its augmentation that spur him [the capitalist] into action. Fanatically bent on making value expand itself, he ruthlessly forces the human race to produce for production's sake' (I, p. 592). This implies very clearly that γ is considered to be close to 1. This can be explained, first, by simple economic reasons:

> the development of capitalist production makes it constantly necessary to keep increasing the amount of the capital laid out in a given industrial undertaking, and competition makes the immanent laws of capitalist production to be felt by each individual capitalist, as external coercive laws. It compels him to keep constantly extending his capital, in order to preserve it, but extend it he cannot, except by means of progressive accumulation [I, p. 592].

Marx adds to these economic reasons other considerations related to economic power: 'To accumulate, is to conquer the world of social wealth, to increase the mass of human beings exploited by him, and thus to extend both the direct and indirect sway of the capitalist' (I, p. 592).

However, the progress of production involves contradictions: 'But along with this growth, there is at the same time developed in his breast, a Faustian conflict between the passion for accumulation, and the desire for enjoyment' (I, p. 594). And a few lines below 'Accumulate, accumulate! That is Moses and the prophets! ... save, save, i.e. reconvert the greatest possible portion of surplus-value, or surplus-product into capital! Accumulation for accumulation's sake, production for production's sake: by this formula classical economy expressed the historical mission of the bourgeoisie' (I, p. 595). 'If to classical economy, the proletarian is but a machine for the production of surplus-value; on the other hand, the capitalist is in its eyes only a machine for the conversion of this surplus-value into additional capital' (I, p. 595).

To use Marx's words, just what are these 'circumstances that ... determine the amount of accumulation' (I, p. 595)? We have already noted the importance of the parameter γ, the propensity to accumulate, or if one prefers, the propensity to save surplus-value. Marx attempts to analyse the other factors assuming initially that the organic composition of capital is constant and that there is no technical progress. Given these provisional assumptions, he demonstrates among other factors the importance of the degree of exploitation of labour, i.e. of labour productivity (I, p. 599).

Let us try to clarify this with the usual notation:[4]

(i) From the organic composition of capital (k) defined as the ratio of constant capital ($\mathbf{y}_t\mathbf{A}\boldsymbol{\Lambda}$) to variable capital ($\mathbf{y}_t\mathbf{Ld}\boldsymbol{\Lambda}$) and assumed to be constant over time,[5] we can obtain a relation between the growth of variable capital

$$\Delta(\mathbf{y}_t\mathbf{A}\boldsymbol{\Lambda}) = k\,\Delta(\mathbf{y}_t\mathbf{Ld}\boldsymbol{\Lambda})$$

(ii) Furthermore, since a fraction γ of the total surplus-value is allocated to accumulation and since the accumulation takes the form of additional constant capital and variable capital, we can write a second relation:

$$\Delta(\mathbf{y}_t\mathbf{A}\boldsymbol{\Lambda}) + \Delta(\mathbf{y}_t\mathbf{Ld}\boldsymbol{\Lambda}) = \gamma e\mathbf{y}_t\mathbf{Ld}\boldsymbol{\Lambda}$$

Thus we have

$$k\Delta(\mathbf{y}_t\mathbf{Ld}\boldsymbol{\Lambda}) + \Delta(\mathbf{y}_t\mathbf{Ld}\boldsymbol{\Lambda}) = \gamma e\mathbf{y}_t\mathbf{Ld}\boldsymbol{\Lambda}$$

The relative rate of growth (in value) of the variable capital can therefore be written

$$\frac{\Delta(\mathbf{y}_t\mathbf{Ld}\boldsymbol{\Lambda})}{\mathbf{y}_t\mathbf{Ld}\boldsymbol{\Lambda}} = \gamma\frac{e}{1+k} \tag{1}$$

We can write the rate of growth of constant capital in the same way:

$$\frac{\Delta(\mathbf{y}_t\mathbf{A}\boldsymbol{\Lambda})}{\mathbf{y}_t\mathbf{A}\boldsymbol{\Lambda}} = \gamma\frac{e}{1+k} \tag{2}$$

From (1) and (2) and since the rate of exploitation is assumed to be constant, we can write the total value of the commodities produced at $t+1$ as:

$$\mathbf{y}_{t+1}\boldsymbol{\Lambda} = \mathbf{y}_t\mathbf{A}\boldsymbol{\Lambda}\left(1+\gamma\frac{e}{1+k}\right) + \mathbf{y}_t\mathbf{Ld}\boldsymbol{\Lambda}\left(1+\gamma\frac{e}{1+k}\right)$$
$$+\, e\mathbf{y}_t\mathbf{Ld}\boldsymbol{\Lambda}\left(1+\gamma\frac{e}{1+k}\right)$$

or

$$\mathbf{y}_{t+1}\boldsymbol{\Lambda} = \left(1+\gamma\frac{e}{1+k}\right)[\mathbf{y}_t\mathbf{A}\boldsymbol{\Lambda} + \mathbf{y}_t\mathbf{Ld}\boldsymbol{\Lambda} + e\mathbf{y}_t\mathbf{Ld}\boldsymbol{\Lambda}]$$

or

$$\mathbf{y}_{t+1}\mathbf{\Lambda} = \left(1 + \gamma\frac{e}{1+k}\right)\mathbf{y}_t\mathbf{\Lambda}$$

Defining g' as the relative rate of growth of the system, we have

$$g' = \frac{\mathbf{y}_{t+1}\mathbf{\Lambda} - \mathbf{y}_t\mathbf{\Lambda}}{\mathbf{y}_t\mathbf{\Lambda}} = \gamma\frac{\mathrm{e}}{1+k}$$

It must be noted that $\mathbf{y}_t$ and $\mathbf{y}_{t+1}$ are vectors representing heterogeneous physical productions; the aggregation is made using the vector of values which is invariant since the methods of production are invariant by assumption. This is a case of non-proportional growth, the various outputs normally grow at different rates, g_i, except for a particular case which we shall consider later (see Section 6.3, below).

At this stage we can draw a number of important conclusions:

(a) the relative rate of growth of the system previously defined (g') depends essentially on three parameters:

- e the rate of exploitation defined by $e = (1 - \mathbf{d\Lambda})/\mathbf{d\Lambda}$ which is a reflection of the 'level of the real wages' per worker and at the same time of the 'productivity' of labour,
- k the organic composition of capital expressed in values,
- γ the 'propensity to accumulate surplus-value' of the capitalists.

Of course, the growth in absolute value of the system, or, in Marx's words, the accumulation, is a function of 'the mass of the capital advanced' (I, p. 608), i.e. $\gamma\,e\mathbf{y}_t\mathbf{Ld\Lambda}$.

(b) We again note the close link, established by modern growth theory (see Chapter 5, above), between the rate of growth, the capitalists' propensity to save, and the rate of profit ($r = g/s_c$). The expression $e/(1+k)$ is simply the rate of profit, as defined by Marx, i.e. as the ratio of total surplus-value to total advanced capital. This formulation, as we know (see Chapter 1), is, if not erroneous, only approximate.

The global rate of growth of the system[6] *is therefore equal* (and determined by) *the product of the propensity to accumulate surplus-value by the rate of profit as it is defined by Marx*, i.e.

$$g' = \gamma\frac{e}{1+k}$$

Recall that this relation is true only under certain assumptions. The most important are:

(i) the absence of technical progress (there is no change of technique),
(ii) a constant rate of exploitation,
(iii) the 'realisation' of the commodities at their values,

(iv) existence of a reserve army of labour allowing the expansion of the system considered,

(v) accumulation based on the fraction of surplus-value appropriated by the capitalists.

6.2 Duality: the second fundamental Marxian theorem

The fundamental Marxian theorem (see Chapter 1, above) states that the necessary and sufficient condition for the existence of a positive uniform rate of profit is the existence of a positive rate of exploitation: $R > 0 \Leftrightarrow e > 0$. We shall prove a perfectly symmetric proposition for a basic system which states that *the necessary and sufficient condition for the existence of a positive uniform rate of growth of the means of production is the existence of a positive rate of exploitation*: $G > 0 \Leftrightarrow e > 0$.

In order to ensure a perfect comparison between the two demonstrations we shall again assume that the system has only single-product industries and circulating capital with wages 'advanced' by capitalists. Thus:

A and **I** are, respectively, the input and output matrices, **A** being indecomposable by assumption,

L is the vector of the needs of direct labour,

d is the vector representing the 'consumption basket' of workers,

Ω is the vector of activity levels[7] corresponding to the production of the 'consumption basket' determined by

$$\mathbf{\Omega} = \mathbf{\Omega A} + \mathbf{d}$$

Consequently the necessary labour associated with the production of **d** is **ΩL**. Given the value system $\mathbf{\Lambda} = \mathbf{A\Lambda} + \mathbf{L}$, we have

$$\mathbf{L} = (\mathbf{I} - \mathbf{A})\mathbf{\Lambda}$$

whence $\quad \mathbf{\Omega L} = \mathbf{\Omega}(\mathbf{I} - \mathbf{A})\mathbf{\Lambda}$

and since $\quad \mathbf{\Omega}(\mathbf{I} - \mathbf{A}) = \mathbf{d}$

we have $\quad \mathbf{\Omega L} = \mathbf{d\Lambda}$

This shows that the value of labour-power can be obtained equivalently from either the value of the goods basket (**dΛ**) or from the necessary social labour required for the production of the basket (**ΩL**) (cf. Section 3.5).

Hence the double definition of the rate of exploitation, either as the ratio of surplus-value to the value of labour-power, or as the ratio of surplus-labour to necessary labour:

$$\frac{1 - \mathbf{d\Lambda}}{\mathbf{d\Lambda}} = e = \frac{1 - \mathbf{\Omega L}}{\mathbf{\Omega L}}$$

or

$$(1+e)\mathbf{d}\mathbf{\Lambda} = 1 = (1+e)\mathbf{\Omega}\mathbf{L}$$

We can thus rewrite the system of the activity levels corresponding to the production of the 'consumption basket' necessary to reproduce the labour force as

$$\mathbf{\Omega} = \mathbf{\Omega}\mathbf{A} + \mathbf{d} = \mathbf{\Omega}\mathbf{A} + (1+e)\mathbf{\Omega}\mathbf{L}\mathbf{d}$$

$$\mathbf{\Omega} = \mathbf{\Omega}\mathbf{A} + \mathbf{\Omega}\mathbf{L}\mathbf{d} + e\mathbf{\Omega}\mathbf{L}\mathbf{d}$$

This latter formulation shows that an intermediate consumption of $\mathbf{\Omega}\mathbf{A}$ is required for a production $\mathbf{\Omega}$. With workers' consumption written as $\mathbf{\Omega}\mathbf{L}\mathbf{d}$, the share of surplus-value appropriated by the capitalists becomes $(1-\mathbf{\Omega}\mathbf{L})\mathbf{d} = e\mathbf{\Omega}\mathbf{L}\mathbf{d}$. But it is necessary that e be positive, as Marx points out in the following passage:

> If man were not capable of producing in one working-day more means of subsistence... than every labourer needs for his own reproduction, if the daily expenditure of his entire labour-power sufficed merely to produce the means of subsistence indispensable for his own individual requirements, then one could not speak at all either of surplus-product or surplus-value [II, p. 766].

With this assumption in mind, we can simplify the expression for $\mathbf{\Omega}$ by stating $\mathbf{A}^* = \mathbf{A} + \mathbf{L}\mathbf{d}$:

$$\mathbf{\Omega} = \mathbf{\Omega}\mathbf{A}^* + e\mathbf{\Omega}\mathbf{L}\mathbf{d}$$

When the rate of growth of the means of production is positive ($g > 0$) we know that (see Chapter 5) the general expression of the system of activity levels is

$$\mathbf{y} = (1+g)\mathbf{y}\mathbf{A} + \xi\boldsymbol{\delta}$$

A new formulation is here necessary because of the Marxian assumption according to which wages are *completely* advanced. Symmetrically we shall assume that there is no consumption out of the surplus, only workers' consumption is considered (now represented by $\mathbf{d}$, not $\boldsymbol{\delta}$), completely 'advanced' by capitalists at level $\xi = \mathbf{y}\mathbf{L}$.

With G as the rate of growth we have

$$\mathbf{y} = (1+G)[\mathbf{y}\mathbf{A} + \xi\mathbf{d}] = (1+G)[\mathbf{y}\mathbf{A} + \mathbf{y}\mathbf{L}\mathbf{d}]$$

or

$$\mathbf{y} = (1+G)\mathbf{y}[\mathbf{A} + \mathbf{L}\mathbf{d}]$$

or

$$\mathbf{y} = (1 + G)\mathbf{y}\mathbf{A}^*$$

If we compare the systems that determine $\mathbf{y}$ and $\boldsymbol{\Omega}$ we observe that

$$-G > 0 \Leftrightarrow \alpha^*(\mathbf{A}^*) = \frac{1}{1+G} < 1$$

$-\alpha^*(\mathbf{A}^*) < 1 \Leftrightarrow e > 0$ because $\boldsymbol{\Omega} = \boldsymbol{\Omega}(\mathbf{A}^* + e\mathbf{Ld})$
or $\alpha^*(\mathbf{A}^* + e\mathbf{Ld}) = 1$, and thus
$\alpha^*(\mathbf{A}^*) < 1$ is equivalent to $\mathbf{A}^* \leq \mathbf{A}^* + \mathrm{e}\mathbf{Ld}$ where $\mathbf{Ld} \geq 0$

Thus

$$G > 0 \Leftrightarrow e > 0$$

This result constitutes the second fundamental Marxian theorem and can be stated as follows:

In an indecomposable system *the exploitation of workers is the necessary and sufficient condition for the existence of a positive uniform rate of growth of the means of production and of subsistence.*

PRIMAL	*DUAL*
$\boldsymbol{\Lambda} = \mathbf{A}\boldsymbol{\Lambda} + \mathbf{L}$	$\boldsymbol{\Omega} = \boldsymbol{\Omega}\mathbf{A} + \mathbf{d}$
value of labour-power: $\mathbf{d}\boldsymbol{\Lambda} = \boldsymbol{\Omega}\mathbf{L}$	: social labour necessary to produce d
$\dfrac{1 - \mathbf{d}\boldsymbol{\Lambda}}{\mathbf{d}\boldsymbol{\Lambda}} = e$	$e = \dfrac{1 - \boldsymbol{\Omega}\mathbf{L}}{\boldsymbol{\Omega}\mathbf{L}}$
$\mathbf{p} = (1 + R)(\mathbf{Ap} + \mathbf{L}w)$ or	$\mathbf{y} = (1 + G)(\mathbf{yA} + \xi\mathbf{d})$ or
$\mathbf{p} = (1 + R)(\mathbf{Ap} + \mathbf{Ldp}) = (1 + R)\mathbf{A}^*\mathbf{p}$	$\mathbf{y} = (1 + G)(\mathbf{yA} + \mathbf{yLd}) = (1 + G)\mathbf{yA}^*$
R: uniform rate of profit on the means of production and subsistence advanced	G: uniform rate of growth of the means of production and subsistence advanced
$w = \mathbf{dp}$: wage level associated with the prices of production $\mathbf{p}$	$\xi = \mathbf{yL}$: consumption level associated with the activity levels $\mathbf{y}$
First fundamental Marxian theorem	*Second fundamental Marxian theorem*
$R > 0 \Leftrightarrow \alpha^*(\mathbf{A}^*) < 1 \Leftrightarrow e > 0$	$G > 0 \Leftrightarrow \alpha^*(\mathbf{A}^*) < 1 \Leftrightarrow e > 0$

$$(R > 0) \Leftrightarrow e > 0 \Leftrightarrow (G > 0)$$

Note that we have assumed that the consumption of capitalists is zero. If this is not the case, this condition remains necessary, but is no longer sufficient. There is a decreasing relation between the level of consumption of the capitalists (of structure $\boldsymbol{\delta}$) and the rate of growth, G. It is linear, subject to the condition that the activity levels are normalised by the prices, $\bar{\mathbf{p}}$, defined as

$$\bar{\mathbf{p}} = (1 + R)\mathbf{A}^*\bar{\mathbf{p}}.$$

6.3 The standard commodity and 'transformation'

It is now possible to return to the problem of the 'transformation' of values into prices of production and of the mass of surplus-value into aggregate profits. Starting from the recent work of M. Morishima[8] we shall first show that 'transformation' is ensured when capitalists accumulate the whole surplus-value. We shall identify such conditions with the name 'Marx–von Neumann system.' We shall thus be able to see clearly the advantages associated with the analysis of the problem in terms of a standard system based on the assumption of wages 'advanced' for the general case where capitalists do not reinvest the whole of their profits. The average rate of profit of the real system is determined, not as Marx thought by the conditions of production of the 'average' commodity, but rather by the conditions of production of the 'standard' commodity.

6.3.1 The transformation of values into prices of production in a Marx–von Neumann system

By a Marx–von Neumann growth system we shall mean a growth system with the following two-fold characteristic:

(i) as in a von Neumann model we assume that capitalists save the entire surplus and that all sectors grow at the same maximum rate. We shall start by assuming that we are in a system of single-product industries and circulating capital. This restrictive assumption will be relaxed later.

(ii) as in Marxian analysis we assume that complex labour has been reduced into simple labour equivalents and that every worker receives a certain quantity of means of subsistence for every hour of work. This amount is fixed in any given historical period and 'advanced' by the capitalist.

To simplify the exposition we shall use the socio-technological matrix $\mathbf{A}^*$ defined by $\mathbf{A}^* = \mathbf{A} + \mathbf{Ld}$ assumed to be indecomposable.

– The quantity equations can then be written as

$$\mathbf{y} = (1 + G)\mathbf{y}\mathbf{A}^* \Leftrightarrow \mathbf{y}\mathbf{A}^* = \frac{1}{1+G}\mathbf{y} = \alpha^*\mathbf{y} \tag{1}$$

By the Perron–Frobenius theorem, we know that $\mathbf{y}$, the eigenvector on the left associated with the dominant eigenvalue $\alpha^* = 1/(1 + G)$, is strictly positive when matrix $\mathbf{A}^*$ is indecomposable.

Furthermore, $G > 0 \Leftrightarrow \alpha^*(= 1/(1 + G)) < 1$, i.e. the rate of growth (identical for the production of all commodities) will be positive if, and only if, the dominant eigenvalue of matrix $\mathbf{A}^*$ is less than 1.

In the Marx–von Neumann system the quantities of the various commodities produced ($\mathbf{y}$) grow at the same rate G determined by the dominant eigenvalue α^* of the socio-technological matrix $\mathbf{A}^*$

$$\alpha^* = \frac{1}{1+G}$$

– The price equations, dual to the quantity equations, can be written as

$$\mathbf{p} = (1+R)\mathbf{A}^*\mathbf{p} \Leftrightarrow \mathbf{A}^*\mathbf{p} = \frac{1}{1+R}\mathbf{p} \tag{2}$$

Here again, $\mathbf{p}$, the eigenvector on the right associated with the dominant eigenvalue $\beta^* = 1/(1+R)$, is strictly positive since matrix $\mathbf{A}^*$ is indecomposable. Furthermore, $R > 0 \Leftrightarrow \beta^*(=1/(1+R)) < 1$, i.e. the rate of profit, R, uniform in all industries, will be positive if, and only if, the dominant eigenvalue of matrix $\mathbf{A}^*$ is less than 1.

Of course, α^* and β^*, being dominant eigenvalues of the same matrix $\mathbf{A}^*$, are identical and

$$\alpha^* = \beta^* \Rightarrow R = G \tag{3}$$

Thus the rate of profit and the rate of growth are equal in the Marx–von Neumann system; they are determined by the dominant eigenvalue of the socio-technological matrix $\mathbf{A}^*$

$$\alpha^* = \frac{1}{1+G} = \frac{1}{1+R}$$

Now, if we go back to the value system, we know that we have

$$\frac{\mathbf{y}_{t+1}\mathbf{\Lambda} - \mathbf{y}_t\mathbf{\Lambda}}{\mathbf{y}_t\mathbf{\Lambda}} = g' = \gamma\frac{e}{1+k}$$

In the general case considered in Section 6.1 we noted that it was a non-proportional growth system, with the outputs of the various industries, sectors or sections growing at different rates, g_i. But in the particular case of the Marx–von Neumann system under consideration here, the rate of growth of the production of the various commodities is by assumption identical:

$g_i = G =$ a constant for all i.

Now we have

$$g_i = \frac{y_{i,t+1} - y_{i,t}}{y_{i,t}} = \frac{\lambda_i y_{i,t+1} - \lambda_i y_{i,t}}{\lambda_i y_{i,t}}$$

$$= \frac{(\lambda_1 y_{1,t+1} + \ldots + \lambda_i y_{i,t+1} + \ldots + \lambda_n y_{n,t+1}) - (\lambda_1 y_{1,t} + \ldots + \lambda_i y_{i,t} + \ldots + \lambda_n y_{n,t})}{\lambda_1 y_{1,t} + \ldots + \lambda_i y_{i,t} + \ldots + \lambda_n y_{n,t}}$$

$$= \frac{\mathbf{y}_{t+1}\mathbf{\Lambda} - \mathbf{y}_t\mathbf{\Lambda}}{\mathbf{y}_t\mathbf{\Lambda}} = g'$$

and thus $G = g'$ since $G = g_i$.

Recalling that in the Marx–von Neumann system the capitalists accumulate the whole of the surplus-value ($\gamma = 1$) and taking into account the general expression of g' and g_i

$$g' = \gamma \frac{e}{1+k} \qquad g_i = G = \frac{e}{1+k} \tag{4}$$

and the equality of the rate of profit and the rate of growth established in (3) gives the fundamental result:

$$G = R = \frac{e}{1+k}$$

To sum up the analysis of the Marx–von Neumann growth system where capitalists save the whole surplus-value and where all output grows at the same rate, the rate of profit earned in each industry is equal to the maximum rate of profit, R (the maximum rate of profit, R, is the rate of profit obtained when wages are completely advanced). This rate of profit can be obtained using Marx's formula

$$R = \frac{e}{1+k} \tag{5}$$

The prices of production $\mathbf{p} = (1+R)\mathbf{A}^*\mathbf{p}$ can be reformulated in the following way:

$$\mathbf{p} = \mathbf{H}\mathbf{p} \qquad \text{where } \mathbf{H} = (1+R)\mathbf{A}^* \tag{6}$$

$\mathbf{H}$ is a nonnegative indecomposable matrix whose dominant eigenvalue is equal to 1 ($\mathbf{p}1 = \mathbf{H}\mathbf{p}$). This formulation is of interest since Marx, in his formulation of the transformation problem, started from values in order to define prices of production in the following way:

$$\mathbf{p}_1 = (1 + R)\mathbf{A}\boldsymbol{\Lambda} \tag{7}$$

$\mathbf{p}_1$ is the vector of prices of production obtained by Marx. But, Marx should have repeated the iteration (7) to reach the following general expression:[9]

$$\mathbf{p}_t = (1 + R)\mathbf{A}^*\mathbf{p}_{t-1} \qquad \mathbf{p}_0 = \boldsymbol{\Lambda} \tag{8}$$

Now the problem is to determine if the iteration is indeed convergent in the particular case of a Marx–von Neumann system where $R = e/(1 + k)$. Since matrix $\mathbf{H} = (1 + R)\mathbf{A}^*$ is indecomposable,[10] we know[11] that the limit solution or the eigenvector associated with the dominant eigenvalue 1 is obtained as the limit of the infinite sequence $\mathbf{p}_0, \mathbf{p}_1, \ldots, \mathbf{p}_t, \ldots$ starting with an arbitrary $\mathbf{p}_0$ (nonnegative and non-zero) and following the sequence $\mathbf{p}_t = (1 + R)\mathbf{A}^*\mathbf{p}_{t-1}$.

This sequential process starting from $t = 1$ where $\mathbf{p}_0 = \boldsymbol{\Lambda}$ thus leads to $\mathbf{p}_t = \mathbf{p}$ when $t \to \infty$ and *will ensure the transformation of values into prices of production in a Marx–von Neumann system.* It can thus be seen that Marx had only taken the first step towards the solution of the problem.

We shall now show that *in the Marx–von Neumann system the sum of prices is indeed equal to the sum of values* and that *aggregate profits equal the mass of surplus-value.*

(a) *The sum of prices is equal to the sum of values.*

Premultiplying (8) by $\mathbf{y}$ we have

$$\mathbf{y}\mathbf{p}_t = (1 + R)\mathbf{y}\mathbf{A}^*\mathbf{p}_{t-1} \tag{9}$$

From (1) and (3) we have

$$\mathbf{y} = (1 + G)\mathbf{y}\mathbf{A}^* = (1 + R)\mathbf{y}\mathbf{A}^* \tag{10}$$

Substituting in (9), we have

$$\mathbf{y}\mathbf{p}_t = \mathbf{y}\mathbf{p}_{t-1} \qquad \forall t \tag{11}$$

Since we have established that $\mathbf{p}_0 = \boldsymbol{\Lambda}$ and $\mathbf{p} = \lim_{t \to \infty} \mathbf{p}_t$ we have

$$\mathbf{y}\mathbf{p} = \mathbf{y}\boldsymbol{\Lambda} \tag{12}$$

(b) *Aggregate profits equal the mass of surplus-value*

From the previous equations we have

$$\begin{cases} \mathbf{y}\mathbf{p}_1 = (1 + R)\mathbf{y}\mathbf{A}^*\boldsymbol{\Lambda} \\ \mathbf{y}\mathbf{p} \;\; = (1 + R)\mathbf{y}\mathbf{A}^*\mathbf{p} \\ \mathbf{y}\mathbf{p}_1 = \mathbf{y}\mathbf{p} \end{cases}$$

and thus $\quad \mathbf{yA^*\Lambda = yA^*p}$ (13)

using (12) we have

$$\mathbf{y(I - A^*)\Lambda = y(I - A^*)p} \tag{14}$$

From (2) we have $\mathbf{(I - A^*)p} = R\mathbf{A^*p}$; this means that $\mathbf{y(I - A^*)p} = R\mathbf{yA^*p}$ represents aggregate profits. Thus we only have to show that $\mathbf{y(I - A^*)\Lambda}$ represents the mass of surplus-value and this can be easily made on the basis of the definitions of $\mathbf{A^*}$, and of the values $\mathbf{\Lambda}$.

$$\mathbf{y(I - A^*)\Lambda = y(I - A - Ld)\Lambda = y(\Lambda - A\Lambda - Ld\Lambda)} = e\mathbf{yLd\Lambda}$$

Since e is the rate of exploitation, $\mathbf{yL}$ total labour, $\mathbf{d\Lambda}$ the value of the workers' means of subsistence, the previous expression indeed represents the mass of surplus-value.

Thus, (14) is the expression of the equality between the mass of surplus-value and aggregate profits.

6.3.2 The relation between the rate of profit and the rate of exploitation

(*A*) *THE SYSTEM WITH CIRCULATING CAPITAL*

The preceding results can be established more quickly on the basis of the standard commodity.

We know that Sraffa's standard commodity is a composite commodity whose composition is given by the vector $\mathbf{q}$ defined as the strictly positive eigenvector associated with the dominant eigenvalue α^* of the basic commodities matrix $\mathbf{A}$ (which is therefore indecomposable).

$$\mathbf{qA} = \alpha^*\mathbf{q} \tag{15}$$

The prices of the various commodities (and the wage) are given in terms of this particular commodity and the value of the net income of the standard system is assumed to be equal to unity. Thus

$$\mathbf{q(I - A)p} = 1 \tag{16}$$

This approach will have to be appropriately modified. We know that Sraffa assumes that the wage is paid *post factum* and is thus completely paid from the surplus, while Marx and the Classics make a very different assumption. To give a more general presentation we have used the assumption[12] that the wage, w, is composed of two parts: one part $w_0 = \mathbf{dp}$ 'advanced' by the capitalist and fixed by the given historical period and another, w', variable and paid from the surplus. Thus:

$$w = w_0 + w' \qquad \text{with} \quad w_0 = \mathbf{dp} \tag{17}$$

Marx's and Sraffa's assumptions represent two particular cases:
– Marx's assumption (wage totally advanced)

$$w = w_0 = \mathbf{dp} \qquad (w' = 0) \tag{17a}$$

– Sraffa's assumption (wage completely taken out of the surplus)

$$w = w' \qquad (w_0 = 0) \tag{17b}$$

The 'generalised' prices of production are then

$$\mathbf{p} = (1 + r)\mathbf{A}^*\mathbf{p} + w'\mathbf{L}$$

$$\text{with} \quad w = w_0 + w' = \mathbf{dp} + w' \qquad \text{and} \quad \mathbf{A}^* = \mathbf{A} + \mathbf{Ld}$$

In the new framework the capitalist advances the means of production (constant capital) as well as the means of subsistence necessary for the reproduction of labour-power (variable capital). We thus come back to a socio-technological matrix of the type $\mathbf{A}^*$ for which we can define a standard commodity, that is, a composite commodity whose composition is given by a strictly positive vector $\mathbf{q}$ associated with the dominant eigenvalue α^* of the $\mathbf{A}^*$ matrix assumed to be indecomposable.

$$\mathbf{qA}^* = \alpha^*\mathbf{q} \Leftrightarrow \mathbf{q} = (1 + R)\mathbf{qA}^* \qquad \text{with } \alpha^* = \frac{1}{1+R} \tag{18}$$

This composite commodity is such that any variation in the way the surplus is divided (with $0 \leq r \leq R$ and $0 \leq w' \leq w'_{max}$ or $w_0 \leq w \leq w_{max}$) is of no consequence for its price. The value of the net income of the new standard system so defined will be assumed equal to 1:

$$\mathbf{q}(\mathbf{I} - \mathbf{A}^*)\mathbf{p} = 1 \tag{19}$$

The prices of production when the part of the wage deducted from the surplus is zero (i.e. $w' = 0$ and $w = w_0 = \mathbf{dp}$) and therefore when the rate of profit is at its maximum ($r = R$) are given by

$$\mathbf{p} = (1 + R)\mathbf{A}^*\mathbf{p} \tag{20}$$

thus

$$R\mathbf{A}^*\mathbf{p} = (\mathbf{I} - \mathbf{A}^*)\mathbf{p} \tag{21}$$

Since $\mathbf{A}^*$ is indecomposable, $\mathbf{qA}^*\mathbf{p}$ is positive. Hence we have

$$R = \frac{\mathbf{q}(\mathbf{I}-\mathbf{A}^*)\mathbf{p}}{\mathbf{qA}^*\mathbf{p}} \tag{22}$$

On the other hand we know that when the rate of profit is zero and the whole of the surplus goes to workers, 'the relative values of commodities are in proportion to their labour cost, that is to say to the quantity of labour which directly and indirectly has gone to produce them' (P.S., § 14, p. 12). This means that labour-values are a particular case:

$$\begin{aligned} \mathbf{\Lambda} &= \mathbf{A\Lambda} + \mathbf{L} \\ 1 &= (1+e)\mathbf{d\Lambda} \end{aligned}$$

Since prices defined by (20) (and already defined in 1.2) are relative prices, we can normalise them by statuing:

$$\mathbf{q}(\mathbf{I}-\mathbf{A}^*)\mathbf{p} = \mathbf{q}(\mathbf{I}-\mathbf{A}^*)\mathbf{\Lambda} \tag{23}$$

Using (18) we have

$$\mathbf{q}(\mathbf{I}-\mathbf{A}^*)\mathbf{p} = (R\mathbf{qA}^*)\mathbf{p} = (R\mathbf{qA}^*)\mathbf{\Lambda}$$

and thus

$$\mathbf{qA}^*\mathbf{p} = \mathbf{qA}^*\mathbf{\Lambda} \tag{24}$$

Combining (22), (23) and (24) we get the fundamental result:[13]

$$R = \frac{\mathbf{q}(\mathbf{I}-\mathbf{A}^*)\mathbf{\Lambda}}{\mathbf{qA}^*\mathbf{\Lambda}} = \frac{e\mathbf{qLd\Lambda}}{\mathbf{q}[\mathbf{A}+\mathbf{Ld}]\mathbf{\Lambda}} = \frac{e\mathbf{qLd\Lambda}}{\mathbf{qLd\Lambda}+\mathbf{qA\Lambda}}$$

Defining $k_q = \dfrac{\mathbf{qA\Lambda}}{\mathbf{qLd\Lambda}}$ we have

$$R = \frac{e}{1+k_q} \tag{25}$$

In the new standard system based on matrix $\mathbf{A}^*$ the rate of profit R is indeed the standard ratio but R is also the rate of profit of a real system in which the wage is totally 'advanced', hence the expression of R as a function of the rate of exploitation and of the organic composition of capital k_q characterising the standard commodity $R = e/(1+k_q)$.

Consequently we must distinguish two series of cases according to whether the system follows, or does not follow, a Marx–von Neumann system.

In the case where the economic system under consideration follows a Marx–von Neumann system, Marx's analysis is correct and we can accept word for word the argument of Chapter X in the second Part of Volume III:

> The capital invested in some spheres of production has a mean, or average, composition, that is, it has the same, or almost the same composition as the average social capital.
>
> In these spheres the price of production is exactly or almost the same as the value of the produced commodity expressed in money ... [The] average rate of profit, however, is the percentage of profit in that sphere of average composition in which profit, therefore, coincides with surplus-value. Hence, the rate of profit is the same in all spheres of production, for it is equalized on the basis of those average spheres of production which has the average composition of capital. Consequently, the sum of the profits in all spheres of production must equal the sum of the surplus-values, and the sum of the prices of production of the total social product equal the sum of its value ... the tendency necessarily prevails to make the prices of production merely converted forms of value, or to turn profits into mere portions of surplus-value. However, these are not distributed in proportion to the surplus-value produced in each special sphere of production, but rather in proportion to the mass of capital employed in each sphere, so that equal masses of capital, whatever their composition, receive equal aliquot shares of the total surplus-value produced by the total social capital [I, pp. 170–1].

We can easily identify the differences between prices and values in the sectors where the organic composition of capital is different from the average composition and thus from the social composition; of course the rate of profit, R, the maximum rate of profit of the system where the wage is totally advanced, is equal to the ratio of total surplus-value to the value of total advanced capital. Since the mathematical structure of the dynamic Marx–von Neumann system is identical to that of Sraffa's standard system, the organic composition of the 'average' commodity k is identical to that of the standard commodity, k_q, hence the well-known formula $R = e/(1 + k)$ is absolutely correct for the case considered, since $k = k_q$.

In the case where the economic system does not follow a Marx–von Neumann regime because capitalists consume part of their income, it is always possible (in the case of single-product industries with circulating and/or fixed capital) to define the standard system on the basis of the $\mathbf{A}^*$ matrix. We know that the standard-ratio, or maximum rate of profit R, can be defined as $R = e/(1 + k_q)$ where $k_q = \mathbf{qA\Lambda}/\mathbf{qLd\Lambda}$ is the organic composition, in values, representing the standard commodity, while the organic composition, in values, of the average commodity is given by

$k = \mathbf{yA\Lambda}/\mathbf{yLd\Lambda}$, $\mathbf{y}$ being the structure of activities of the real system while $\mathbf{q}$ is that of the standard system.

Since the wage is, by assumption, completely advanced, no part of the surplus is allocated to workers. Therefore the maximum rate of profit or the standard-ratio, R, will determine the average rate of profit in the real system:

$$R = \frac{e}{1 + k_q}$$

Of course, if matrix $\mathbf{A}$ is decomposable Sraffa's 'beans' case may occur.

There is indeed a relation between rate of profit and rate of exploitation; but while Marx thought that this relation depended on the organic composition of capital (k) representing a commodity produced under 'average' conditions, it in fact depends on the organic composition of capital (k_q) which is used to produce the standard commodity.

We know that the decreasing linear relation between the wage paid from the surplus and the rate of profit is not limited to the imaginary standard system but can be applied to the actual economic system. The rate of profit of the real system is thus determined by the standard-ratio (since by assumption the whole surplus goes to capitalists) and is linked to the rate of exploitation through the intermediary of k_q, the organic composition of capital of the standard commodity. *Marx's analysis given above maintains its validity in the general case subject to the single condition that 'average' commodity or 'average' composition be replaced by 'standard' commodity or 'standard' composition.*

Obviously, in the general case, we no longer have the equality between the sum of profits and the sum of surplus-values at the same time as the equality between the sum of prices and the sum of values.

We note finally that when capitalists consume part of the surplus we still have the decreasing linear relation between the rate of growth, g, of the means of production and the level of consumption in terms of the standard system of the activity levels defined from matrix $\mathbf{A}$ (cf. Section 5.2). Since by assumption the system is indecomposable, the maximum rate of growth, G, is equal to the rate of profit, R. Thus

$$g = (1 - \xi_s)G = (1 - \xi_s)R = (1 - \xi_s)\frac{e}{1 + k_q}$$

This again demonstrates, in a more general sense, Sraffa's assertion that 'Particular proportions, such as the Standard ones, may give transparency to a system and render visible what was hidden' (P.S., §31, p. 23).

(B) *EXTENSION TO SYSTEMS WITH FIXED CAPITAL*

The preceding analysis concerned a system of single-product industries and circulating capital. The extension to fixed capital does not present any difficulty if machines are treated according to the von Neumann–Sraffa method which can be summarised with a simple example (see Section 3.1).

Let machine M have a working life of T years. Using the equations of the separate processes corresponding to the successive ages of the machine $M_0, M_1, \ldots, M_h, \ldots, M_{T-1}$ with $0 \leq h \leq T-1$ and $M_T = 0$ (the machine 'disappears' after T periods of use) the various machines (or rather the new as well as the old machines) produce the same quantities $b_{g,h}$ of the same final good g and the respective prices or book values of the various machines are given by $p_{m,0}, p_{m,1}, \ldots, p_{m,h}, \ldots, p_{m,T-1}$. Calling $\mathbf{a}_0^*, \mathbf{a}_1^*, \ldots, \mathbf{a}_h^*, \ldots, \mathbf{a}_{T-1}^*$ the consumption vector of intermediate goods necessary to produce the final good, used in the maintenance of the machine and for the maintenance of the labour force,[14] we can write the equations of the T production processes in which the machine appears as a means of production in the following form (we can, without restricting the analysis, set $M_0 = M_1 = \ldots = M_h = \ldots = M_{T-1} = 1$):

$$\begin{cases} (1+R)[\mathbf{a}_0^*\mathbf{p} + p_{m,0}] = b_{g,0}p_g + p_{m,1} \\ \ldots\ldots\ldots\ldots\ldots\ldots\ldots\ldots \\ (1+R)[\mathbf{a}_h^*\mathbf{p} + p_{m,h}] = b_{g,h}p_g + p_{m,h+1} \\ \ldots\ldots\ldots\ldots\ldots\ldots\ldots\ldots \\ (1+R)[\mathbf{a}_{T-1}^*\mathbf{p} + p_{m,T-1}] = b_{g,T-1}p_g \end{cases} \tag{26}$$

Of course, it is also possible to write the value equations of the various machines $\lambda_{m,0}, \ldots, \lambda_{m,h}, \ldots, \lambda_{m,T-1}$ using the technical conditions of production, the requirements of direct labour $l_{m,h}$ in each process, the vector of values $\mathbf{\Lambda}$, the consumption vector of intermediate goods $(\mathbf{a}_h)$ and the value λ_g of the final good produced by the machine during its working life. The value of the new machine, $\lambda_{m,0}$, is determined as usual by the value system $\mathbf{\Lambda} = \mathbf{A}\mathbf{\Lambda} + \mathbf{L}$.

$$\begin{cases} l_{m,0} + \mathbf{a}_0\mathbf{\Lambda} + \lambda_{m,0} = b_{g,0}\lambda_g + \lambda_{m,1} \\ \ldots\ldots\ldots\ldots\ldots\ldots\ldots\ldots \\ l_{m,h} + \mathbf{a}_h\mathbf{\Lambda} + \lambda_{m,h} = b_{g,h}\lambda_g + \lambda_{m,h+1} \\ \ldots\ldots\ldots\ldots\ldots\ldots\ldots\ldots \\ l_{m,T-1} + \mathbf{a}_{T-1}\mathbf{\Lambda} + \lambda_{m,T-1} = b_{g,T-1}\lambda_g \end{cases} \tag{27}$$

Marx had anticipated this method of treating fixed capital, as can be seen in the following quotation:

> we reckon as advanced for the purpose of turning out the product, the sum of £ 54 alone, which the machinery loses by wear and tear in the process, for it is all it parts with to the product.[15] Now if we reckon the remaining £ 1,000, which still continues in the machinery, as transferred to the product, we ought also to reckon it as part of the value advanced, and thus make it appear on both sides of our calculation [I, p. 213].

The results reached previously in the case of a system of single-product industries and circulating capital can be extended without difficulty to systems with fixed capital. Prices and values can be determined without ambiguity since we always have as many methods (or processes) as we have machines for any old machine still in use is considered as a new commodity which uses a new process, i.e. that same process in which it enters, one period later, as a 'new' means of production.

Of course, the essential difference for the system of simple production is to be found in the quantities produced; these quantities can no longer be represented by the diagonal identity matrix $\mathbf{B} = \mathbf{I}$ since some processes produce final goods and intermediate goods (used machines) at the same time.

Values will thus be determined by the following system where $\mathbf{B}$ is the output matrix (final goods and used machines), $\mathbf{A}$ the technology matrix (including the old machines used as means of production), $\mathbf{L}$ the vector of direct labour requirements for all processes:

$$\mathbf{B\Lambda} = \mathbf{A\Lambda} + \mathbf{L} \tag{28}$$

Assuming that the inverse of $(\mathbf{B} - \mathbf{A})$ exists, it follows that

$$\mathbf{\Lambda} = (\mathbf{B} - \mathbf{A})^{-1}\mathbf{L} \tag{29}$$

The prices of production can be determined in the same way from the following system (with $\mathbf{A}^*$ including old machines used as means of production as well as the wage advanced to workers). If the wage is completely advanced we then have:

$$\mathbf{Bp} = (1 + R)\mathbf{A}^*\mathbf{p} \tag{30}$$

We have shown (see Section 3.4) that the standard-ratio, R, always exists and that the prices of the used machines are positive when their efficiency is constant or increasing; in the case of decreasing efficiency the prices of the used machines can become negative. In this case the prices of the machines remain negative in the following periods and their utilisation is limited to the periods where their prices are positive. However, since we have both R and a standard system, there is no difficulty in duplicating the results previously obtained for a system of single-product industries and circulating capital.

CONCLUSION

The transformation of surplus-value into profit and of values into prices of production is therefore possible in a system of single-product industries and circulating capital as well as in a more general system using fixed capital when the fixed capital is valued by the von Neumann–Sraffa method. The two important results stressed by Marx, the equality between the sum of prices and the sum of values and the equality between aggregate profits and the mass of surplus-value can also be demonstrated.

The fundamental condition required for these results is that the economic system should follow a so-called Marx–von Neumann growth regime where the capitalists accumulate the whole of the surplus-value and all sectors grow at the same rate. This rate (which is at the same time the maximum rate of growth of the system and the maximum rate of profit) is determined by the dominant eigenvalue of the socio-technological matrix $\mathbf{A}^*$ which includes the means of subsistence of the workers, the wage being completely 'advanced'. Of course, neither technical progress nor change in the methods of production are considered.

The assumptions necessary to verify Marx's position on the transformation problem may seem very restrictive; however, Marx's thesis is that 'it is not values in use and the enjoyment of them, but exchange-value and its augmentation that spur the capitalist into action. Fanatically bent on making value expand itself, he ruthlessly forces the human race to produce for production's sake' (I, p. 592). 'Accumulate, accumulate! That is Moses and the prophets!' (I, p. 595). This means, implicitly, but very clearly, that the propensity to accumulate surplus-value is assumed to be close to 1. As we have seen, the transformation of surplus-value into profit and of values into prices of production is only realised under assumptions that seem very restrictive. But we should perhaps point out that in certain historical situations they represent acceptable approximations.

It should also be pointed out that we could have reached the same results on the basis of Sraffa's standard system. Of course, as Sraffa himself notes, the standard system and the standard commodity are only analytical constructions built to 'give transparency to a system and render visible what was hidden' (P.S. §31, p. 23), while the Marx–von Neumann growth system is a dynamic state based on particular behavioural assumptions ('subsistence' wage completely advanced and consumed, non-consuming capitalists accumulating the whole of the surplus-value). However, we have noted that the mathematical structure of the standard system constructed after taking account of the socio-technological matrix $\mathbf{A}^*$ which includes the wage 'advanced' to workers was identical to the structure of the Marx–von Neumann growth system previously defined. Thus the structure common to the model of Marx, von Neumann and Sraffa would appear to have great analytical importance. In the general case where the real economic system does not follow a Marx–von Neumann system (the structure of the activity levels $\mathbf{y}$ being different from the structure $\mathbf{q}$ that would appear in this hypothetical case) the organic composition k of the actual system is different from the composition (k_q) characterising the standard system and the Marx–von Neumann system. The average rate of profit of the actual system is R, the standard ratio, i.e. the relation with the rate of exploitation (e) defined by means of the organic composition characterising the standard commodity

$$R = \frac{e}{1 + k_q}$$

If part of the surplus is consumed by capitalists (the assumption that the wage is *completely* advanced excludes the possibility that the workers receive anything from the surplus) and if the consumption level is measured in terms of the standard commodity of the activity levels, we can again derive the decreasing linear relation between the rate of growth of the means of production (g) and the consumption level ξ_s

$$g = (1 - \xi_s)G = (1 - \xi_s)\frac{e}{1 + k_q} \text{ since } R = G$$

Now, the vector $\bar{\mathbf{p}}$ of Marx's prices of production defined as

$$\bar{\mathbf{p}} = (1 + R)\mathbf{A}^*\bar{\mathbf{p}}$$

is no different from the vector defining the 'virtual' standard commodity of the activity levels. Therefore Marx's system of prices of production is the dual standard system in which we have $\xi = \xi_s$ and consequently

$$g = (1 - \xi)G = (1 - \xi)\frac{e}{1 + k_q}.$$

6.4 'Transformation' and the proportion of labour to means of production

In this section we shall consider the cases in which the rate of profit is effectively determined by the ratio of total surplus-value to the total value of the advanced capital.

We shall call[16]

$\alpha > 0, \alpha_2, \alpha_3, \ldots$ the eigenvalues of the square matrix $\mathbf{A}$

$\mathbf{q} > \mathbf{0}, \mathbf{q}_2, \mathbf{q}_3, \ldots$ and $\bar{\mathbf{p}} > \mathbf{0}, \bar{\mathbf{p}}_2, \bar{\mathbf{p}}_3, \ldots$ the eigenvectors on the left and on the right of matrix $\mathbf{A}$ associated with the eigenvalues $\alpha, \alpha_2, \alpha_3, \ldots$

$\alpha^* > 0, \alpha_2^*, \alpha_3^*, \ldots$ the eigenvalues of matrix $\mathbf{A}^* = \mathbf{A} + \mathbf{Ld}$

$\mathbf{q}^* > \mathbf{0}, \mathbf{q}_2^*, \mathbf{q}_3^*, \ldots$ and $\mathbf{p}^* > \mathbf{0}, \mathbf{p}_2^*, \mathbf{p}_3^*, \ldots$ the eigenvectors on the left and on the right of matrix $\mathbf{A}^*$ associated with the eigenvalues $\alpha^*, \alpha_2^*, \alpha_3^*, \ldots$

The rate of profit defined by Marx for the value system can be written as

$$\mathbf{R}_\Lambda = \frac{\mathbf{y}(\mathbf{I} - \mathbf{A}^*)\mathbf{\Lambda}}{\mathbf{yA}^*\mathbf{\Lambda}} = \frac{e\mathbf{yLd\Lambda}}{\mathbf{yA\Lambda} + \mathbf{yLd\Lambda}} = \frac{e}{1+k}$$

where $k = \dfrac{\mathbf{yA\Lambda}}{\mathbf{yLd\Lambda}}$ is the organic composition of capital

Von Bortkiewicz has pointed out that it is illogical to introduce a rate of profit calculated in terms of value into a system of prices of production where there is simultaneous co-determination of the prices and the distributive variables.

In the case considered by Marx where the wage is *completely* advanced, the rate of profit R is determined in the system of prices of production

$$\mathbf{p}^* = (1 + R)(\mathbf{Ap}^* + \mathbf{L}w) \quad \text{with } w = \mathbf{dp}^*$$

$$\mathbf{p}^* = (1 + R)(\mathbf{Ap}^* + \mathbf{Ldp}^*) = (1 + R)(\mathbf{A} + \mathbf{Ld})\mathbf{p}^* = (1 + R)\mathbf{A}^*\mathbf{p}^*$$

The price vector $\mathbf{p}^*$, the eigenvector on the right of matrix $\mathbf{A}^*$ associated with the dominant eigenvalue $\alpha^* = 1/(1 + R)$, is defined up to the multiplication by scalars. We can normalise the prices of production $\mathbf{p}^*$ by setting $\mathbf{yp}^* = \mathbf{y\Lambda}$, making prices and values commensurate.

The system of prices of production can be written as

$$(\mathbf{I} - \mathbf{A}^*)\mathbf{p}^* = R\mathbf{A}^*\mathbf{p}^*$$

Premultiplying by $\mathbf{y}$ we have

$$\mathbf{y}(\mathbf{I} - \mathbf{A}^*)\mathbf{p}^* = R\mathbf{yA}^*\mathbf{p}^*$$

and thus

$$R = \frac{\mathbf{y}(\mathbf{I} - \mathbf{A}^*)\mathbf{p}^*}{\mathbf{yA}^*\mathbf{p}^*}$$

We can then state that *there are always two cases in which Marx's proposition, i.e.* $R_\Lambda = R$, *is rigorously true.*

FIRST CASE

The labour vector $\mathbf{L}$ is an eigenvector on the right of matrix $\mathbf{A}$, or, equivalently, all sectors have the same organic composition. We shall show that in this case we have $\mathbf{p}^* = \mathbf{\Lambda}$.

If $\mathbf{L}$ is an eigenvector on the right of $\mathbf{A}^*$, we have

$$\mathbf{A}^*\mathbf{L} = (\mathbf{A} + \mathbf{Ld})\mathbf{L} = \mathbf{AL} + \mathbf{LdL} = \alpha\mathbf{L} + \mathbf{LdL} = (\alpha + \mathbf{dL})\mathbf{L}$$

i.e. the dominant eigenvalue of $\mathbf{A}^*$ is $\alpha^* = \alpha + \mathbf{dL}$ and $\mathbf{L}$ is the eigenvector on the right of $\mathbf{A}^*$ associated with α^*.

The vector of the prices of production $\mathbf{p}^*$ such that

$$\mathbf{p}^* = (1 + R)\mathbf{A}^*\mathbf{p}^*$$

where $(1 + R) = 1/\alpha^*$ is, just as is $\mathbf{L}$, the eigenvector on the right of $\mathbf{A}^*$ associated with the dominant eigenvalue α^*. Therefore the vector $\mathbf{p}^*$ is *proportional* to $\mathbf{L}$.

The vector $\mathbf{\Lambda}$ is such that $\mathbf{\Lambda} = \mathbf{A\Lambda} + \mathbf{L}$ or $(\mathbf{I} - \mathbf{A})\mathbf{\Lambda} = \mathbf{L}$ and can be written as

$$\mathbf{\Lambda} = (\mathbf{I} - \mathbf{A})^{-1}\mathbf{L} = \frac{1}{1-\alpha}\mathbf{L} \text{ (Property 1)}^{17} \text{ (see mathematical appendix)}$$

Thus the value vector $\mathbf{\Lambda}$ is also *proportional* to $\mathbf{L}$.

The vectors $\mathbf{p}^*$ and $\mathbf{\Lambda}$ are therefore proportional and we have normalised the prices of production $\mathbf{p}^*$ by $\mathbf{yp}^* = \mathbf{y\Lambda}$; thus $\mathbf{p}^* = \mathbf{\Lambda}$.

We now show that for $\mathbf{L}$ to be eigenvector on the right of $\mathbf{A}$ is equivalent to the equality of the organic composition of all sectors.

If $\mathbf{AL} = \alpha\mathbf{L}$, we have

$$\mathbf{A\Lambda} = \mathbf{A}(\mathbf{I} - \mathbf{A})^{-1}\mathbf{L} = \frac{\alpha}{1-\alpha}\mathbf{L} \text{ (Property 1) and}$$

$$\mathbf{a}_i\mathbf{\Lambda} = \frac{\alpha}{1-\alpha}l_i = \frac{\alpha}{(1-\alpha)\mathbf{d\Lambda}}l_i\mathbf{d\Lambda} \text{ for all } i = 1, 2, \ldots, k \text{ where } \mathbf{d\Lambda} \text{ is the}$$

wage and thus

$$k_i = \frac{\mathbf{a}_i\mathbf{\Lambda}}{l_i\mathbf{d\Lambda}} = \frac{\alpha}{(1-\alpha)\mathbf{d\Lambda}} = k \quad \text{for all } i$$

Note that $\frac{\mathbf{a}_i\mathbf{\Lambda}}{l_i} = \frac{\alpha}{1-\alpha}$ for all $i = 1, 2$ and 3, i.e. the ratio between the value of the means of production and labour is equal in all sectors.

Reciprocally, if for all $i = 1, 2, \ldots, k$ we have

$$\frac{\mathbf{a}_i \mathbf{\Lambda}}{l_i \mathbf{d\Lambda}} = k \text{ then } \mathbf{a}_i \mathbf{\Lambda} = k\mathbf{d\Lambda}\, l_i \text{ or } \mathbf{A\Lambda} = k\mathbf{d\Lambda L}$$

and since $\mathbf{\Lambda} = \mathbf{A\Lambda} + \mathbf{L}$, it follows that $\mathbf{\Lambda} = (1 + k\mathbf{d\Lambda})\mathbf{L}$ that is, $\mathbf{\Lambda}$ and $\mathbf{L}$ are proportional and thus are eigenvectors on the right of $\mathbf{A}$ associated with the dominant eigenvalue α.

SECOND CASE

This case occurs when the actual system and standard system are identical,[18] that is, in what we have called a 'Marx–von Neumann system' characterised by a very particular behaviour on the part of capitalists who accumulate the whole surplus-value. In these conditions, the vector of activity levels of the actual system $\mathbf{y}$ has the same structure as the vector $\mathbf{q}^*$, the eigenvector on the left associated with the dominant eigenvalue $1/(1 + R)$ of matrix $\mathbf{A}^*$:

$$\mathbf{q}^* = (1 + R)\mathbf{q}^*\mathbf{A}^*$$

or $\quad \mathbf{q}^*(\mathbf{I} - \mathbf{A}^*) = R\mathbf{q}^*\mathbf{A}^* \quad$ where R is the rate of profit defined

by $\quad \mathbf{p}^* = (1 + R)\mathbf{A}^*\mathbf{p}^*$.

Multiplying both sides by the vector $\mathbf{\Lambda}$, we have

$$\mathbf{q}^*(\mathbf{I} - \mathbf{A}^*)\mathbf{\Lambda} = R\mathbf{q}^*\mathbf{A}^*\mathbf{\Lambda}$$

or

$$R = \frac{\mathbf{q}^*(\mathbf{I} - \mathbf{A}^*)\mathbf{\Lambda}}{\mathbf{q}^*\mathbf{A}^*\mathbf{\Lambda}} = R_\Lambda$$

In this case Marx's analysis is strictly validated: the rate of profit R is equal to the ratio of total surplus-value to the value of total advanced capital. Since we normalise the prices $\mathbf{p}^*$ by $\mathbf{q}^*\mathbf{p}^* = \mathbf{q}^*\mathbf{\Lambda}$, that is, the sum of prices equals the sum of values, total profit equals the mass of surplus-value. Furthermore we again discover the well-known divergence of prices from values in the sectors where the organic composition is different from the average composition and thus from the social composition.

Note that this second case includes Samuelson's case of 'equal *internal* compositions of (constant) capitals'. Samuelson assumes first that 'every one of the departments happens to use the various raw materials and machine services in the same proportions that society produces them in toto... We must also assume that the minimum-subsistence budget is a market basket of goods that comes in those same relative proportions as the goods are used as inputs in production'.[19] This means that if the output matrix is the identity matrix **I**, i.e. we take as unit for each commodity the production of each activity, then all columns of the input matrix **A** are identical because each activity uses various inputs in the same proportions $(1, 1, \ldots, 1)$ as they are globally produced by the society and the ith line of matrix **A** is $a_i[1, 1, \ldots, 1] = [a_i, \ldots, a_i]$

$$\mathbf{A} = \begin{bmatrix} a_1 & a_1 \ldots a_1 \\ a_2 & a_2 \ldots a_2 \\ \vdots & \vdots \\ a_k & a_k \ldots a_k \end{bmatrix}$$

and all components of vector $\mathbf{d} = (d_1, d_1, \ldots, d_1)$ are equal. The vector $[1, 1, \ldots, 1]$ is an eigenvector on the left of **A** and **A***. The case of equal internal composition is thus only a very special version of the second case in which the transformation is possible. It appears therefore that there are always two cases where it is possible to show the validity of transformation in Marx's sense; either the vector of activity levels is the eigenvector on the left associated with the dominant eigenvalue of matrix **A***, or the labour vector **L** is the eigenvector on the right of **A*** (or of **A**).

The first case is based on a behavioural assumption (capitalists do not consume) and consequently the actual economy has a productive structure which is identical to that of Sraffa's standard commodity of prices (associated to matrix $\mathbf{A}^* = \mathbf{A} + \mathbf{Ld}$). The second case is based on a technological peculiarity: **L** is the eigenvector on the right of matrix **A** or, equivalently, the organic composition of the various sectors are equal.

Let us call $E_1 = \{\bar{\mathbf{p}}\}$ the vector sub-space determined by the eigenvector $\bar{\mathbf{p}}$ on the right of **A** associated with α and $F_1^* = \{\mathbf{q}^*\}$ the vector sub-space determined by the eigenvector $\mathbf{q}^*$ on the left of **A*** associated with α^*.

We have already demonstrated the transformation process when $\mathbf{L} \in E_1$ or $\mathbf{y} \in F_1^*$, i.e. when **L** is the eigenvector on the right of **A** associated with α or when **y** is the eigenvector on the left of **A*** associated with α^*.

The double entry table given below shows four cases given by the following conditions:

$\mathbf{L} \in E_1$ or $\mathbf{L} \notin E_1$

$\mathbf{y} \in F_1^*$ or $\mathbf{y} \notin F_1^*$

The table shows the relations between the rate of profit R and the rate

y \ L	$\mathbf{L} \in E_1$	$\mathbf{L} \notin E_1$
$\mathbf{y} \in F_1$	$\mathbf{p}^* = \mathbf{\Lambda} \quad k = k_{q*}$ $R = \dfrac{e}{1+k}$ $\mathbf{y}(\mathbf{I}-\mathbf{A}^*)\mathbf{p}^* = \mathbf{y}(\mathbf{I}-\mathbf{A}^*)\mathbf{\Lambda}$	$k = k_{q*}$ $R = \dfrac{e}{1+k}$ $\mathbf{q}^*(\mathbf{I}-\mathbf{A}^*)\mathbf{p}^* = \mathbf{y}(\mathbf{I}-\mathbf{A}^*)\mathbf{\Lambda}$
$\mathbf{y} \notin F_1^*$	$\mathbf{p}^* = \mathbf{\Lambda}$ $R = \dfrac{e}{1+k}$ $\mathbf{y}(\mathbf{I}-\mathbf{A}^*)\mathbf{p}^* = \mathbf{y}(\mathbf{I}-\mathbf{A}^*)\mathbf{\Lambda}$	?

of exploitation e and between aggregate profits $\mathbf{y}(\mathbf{I}-\mathbf{A}^*)\mathbf{p}^*$ and the mass of surplus-value $\mathbf{y}(\mathbf{I}-\mathbf{A}^*)\mathbf{\Lambda}$.

While transformation is *always realised* in the first three cases of the table, *it is not necessarily excluded in the last case.*

To simplify the exposition we shall take a 3×3 indecomposable matrix $\mathbf{A}$ and assume that the eigenvalues of $\mathbf{A}, \alpha > 0, \alpha_2$ and α_3 are real and distinct and that matrix $\mathbf{A}^*$ is such that the eigenvalues of matrix $\mathbf{A}^*, \alpha^* > 0, \alpha_2^*$ and α_3^* are also real and distinct (the generalisation to a $k \times k$ matrix is immediate).

We shall show that if $\mathbf{L} \in E_2 = \{\bar{\mathbf{p}}, \bar{\mathbf{p}}_2\}$, the vector sub-space of $\mathbf{R}^3$ determined by the eigenvectors $\bar{\mathbf{p}}$ and $\bar{\mathbf{p}}_2$ on the right of $\mathbf{A}$ associated with α and α_2, and if $\mathbf{y} \in F_2^* = \{\mathbf{q}^*, \mathbf{q}_3^*\}$, the vector sub-space of $\mathbf{R}^3$ determined by the eigenvectors $\mathbf{q}^*$ and $\mathbf{q}_3^*$ of $\mathbf{A}^*$ associated with α^* and α_3^*, the transformation is realised. Obviously the transformation is also realised when $\mathbf{L} \in E_2' = \{\bar{\mathbf{p}}, \bar{\mathbf{p}}_3\}$ and $\mathbf{y} \in F'^*_2 = \{\mathbf{q}^*, \mathbf{q}_2^*\}$.

Let us first show that if $\mathbf{L} \in E_2, \mathbf{p}^*$ and $\mathbf{p}_2^*$ also belong to E_2. The indecomposable matrix $\mathbf{A}^* = \mathbf{A} + \mathbf{L}\mathbf{d} \geq \mathbf{A}$, thus its dominant eigenvalue $\alpha^* > \alpha$ and α^* is not an eigenvalue of $\mathbf{A}$. Therefore matrix $[\alpha^*\mathbf{I} - \mathbf{A}]$ is non-singular. We have

$$\alpha^*\mathbf{p}^* = \mathbf{A}^*\mathbf{p}^* = \mathbf{A}\mathbf{p}^* + \mathbf{L}\mathbf{d}\mathbf{p}^* = \mathbf{A}\mathbf{p}^* + \mathbf{d}\mathbf{p}^*\mathbf{L}$$

or

$$(\alpha^*\mathbf{I} - \mathbf{A})\mathbf{p}^* = (\mathbf{d}\mathbf{p}^*)\mathbf{L}$$

or, since $[\alpha^*\mathbf{I} - \mathbf{A}]$ is non-singular

$$\mathbf{p}^* = (\alpha^*\mathbf{I} - \mathbf{A})^{-1}(\mathbf{d}\mathbf{p}^*)\mathbf{L} \in E_2 \qquad \text{(Property 3')}$$

On the other hand we have $\mathbf{p}_2^* \in E_2$ because

– either α_2^* is not an eigenvalue of matrix $\mathbf{A}$ and $\alpha_2^*\mathbf{I} - \mathbf{A}$ is not singular. We have

$$\alpha_2^*\mathbf{p}_2^* = \mathbf{A}^*\mathbf{p}_2^* = \mathbf{A}\mathbf{p}_2^* + (\mathbf{Ld})\mathbf{p}_2^* = \mathbf{A}\mathbf{p}_2^* + (\mathbf{d}\mathbf{p}_2^*)\mathbf{L}$$

or $\quad (\alpha_2^*\mathbf{I} - \mathbf{A})\mathbf{p}_2^* = (\mathbf{d}\mathbf{p}_2^*)\mathbf{L}$

or since $[\alpha_2^*\mathbf{I} - \mathbf{A}]$ is non-singular,

$$\mathbf{p}_2^* = (\alpha_2^*\mathbf{I} - \mathbf{A})^{-1}(\mathbf{d}\mathbf{p}_2^*)\mathbf{L} \in E_2 \qquad \text{(Property 3')}$$

– or $\alpha_2^* = \alpha_2$ and by Property 4 we have $\mathbf{p}_2^* = \mathbf{p}_2 \in E_2$

since $\quad \mathbf{q}_2\mathbf{A}^* = \mathbf{q}_2\mathbf{A} + \mathbf{q}_2(\mathbf{Ld}) = \mathbf{q}_2\mathbf{A} + (\mathbf{q}_2\mathbf{L})\mathbf{d} \neq \mathbf{q}_2\mathbf{A}$

because $\mathbf{L} \in E_2 = \{\bar{\mathbf{p}}, \bar{\mathbf{p}}_2\}$ and this implies that $\mathbf{q}_2\mathbf{L} \neq 0$.

Thus $\mathbf{p}^*$ and $\mathbf{p}_2^*$ associated with two distinct eigenvalues α^* and α_2^* are linearly independent and belong to the two-dimensional vector sub-space E_2. They thus form a base of E_2.

The vector $\mathbf{\Lambda} = (\mathbf{I} - \mathbf{A})^{-1}\mathbf{L} \in E_2$ (Property 3') can be expressed in the base $\{\mathbf{p}^*, \mathbf{p}_2^*\}$ of E_2, i.e. there exist scalars μ and μ_2 such that

$$\mathbf{\Lambda} = \mu\mathbf{p}^* + \mu_2\mathbf{p}_2^*$$

If the vector $\mathbf{y} \in F_2^* = \{\mathbf{q}^*, \mathbf{q}_3^*\}$ there exist scalars ν and ν_3 such that

$$\mathbf{y} = \nu\mathbf{q}^* + \nu_3\mathbf{q}_3^*$$

and we have

$$\frac{\mathbf{y}(\mathbf{I} - \mathbf{A}^*)\mathbf{\Lambda}}{\mathbf{y}\mathbf{A}^*\mathbf{\Lambda}} = \frac{(\nu\mathbf{q}^* + \nu_3\mathbf{q}_3^*)(\mathbf{I} - \mathbf{A}^*)(\mu\mathbf{p}^* + \mu_2\mathbf{p}_2^*)}{(\nu\mathbf{q}^* + \nu_3\mathbf{q}_3^*)\mathbf{A}^*(\mu\mathbf{p}^* + \mu_2\mathbf{p}_2^*)} = \frac{\nu\mu(1 - \alpha^*)\mathbf{q}^*\mathbf{p}^*}{\nu\mu\alpha^*\mathbf{q}^*\mathbf{p}^*}$$

$$= \frac{1 - \alpha^*}{\alpha^*} = R$$

because the following products are zeros by Property 2:

$$\nu_3\mathbf{q}_3^*(\mathbf{I} - \mathbf{A}^*)(\mu\mathbf{p}^* + \mu_2\mathbf{p}_2^*) = (1 - \alpha_3^*)(\nu_3\mu\mathbf{q}_3^*\mathbf{p}^* + \nu_3\mu_2\mathbf{q}_3^*\mathbf{p}_2^*)$$

$$\nu\mathbf{q}^*(\mathbf{I} - \mathbf{A}^*)\mu_2\mathbf{p}_2^* = \nu\mu_2(1 - \alpha^*)\mathbf{q}^*\mathbf{p}_2^*$$

$$\nu_3\mathbf{q}_3^*\mathbf{A}^*(\mu\mathbf{p}^* + \mu_2\mathbf{p}_2^*) = \alpha_3^*(\nu_3\mu\mathbf{q}_3^*\mathbf{p}^* + \nu_3\mu_2\mathbf{q}_3^*\mathbf{p}_2^*)$$

$$\nu\mathbf{q}^*\mathbf{A}^*\mu_2\mathbf{p}_2^* = \alpha^*\nu\mu_2\mathbf{q}^*\mathbf{p}_2^*$$

We thus have

$$\frac{\mathbf{y}(\mathbf{I} - \mathbf{A}^*)\mathbf{\Lambda}}{\mathbf{y}\mathbf{A}^*\mathbf{\Lambda}} = R = \frac{\mathbf{y}(\mathbf{I} - \mathbf{A}^*)\mathbf{p}^*}{\mathbf{y}\mathbf{A}^*\mathbf{p}^*}$$

and the transformation is realised in the sense that the rate of profit R is effectively determined by the ratio of the mass of surplus-value to the total value of the advanced capital.

To sum up, the transformation is realised

(i) when $\mathbf{L} \in E_1$ and $\mathbf{y}$ is unspecified

(ii) when $\mathbf{L} \in E_2 = \{\bar{\mathbf{p}}, \bar{\mathbf{p}}_2\}$ and $\mathbf{y} \in F_2^* = \{\mathbf{q}^*, \mathbf{q}_3^*\}$

(iii) when $\mathbf{L}$ is unspecified and $\mathbf{y} \in F_1^*$.

If $\mathbf{L} \in E_1$ the vectors $\mathbf{L}, \mathbf{AL}, \mathbf{A}^2\mathbf{L}$ are proportional and the rank of the system of vectors $\{\mathbf{L}, \mathbf{AL}, \mathbf{A}^2\mathbf{L}\}$ is 1. We have already shown that in this case

$$\frac{\mathbf{A\Lambda}}{\mathbf{L}} = \frac{\alpha}{1-\alpha} \quad \text{or}$$

$\dfrac{\mathbf{a}_i\mathbf{\Lambda}}{l_i} = \dfrac{\alpha}{1-\alpha}$ for all $i = 1, 2, 3$, that is, the ratio between means of production and labour is equal in all sectors (or in other words all sectors have the same organic composition).

If $\mathbf{L} \in E_2 = \{\bar{\mathbf{p}}, \bar{\mathbf{p}}_2\}$ all three vectors $\mathbf{L}$, $\mathbf{AL}$ and $\mathbf{A}^2\mathbf{L}$ belong to E_2 and the rank of the system of vectors $\{\mathbf{L}, \mathbf{AL}, \mathbf{A}^2\mathbf{L}\}$ is 2. In this case there exist two constant numbers θ and θ_2 such that $\mathbf{L} = \theta\bar{\mathbf{p}} + \theta_2\bar{\mathbf{p}}_2$ and we have

$$\mathbf{A\Lambda} = \mathbf{A}(\mathbf{I}-\mathbf{A})^{-1}\mathbf{L} = \frac{\alpha}{1-\alpha}\theta\bar{\mathbf{p}} + \frac{\alpha_2}{1-\alpha_2}\theta_2\bar{\mathbf{p}}_2$$

If $\mathbf{U}$ is a row-vector of dimension 3, the ratio

$$\frac{\mathbf{UA\Lambda}}{\mathbf{UL}} = \frac{\dfrac{\alpha}{1-\alpha}\theta\mathbf{U}\bar{\mathbf{p}} + \dfrac{\alpha_2}{1-\alpha_2}\theta_2\mathbf{U}\bar{\mathbf{p}}_2}{\theta\mathbf{U}\bar{\mathbf{p}} + \theta_2\mathbf{U}\bar{\mathbf{p}}_2} = \frac{\alpha}{1-\alpha} \quad \text{if} \quad \mathbf{U}\bar{\mathbf{p}}_2 = 0$$

that is, if $\mathbf{U}$ is orthogonal to the eigenvector $\bar{\mathbf{p}}_2$.

If one of the components U_1 of such a vector $\mathbf{U} \neq 0$ is zero, the two other components U_i and U_j satisfy

$$U_i\bar{p}_{i2} + U_j\bar{p}_{j2} = 0$$

and except in the case where $\bar{p}_{i2} = 0$ or $\bar{p}_{j2} = 0$, there is a fixed ratio between U_i and U_j:

$$\frac{U_i}{U_j} = \lambda - \frac{\bar{p}_{j2}}{\bar{p}_{i2}}$$

This means that, whatever the couple of activities (i, j), the ratio between means of production and labour for the composite activity $U_i\mathbf{a}_i + U_j\mathbf{a}_j$ is fixed and equal to $\alpha/(1-\alpha)$ since

$$\frac{(U_i\mathbf{a}_i + U_j\mathbf{a}_j)\mathbf{\Lambda}}{U_il_i + U_jl_j} = \frac{\mathbf{U}\mathbf{A}\mathbf{\Lambda}}{\mathbf{UL}} = \frac{\alpha}{1-\alpha}$$

If **L** is unspecified in the sense that the system of vectors $\{\mathbf{L}, \mathbf{AL}, \mathbf{A}^2\mathbf{L}\}$ is of rank 3 (Schefold calls this case the 'regular' case), only the composite commodity $\mathbf{q} = (q_1, q_2, q_3)$ (where **q** is an eigenvector on the left of **A** associated with α) is such that the ratio between its means of production and labour is equal to $\alpha/(1-\alpha)$ since

$$\frac{\mathbf{q}\mathbf{A}\mathbf{\Lambda}}{\mathbf{qL}} = \frac{\mathbf{q}\mathbf{A}(\mathbf{I}-\mathbf{A})^{-1}\mathbf{L}}{\mathbf{qL}} = \frac{\frac{\alpha}{1-\alpha}\mathbf{qL}}{\mathbf{qL}} = \frac{\alpha}{1-\alpha}$$

To sum up, the ratio of means of production to labour is equal to the 'critical' proportion $\alpha/(1-\alpha)$

(i) in each activity if the system of vectors $\{\mathbf{L}, \mathbf{AL}, \mathbf{A}^2\mathbf{L}\}$ is of rank 1,

(ii) for a particular combination (U_i, U_j) of any couple (i,j) of activities if the system of vectors $\{\mathbf{L}, \mathbf{AL}, \mathbf{A}^2\mathbf{L}\}$ is of rank 2,

(iii) only for the linear combination $q_1\mathbf{a}_1 + q_2\mathbf{a}_2 + q_3\mathbf{a}_3$ of the three activities where $\mathbf{q} = (q_1, q_2, q_3)$ is the eigenvector on the left of **A** associated with α (i.e. Sraffa's standard commodity) if the system of vectors $\{\mathbf{L}, \mathbf{AL}, \mathbf{A}^2\mathbf{L}\}$ is of rank 3.

In the general case where **A** is a $k \times k$ indecomposable matrix, the transformation is realised if $\mathbf{L} \in E_m = \{\bar{\mathbf{p}}, \bar{\mathbf{p}}_2, \ldots, \bar{\mathbf{p}}_m\}$ and $\mathbf{y} \in F_n^* = \{\mathbf{q}^*, \mathbf{q}_a, \ldots, \mathbf{q}_n\}$ where the eigenvalues $\alpha_a, \ldots, \alpha_n$ are real, distinct and different from the eigenvalues $\alpha_2, \ldots, \alpha_m$ to which are associated the eigenvectors $\bar{\mathbf{p}}_2, \ldots, \bar{\mathbf{p}}_m$.

In this case, the system of vectors $\{\mathbf{L}, \mathbf{AL}, \mathbf{A}^2\mathbf{L} \ldots, \mathbf{A}^{k-1}\mathbf{L}\}$ is of rank m, i.e. the ratio of means of production to labour is equal to the 'critical' proportion $\alpha/(1-\alpha)$ for a determined combination of any sub-set of m activities.

The transformation problem as stated by Marx can only be solved in very particular cases.[20] However, in the general case where the system of vectors $\{\mathbf{L}, \mathbf{AL}, \ldots, \mathbf{A}^{k-1}\mathbf{L}\}$ is of rank k and where **y** is not proportional to $\mathbf{q}^*$ a relation between the rate of profit and the rate of exploitation still exists. This relation does not use the average organic composition of capital but the organic composition of the standard commodity

$$R = \frac{e}{1+k_{q^*}} \qquad \text{where} \qquad k_{q^*} = \frac{\mathbf{q}^*\mathbf{A}\mathbf{\Lambda}}{\mathbf{q}^*\mathbf{L}d\mathbf{\Lambda}}.$$

6.5 Conclusion

The rate of profit, R, is thus the keystone of the system since, as we have seen above, it appears as the rate of profit in von Neumann's analysis, as the standard ratio in Sraffa's system, and finally, as the rate of profit which determines Marx's prices of production when wages are advanced. We have shown, in particular, that the 'transformation' problem, as stated by Marx, can be solved by means of concepts proposed by Sraffa. Values and prices of production indeed constitute two independent systems. If we assume that the wage is advanced, we can identify easily a special case in which 'transformation' is assured, i.e. the case where capitalists' consumption is zero and the entire surplus is reinvested. This is what we have called a Marx–von Neumann growth system. The structure of the activity levels is then the structure of Sraffa's standard commodity; it is also the eigenvector corresponding to the dominant eigenvalue of the indecomposable socio-technological matrix.

While it is unlikely for such conditions to exist in reality, it is always possible to derive a relation between the rate of exploitation and the rate of profit. This relation does not occur, as Marx thought, through the social or organic composition of capital, but through the organic composition of the standard commodity constructed under the assumption that wages are 'advanced'.

The treatment of labour, which is assumed to be homogeneous in all the analyses considered, is nonetheless distinct. The role of labour in Sraffa's analysis is explicit to the extent that the wage is paid *post-factum* from the produced surplus. It also appears clearly in Marx's analysis of labour-values where commodities can be considered, from a particular point of view, as embodied labour. On the other hand, Marx's prices of production tend to mask the role of labour which is hidden within the elements of the socio-technological matrix. Finally, in von Neumann's analysis the role of labour completely disappears. It can, however, be reintroduced by considering the goods necessary for workers' subsistence just 'as the fuel for engines... among the means of production' (in Sraffa's words, P.S. p. 9, §8) as indeed Marx did.

However, it would be a mistake to define a formal link between the various different methods of analysis. It is true that the treatment of joint production is the same in von Neumann and Sraffa, while it is absent (for obvious reasons) from Marx's analysis (although Marx considered fixed capital as a joint product—which may be sufficient justification for the generalisation we have proposed for the treatment of this aspect of his system). There are, however, two objections that immediately come to mind. First, the problem of the choice of techniques is dealt with in very different ways in the various models considered. The choice of technique is at the centre of von Neumann's analysis since it determines the systems of equilibrium prices and activity levels that ensure proportional growth. The problem is considered differently in Sraffa since his analysis is of systems that can be represented by square matrices, with the choice of technique only considered secondarily. Moreover, the distinction between market goods and free goods is only relevant to von Neumann's analysis. The notion of superprofit is *a priori* excluded from Sraffa's analysis, as it is with von Neumann's which only deals with steady state solutions. Outside such a framework the output of the process of production chosen may not be sufficient to satisfy total demand. In this case several processes may be used simultaneously, which leads to the possibility of quasi-rents or superprofits being earned by some processes. As we have seen above, this possibility allows the derivation of a relation between prices of production and market prices to be identified. Marx's analysis is especially instructive in this regard.

The second objection is more fundamental. It concerns the analysis of production in the strict sense. In fact, von Neumann's and Marx's approach contrasts with that of Sraffa. The first two, as is well known, are concerned with the analysis of accumulation, while *Production of Commodities by Means of Commodities* is in no way dynamic. It deals essentially with the consequences of variations in the distribution of a given output. No change in output is ever taken into consideration: 'no question arises as to the variation or constancy of returns' (P.S., p. v). Obviously, in order to study the dual of the problem posed by Sraffa constant returns to scale had to be assumed, but this working hypothesis was not absolutely ruled out by Sraffa and it allows us to contrast the conflict of distribution and the conflict of accumulation. We know that the first type of conflict is clearly analysed by Sraffa in terms of the linear wage–profit relation (subject to the condition that prices are normalised by an appropriate composite commodity). Furthermore, we have shown that a conflict between the rhythm of accumulation and the level of consumption can exist. This negative relation is linear if activity levels are normalised by an appropriate 'virtual' commodity. This dual approach leads to the determination of a standard of activity levels that does not vary with changes in the distribution of the net product between the level of final consumption and accumulation.

It is also possible to show the construction and existence of norms for prices of production and activity levels such that the wage–profit curve and the consumption–accumulation curve are identical. Von Neumann's analysis totally ignores these two types of conflict since it does not involve either workers receiving part of the surplus as wages or final consumption diminishing the surplus available for investment. The class struggle considered by Marx relates to a different aspect of the distribution conflict. Yet, it is indeed the other type of conflict that determines the scale of accumulation, and which is considered by Marx in terms of the 'Faustian conflict between the passion for accumulation and the desire for enjoyment' (I, p. 592).

The Perron–Frobenius theorem, and more generally the orthogonality properties between the vectors of activity levels and the labour vector give a better understanding of certain problems linked to the three analyses here considered.

On the one hand, Sraffa demonstrated the existence of a standard of prices that was invariant to change in the distribution of income. On the other hand, we have shown that other standards of prices exist when the labour vector belongs to a vector subspace made up of only part of the eigenvectors on the right of the input matrix. Similarly, it appears that the transformation of values into prices of production and of surplus-value into profit is only assured in special cases. These cases occur when the vector of activity levels satisfies the critical proportion of labour to means of production. Finally, if we normalise prices of production by a standard invariant to changes in distribution then the wage–profit curve is a straight line. Cf. G. Abraham-Frois and E. Berrebi: 'Pluralité des marchandises etalons: existence et construction', *Revue d'Economie Politique*, no. 5, 1978; and 'Etalon(s) et "transformation" pour close un débat', *Econometrica*, November 1979.

In this way the solution to the three problems considered—the existence of a standard invariant to a change in the distribution of income, the demonstration of transformation, the linearity of the wage–profit curves—depends on the existence of the critical proportion of labour to means of production in the system.

Mathematical appendix

A.1 Eigenvalues and eigenvectors

Given a square matrix $\mathbf{A}$ composed of real number a_{ij} consider the vectors $\mathbf{x}$ such that $\mathbf{Ax} = \alpha\mathbf{x}$. Obviously the vector $\mathbf{x} = \mathbf{0}$ satisfies the equality $\mathbf{Ax} = \alpha\mathbf{x}$ for any real number α. Our aim is to determine the non-zero vectors $\mathbf{x}$ and the real numbers α such that $\mathbf{Ax} = \alpha\mathbf{x}$.

Consider a square matrix $\mathbf{A}$ of order k. If there exists a real number α and a non-zero vector $\mathbf{x}$ such that $\mathbf{Ax} = \alpha\mathbf{x}$, α is said to be an eigenvalue of $\mathbf{A}$ and $\mathbf{x}$ an eigenvector of $\mathbf{A}$ corresponding to α.

DETERMINATION OF THE EIGENVALUES OF **A**

Any eigenvalue α of $\mathbf{A}$ is such that there exists a non-zero vector $\mathbf{x}$ which satisfies $\mathbf{Ax} = \alpha\mathbf{x} = \alpha\mathbf{Ix}$ where $\mathbf{I}$ is the identity matrix of the same order k as the square matrix $\mathbf{A}$. Thus any eigenvalue α of $\mathbf{A}$ satisfies $(\mathbf{A} - \alpha\mathbf{I})\mathbf{x} = \mathbf{0}$. Since $\mathbf{A} - \alpha\mathbf{I}$ is a non-zero matrix and since $\mathbf{x}$ is a non-zero vector we must have $|\mathbf{A} - \alpha\mathbf{I}| = 0$ (recall that $|\mathbf{A} - \alpha\mathbf{I}|$ is the determinant of the square matrix $\mathbf{A} - \alpha\mathbf{I}$), i.e. α is a solution of the equation of the kth degree $|\mathbf{A} - \alpha\mathbf{I}| = 0$ since the square matrix $\mathbf{A} - \alpha\mathbf{I}$ is of order k.

The equation $|\mathbf{A} - \alpha\mathbf{I}| = 0$ is called the *characteristic equation* of matrix $\mathbf{A}$ and has at most k real solutions. If the characteristic equation has no real solution, matrix $\mathbf{A}$ has neither real eigenvalues nor eigenvectors with real components.

DETERMINATION OF THE EIGENVECTORS OF **A**

If the real number $\bar{\alpha}$ is a solution of the characteristic equation $|\mathbf{A} - \alpha\mathbf{I}| = 0$ of the square matrix $\mathbf{A}$, $\bar{\alpha}$ is an eigenvalue of $\mathbf{A}$. Any non-zero eigenvector $\mathbf{x}$ of $\mathbf{A}$ associated with $\bar{\alpha}$ satisfies the matrix equation $\mathbf{Ax} = \bar{\alpha}\mathbf{x} = \bar{\alpha}\mathbf{Ix}$ or $(\mathbf{A} - \bar{\alpha}\mathbf{I})\mathbf{x} = 0$. This equation in fact represents a system of k homogeneous linear equations with k unknowns, i.e. the components $x_1, x_2, \ldots, x_k$ of the eigenvector $\mathbf{x}$. Since $|\mathbf{A} - \bar{\alpha}\mathbf{I}| = 0$, the rank of matrix $\mathbf{A} - \bar{\alpha}\mathbf{I}$ is at most equal to $k - 1$. We can then distinguish the following cases:

–rank$(\mathbf{A}-\bar{\alpha}\mathbf{I}) = k-1$: one of the components, say x_1, can be arbitrarily chosen and the $k-1$ others are uniquely determined by the value chosen for x_1. The eigenvector $\mathbf{x}$ is thus *uniquely defined up to the multiplication by scalars.*

–rank $(\mathbf{A}-\bar{\alpha}\mathbf{I}) \leq k-2$: p components $(p \geq 2)$, say $x_1, x_2, \ldots, x_p$, can be arbitrarily chosen and the $k-p$ others are determined by $x_1, x_2, \ldots, x_p$. We can then have p linearly *independent* eigenvectors corresponding to the *same* eigenvalue $\bar{\alpha}$.

Only one eigenvector $\mathbf{x}$ (up to the multiplication by scalars) corresponds to the real eigenvalue $\bar{\alpha}$ when $\bar{\alpha}$ is a simple root of the characteristic equation. But when the eigenvalue $\bar{\alpha}$ is a multiple root of order $\mathbf{p}$ of the characteristic equation, we have

– *either one* eigenvector $\mathbf{x}$ (up to the multiplication by scalars) associated with $\bar{\alpha}$, in this case $\bar{\alpha}$ is said to be a *semi-simple* eigenvalue;

– *or several* linearly *independent* eigenvectors corresponding to $\bar{\alpha}$.

Remark

We can also determine a vector $\mathbf{y}$ such that $\mathbf{yA} = \alpha\mathbf{y}$. Call $\mathbf{y}$ the eigenvector on the left of $\mathbf{A}$ associated with the eigenvalue α. The vector $\mathbf{x}$ such that $\mathbf{Ax} = \alpha\mathbf{x}$ is then the eigenvector on the right of $\mathbf{A}$ associated with α.

Example

Let us determine the eigenvalues and the eigenvectors of the matrix (cf. Chapters 2 and 5)

$$\mathbf{A} = \begin{bmatrix} \frac{1}{2} & \frac{4}{15} & \frac{1}{8} \\ \frac{5}{18} & \frac{5}{18} & \frac{5}{16} \\ \frac{2}{9} & \frac{4}{45} & \frac{5}{12} \end{bmatrix}$$

The eigenvalues α of matrix $\mathbf{A}$ are the solutions of a third degree equation $|\mathbf{A}-\alpha\mathbf{I}| = 0$ where

$$|\mathbf{A}-\alpha\mathbf{I}| = \begin{vmatrix} \frac{1}{2}-\alpha & \frac{4}{15} & \frac{1}{8} \\ \frac{5}{18} & \frac{5}{18}-\alpha & \frac{5}{16} \\ \frac{2}{9} & \frac{4}{45} & \frac{5}{12}-\alpha \end{vmatrix}$$

$$=\left(\frac{1}{2}-\alpha\right)\begin{vmatrix}\frac{5}{18}-\alpha & \frac{5}{16}\\ \frac{4}{45} & \frac{5}{12}-\alpha\end{vmatrix}-\frac{4}{15}\begin{vmatrix}\frac{5}{18} & \frac{5}{16}\\ \frac{2}{9} & \frac{5}{12}-\alpha\end{vmatrix}$$

$$+\frac{1}{8}\begin{vmatrix}\frac{5}{18} & \frac{5}{18}-\alpha\\ \frac{2}{9} & \frac{4}{45}\end{vmatrix}$$

$$|\mathbf{A}-\alpha\mathbf{I}|=\left(\frac{1}{2}-\alpha\right)\left[\left(\frac{5}{18}-\alpha\right)\left(\frac{5}{12}-\alpha\right)-\frac{5}{16}\cdot\frac{4}{45}\right]$$

$$-\frac{4}{15}\left[\frac{5}{18}\cdot\frac{5}{12}-\frac{5}{18}\alpha-\frac{5}{16}\cdot\frac{2}{9}\right]+\frac{1}{8}\left[\frac{5}{18}\cdot\frac{4}{45}-\frac{2}{9}\cdot\frac{5}{18}+\frac{2}{9}\alpha\right]$$

$$=\left(\frac{1}{2}-\alpha\right)\left(\alpha^2-\frac{25}{36}\alpha+\frac{19}{216}\right)+\frac{2}{27}\alpha-\frac{1}{81}+\frac{1}{36}\alpha-\frac{3}{648}$$

$$=-\alpha^3+\frac{43}{36}\alpha^2-\frac{1}{3}\alpha+\frac{35}{1296}$$

The equation $-\alpha^3+(43/36)\alpha^2-\frac{1}{3}\alpha+(35/1296)=0$ can be written in the form $-(\alpha-\frac{5}{6})(\alpha-7/36)(\alpha-\frac{1}{6})=0$ and thus $\mathbf{A}$ has three eigenvalues: $\frac{5}{6}$, 7/36 and $\frac{1}{6}$ which are the simple roots of the characteristic equation.

Let us determine an eigenvector on the right $\bar{\mathbf{p}}$ and an eigenvector on the left $\mathbf{q}$ of matrix $\mathbf{A}$ associated with the highest eigenvalue $\alpha=\frac{5}{6}$.

An eigenvector on the right $\bar{\mathbf{p}}=\begin{bmatrix}p_1\\p_2\\p_3\end{bmatrix}$ of $\mathbf{A}$ associated with the eigenvalue $\alpha=\frac{5}{6}$ satisfies the matrix equation $(\mathbf{A}-\frac{5}{6}\mathbf{I})\bar{\mathbf{p}}=\mathbf{0}$ or

$$\begin{bmatrix}-\frac{1}{3} & \frac{4}{15} & \frac{1}{8}\\ \frac{5}{18} & -\frac{5}{9} & \frac{5}{16}\\ \frac{2}{9} & \frac{4}{45} & -\frac{5}{12}\end{bmatrix}\begin{bmatrix}p_1\\p_2\\p_3\end{bmatrix}=\begin{bmatrix}0\\0\\0\end{bmatrix}$$

and its components p_1, p_2 and p_3 are the solutions of the system of homogeneous equations:

$$\begin{cases} -\dfrac{1}{3}p_1 + \dfrac{4}{15}p_2 + \dfrac{1}{8}p_3 = 0 \\[2ex] \dfrac{5}{18}p_1 - \dfrac{5}{9}p_2 + \dfrac{5}{16}p_3 = 0 \\[2ex] \dfrac{2}{9}p_1 + \dfrac{4}{45}p_2 - \dfrac{5}{12}p_3 = 0 \end{cases}$$

which is an undetermined system of rank 2. If we give to p_1 the value 11, we have $p_2 = 10$ and $p_3 = 8$, that is, $\bar{\mathbf{p}} = \begin{bmatrix} 11 \\ 10 \\ 8 \end{bmatrix}$ is an eigenvector on the right of $\mathbf{A}$ associated with $\alpha = \frac{5}{6}$, and any vector $\begin{bmatrix} 11\mu \\ 10\mu \\ 8\mu \end{bmatrix}$ where μ is any scalar, is also an eigenvector on the right associated with $\alpha = \frac{5}{6}$.

Similarly, an eigenvector on the left $\mathbf{q} = (q_1, q_2, q_3)$ of $\mathbf{A}$ associated with the eigenvalue $\alpha = \frac{5}{6}$ satisfies the matrix equation:

$$\mathbf{q}\left(\mathbf{A} - \frac{5}{6}\mathbf{I}\right) = \mathbf{0} \quad \text{or}$$

$$(q_1\, q_2\, q_3)\begin{bmatrix} -\dfrac{1}{3} & \dfrac{4}{15} & \dfrac{1}{8} \\[2ex] \dfrac{5}{18} & -\dfrac{5}{9} & \dfrac{5}{16} \\[2ex] \dfrac{2}{9} & \dfrac{4}{45} & -\dfrac{5}{12} \end{bmatrix} = (0 \quad 0 \quad 0)$$

and its components q_1, q_2 and q_3 are the solutions of the system of homogeneous equations:

$$\begin{cases} -\dfrac{1}{3}q_1 + \dfrac{5}{18}q_2 + \dfrac{2}{9}q_3 = 0 \\[2ex] \dfrac{4}{15}q_1 - \dfrac{5}{9}q_2 + \dfrac{4}{45}q_3 = 0 \\[2ex] \dfrac{1}{8}q_1 + \dfrac{5}{16}q_2 - \dfrac{5}{12}q_3 = 0 \end{cases}$$

which is an undetermined system of rank 2. If we assume that $q_1 = 1$, we have $q_2 = \frac{3}{5}$ and $q_3 = \frac{3}{4}$, that is, $\mathbf{q} = (1, \frac{3}{5}, \frac{3}{4})$ is an eigenvector on the left of $\mathbf{A}$ associated with $\alpha = \frac{5}{6}$ and any vector $(\mu, \frac{3}{5}\mu, \frac{3}{4}\mu)$ where μ is any scalar, is also an eigenvector on the left associated with $\alpha = \frac{5}{6}$.

PROPERTIES OF THE EIGENVECTORS OF A SQUARE MATRIX

Property 1

If $\mathbf{q}_i$ is an eigenvector on the left of the square matrix $\mathbf{A}$ associated with the eigenvalue α_i, i.e. $\mathbf{q}_i\mathbf{A} = \alpha_i\mathbf{q}_i$ we have in particular

$$\mathbf{q}_i\mathbf{A}^n = \alpha_i^n\mathbf{q}_i$$

$$\mathbf{q}_i(\mathbf{I} - \mathbf{A}) = (1 - \alpha_i)\mathbf{q}_i$$

$$\mathbf{q}_i[\mathbf{I} - (1 + r)\mathbf{A}] = [1 - \alpha_i(1 + r)]\mathbf{q}_i$$

$$\mathbf{q}_i[\mathbf{I} - (1 + r)\mathbf{A}]^{-1} = \frac{\mathbf{q}_i}{1 - \alpha_i(1 + r)}$$

if $\mathbf{I} - (1 + r)\mathbf{A}$ is nonsingular.

Property 1′

If $\bar{\mathbf{p}}_i$ is an eigenvector on the right of the square matrix $\mathbf{A}$ associated with the eigenvalue α_i, i.e. $\mathbf{A}\bar{\mathbf{p}}_i = \alpha_i\bar{\mathbf{p}}_i$ we have in particular

$$\mathbf{A}^n\bar{\mathbf{p}}_i = \alpha_i^n\bar{\mathbf{p}}_i$$

$$(\mathbf{I} - \mathbf{A})\bar{\mathbf{p}}_i = (1 - \alpha_i)\bar{\mathbf{p}}_i$$

$$[\mathbf{I} - (1 + r)\mathbf{A}]\bar{\mathbf{p}}_i = [\mathbf{I} - (1 + r)\alpha_i]\bar{\mathbf{p}}_i$$

$$[\mathbf{I} - (1 + r)\mathbf{A}]^{-1}\bar{\mathbf{p}}_i = \frac{\bar{\mathbf{p}}_i}{1 - \alpha_i(1 + r)} \text{ if } \mathbf{I} - (1 + r)\mathbf{A} \text{ is nonsingular.}$$

Property 2

If the eigenvalues α_i and α_j of a square matrix $\mathbf{A}$ are distinct, the eigenvector $\mathbf{q}_i$ on the left of $\mathbf{A}$ associated with α_i is orthogonal to the eigenvector $\bar{\mathbf{p}}_j$ on the right of $\mathbf{A}$ associated with α_j.

We have

$$\alpha_i\mathbf{q}_i\bar{\mathbf{p}}_j = (\mathbf{q}_i\mathbf{A})\bar{\mathbf{p}}_j = \mathbf{q}_i(\mathbf{A}\bar{\mathbf{p}}_j) = \mathbf{q}_i\alpha_j\bar{\mathbf{p}}_j = \alpha_j\mathbf{q}_i\bar{\mathbf{p}}_j$$

or $\quad(\alpha_i - \alpha_j)\mathbf{q}_i\bar{\mathbf{p}}_j = 0$

and this implies $\mathbf{q}_i\bar{\mathbf{p}}_j = 0$ since $\alpha_i - \alpha_j \neq 0$.

VECTOR SUBSPACES DETERMINED BY THE EIGENVECTORS OF A MATRIX

Property 3

Consider a square $(k \times k)$ matrix $\mathbf{A}$.

If $\mathbf{q}_1, \mathbf{q}_2, \ldots, \mathbf{q}_m$ are the eigenvectors on the left of $\mathbf{A}$ associated with the real eigenvalues $\alpha, \alpha_2, \ldots, \alpha_m$, they determine a vector subspace $E_m = \{\mathbf{q}, \mathbf{q}_2, \ldots \mathbf{q}_m\}$ of $\mathbf{R}^k$ (Euclidean space of dimension k) *invariant on the left* by matrix $\mathbf{A}$ in the sense that for any vector $\mathbf{u} \in E_m$ we have $\mathbf{uA} \in E_m$.

Since $\mathbf{q}, \mathbf{q}_2, \ldots, \mathbf{q}_m$ form a basis of E_m we can write vector $\mathbf{u}$ as

$$\mathbf{u} = \mu\mathbf{q} + \mu_2\mathbf{q}_2 + \ldots + \mu_m\mathbf{q}_m$$

and thus we have

$$\begin{aligned}\mathbf{uA} &= \mu\mathbf{qA} + \mu_2\mathbf{q}_2\mathbf{A} + \ldots + \mu_m\mathbf{q}_m\mathbf{A} \\ &= \alpha\mu\mathbf{q} + \alpha_2\mu_2\mathbf{q}_2 + \ldots + \alpha_m\mu_m\mathbf{q}_m \in E_m\end{aligned}$$

Note that if $\mathbf{u} \in E_m$ we have in particular $\mathbf{uA}^p \in E_m$ and $\mathbf{u}(\mu\mathbf{I} - \mathbf{A})^{-1} \in E_m$ if μ is not an eigenvalue of A.

Property 3′

If $\bar{\mathbf{p}}, \bar{\mathbf{p}}_2, \ldots, \bar{\mathbf{p}}_n$ are the eigenvectors on the right of $\mathbf{A}$ associated with the eigenvalues $\alpha, \alpha_2, \ldots, \alpha_n$, they determine a subspace $F_n = \{\bar{\mathbf{p}}, \bar{\mathbf{p}}_2, \ldots, \bar{\mathbf{p}}_n\}$ of $\mathbf{R}^k$ *invariant on the right* by matrix $\mathbf{A}$ in the sense that, for any vector $\mathbf{v} \in F_n$ we have $\mathbf{Av} \in F_n$.

Note in particular that if $\mathbf{v} \in F_n$ we have $\mathbf{A}^p\mathbf{v} \in F_n$ and $(\mu\mathbf{I} - \mathbf{A})^{-1}\mathbf{v} \in F_n$ if μ is not an eigenvalue of $\mathbf{A}$.

RELATIONS BETWEEN EIGENVALUES AND EIGENVECTORS OF THE A* *AND* A *MATRICES*

Let $\mathbf{A}^* = \mathbf{A} + \mathbf{Ld}$. Call $\alpha^*, \alpha_2^*, \alpha_3^*, \ldots$ its eigenvalues, $\mathbf{q}^*, \mathbf{q}_2^*, \mathbf{q}_3^*, \ldots$ its eigenvectors on the left and $\mathbf{p}^*, \mathbf{p}_2^*, \mathbf{p}_3^*, \ldots$ its eigenvectors on the right.

Let us consider some cases where the $\mathbf{A}^*$ and $\mathbf{A}$ matrices have common eigenvalues and common eigenvectors on the right or on the left.

Property 4

If the $\mathbf{A}^*$ and $\mathbf{A}$ matrices have a common eigenvalue $\alpha_i^* = \alpha_i$, we have either $\mathbf{q}_i^* = \mathbf{q}_i$ or $\mathbf{p}_i^* = \bar{\mathbf{p}}_i$.

Since by assumption we have

$$\alpha_i\mathbf{q}_i = \mathbf{q}_i\mathbf{A} \qquad \text{and} \qquad \alpha_i\mathbf{p}_i^* = \mathbf{A}^*\mathbf{p}_i^* = (\mathbf{A} + \mathbf{Ld})\mathbf{p}_i^*$$

it follows that

$$\begin{aligned}\alpha_i \mathbf{q}_i \mathbf{p}_i^* = \mathbf{q}_i \mathbf{A} \mathbf{p}_i^* = \mathbf{q}_i (\mathbf{A}^* - \mathbf{L}\mathbf{d}) \mathbf{p}_i^* = \mathbf{q}_i \mathbf{A}^* \mathbf{p}_i^* - \mathbf{q}_i \mathbf{L}\mathbf{d}\mathbf{p}_i^* \\ = \alpha_i \mathbf{q}_i \mathbf{p}_i^* - \mathbf{q}_i \mathbf{L}\mathbf{d}\mathbf{p}_i^*\end{aligned}$$

this implies that $\mathbf{q}_i \mathbf{L}\mathbf{d}\mathbf{p}_i^* = 0$ or $(\mathbf{q}_i \mathbf{L})(\mathbf{d}\mathbf{p}_i^*) = 0$.
We thus have

- either $\mathbf{q}_i \mathbf{L} = 0$ and $\alpha_i \mathbf{q}_i = \mathbf{q}_i \mathbf{A} = \mathbf{q}_i \mathbf{A} + (\mathbf{q}_i \mathbf{L})\mathbf{d} = \mathbf{q}_i(\mathbf{A} + \mathbf{L}\mathbf{d}) = \mathbf{q}_i \mathbf{A}^*$ thus $\mathbf{q}_i^* = \mathbf{q}_i$
- or $\mathbf{d}\mathbf{p}_i^* = 0$ and $\alpha_i \mathbf{p}_i^* = \mathbf{A}^* \mathbf{p}_i^* = (\mathbf{A} + \mathbf{L}\mathbf{d})\mathbf{p}_i^* = \mathbf{A}\mathbf{p}_i^* + \mathbf{L}\mathbf{d}\mathbf{p}_i^* = \mathbf{A}\mathbf{p}_i^*$ thus $\bar{\mathbf{p}}_i = \mathbf{p}_i^*$.

Property 5

If the labour vector **L** belongs to the vector subspace $E_m = \{\bar{\mathbf{p}}, \bar{\mathbf{p}}_2, \ldots, \bar{\mathbf{p}}_m\}$ any eigenvalue α_i different from the eigenvalues $\alpha, \alpha_2, \ldots, \alpha_m$ is an eigenvalue of $\mathbf{A}^*$ and $\mathbf{q}_i$ is a common eigenvector on the left of **A** and $\mathbf{A}^*$.

Since $\mathbf{q}_i \mathbf{A} = \alpha_i \mathbf{q}_i$ we have

$$\mathbf{q}_i \mathbf{A}^* = \mathbf{q}_i \mathbf{A} + \mathbf{q}_i \mathbf{L}\mathbf{d} = \mathbf{q}_i \mathbf{A} + (\mathbf{q}_i \mathbf{L})\mathbf{d} = \mathbf{q}_i \mathbf{A} = \alpha_i \mathbf{q}_i$$

since $\mathbf{q}_i$, being orthogonal to $\bar{\mathbf{p}}, \bar{\mathbf{p}}_2, \ldots, \bar{\mathbf{p}}_m$ (cf. property 2), is also orthogonal to **L**.

Property 5′

If the vector **d** belongs to the vector subspace $F_n = \{\mathbf{q}, \mathbf{q}_2, \ldots, \mathbf{q}_n\}$ any eigenvalue α_j of **A** different from the eigenvalues $\alpha, \alpha_2, \ldots, \alpha_n$ is an eigenvalue of $\mathbf{A}^*$ and $\bar{\mathbf{p}}_j$ is a common eigenvector on the right of **A** and $\mathbf{A}^*$.

Since $\mathbf{A}\bar{\mathbf{p}}_j = \alpha_j \bar{\mathbf{p}}_j$ we have

$$\mathbf{A}^* \bar{\mathbf{p}}_j = \mathbf{A}\bar{\mathbf{p}}_j + (\mathbf{L}\mathbf{d})\bar{\mathbf{p}}_j = \mathbf{A}\bar{\mathbf{p}}_j + \mathbf{L}(\mathbf{d}\bar{\mathbf{p}}_j) = \mathbf{A}\bar{\mathbf{p}}_j = \alpha_j \bar{\mathbf{p}}_j$$

since $\bar{\mathbf{p}}_j$, being orthogonal to $\mathbf{q}, \mathbf{q}_2, \ldots, \mathbf{q}_n$, is also orthogonal to **d**.

A.2 Decomposable and indecomposable matrices

PERMUTATION MATRIX

A square matrix **P** is said to be a permutation matrix when its elements are either 0 or 1, each row and each column containing one 1 and only one. Any permutation matrix P is nonsingular and is such that $\mathbf{P}'\mathbf{P} = \mathbf{P}\mathbf{P}' = \mathbf{I}$, i.e., it has as inverse its transpose $\mathbf{P}'$.

The pre-multiplication or post-multiplication of a square matrix **A** by a permutation matrix **P** will produce respectively either a permutation of its rows or a permutation of its columns.

PERMUTATION OF A SQUARE MATRIX

We call permutation of a square matrix $\mathbf{A}$ the square matrix $\bar{\mathbf{A}}$ obtained by the permutation of the rows of $\mathbf{A}$ combined with the *same* permutation of the columns.

Any permutation $\bar{\mathbf{A}}$ of a square matrix $\mathbf{A}$ can be written as $\bar{\mathbf{A}} = \mathbf{PAP}'$ where $\mathbf{P}$ is a permutation matrix. In particular, when the same permutation of the rows and the columns is performed on the identity matrix $\mathbf{I}$, the result is always matrix $\mathbf{I}$ since $\mathbf{PIP}' = \mathbf{PP}' = \mathbf{I}$ for any matrix $\mathbf{P}$. Note that $\mathbf{A}$ and $\bar{\mathbf{A}}$ have the *same rank* since matrix $\mathbf{P}$ is nonsingular.

INDECOMPOSABLE MATRIX

A square matrix is said to be *decomposable* or *reducible* if there exists a permutation $\bar{\mathbf{A}}$ of $\mathbf{A}$

$$\bar{\mathbf{A}} \begin{bmatrix} \mathbf{A}_1^1 & \mathbf{0} \\ \mathbf{A}_2^1 & \mathbf{A}_2^2 \end{bmatrix} \text{ where } \mathbf{A}_1^1 \text{ and } \mathbf{A}_2^2 \text{ are square matrices.}$$

$\bar{\mathbf{A}}$ is said to be a *quasi-triangular* matrix, that is, it contains only zeros at the intersection of its first rows and its last columns.

When a square matrix is not decomposable, it is said to be *indecomposable* or *irreducible*.

A.3 Matrices with nonnegative elements

With the usual notation

$\mathbf{A} \geqq \mathbf{0}$ $\mathbf{A}$ is said to be *nonnegative* when $a_{ij} \geq 0$ for any i and any j;

$\mathbf{A} \geq \mathbf{0}$ $\mathbf{A}$ is said to be *semi-positive* when $a_{ij} \geq 0$ for any i and any j and $\mathbf{A} \neq \mathbf{0}$;

$\mathbf{A} > \mathbf{0}$ $\mathbf{A}$ is said to be *positive* when $a_{ij} > 0$ for any i and any j.

SUPPORT OF A VECTOR

Given a nonnegative vector $\mathbf{u} = (u_1, \dots, u_j, \dots, u_n)$ we call the support of the vector $\mathbf{u}$ the set of the subscripts of the strictly positive elements u_j of $\mathbf{u}$, i.e.

$$\text{supp}(\mathbf{u}) = \{j \,|\, u_j > 0\}.$$

A.4 Properties of the elements of an indecomposable semi-positive square matrix

Property I

If the square matrix **A** is semi-positive and indecomposable and if $\mathbf{x} > \mathbf{0}$, the vector $\mathbf{z} = (\mathbf{I} + \mathbf{A})\mathbf{x}$ always has a number of zero elements lesser than that of **x**.

Property II

If the square matrix **A** of order $(k \times k)$ is semi-positive and indecomposable, the $(\mathbf{I} + \mathbf{A})^{k-1}$ and $\mathbf{A}(\mathbf{I} + \mathbf{A})^{k-1}$ matrices are strictly positive.

Property III

If the $(k \times k)$ square matrix **A** is semi-positive and indecomposable, for all index pairs (i, j) we have:

$$\text{either } a_{ij} > 0$$

or there exists a series of subscripts $j_1, j_2, \ldots, j_l$ such that $a_{ij_1}, a_{j_1 j_2}, \ldots, a_{j_1 j} > 0$.

A.5 Spectral properties of indecomposable semi-positive matrices

Let **A** be an indecomposable and semi-positive $(k \times k)$ square matrix. Its transpose **A**′ is also semi-positive and indecomposable. We shall establish five lemmas leading to the well-known Perron–Frobenius Theorem.

Lemma 1

For any vector $\mathbf{x} \geq \mathbf{0}$, we have $\mathbf{Ax} \geq \mathbf{0}$.

Lemma 2

There exists a positive number α such that the equation $\mathbf{Ax} = \alpha\mathbf{x}$ has a solution $\mathbf{x} \geq \mathbf{0}$.

Lemma 3

If $\alpha > 0$, any solution $\mathbf{x} \geq \mathbf{0}$ of the equation $\mathbf{Ax} = \alpha\mathbf{x}$ is positive.

Lemma 4

The equation $\mathbf{Ax} = \alpha\mathbf{x}$ has only one solution $\alpha > 0, \mathbf{x} > \mathbf{0}$ with **x** defined up to the multiplication by scalars.

Lemma 5

Let $\alpha(\mathbf{A})$ be the solution of the equation $\mathbf{Ax} = \alpha\mathbf{x}$ with $\alpha > 0$ and $\mathbf{x} > \mathbf{0}$ and r be a given positive number

– if there exists a vector $\mathbf{z} \geq \mathbf{0}$ such that $\mathbf{Az} \geqq r\mathbf{z}$, we have $\alpha(\mathbf{A}) \geq r$;

– if there exists a vector $\mathbf{z} \geq \mathbf{0}$ such that $\mathbf{Az} \leqq r\mathbf{z}$, we have $\alpha(\mathbf{A}) \leq r$.

Lemma 5′

Let $\alpha(\mathbf{A})$ be the solution of the equation $\mathbf{Ax} = \alpha\mathbf{x}$ with $\alpha > 0, \mathbf{x} > \mathbf{0}$ and r be a given positive number

(i) if there exists a vector $\mathbf{z} \geq \mathbf{0}$ such that $\mathbf{Az} \geq r\mathbf{z}$, we have $\alpha(\mathbf{A}) > r$;

(ii) if there exists a vector $\mathbf{z} \geq \mathbf{0}$ such that $\mathbf{Az} \leq r\mathbf{z}$, we have $\alpha(\mathbf{A}) < r$.

PERRON–FROBENIUS THEOREM

Any indecomposable semi-positive square matrix $\mathbf{A}$ possesses a positive eigenvalue $\alpha(\mathbf{A})$ and a positive eigenvector $\mathbf{x}$ corresponding to $\alpha(\mathbf{A})$. The positive number $\alpha(\mathbf{A})$, the only eigenvalue of matrix $\mathbf{A}$ with an associated positive eigenvector, is a simple root of the characteristic equation $|\mathbf{A} - \alpha\mathbf{I}| = 0$. The absolute values of the $k-1$ other eigenvalues of matrix $\mathbf{A}$ are not greater than $\alpha(\mathbf{A})$.

DOMINANT EIGENVALUE OF AN INDECOMPOSABLE MATRIX

Definition

The positive eigenvalue $\alpha(\mathbf{A})$ (or equivalently α^*) of the indecomposable nonnegative square matrix $\mathbf{A}$ with an associated eigenvector $\mathbf{x} > \mathbf{0}$ is called the dominant eigenvalue of matrix $\mathbf{A}$.

We call

$$c_j = \sum_{i=1}^{k} a_{ij} \quad \text{the sum of the elements of the } j\text{th column of matrix } \mathbf{A}$$

$$l_i = \sum_{j=1}^{k} a_{ij} \quad \text{the sum of the elements of the } i\text{th row of matrix } \mathbf{A}.$$

Since the semi-positive square matrix $\mathbf{A}$ is indecomposable we have $c_j > 0$ for any $j \in \{1, 2, \ldots, k\}$ and $l_i > 0$ for any $i \in \{1, 2, \ldots, k\}$.

In the following theorems we determine the limits of the dominant eigenvalue $\alpha(\mathbf{A})$ of an indecomposable matrix $\mathbf{A}$ using the sums c_j and l_i and we consider the variations of the number $\alpha(\mathbf{A})$ for increasing and continuous variations of matrix $\mathbf{A}$.

Theorem 1

The dominant eigenvalue $\alpha(\mathbf{A})$ of the indecomposable matrix **A** satisfies the inequalities:

$$\cdot \min_{1 \leq j \leq k} c_j \leq \alpha(\mathbf{A}) \leq \max_{1 \leq j \leq k} c_j$$

$$\cdot \min_{1 \leq i \leq k} l_i \leq \alpha(\mathbf{A}) \leq \max_{1 \leq i \leq k} l_i$$

Theorem 2

The mapping $\mathbf{A} \to \alpha(\mathbf{A})$ associating its dominant eigenvalue to any indecomposable semi-positive $(k \times k)$ square matrix is increasing, i.e. if $\mathbf{A} \leq \bar{\mathbf{A}}$ we have $\alpha(\mathbf{A}) < \alpha(\bar{\mathbf{A}})$.

Theorem 3

The mapping $\mathbf{A} \to \alpha(\mathbf{A})$ is a continuous mapping from the set of the indecomposable nonnegative square matrices in $\mathbf{R}^+$ (the set of positive real numbers).

Theorem 4

If $\rho > \alpha(\mathbf{A})$ we have $(\rho\mathbf{I} - \mathbf{A})^{-1} > \mathbf{0}$.

Corollary

If the square matrix **A** is semi-positive and indecomposable, the mapping $r \to [\mathbf{I} - (1 + r)\mathbf{A}]^{-1}$ is an increasing function of r on the interval $[0\,R[$ where $1/(1 + R)$ is the dominant eigenvalue of matrix **A**.

A.6 Primitive and non-primitive matrices

Definition

If an indecomposable semi-positive square matrix **A** has h eigenvalues $\alpha_1 = \alpha(\mathbf{A}), \alpha_2, \ldots, \alpha_h$ of modulus $\alpha(\mathbf{A})$, then **A** is primitive if $h = 1$ and non-primitive if $h > 1$. In the latter case h is called the index of non-primitiveness.

Theorem 1

A matrix $\mathbf{A} \geq \mathbf{0}$ is indecomposable and primitive if, and only if, a power of **A** is positive: $\mathbf{A}^p > \mathbf{0}$.

Theorem 2

If an indecomposable semi-positive square matrix $\mathbf{A}$ has at least one nonzero element on the principal diagonal, it is primitive.

A.7 Properties of decomposable matrices

If a square matrix $\mathbf{A}$ is decomposable there exists a permutation $\bar{\mathbf{A}}$ of $\mathbf{A}$ which can be written in the triangular form:

$$\bar{\mathbf{A}} = \begin{bmatrix} \mathbf{A}_{11} & 0 & 0 & 0 \\ \mathbf{A}_{21} & \mathbf{A}_{22} & 0 & 0 \\ \vdots & \vdots & & \vdots \\ \mathbf{A}_{s1} & \mathbf{A}_{s2} & & \mathbf{A}_{ss} \end{bmatrix}$$

where the diagonal blocks $\mathbf{A}_{11}, \mathbf{A}_{22}, \ldots, \mathbf{A}_{ss}$ are indecomposable square matrices.

A diagonal block $\mathbf{A}_{ii}$ is said to be

– isolated in row if $\mathbf{A}_{ik} = \mathbf{0}$ for any $k \neq i$

– isolated in column if $\mathbf{A}_{ji} = \mathbf{0}$ for any $j \neq i$.

We call the *normal form* of a decomposable matrix a permutation $\bar{\mathbf{A}}$ of matrix $\mathbf{A}$ where all the blocks in the first positions of the principal diagonal are isolated in row and all the blocks in the last positions of the principal diagonal are isolated in column:

$$\begin{bmatrix}
\mathbf{A}_{11} & \mathbf{0} & \ldots \mathbf{0} & \mathbf{0} & \ldots \mathbf{0} & \mathbf{0} & \ldots \mathbf{0} \\
\mathbf{0} & \mathbf{A}_{22} & \ldots \mathbf{0} & \mathbf{0} & \ldots \mathbf{0} & \mathbf{0} & \ldots \mathbf{0} \\
\vdots & \vdots & \vdots & \vdots & \vdots & \vdots & \vdots \\
\mathbf{0} & \mathbf{0} & \ldots \mathbf{A}_{gg} & \mathbf{0} & \ldots \mathbf{0} & \mathbf{0} & \ldots \mathbf{0} \\
\mathbf{A}_{g+1,1} & & \ldots \mathbf{A}_{g+1,g} & \mathbf{A}_{g+1,g+1} & \mathbf{0} & \cdot & \cdot \\
\vdots & & \vdots & \vdots & \vdots & \vdots & \vdots \\
\mathbf{A}_{r,1} & & \ldots \mathbf{A}_{r,g} & \mathbf{A}_{r,g+1} & \ldots \mathbf{A}_{r,r} & \mathbf{0} & \ldots \mathbf{0} \\
\mathbf{A}_{r+1,1} & & \ldots \mathbf{A}_{r+1,g} & & \ldots \mathbf{A}_{r+1,r} & \mathbf{A}_{r+1,r+1} & \ldots \mathbf{0} \\
\vdots & & \vdots & & \vdots & \vdots & \vdots \\
\mathbf{A}_{s,1} & & \ldots \mathbf{A}_{s,g} & & \ldots \mathbf{A}_{s,r} & \mathbf{0} & \ldots \mathbf{A}_{s,s}
\end{bmatrix}$$

The normal form of a decomposable matrix is unique (up to the permutations).

Theorem 1

To the dominant eigenvalue α of matrix $\mathbf{A} \geq \mathbf{0}$ corresponds a (strictly) positive eigenvector on the right if, and only if, in the normal form of $\mathbf{A}$, α is the dominant eigenvalue of each matrix $\mathbf{A}_{11}, \mathbf{A}_{22}, \ldots, \mathbf{A}_{gg}$ and the eigenvalues of each matrix $\mathbf{A}_{g+1,g+1}, \ldots, \mathbf{A}_{s,s}$ are strictly less than α.

Theorem 2

To the dominant eigenvalue α of matrix $\mathbf{A} \geq \mathbf{0}$ corresponds a (strictly) positive eigenvector on the left if, and only if, in the normal form of $\mathbf{A}$, α is the dominant eigenvalue of each matrix $\mathbf{A}_{r+1,r+1}, \ldots, \mathbf{A}_{s,s}$ and the eigenvalues of each matrix $\mathbf{A}_{11}, \mathbf{A}_{22}, \ldots, \mathbf{A}_{r,r}$ are strictly less than α.

Corollary

A necessary and sufficient condition for the existence of (strictly) positive eigenvectors on the right and on the left of $\mathbf{A}$ corresponding to the dominant eigenvalue of the decomposable square matrix $\mathbf{A} \geq \mathbf{0}$ is for matrix $\mathbf{A}$ to be quasi-diagonal and for all its diagonal blocks to have α as dominant eigenvalue, thus:

$$\mathbf{A} = \begin{bmatrix} \mathbf{A}_{11} & \mathbf{0} & \ldots \mathbf{0} & \ldots \mathbf{0} \\ \mathbf{0} & \mathbf{A}_{22} & \ldots \mathbf{0} & \ldots \mathbf{0} \\ \vdots & \vdots & \vdots & \vdots \\ \mathbf{0} & \mathbf{0} & \mathbf{A}_{ii} & \ldots \mathbf{0} \\ \vdots & \vdots & \vdots & \vdots \\ \mathbf{0} & \mathbf{0} & \ldots \mathbf{0} & \ldots \mathbf{A}_{ss} \end{bmatrix}$$

with $\alpha(\mathbf{A}_{ii}) = \alpha$ for any $i = 1, 2, \ldots, s$.

Remark

In a decomposable matrix $\mathbf{A} \geq \mathbf{0}$ there exist eigenvalues $\alpha_i < \alpha$ with corresponding semi-positive eigenvectors $\mathbf{q}_i$ on the left and/or $\bar{\mathbf{p}}_i$ on the right.

Theorem 3

Let $\mathbf{A}$ be a semi-positive decomposable square matrix and r be a given positive number.

When $\mathbf{A}$ has an eigenvector on the left $\mathbf{y} > \mathbf{0}$,

– we have $\alpha(\mathbf{A}) \geq r$ if there exists a vector $\mathbf{z} \geq \mathbf{0}$ such that $\mathbf{Az} \geqq r\mathbf{z}$

– we have $\alpha(\mathbf{A}) \leq r$ if there exists a vector $\mathbf{z} \geq \mathbf{0}$ such that $\mathbf{Az} \leqq r\mathbf{z}$.

When $\mathbf{A}$ has an eigenvector on the right $\mathbf{x} > \mathbf{0}$,
– we have $\alpha(\mathbf{A}) \geq r$ if there exists a vector $\mathbf{z} \geq \mathbf{0}$ such that $\mathbf{zA} \geqq r\mathbf{z}$
– we have $\alpha(\mathbf{A}) \leq r$ if there exists a vector $\mathbf{z} \geq \mathbf{0}$ such that $\mathbf{zA} \leqq r\mathbf{z}$.

Theorem 4

If a semi-positive square matrix $\mathbf{A}$ is decomposable, any power $\mathbf{A}^q$ of $\mathbf{A}$ is a decomposable matrix.

If a semi-positive indecomposable square matrix $\mathbf{A}$ is non-primitive with an index of non-primitiveness h matrix $\mathbf{A}^h$ is a quasi-diagonal matrix of the form:

$$\mathbf{A} = \begin{bmatrix} \mathbf{A}_{11} & \mathbf{0} & \mathbf{0} \dots \mathbf{0} \\ \mathbf{0} & \mathbf{A}_{22} & \mathbf{0} \dots \mathbf{0} \\ \vdots & \vdots & \vdots \quad \vdots \\ \mathbf{0} & \mathbf{0} & \mathbf{0} \dots \mathbf{A}_{hh} \end{bmatrix}$$

the diagonal blocks $\mathbf{A}_{11}, \mathbf{A}_{22}, \dots, \mathbf{A}_{hh}$ are indecomposable matrices and have the same dominant eigenvalue.

Notes

Introduction

1 *Production of Commodities by Means of Commodities* (Cambridge University Press, 1960).
2 A. Brody, *Proportions, Prices and Planning* (Amsterdam: North Holland, 1970).
3 M. Morishima, *Marx's Economics—A Dual Theory of Value and Growth* (Cambridge University Press, 1973).
4 See C. Benetti, Cl. Berthomieu, J. Cartelier, *Economie Classique, Economie Vulgaire* (Presses Universitaires de Grenoble & F. Maspero, 1975) and P. Salama, *Sur la Valeur* (F. Maspero, 1975).
5 G. Maarek, *Introduction au Capital de Karl Marx* (Paris: Calmann-Levy, 1975).
6 See H. Nikaïdo, *Introduction to Sets and Mappings in Modern Economics* (Amsterdam: North Holland, 1970) and J. T. Schwartz, *Lectures on the Mathematical Method in Analytical Economics* (Gordon & Breach, 1961); see also mathematical appendix above.
7 See P. Maurisson, *La Théorie des Prix de Production–Essai sur les Travaux de P. Sraffa*, Doctoral Dissertation (Paris I, 1974).
8 B. Schefold, 'Theorie der Kuppelproduktion' (Basel, 1972, mimeo).
9 See C. F. Manara, 'Il Modello di Piero Sraffa per la Produzione Congiunta di Merci a mezzo di Merci', *L'Industria*, no. 1 (1968).
10 J. von Neumann, 'A Model of General Equilibrium', *Review of Economic Studies*, XIII (1945–46).

1 From the theory of value to the explanation of profit

1 Cf. Marx, 'Nothing can have value, without being an object of utility' (I, p. 40). (Note: References to *Capital* are given by Volume number and page only).
2 Cf. Marx, 'The different proportions in which different sorts of labour are reduced to unskilled labour as their standard, are established by a social process that goes on behind the backs of the producers, and, consequently, appear to be fixed by custom' (I, p. 44).
3 See A. Brody: *Proportions, Prices and Planning* (Amsterdam: North Holland, 1970) pp. 76 & ff.
4 The theory of prices of production will be considered at length below.

5 A. Medio, 'Profit and Surplus-Value: Appearance and Reality in Capitalist Production' in *A Critique of Economic Theory*, E. K. Hunt and J. G. Schwartz (Harmondsworth: Penguin, 1972) pp. 315–16.

6 M. Morishima, *Marx's Economics—A Dual Theory of Value and Growth* (Cambridge University Press, 1973) p. 11.

7 Engels adds an interesting point to this discussion: wheat paid in tithes is not a commodity; to become a commodity, a product must be exchanged and have a use-value for the other person making the exchange.

8 Cf. M. Morishima, *op. cit.*

9 This assumption is implicitly made by Marx on several occasions, as in the following passage where he assumes constant returns together with strict complementarity: 'Just as during the six hours' process our 10 lbs. of cotton absorbed six hours' labour, and became 10 lbs. of yarn, so now, 20 lbs. of cotton will absorb 12 hours' labour and be changed into 20 lbs. of yarn' (I, p. 194).

10 'Capitalist production, therefore, of itself, reproduces the separation between labour-power and the means of labour' (I, p. 577); and further on 'Capitalist production, therefore, under its aspect of a continuous connected process, of a process of reproduction, produces not only commodities, not only surplus-value, but it also produces and reproduces the capitalist relation' (I, p. 578). For Marx, the capital cannot be reduced to a simple technological datum, it is essentially a *social relation.*

11 This much debated problem will not be considered in this book. See M. Morishima and G. Catephores, 'Is there an Historical Transformation Problem?', *Economic Journal*, LXXXV (June 1975).

12 See in particular Chapter IX (Part II of Volume III) entitled 'Formation of a general rate of profit [average rate of profit] and transformation of the values of commodities into prices of production', pp. 154–72.

13 For any commodity we have

$$\lambda_i = \mathbf{a}_i\mathbf{\Lambda} + l_i\mathbf{d}\mathbf{\Lambda} + el_i\mathbf{d}\mathbf{\Lambda} \qquad \text{with } \mathbf{a}_i = [a_{i1}, a_{i2}, \ldots, a_{in}]$$

This is equivalent to Marx's formulation: 'When the process of production is finished, we get a commodity whose value $= (c + v) + s$' (I, p. 212) where c (here $\mathbf{a}_i\mathbf{\Lambda}$) and v (here $l_i\mathbf{d}\mathbf{\Lambda}$) are respectively the value of constant capital and the value of variable capital used up during the production process and s (here $el_i\mathbf{d}\mathbf{\Lambda}$) is the surplus-value.

14 Recall that only systems with circulating capital are considered here. The extension of the analysis to the case of fixed capital will be made below.

15 The organic composition of capital in a sector is given by

$$k_i = \frac{\mathbf{a}_i\mathbf{\Lambda}}{l_i\mathbf{d}\mathbf{\Lambda}} \quad \text{with } k_i >, = \text{ or } < k, \text{ the average composition of all sectors.}$$

16 L. von Bortkiewicz, 'Value and Price in the Marxian System', *International Economic Papers* no. 2 (1952).

17 This is not absolutely exact: the rate of profit is, indeed, co-determined simultaneously with the prices of production of the basic commodities in the basic sector but it can be limited by the conditions of production of luxury goods (cf. Sraffa's famous 'beans' example).

18 P. A. Samuelson, 'Understanding the Marxian Notion of Exploitation: A Summary of the So-Called Transformation Problem between Marxian Values and Competitive Prices', *Journal of Economic Literature*, IX (June 1971).

19 The fundamental Marxian theorem has been presented by M. Okishio, 'A Mathematical Note on Marxian Theorems', *Weltwirtschaftliches Archiv*, Vol. XCI (1963) pp. 287–91; and again by M. Morishima, *op. cit.* pp. 53–5. The usual demonstration is based on the Hawkins–Simon conditions while here we are using the Perron–Frobenius theorem (see mathematical appendix) for it allows a simpler demonstration and underlines the necessity of an eventual distinction between basic and non-basic products.

20 On this point, see Section 1.2.2 and Chapter 2 and 3.

21 See above Section 1.1.2, for the other characteristics of the system.

22 But we always assume that at least one basic commodity exists, or matrix $\mathbf{A}^*$ would be completely decomposable and we would have several disjointed sub-economies.

2 Prices of production

1 Cambridge University Press (1972). We shall hereafter refer to Sraffa's book by the initials P. S. followed by the number of the relevant page, section or chapter.

2 To simplify the exposition we shall not consider here the problem of the 'Reduction to dated quantities of labour' (P.S. Ch. VI).

3 See the mathematical appendix, Section, A. 5.

4 P.S. p.v. See also G. Abraham-Frois: 'Préface aux *Ecrits d'Economie Politique* de P. Sraffa', *Economica* (1975).

5 P.S. p.v: 'If such a proposition is found helpful, there is no harm in the reader's adopting it as a temporary working hypothesis.'

6 See G.C. Harcourt: *Some Cambridge Controversies in the Theory of Capital* (Cambridge University Press, 1972).

7 For the definition of eigenvalue and eigenvector, see the mathematical appendix, above.

8 Since it is implicitly assumed here that all goods are basic, all prices are strictly positive. The importance of this assumption will be dealt with in more detail below.

9 Note that by the Perron–Frobenius theorem (see mathematical appendix) the dominant eigenvalue $1/(l+r)$ has a value between 1 and zero, since the sum of the elements of each column lies between 0 and 1. This implies that r is positive and finite.

10 Recall that Marx's prices of production, as they have been defined in Chapter 1, are the components of the eigenvector associated with the dominant eigenvalue of matrix $\mathbf{A}^* = \mathbf{A} + \mathbf{Ld}$ and not of matrix $\mathbf{A}$.

11 We have:

$$\det[\mathbf{A} - \alpha\mathbf{I}] = \alpha^2 - \alpha\left[\frac{56}{115} + 0.4\right] + \frac{22.4 - 14.4}{115} = 0$$

or $\alpha^2 - \frac{102}{115}\alpha + \frac{8}{115} = 0$ whose discriminant is

$$\Delta = \left(\frac{102}{115}\right)^2 - \frac{4 \times 8}{115} = \frac{6724}{(115)^2} = \left(\frac{82}{115}\right)^2$$

and thus $\alpha^* = \frac{102 + 82}{2 \times 115} = \frac{92}{115} \Rightarrow r = 25\%$

Note that the dominant eigenvalue $\alpha^* = 92/115$ is indeed less than 1 in this case of production with a surplus, while $\alpha^* = 1$ in the case of subsistence production.

12 The same result can be reached with the second equation:

$$\frac{24}{115}p_1 + 0.4p_2 = \frac{92}{115}p_2 \Rightarrow p_2 = \frac{12}{23}p_1$$

13 The analysis carried out in Section 2.1 above can throw some light on this sentence: it is, in fact, the assumption of the classical economists, i.e. the assumption that wages are advanced prior to production, which Sraffa later abandons.

14 This point will be considered in detail below.

15 See Section 2.2.2, below.

16 The assumption of an annual production cycle is retained.

17 In the notation of the blocks the subscript indicates a group of rows, the superscript a group of columns: in the case considered above of a decomposable matrix the block $\mathbf{A}_1^2$ contains only zero elements.

18 With the additional condition that $\mathbf{A}_2^1$ contains at least one strictly positive element, otherwise the matrix would be totally decomposable.

19 We have $\det[\mathbf{A} - \alpha\mathbf{I}] = -\alpha^3 + \frac{43}{36}\alpha^2 - \frac{1}{3}\alpha + \frac{35}{1296} = 0$

whose roots are $\frac{5}{6}, \frac{1}{6}$ and $7/36$; the maximum root is thus $\alpha^* = \frac{5}{6}$ (thus $R = \frac{1}{5} = 20\%$).

20 Sraffa adds: 'We shall as a rule find it convenient to take as unit of the Standard commodity the quantity of it that would form the net product of a Standard system employing the whole annual labour of the actual system. (For such a unit to form the net product in the above example, each industry must be increased by $\frac{1}{3}$, the aggregate labour employed being thereby raised from 12/16 to 16/16; as a result the unit would consist of 40 t. iron, 60 t. coal and 80 qr. wheat.) Such a unit we shall call the *Standard net product* or *Standard national income*' (P.S. §26, p. 20).

21 It is obviously impossible for the non-basic products to belong to the standard system for they are completely excluded from the means of production. Thus the appropriate multiplier for their equations can only be zero. The same is true for the non-basic products entering only the production of non-basic goods. In this way, all non-basic equations are eliminated and only the basic industries enter the standard system.

22 The only basic good, B_1, is the standard; this explains why its price is independent of r.

3 General analysis of prices

1 B. Schefold's 'Theorie der Kuppelproduktion' (Basel, 1972, mimeo), has been an invaluable aid to the exposition given here.

2 J. V. Neumann, 'A model of General Equilibrium', *Review of Economic Studies*, XIII (I) (1945–46) pp. 1–9 (translated from the original German).

3 This rather unrealistic assumption does not modify the analysis and will be relaxed later (Section 3.1.5) when we consider the completed input matrix $\mathbf{A}^*$ which takes the worker's needs implicitly into account.

4 This is not to be confounded with Sraffa's analysis which considers the production of commodities by means of commodities and labour. The two analyses coincide in the particular case where Sraffa assumes that the wage paid out of the surplus is zero.

5 Cf. the assumption that, initially, labour is not taken explicitly into account in the system.

6 It is essential to note that R corresponds to Sraffa's maximum rate of profit since labour is not considered separately from other means of production and thus $w = 0$.

7 supp($\mathbf{Bp}$) is the support of the vector $\mathbf{Bp}$. For the definition of a support of a vector, see the mathematical appendix, A.3. If $\mathbf{x} = (x_1, x_2, x_3, x_4, x_5)$ is a vector input, supp $(\mathbf{x}) = \{2,4\}$ implies $\mathbf{x} = (0, x_2, 0, x_4, 0)$, with $x_2 > 0$ and $x_4 > 0$; i.e. only goods 2 and 4 are used.

8 In the simple production case previously considered, matrix $\mathbf{B}$ was the diagonal unit matrix, $\mathbf{B} = \mathbf{I}$. The framework presented above is therefore completely general, the case of simple production being a particular case of joint production:

$$\mathbf{A}\mathbf{p}(1 + r) + \mathbf{L}w = \mathbf{B}\mathbf{p} = \mathbf{I}\mathbf{p} = \mathbf{p}.$$

9 It should, perhaps, be pointed out that Sraffa had initially (P.S. p. 12) considered the wage as independent variable, but subsequently decided to take the rate of interest as independent variable (see P.S. p. 31). This does not, however, modify the analysis in any way.

10 Note first that we are speaking here of an indecomposable *system* and not of an indecomposable *matrix*, and second that in the case of simple production there is an equivalence between a basic system and an indecomposable system. We shall return to these two points below.

11 In the case of simple production $\mathbf{B} = \mathbf{I}$ remains invariant whatever the permutation made on the rows and columns since $\mathbf{I}$ is a diagonal matrix and this implies that a simple production system $[\mathbf{A}, \mathbf{I}]$ is decomposable if, and only if, $\mathbf{A}$ is a decomposable matrix.

12 Obviously the system formed by the $\mathbf{A}$ and $\mathbf{B}$ matrices is indecomposable if there are no such permutations. Similarly a simple production system $[\mathbf{A}, \mathbf{I}]$ is indecomposable if, and only if, $\mathbf{A}$ is an indecomposable matrix.

13 See P. Maurisson, 'La Théorie des prix de production', Doctoral Dissertation (University of Paris I, 1974), and C. F. Manara, 'Il modello di Piero Sraffa per la produzione congiunta di merci a mezzo di merci', *l'Industria*, 1968, no. 1.

14 This relation means that the rank of the $[\mathbf{A}^2, \mathbf{B}^2]$ matrix $\begin{bmatrix} a_{12} & b_{12} \\ a_{22} & b_{22} \end{bmatrix} = \begin{bmatrix} \beta a_{22} & \beta b_{22} \\ a_{22} & b_{22} \end{bmatrix}$ is equal to 1 (there is only one independent row-vector).

15 Recall that this means that rank $[\mathbf{A}^2, \mathbf{B}^2] = 1$. In other words the rank of the matrix formed by the *last* column of **A** and **B** (and thus of dimension (2×2)) is equal to 1.

16 In the preceding simple example $k = 2$, $m = 1$, the dimension of matrix $\mathbf{H}(k - m, 1)$ *is reduced* to 1×1, i.e. a scalar. The matrix $[\mathbf{A}^2, \mathbf{B}^2]$ of dimension $(k, 2m) = (2, 2)$ is at most of rank $m = 1$.

17 We also have $\mathbf{ML} = \begin{bmatrix} \mathbf{L}_1 - \mathbf{HL}_1 \\ \mathbf{L}_2 \end{bmatrix}$

18 Let us recall that in simple production we have $0 < \alpha^* < 1$ when the system is productive and that the eigenvector **q** associated with the dominant eigenvalue α^* is strictly positive if matrix **A** is indecomposable, semi-positive if **A** is decomposable.

19 In simple production, $\mathbf{B}^{-1} = \mathbf{B} = \mathbf{I}$, hence $\alpha^* \mathbf{q} = \mathbf{qA}$; this eliminates any complication since the Perron–Frobenius theorem ensures that there cannot be any negative component in vector **q**, the eigenvector associated with the dominant eigenvalue $\alpha^*(\mathbf{A})$.

20 The system of homogeneous equations $\mathbf{q}\,[\alpha^* \bar{\mathbf{B}} - \bar{\mathbf{A}}] = 0$ has a unique (up to the multiplication by scalars) solution only if the rank of matrix $[\alpha^* \bar{\mathbf{B}} - \bar{\mathbf{A}}]$ is equal to $k - m - 1$.

21 Note that in Manara's example the first process 'dominates' the second one in the sense that $\frac{b_{1j} - a_{1j}}{a_{1j}} > \frac{b_{2j} - a_{2j}}{a_{2j}}$ for $j = 1$ and $j = 2$.

22 As an example, we could conceive of a composite, standard commodity made of 1 ton of iron, 1.5 tons of coal less 2 quarters of wheat.

23 Note that the third property is simply the simultaneous realisation of the first two properties which are not exclusive despite appearances.

24 This restriction can be discarded by combining the results previously obtained with the following analyses.

25 As previously indicated, at this stage joint production is excluded.

26 Recall that, in physical terms, there is by assumption only one machine. But in economic terms there are as many 'machines' as there are years of utilisation: the same machine will thus have various prices throughout its working life.

27 Without restricting the analysis we can assume $M_o = M_h = \ldots = M_{T-1} = 1$. Note that, the lifetime of the machine being T, h takes on integer values between 0 and $T - 1$.

28 Furthermore note that

$$F \sum_{t=1}^{T-h} (1+r)^{T-h-t} = (1+r)^{T-h} p_{m,h}$$

29 P.S. §77. Generally speaking, we shall say that the efficiency of the machine throughout its working life is constant, increasing or decreasing according as

$$b_0 = \ldots = b_{T-1}, \mathbf{a}_0 = \ldots = \mathbf{a}_{T-1}, \quad l_0 = \ldots = l_{T-1}$$
$$b_0 \leq \ldots \leq b_{T-1}, \mathbf{a}_0 \geqq \ldots \geqq \mathbf{a}_{T-1}, \quad l_0 \geq \ldots \geq l_{T-1}$$
$$b_0 \geq \ldots \geq b_{T-1}, \mathbf{a}_0 \leqq \ldots \leqq \mathbf{a}_{T-1}, \quad l_0 \leq \ldots \leq l_{T-1}$$

30 Note that in the limit case $r = 0$, we have $p_{m,h} = (1 - h/T)p_{m,0}$ since when r tends towards 0, $p_{m,h}$ is equivalent to

$$\frac{1 + Tr - (1 - hr)}{1 + Tr - 1} p_{m,0} = \frac{(T-h)r}{Tr} p_{m,0} = 1 - \frac{h}{T} p_{m,0}$$

31 It is obvious that this is true only when the efficiency of the machine remains constant through time. Schefold showed (*op. cit.*) that two cases must be distinguished: when the efficiency is constant or increasing, the successive prices of a machine (the $p_{m,h}$s) are always positive but they *could* become negative in the case of decreasing efficiency. We shall return to this point later.

32 This assumption is made to simplify the exposition, it is not absolutely necessary. For the construction of an integrated sector of an unspecified (thus not unique) system of industries using fixed capital, see Schefold, *op. cit.*

33 This removal is in fact a pseudo-removal since the term F represents the constant charge of any intermediate process thus 'hiding' the fact that intermediate machines are taken into account. We have by definition (see Section 3.3.2, above):

$$\begin{cases} F = (1+r)p_{m0} - p_{m1} & = rp_{m0} + p_{m0} - p_{m1} \\ F = (1+r)p_{m1} - p_{m2} & = rp_{m1} + p_{m1} - p_{m2} \\ \cdots\cdots\cdots & \\ F = (1+r)p_{mh} - p_{m,h+1} & = rp_{mh} + p_{mh} - p_{m,h+1} \\ \cdots\cdots\cdots & \\ F = (1+r)p_{m,T-1} & = rp_{m,T-1} + p_{m,T-1} \\ \hline \end{cases}$$

$$\text{thus} \quad TF = r \sum_{h=0}^{h=T-1} p_{m,h} + p_{m0}$$

$$\text{and the expression for } F = \frac{1}{T}\left[r \sum_{h=0}^{h=T-1} p_{m,h} + p_{m0} \right]$$

Note that in this way we can obtain the global value of a complete set of instruments of all ages:

$$\sum_{h=0}^{T-1} p_{m,h} = \frac{TF - p_{m0}}{r}$$

34 While they were constant in the construction of the basic system (cf. Manara's *matrix* **M**) and were the pure and simple reflection of the state of technology.

35 (a) in the case of constant or increasing efficiency, we must distinguish two cases in order to show that $p_{m,h} > 0$.

$F_h > 0$ (this is always true in a situation of constant efficiency of the machines).

From $(1+r)p_{mh} = F_h + p_{m,h+1}$, we have:

$$p_{mh} = \frac{1}{1+r}F_h + \frac{1}{(1+r)^2}F_{h+1} + \ldots + \frac{F_{T-1}}{(1+r)^{T-H}} > 0$$

since $F_{T-1} \geq \ldots \geq F_h > 0$

$F_h < 0$ (this may occur in the case of increasing efficiency during the first phases of the process since $F_0 \leq \ldots \leq F_h \leq \ldots \leq F_{T-1}$).
If for example $F_0 < 0$, we have:

$(1+r)p_{m0} = F_0 + p_{m1}$
thus with $-F_0 > 0, p_{m1} \geq (1+r)p_{m0} > 0$

(b) In the case of decreasing efficiency, it is possible for the prices of the used machines to become negative after a certain period of utilisation. Since the machine is only used during the $T-1$ periods where the value of the net current production is positive, we have: $F_h > 0$ for all $h \leq T-1$.

Thus since $p_{m,h+1} = -F_h + (1+r)p_{m,h}$, if the price of the machine becomes negative in period (t) it will remain so in the following periods since $p_{m,t} < 0 \Rightarrow p_{m,t+1} = -F_t + (1+r)p_{m,t} < 0$.

36 From the technical point of view the maximum lifetime of a machine can be defined as the maximum age for which $\mathbf{u}(\mathbf{B}-\mathbf{A}) \geq 0$, i.e. the maximum age compatible with the production of a surplus.

37 The first process produces only the new machine, taking into account the (fundamental) assumption previously made that 'traditional' joint production is here excluded. The generalisation to the case of n goods used to produce the machine can be made without difficulty other than of exposition.

38 Which is indeed the present case, for wheat and the new machine are basic commodities. Note, however, that it is possible for some machines to be non-basic commodities.

39 With our notation, it comes with $R = 10\%$ and $q_4 = 100$ $q_3 = (1+R)q_4 = 110$ and $q_2 = (1+R)q_3 = 121$.

40 Whether these 'repairs' are worthwhile or whether it would be better to replace the entire machine is another problem (related, in any case, to the problem of the choice of techniques).

41 We shall assume for the sake of simplicity that the rate of profit and the rate of interest are identical.

42 G. Montani: 'La teoria ricardiana della rendita', *l'Industria* no. 3–4 (1972).

43 If this is not the case and there are k basic goods (including corn) we have $(k+1)$ equations and $(k+3)$ unknowns: k prices, the two distributive variables and rent. The system can be solved as usual by choosing a numeraire and the level of the exogenous distributive variable.

44 Schefold (*op. cit.* p. 83) gives a very clear example of rent of this type outside the agricultural sector. Consider two types of building in an urban zone; the rents are reflected in the value of the land while the duality of methods is given by the different heights of the buildings.

45 The only exception (i.e. more than one crop per type of land) occurs when we are at a switch point of techniques (see below) where two techniques (two methods of cultivation) are equally 'profitable'.

46 Note that here we no longer assume (as in the second case) that there is necessarily a uniform quality of land, i.e. a unique type of land. See Sraffa, §29, p. 76, for the case of multiple crops with a single quality of land.

47 These conditions are not, however, sufficient to ensure that the mathematically determined prices and rents are positive.

48 Obviously the analysis would be much more complex if we were to introduce the possibility of joint production. Schefold (*op. cit.* p. 86) gives an interesting and not very obvious case of joint production: that of the system of crop rotation. Although the various crops are not simultaneously produced in the same place, there is joint production in the sense that rotation increases the fertility of the land and requires a technical interdependence of the crops concerned.

49 Subject to the condition that there are only basic goods in the system (land excluded). Corn in the previous example must therefore be a basic good. This is the case if a_i represents the quantity of corn used in the ith method to produce corn.

50 Sraffa adds: 'And like land such obsolescent instruments have the properties of non-basics and are excluded from the composition of the Standard commodity' (P.S. §91, p. 78).

51 The formulation remains voluntarily vague. We should distinguish whether the 'everlasting' machine is a basic good or not.

52 P. A. Samuelson, 'Abstract of a Theorem concerning Substitution in Open Leontief Models', and T. C. Koopmans, 'Maximisation and Substitution' in *Activity Analysis of Production and Allocation*, ed. T. C. Koopmans (New York, 1971). See also J. A. Mirrlees, 'The Dynamic Non-Substitution Theorem', *Review of Economic Studies*, XXXVI(1) (1969).

53 Recall that it is not certain that these prices are always strictly positive. See Section 3.2.

54 Of course, this is true only if matrix **A** is a square matrix, i.e. if one good is produced by a single process. We shall return to this point in Section 5.5.

55 Cf. Sraffa's sub-system and Morishima's dual definition of value.

56 This problem is pointed out by Sraffa §66, footnote 1. A process may be said to operate at a negative level when it operates inversely, consuming outputs and producing inputs and labour.

57 Furthermore, if no assumption is made on the model $[\mathbf{A}, \mathbf{B}, \mathbf{L}]$, a negative surplus (in values) can occur in the economy simultaneously with a positive profit. But this case is practically excluded in a real economy. See I. Steedman's and M. Morishima's contributions in the *Economic Journal* (1976 and 1977).

58 Cf. Marx, 'Out of this latter sum, then, we reckon as advanced for the purpose of turning out the product, the sum of £54 alone, which the machinery loses by wear and tear in the process; for this is all it parts with to the product' (I, p. 213).

59 The value of an 'everlasting' machine is always constant since it does not transmit any value to the newly produced goods:

$$\lambda_{m,h} = \left(1 - \frac{h}{T}\right)\lambda_{m,0} \rightarrow \lambda_{m,0} \qquad \text{when} \qquad T \rightarrow +\infty.$$

60 Cf. the difficulties previously pointed out Chapter 1.

4 Proportional growth–duality

1 Gale, D., *The Theory of Linear Economic Models* (New York: McGraw-Hill, 1960).
2 Robinson, S. M., 'Irreducibility in the von Neumann Model', *Econometrica*, 41 (1973).
3 The reader may, if he wishes, go directly to Chapters 5 and 6, referring back to the present chapter only when necessary.
4 Note that several optimal techniques of production may correspond to a rate of growth G. See example (1), below.
5 $\sup\{\beta \geq 0 | \beta \mathbf{y}_0 \mathbf{A} \leqq \mathbf{c}_0\}$ is the highest β such that $\mathbf{y}(G) = \beta\mathbf{y}$ and $\beta\mathbf{y}_0\mathbf{A} \leqq \mathbf{c}_0$.
6 $\mathbf{yA} \not> \mathbf{0}$ means that at least one component of the semi-positive vector $\mathbf{yA}$ is zero.
7 See D. Gale, *op. cit.*, p. 49, Theorem 2.10.
8 We assume that $b_{ij} = 0$ when $a_{ij} = 0$.

5 Accumulation, conflicts and quasi-duality

1 $w = \dfrac{1-(1+r)a_{11}}{l_2 - \Delta(1+r)}$ hence $\dfrac{dw}{dr} = \dfrac{\Delta - l_2 a_{11}}{[l_2 - \Delta(1+r)]^2} = \dfrac{-l_1 a_{21}}{[l_2 - \Delta(1+r)]^2} < 0$

$$\frac{d^2w}{dr^2} = \frac{-2l_1 a_{21}\Delta}{[l_2 - \Delta(1+r)]^3}$$

2 In this case $\mathbf{L}$ is an eigenvector on the right of matrix $\mathbf{A}$. Cf. Section 5.3.
3 The relation between w and r is necessarily of degree one, thus there cannot be an inflexion point.
4 Note that $\mathbf{A}^*$ is indecomposable while $\mathbf{A}$ was decomposable.
5 This is the assumption that was made initially by Sraffa (see P.S. §8).
6 The analysis can be easily generalised: if we have several qualities of land or several scarce natural resources (paying rents), the analysis will take place in the $\mathbf{R}^{n+2}$ space, where n is the number of natural resources considered.
7 See J. S. Metcalfe and I. Steedman, 'Reswitching and Primary Input Use', *Economic Journal* (March 1972).
8 From the definition of $\mathbf{q}$ and R

$$\mathbf{q}(\mathbf{I}-\mathbf{A}) - R\mathbf{qA} = \mathbf{0}$$

hence $\mathbf{q}(\mathbf{I}-\mathbf{A}) + R\mathbf{q} - R\mathbf{qA} = R\mathbf{q}$

or $\mathbf{q}(\mathbf{I}-\mathbf{A})(1+R) = R\mathbf{q}$

9 $\mathbf{y}$ represents here in an equivalent way quantity produced as well as activity levels since we are in a single-product system.
10 This equation can be compared with the equation used for the determination of values. These developments can be compared more generally with those of Section 2.3 and with P.S. §§13–16, pp. 12–13.
11 The system considered here is basic. The case where the $\mathbf{A}$ matrix is decomposable will be considered below.
12 1650 ($= 990 + 480 + 180$) is the sum of the values of the inputs of the first

process. Similarly, 1500 (= 550 + 500 + 450), the second, and 1200 (= 440 + 160 + 600) the third.

13 By transposing the preceding analysis into the 'primal'. See Section 2.2 and P.S. chs. IV and V.

14 Cf. the m last processes of matrix **A**.

15 We assume in this configuration and in the following two that the matrices $\mathbf{A}_1^1, \mathbf{A}_2^2$ and $\mathbf{A}_3^3$ are indecomposable.

16 Taking into account the new presentation made here. Note again that this condition is necessary but not sufficient.

17 Cf. Chenery and Watanabe in A. O. Hirschman, *The Strategy of Economic Development* (New Haven and London: Yale University Press, 1958) pp. 105–19. See also G. Abraham-Frois, *Essai sur les problèmes d'investissement en pays sous-développé* SEDES 1962. On the planification in a socialist economy when the matrix is decomposable, see O. Lange, *Introduction to Econometrics*, in particular Chapter IV.

18 See P. A. Samuelson, 'Parable and Realism in Capital Theory: the Surrogate Production Function', *Review of Economic Studies*, XXIX; P. Sraffa, *ibid.*; J. R. Hicks, *Capital and Growth* (Oxford, 1965) p. 140.

19 A third solution, not considered here, would be to assume $\xi = w = 1$, that is, to reason in terms of wage prices $\hat{\mathbf{p}} = \mathbf{p}/w$.

20 L. Spaventa, 'Rate of Profit, Rate of Growth and Capital Intensity in a Simple Production model', *Oxford Economic Papers*, Vol. XXII. (July 1970).

21 M. Bruno, 'Fundamental Duality Relation in the Pure Theory of Capital and Growth', *Review of Economic Studies* (January 1969).

22 C. C. von Weizsäcker, *Steady State Capital Theory*, Springer Verlag, 1971.

23 Sraffa chooses as numeraire $\mathbf{q}(\mathbf{I}-\mathbf{A})\mathbf{p}\ (=1)$ where $\mathbf{q}$ is the eigenvector on the left of $\mathbf{A}$ and is such that $\mathbf{qL} = 1$ or $\mathbf{q}(\mathbf{I}-\mathbf{A})(\mathbf{I}-\mathbf{A})^{-1}\mathbf{L} = 1$, i.e. in this case $\mathbf{u} = \mathbf{q}(\mathbf{I}-\mathbf{A})$ with $\mathbf{qL} = 1$.

24 Note that here the vector $\bar{\mathbf{p}}$ is such that $\boldsymbol{\delta}(\mathbf{I}-\mathbf{A})\bar{\mathbf{p}} = 1$ while in the preceding section we chose for $\bar{\mathbf{p}}$ a proportional vector such that $\boldsymbol{\delta}\bar{\mathbf{p}} = 1$.

25 When we choose the normalisation vector $\beta\boldsymbol{\delta}\mathbf{p} = 1$, we have $w = \frac{w}{\beta\boldsymbol{\delta}\mathbf{p}} = \frac{1}{\beta}\frac{w}{\boldsymbol{\delta}\mathbf{p}}$ where $\frac{w}{\boldsymbol{\delta}\mathbf{p}}$ is the real wage and when we choose the normalisation vector $\mathbf{y}\beta\mathbf{L} = 1$ we have $\xi = \frac{\xi}{\beta\mathbf{yL}} = \frac{1}{\beta}\frac{\xi}{\mathbf{yL}}$ where $\frac{\xi}{\mathbf{yL}}$ represents consumption per capita. And so the rate-of-profit–wage curve

$r \to \frac{w(r)}{\boldsymbol{\delta}\mathbf{p}}$ is identical to the rate-of-accumulation–consumption per capita curve

$$g \to \frac{\xi(g)}{\mathbf{yL}}.$$

26 The case considered by Hicks, and Spaventa (*op. cit.*) is very special on two accounts: first, $\mathbf{A} = \begin{bmatrix} a_{11} & 0 \\ a_{21} & 0 \end{bmatrix}$ and only the second good is consumed: that is, $\boldsymbol{\delta}$ is defined up to the multiplication by scalars as $\boldsymbol{\delta} = [0, 1]$; and second, the assumption that $p_2 = 1$ is equivalent to normalising $\mathbf{p}$ by $\boldsymbol{\delta}\mathbf{p} = 1$. The generali-

sation made by Bruno (*op. cit.*) concerns only the dimension of matrix **A**, the last column is still made of zeros and only the last good is consumed.

27 The two dual normalisation vectors pointed out above are not the only ones that make the curves (w, r) and (ξ, g) identical. For a more complete analysis, see G. Abraham-Frois and E. Berrebi, 'Conflit de Répartition et Conflit d'Accumulation. Normes Duales', *Revue d'Economie Politique* (1977).

28 N. Kaldor, 'Marginal Productivity and the Macro-Economic Theories of Distribution', *Review of Economic Studies*, XXXIII (October 1966).

29 In particular Section II. See also R. Rosdolsky, *La Genése du 'Capital' chez Karl Marx* (Maspero 1976) pp. 112–40.

30 The generalisation to a system of multiple-product industries can be made without difficulty.

31 When workers save part of their wages, the relation between r and g takes the following form: $r = g(1 - i)/s_c$. A more general formulation is given by substituting this relation for the relation used in the analysis above.

32 Recall that we assumed the dominant eigenvalue of $\mathbf{A}_2^2$ to be inferior to those of $\mathbf{A}_1^1$ and $\mathbf{A}_3^3$.

6 Value

1 Cf. M. Morishima and G. Catephores, 'Is there an Historical Transformation problem?', *Economic Journal*, LXXXV (June 1975). Cf. also, L. Althusser: 'Just as we can say that we possess only the outline of a marxist theory of the modes of production before the capitalist mode of production ... We must say that *Marx did not give us any theory of the transition from one mode of production to another, i.e., of the constitution of a mode of production*', *Reading Capital* (London: New Left Books, 1970) p. 197 (trans. B. Brewster) (italics added).

2 Italics added.

3 For an algebraic formulation of Marx's arithmetical examples see O. Lange, *Introduction to Econometrics*; see also Morishima, *op. cit.*

4 On this point see B. Rosier, *Croissance et Crise Capitaliste* (Paris: Presses Universitaires de France, 1975) pp. 126–7, who uses a different notation.

5 Note that the assumption of no technical progress or of constant technology is indeed a necessary condition for the organic composition of capital (in values) to be constant, but not a sufficient condition. The structure of the levels of activity (or of quantities) would also have to be invariant for this to be the case, i.e. γ should be a (positive) constant, and the structure of final demand should be constant.

6 Recall that we are assuming that the growth of output of the various commodities is non-proportional.

7 Which is here the system determining the quantities produced $(\mathbf{B} = \mathbf{I}) \Rightarrow \mathbf{\Omega}$ (levels of activity) $= \mathbf{\Omega I}$ (outputs). The relation $\mathbf{\Omega} = \mathbf{\Omega A} + \mathbf{d}$ can also be written as $\mathbf{\Omega} = \mathbf{d}(\mathbf{I} - \mathbf{A})^{-1} = \mathbf{d} + \mathbf{dA} + \mathbf{dA}^2 + \ldots + \mathbf{dA}^n + \ldots$ because the dominant eigenvalue is less than 1 by assumption. $\mathbf{\Omega}$ is therefore determined by the quantity of goods directly ($\mathbf{d}$) and indirectly ($\mathbf{dA}, \mathbf{dA}^2, \ldots, \mathbf{dA}^n, \ldots$) necessary for workers' subsistence and for the reproduction of labour

power. The vector **Ω** is the dual of vector **Λ** just as we must distinguish between the values **Λ** and the prices **p**, it is also imperative to distinguish between **Ω** and **y**. To this end we could call the 'height' the vector **Ω** corresponding to zero accumulation. This 'height' could then be analysed as a particular case of the levels of activity in the same way as values can be interpreted and calculated as a particular case of the more general analysis of prices of production.

8 M. Morishima, 'Marx in the Light of Modern Economic Theory', *Econometrica*, 42 (July 1974).

9 Marx was conscious of the approximative character of his solution, see Chapter 1, above, and *Capital*, Vol. III.

10 It is also necessary to assume that matrix **A*** is primitive. This means that the dominant eigenvalue is strictly greater than the modulus of all other eigenvalues. The primitiveness condition on matrix **A*** is not really a constraint; for an indecomposable matrix to be primitive it only needs one positive element on the principal diagonal. This condition is usually satisfied for obvious economic reasons; see G. H. Nikaïdo, *Introduction to Sets and Mappings in Modern Economics* (Amsterdam: North Holland, 1970); and R. M. Solow, 'On the Structure of Linear Models', *Econometrica*, 20 (1952).

11 See M. Morishima, *op. cit.*

12 See P. Maurisson, *La Théorie des Prix de Production–Essai sur les Travaux de Piero Sraffa*, Doctoral Dissertation, (University of Paris I, 1974) p. 155.

13 A. Medio, 'Profit and Surplus-Value', reached the same result using a slightly different method.

14 Recall that we assume the wage to be completely advanced: **p** is the vector of prices.

15 This corresponds to $\lambda_{m,h} - \lambda_{m,h+1}$ of the preceding formulation.

16 In order to simplify the notation, and because there was no possibility for confusion, we have used the same symbols for the eigenvalues and the eigenvectors of **A** and **A*** in the preceding chapters and the initial sections of this chapter.

17 Properties 1, 2, …, 5 and 5′ used in this section are defined and proved in the mathematical appendix, A.1.

18 Note that the Standard system is defined here in terms of matrix $\mathbf{A}^* = \mathbf{A} + \mathbf{Ld}$, while Sraffa's Standard system is defined in terms of **A** because the wage is paid from the surplus.

19 'Understanding the Marxian Notion of Exploitation'. *Journal of Economic Literature*, 9 (June 1971) p. 415.

20 The preceding analysis indicates that the transformation of values into prices is possible if and only if the vector **y** is one of the standards of the system (**A***, **L**). For an analysis of special cases where there are several standard commodities for prices, see T. Miyao, 'A Generalisation of Sraffa's Standard Commodity and its Complete Characterisation', *International Economic Review*, 18, Feb. 1977.

Bibliography

G. Abraham-Frois, *Essai sur les Problèmes d' Investissement en Pays Sous-Développé* (SEDES, 1962).

G. Abraham-Frois and E. Berrebi, 'Progrès Technique et Théorie du Capital', Paper presented at the Colloque International CNRS–IREP, Université Paris X (November 1976). CNRS edn, Paris (1978).

'Le Problème de la Transformation: Fin(?) d'une Controverse', *Economie Appliquée* no. 4 (1976).

'Conflit de Repartition et Conflit d'Accumulation: Normes Duales', *Revue d'Economie Politique* (October 1977).

'Transformation et proportions entre travail et moyens de production' in Abraham-Frois, Gibert and de Lavergne (1977) Vol. II.

'A propos d'une incohérence logique de P. Sraffa', *Cahiers d'Economie Politique* no. 5, Université de Picardie, PUF edn (1979).

G. Abraham-Frois, P. Gibert and Ph. de Lavergne, *Problématiques de la Croissance*, Vols. I and II (Paris: Economica, 1977).

L. Althusser, *Reading Capital*, trans. B. Brewster (London: New Left Books, 1970).

C. Benetti, *Valeur et Répartition* (Presses Universitaires de Grenoble and Maspero, 1973).

C. Benetti, C. Berthomieu and J. Cartelier, *Economie Classique, Economie Vulgaire* (Presses Universitaires de Grenoble and Maspero, 1975).

C. Berthomieu, J. and L. Cartelier, ed., *Ricardiens, Keynésiens et Marxistes. Essai en Economie Politique Non Néo-Classique*, Actes du Colloque de Nice, September 1972 (Presses Universitaires de Grenoble and F. Maspero, 1976).

L. von Bortkiewicz, 'Value and Price in the Marxian System', *International Economic Papers*, no. 2 (1952).

A. Brody, *Proportions, Price and Planning* (Amsterdam: North Holland, 1970).

M. Bruno, 'Fundamental Duality Relations in the Pure Theory of Capital and Growth', *Review of Economic Studies*, XXXVI (January 1969).

E. Burmeister and A. R. Dobell, *Mathematical Theories of Economic Growth* (London: Macmillan, 1970).

Cahiers d'Economie Politique no. 3, Actes du Colloque SRAFFA 1973 UER d'Economie et de Gestion, Université de Picardie (Amiens, 1976).

G. Dumenil, *La Position de Classe des Cadres et Employés* (Presses Universitaires de Grenoble, 1975).

'Accumulation et Investissement', Doctoral Dissertation (Paris X–Nanterre, 1975).

G. Faccarello, 'A la Limite du Pays Fertile ... : La Nouvelle Ecole de Cambridge', Honours Thesis D.E.S. (Paris X–Nanterre, 1973).

G. Faccarello and Ph. de Lavergne, ed., *Une Nouvelle Approche en Economie Politique* (Paris: Economica, 1977).

G. Ferreira dos Santos, *Valeur et Agrégation dans la Problématique de la Production*, Doctoral Dissertation U.L.P. (Strasbourg, 1974).

D. Gale, *The Theory of Linear Economic Models* (New York: McGraw-Hill, 1960).

F. R. Gantmacher, *The Theory of Matrices*, Vols. I and II (New York: Chelsea, Bronx, 1960).

G. C. Harcourt, *Some Cambridge Controversies in the Theory of Capital* (Cambridge University Press, 1972).

J. R. Hicks, *Capital and Growth* (Oxford: Clarendon Press, 1965).

A. O. Hirschman, *The Strategy of Economic Development* (New Haven and London: Yale University Press, 1958).

N. Kaldor, 'Marginal Productivity and the Macro-Economic Theories of Distribution', *Review of Economic Studies*, XXXIII (October 1966).

T. C. Koopmans, 'Maximisation and Substitution' in *Activity Analysis of Production and Allocation*, ed. T. C. Koopmans (New York, 1971).

D. Lacaze, *Valeurs, Prix de Production et Dualité Mathématique*, Groupe de Mathématique Economique, Universités Paris I–Paris IV (November 1974).

O. Lange, *Introduction to Econometrics* (New York: Pergamon, 1959).

G. Maarek, *Introduction au Capital de Karl Marx* (Paris: Calmann-Lévy, 1975).

C. F. Manara, 'Il Modello di Piero Sraffa per la Produzione Congiunta di Merci a mezzo di Merci', *l'Industria*, no. 1 (1968).

K. Marx, *Wages, Price and Profit* (Moscow: Progress Publishers, 1947).

Capital, Volume I (London: Lawrence & Wishart, 1970).

Capital, Volume II (London: Lawrence & Wishart–Moscow: Progress Publishers, 1967).

Capital, Volume III (London: Lawrence & Wishart–Moscow: Progress Publishers, 1962).

A Contribution to the Critique of Political Economy (London: Lawrence & Wishart, 1971).

The Poverty of Philosophy (Chicago: Charles H. Kerr & Co., n.d.).

K. Marx and F. Engels, *Selected Correspondence* (Moscow: Progress Publishers, second edn, 1965).

P. Maurisson, 'La Théorie des Prix de Production. Essai sur les Travaux de Piero Sraffa', Doctoral Dissertation (Paris I, 1974).

A. Medio, 'Profit and Surplus-Value: Appearance and Reality in Capitalist Production' in E. K. Hunt and J. G. Schwartz, *A Critique of Economic Theory* (Harmondsworth: Penguin, 1972).

J. S. Metcalfe and I. Steedman, 'Reswitching and Primary Input Use', *Economic Journal*, LXXXII (March 1972).

J. A. Mirrlees, 'The Dynamic Non-Substitution Theorem', *Review of Economic Studies*, XXXVI (1969).

T. Miyao, 'A generalization of Sraffa's standard commodity and its complete characterization', *International Economic Review*, Vol. 18 (February, 1977).

G. Montani, 'La Teoria Ricardiana della Rendita', *l'Industria*, nos. 3–4 (1972).

'Scarce Natural Resources and Income Distribution', *Metroeconomica*, no. 1 (1976).

M. Morishima, 'Marx in the Light of Modern Economic Theory', *Econometrica*, XLII (July 1974).

Marx's Economics. A Dual Theory of Value and Growth (Cambridge University Press, 1973).

M. Morishima and G. Catephores, 'Is There an Historical Transformation Problem?', *Economic Journal*, LXXXV (June 1975).

M. Morishima and I. Steedman, 'Positive Profits with Negative Surplus-Value. An Interchange', *Economic Journal*, LXXXVI (September 1976).

J. von Neumann, 'A Model of General Equilibrium', *Review of Economic Studies*, XIII (I) (1945–46).

H. Nikaïdo, *Introduction to Sets and Mappings in Modern Economics*, (Amsterdam: North Holland, 1970).

N. Okishio, 'A Mathematical Note on Marxian Theorems', *Weltwirtschaftliches Archiv*, Vol. XCI (1963).

L. Pasinetti, *Lessons in the Theory of Production* (London: Macmillan, 1976).

D. Ricardo, *On the Principles of Political Economy and Taxation* (Cambridge University Press, 1951).

S. M. Robinson, 'Irreducibility in the von Neumann Model', *Econometrica*, XLI (1973).

B. Rosier, *Croissance et Crise Capitaliste* (Presses Universitaires de France, 1975).

P. Salama, *Sur la Valeur* (Paris: F. Maspero, 1975).

P. A. Samuelson, 'Abstract of a Theorem Concerning Substitution in Open Leontief Models' in *Activity Analysis of Production and Allocation*, ed. T. S. Koopmans (New York, 1971).

'Understanding the Marxian Notion of Exploitation: A Summary of the So-Called Transformation Problem between Marxian Values and Competitive Prices', *Journal of Economic Literature*, IX (June 1971).

A. von Schaik, *Reproduction and Fixed Capital* (Tilburg University Press, 1976).

B. Schefold, 'Piero Sraffas Theorie der Kuppelproduktion, des Kapitals und der Rente (Mr Sraffa on Joint Production)', private printing (Basel, 1971).

'Nachworte' (postscript to the German edition of Piero Sraffa's *Production of Commodities by Means of Commodities*) in Piero Sraffa: *Warenproduktion mittels Waren* (Frankfurt: Suhrkamp Verlag, 1976) pp. 131–226.

'Relative Prices as a Function of the Rate of Profit', *Zeitschrift für Nationalökonomie*, 36 (1976) pp. 21–48.

'Different Forms of Technical Progress', *Economic Journal* 86 (December 1976) pp. 806–819; Italian translation in preparation, to be published (Feltrinelli).

'Fixed Capital as a Joint Product', in *Jahrbücher für Nationalökonomie und Statistik* (1977).

'Reduction to Dated Quantities of Labour, Roundabout Processes, and Switches of Techniques in Fixed Capital Systems', *Metroeconomica*, vol. 28 (1976).

'Multiple Product Techniques with Properties of Single Product Systems', to appear in *Zeitschrift für Nationalökonomie*, 37 (1978).

'Von Neumann and Sraffa: Mathematical Equivalence and Conceptual Difference', mimeo, to be published.

'Capital, Growth, and Definitions of Technical Progress', to appear in Festschrift für G. Bombach, *Kyklos*, vol. 32 (1979).

'Energy and Economic Theory', pp. 22, in *Zeitschrift für Wirtschafts- und Sozialwissenschaften*, Heft 3 (1977) pp. 227–249.

J. T. Schwartz, *Lectures on the Mathematical Method in Analytical Economics* (London: Gordon and Breach, 1961).

R. M. Solow, 'On the Structure of Linear Models', *Econometrica*, XX (1952).

L. Spaventa, 'Rate of Profit, Rate of Growth and Capital Intensity in a Simple Production Model', *Oxford Economic Papers*, XXII (July 1970).

P. Sraffa, *Production of Commodities by Means of Commodities* (Cambridge University Press, 1960).

I. Steedman, 'Positive Profits with Negative Surplus-Values', *Economic Journal*, LXXXV (March 1975).

'Marx after Sraffa' (NLB, 1977).

P. Vidonne, 'Une Présentation Critique de la Rente Ricardienne', *Revue Economique* (March 1976).

C. C. von Weizsäcker, *Steady State Capital Theory* (Springer Verlag, 1971).

E. Wolfstetter, 'Positive Profits with Negative Surplus-Value: A Comment', *Economic Journal*, LXXXVI (December 1976).